PENGUIN  CLASSICS

THE PRIVATE JOURNAL OF WILLIAM REYNOLDS

Grandson of Scotch-Irish immigrants, WILLIAM REYNOLDS was born in Lancaster, Pennsylvania, in 1815, the second of thirteen children. After receiving the equivalent of a high school education at a local private academy, he obtained an appointment as a midshipman in the United States Navy in 1831. For the next five years he served his naval apprenticeship on board a succession of vessels that carried him to Africa, South America, Sumatra, and the Mediterranean. In 1836 he returned to the United States to take the examination that qualified him for appointment as a lieutenant. In the absence of any vacancies in that rank, he was warranted as a passed midshipman and assigned to the Depot of Charts and Instruments in Washington. There, in early 1838, he met Lieutenant Charles Wilkes, the newly appointed commander of the United States Exploring Expedition. Full of admiration for Wilkes and eager for adventure, Reynolds joined the expedition, which for the next four years was to range across the Pacific, from Tahiti to the Antarctic, from Australia to the American Northwest coast. That long voyage, with all its delights and terrors, furnished the material for the running chronicle which makes up the *Private Journal*. When Reynolds at last returned to the United States, worn and embittered, he joined the other junior officers of the expedition in the vain hope that the now-hated Wilkes would be punished by court-martial for his abusive treatment of his subordinates. Although Wilkes survived his trial relatively unscathed, Reynolds had other satisfactions: he had received his lieutenant's commission and was able to marry and look forward to a secure and honorable career in the navy. In 1851, however, he was forced by poor health to secure a prolonged leave of absence, but with the outbreak of the Civil War, he insisted on returning to the navy. Recovering his strength by an apparent act of will, he not only served throughout the war but remained on active duty in the ensuing years, rising through the ranks to rear admiral in 1873. In 1879, after suffering two years of illness, he died.

NATHANIEL PHILBRICK is the author of the *New York Times* bestseller *In the Heart of the Sea*, which won the National Book Award and was a finalist for the *Los Angeles Times* Book Prize, and the national bestseller *Sea of Glory*. He is founding director of the Egan Institute of Maritime Studies and a leading authority on the history of Nantucket, where he lives with his wife and two children.

THOMAS PHILBRICK is Professor Emeritus of English at the University of Pittsburgh and a lifelong small boat sailor. He is the author of *James Fenimore Cooper and the Development of American Sea Fiction* and the study *St. John de Crèvecoeur*. He has edited five of Cooper's novels and travel books for the Cooper Edition, as well as Dana's *Two Years Before the Mast* for Penguin Classics.

WILLIAM REYNOLDS

The Private Journal of William Reynolds

UNITED STATES EXPLORING EXPEDITION, 1838–1842

*Edited with an Introduction
and Notes by* NATHANIEL PHILBRICK
and THOMAS PHILBRICK

PENGUIN BOOKS

PENGUIN BOOKS
Published by the Penguin Group
Penguin Group (USA) Inc., 375 Hudson Street, New York, NY 10014, U.S.A.
Penguin Group (Canada), 10 Alcorn Avenue, Toronto,
Ontario, Canada M4V 3B2 (a division of Pearson Penguin Canada Inc.)
Penguin Books Ltd, 80 Strand, London WC2 0RL, England
Penguin Ireland, 25 St Stephen's Green, Dublin 2, Ireland (a division of Penguin Books Ltd)
Penguin Group (Australia), 250 Camberwell Road, Camberwell,
Victoria 3124, Australia (a division of Pearson Australia), Group Pty Ltd)
Penguin Books India Pvt Ltd, 11 Community Centre, Panchsheel Park, New Delhi – 110 017, India
Penguin Group (NZ), cnr Airborne and Rosedale Roads, Albany,
Auckland, New Zealand (a division of Pearson New Zealand Ltd)
Penguin Books (South Africa) Pty) Ltd, 24 Sturdee Avenue
Rosebank, Johannesberg 2196, South Africa

Penguin Books Ltd, Registered Offices:
80 Strand, London WC2R 0RL, England

First published in Penguin Books 2004

The journals of William Reynolds are published by arrangement with Franklin and Marshall College.

LIBRARY OF CONGRESS CATALOGING IN PUBLICATION DATA
Reynolds, William, 1815–1879.
The private journal of William Reynolds : United States Exploring Expedition, 1838–1842 / edited with
an introduction and notes by Nathaniel Philbrick and Thomas Philbrick.
p. cm.
Includes bibliographical references.
ISBN 978-0-143-03905-1
1. Reynolds, William, 1815–1879—Diaries. 2. Sailors—United States—Diaries. 3. Explorers—United
States—Diaries. 4. United States Exploring Expedition (1838–1842) 5. Wilkes, Charles, 1798–1877
6. Seafaring life. 7. Voyages around the world. 8. Scientific expeditions—History—19th century
9. Ethnological expeditions—History—19th century. I. Philbrick, Nathaniel II. Philbrick, Thomas.
III. United States Exploring Expedition (1838–1842) IV. Title.
Q115 .R35
508.3—dc22 2004044725

Set in Sabon

146028962

Contents

Introduction

Passed Midshipman William Reynolds was just twenty-two years old when the six vessels of the U.S. Exploring Expedition set sail from Hampton Roads, embarking on America's first oceangoing voyage of discovery. The second oldest of eight surviving children, Reynolds had long made a habit of keeping a journal of his experiences for his parents and siblings back in Lancaster, Pennsylvania. This meant that when the commander of the expedition, Lieutenant Charles Wilkes, ordered the squadron's officers to begin keeping detailed journals that were to be turned over to him at the completion of the voyage, Reynolds was already three pages into his own, very personal account of the expedition. "I cannot think of letting this go before any ones eyes but those few at home," he wrote. Instead, on September 13, 1838, almost a month into the voyage, he began keeping a second, "official" log of the cruise.

It would prove to be a momentous decision. While his official journal would grow to nearly 86,000 words and provide a workmanlike account of the expedition, Reynolds's personal journal would ultimately take up three notebooks and comprise some 250,000 words. Of the dozens of journals that have survived from the U.S. Exploring Expedition (known as the Ex. Ex. for short), only Reynolds's personal journal begins to tell the full, uncensored story of how a group of young and idealistic officers gradually lost faith in the leader who they had once dared to believe was, in Reynolds's words, "every thing pure and honorable."

But Reynolds's journal is much more than a story of disillusionment and frustration. In spite of being what we would call today "a bad boss," Wilkes managed to lead the U.S. Ex. Ex. to some extraordinary accomplishments—covering more than eighty-seven thousand miles in what turned into a four-year circuit of the globe. Over the course of the voyage, Reynolds would come of age amid the bleak, wave-lashed rocks of Cape Horn, the beckoning paradises of the South Pacific, the gigantic icebergs of Antarctica, and the primeval forests of the Pacific Northwest. By the time he returned to the United States in the summer of 1842, Reynolds had developed into a writer of remarkable power and range, and his journal contains some of the best descriptions of the sea to come from a nineteenth-century American pen.

By the time the squadron reached Cape Horn in February 1839, Reynolds had fallen into the writing routine he would follow for the rest of the voyage. In addition to keeping both the personal and official journals, Reynolds wrote more than twenty letters to his family back in Lancaster. These letters, which have been collected into a volume titled *Voyage to the Southern Ocean,* edited by Reynolds descendant Anne Hoffman Cleaver and E. Jeffrey Stann, are based on material that first appeared in the private journal. Reynolds also possessed a small pocket-sized journal that he took with him into the field, enabling him to record incidents that he would later integrate into the journal.

By this time, too, Reynolds had hit his stride as a writer. While many of the early pages of his journal are full of the sentimental clichés and romantic posturings that were the standard fare of the popular magazines of the period, he now had developed a style that impresses the reader as an authentically personal and direct response to experience. His account of surveying the islands of southern Tierra del Fuego in a thirty-five-foot open boat is a tour de force, combining meticulous observations of the weather, geography, and native inhabitants with a young man's sense of wonder and, on occasion, terror as his little boat is tossed about by the tremendous seas. Reynolds is particularly good at describing how the officers and men interact during the mission. When a sudden change in wind direction threatens to dash the launch against the rocks, Reynolds takes solace in the disciplined resolve of the sailors who are about to go down with him. "My glance went from face to face of the hardy crew, & I read there the same quiet & determined expression that each had worn when so actively at work a few minutes before. *It does one good* to see the way Sailors go on with their duty, when their lives are in imminent & terrible danger."

Later, once he is back aboard the squadron's flagship, the 127-foot sloop of war *Vincennes,* he experiences yet another unforgettable storm, this time amid the emptiness of the Southern Ocean. Reynolds's description of the passage combines a seaman's understanding of the discipline, nerve, and endurance required to drive a ship through several weeks of punishing gales with an artist's appreciation for the wild beauty that surrounds them. "The small portion of canvass that we could Show, was confined to the lower yards & masts," he writes. "The upper ones were bare and as the Ship rolled, swept in huge circles against the Sky. Often even this little spread of sail was too much to expose to the fury of the squalls, & 'all hands' would be called to get it in in time & to Set it again the moment it was possible. The work was hard, killing." Reynolds is up in the rigging at night when the full moon breaks through the clouds. "[T]he play of her placid beams upon the bursting waves & the foamy track of the Ship was beautiful indeed. . . . [T]here was an inconceivable grandeur & Sublimity in the aspect of the Ocean & in the motions of the tempest tossed Ship."

When the squadron reaches Tahiti, Reynolds moves effortlessly from describing life at sea to a candid, refreshingly open-minded examination of what he sees in this new and exotic place. He's shocked by the sexual promiscuity of the islanders and yet he cannot help but wonder if his own preconceptions are getting in the way of a proper appreciation of the Polynesians. Echoing sentiments Herman Melville would voice seven years later in his first book, *Typee,* Reynolds asks, "Who can judge one nation by another? What man can say, this people shall be my standard, by them I will judge all others?"

In addition to writing accounts of maritime experience worthy of a Melville or a Richard Henry Dana, Reynolds was a witness to history. On January 16, 1840, the sloop of war *Peacock* made her way to the edge of the icy barrier that surrounds Antarctica. At this time, there was no clear understanding of what existed to the south. That day Reynolds, along with fellow passed midshipman Henry Eld, climbed to the *Peacock*'s masthead. Many miles away, looming over the glittering sheet of ice, they saw land. "At a great distance over the barrier," Reynolds writes, "were several peaks showing very distinctly, & other summits were hidden in the clouds. They rose to an immense height. We looked for half an hour at least & procured a glass to satisfy ourselves that we were not mistaken. We were convinced that our judgement was correct & that we actually beheld the long sought for Terra Firma of the Antarctic continent." Wilkes would eventually survey a 1,500-mile section of Antarctic coast and provide compelling evidence that it was a continent indeed, but it was Reynolds and Eld who had been the first to sight land.

The journal is inhabited by a wide-ranging and constantly shifting cast of characters as Reynolds is moved from vessel to vessel and the squadron moves from place to place. In addition to more than a dozen officers and sailors, we meet the beautiful Polynesian princess Emma in western Samoa, the grizzled Irish beachcomber Paddy O'Connell in Fiji, the multiracial Birney family at the Hudson's Bay Company trading post on the Columbia River, and a duplicitous American missionary who convinces one of the expedition's marines to desert, forcing Reynolds to undertake an unforgettable all-night chase through the wilderness of the Pacific Northwest.

In addition to all these people, there are the many vessels on which Reynolds serves, including the flagship *Vincennes,* the *Peacock,* and the brig *Porpoise.* But it is the schooners *Sea Gull* and *Flying Fish,* former New York Harbor pilot boats, that prove to be the main characters of the journal. Reynolds began the voyage yearning to serve on one of these flashy little speedsters. But after the *Sea Gull* is lost with all hands in a storm off Cape Horn and Reynolds survives several near-death experiences of his own aboard the *Flying Fish* off Oregon and the Philippines, he is more than ready to return to a larger and safer vessel when it comes time to sell the worn-out schooner in Singapore. In the meantime, his journal brings to life the cramped and boisterous world of the little schooner in the open ocean with such authenticity and verve that the reader cannot help but regret the loss of one of the expedition's most stalwart members. "I had the same sort of regard for her tha[t] a man must entertain for a gallant horse that has carried him safely through the fight," Reynolds writes, "& I almost repented that the poor little craft had been so rudely bartered away."

In the end, it is his relationship with Wilkes that becomes the primary focus of the narrative. One of the more tantalizing episodes occurs at the Columbia River, where Wilkes makes what Reynolds terms "unmistakable" attempts to mend fences with him. But Reynolds will have none of it, and the final pages of the journal are dominated by an intense, almost ferocious hatred for his commander. The strength of his feelings would lead Reynolds to pen yet another account of the voyage—a seventy-eight-page memorandum refuting Wilkes's published account of the expedition. But it is the journal that stands as his most important and vital writing about the Ex. Ex. Indeed, the journal deserves to be recognized as not just the most readable first-person account we have of the U.S. Exploring Expedition, but as one of the finest accounts of a sea voyage to be written in the nineteenth century.

Suggestions for Further Reading

Philbrick, Nathaniel. *Sea of Glory: America's Voyage of Discovery, the U.S. Exploring Expedition, 1838–1842*. New York: Viking, 2003.

Reynolds, William. *Voyage to the Southern Ocean: The Letters of Lieutenant William Reynolds from the U.S. Exploring Expedition, 1838–1842*. Edited by Anne Hoffman Cleaver and E. Jeffrey Stann. Annapolis, Md.: Naval Institute Press, 1988.

Stanton, William. *The Great United States Exploring Expedition of 1838–1842*. Berkeley and Los Angeles: University of California Press, 1975.

Tyler, David. *The Wilkes Expedition: The First United States Exploring Expedition (1838–1842)*. Philadelphia: American Philosophical Society, 1968.

Viola, Herman J., and Carolyn Margolis, eds. *Magnificent Voyagers: The U.S. Exploring Expedition, 1838–1842*. Washington, D.C.: Smithsonian Institution, 1985.

Wilkes, Charles. *Autobiography of Rear Admiral Charles Wilkes, U.S. Navy*. Edited by William James Morgan et al. Washington, D.C.: Naval History Division, Department of the Navy, 1978.

———. *Narrative of the United States Exploring Expedition*. 5 vols. Philadelphia: Lea and Blanchard, 1845. Reprinted Upper Saddle River, N.J.: Gregg Press, 1970.

A Note on the Text

Reynolds's *Private Journal*, housed in the Archives and Special Collections of the Shadek-Fackenthal Library at Franklin and Marshall College, is closely written in three large bound blank books. The first consists of 370 pages of text, the second of 387 pages, and the third of 32 pages. Occasional water staining and crabbed handwriting testify to the extraordinarily difficult conditions under which the manuscript was written and stored in the course of the four-year voyage.

In order to serve the interests of the general reader, the Penguin edition reproduces only slightly more than half of the 253,500 words of the original journal. The omitted material falls into three broad categories: lengthy passages of what would seem to be literary experimentation in which the young Reynolds imitates the sentimental tone and substance of the gift books and magazines of his era; repetitive accounts of routine duties such as surveying and keeping watch; and extended narratives of shore excursions in such places as Madeira, Peru, and Singapore, relatively familiar ground for nineteenth-century travel writers. To facilitate access to the entire journal, the editors have deposited a complete transcript in the library at Franklin and Marshall.

The exigencies of the voyage at times required Reynolds to record events out of their chronological sequence. A month or more of demanding activity would force him to defer writing until an interlude of quiet allowed him to take up his pen once more. As a result, his narrative sometimes moves in mysterious ways, looping confusingly back and forth between past and present. In those rare instances, the Penguin edition rearranges Reynolds's text so as to produce a consecutive account.

Beyond extensive abridgement and infrequent reordering, the Penguin edition silently emends the text of the journal in a few small ways. The editors have supplied punctuation and capitalization where needed to clarify Reynolds's meaning, as when he neglects to indicate the division of his sentences. The names of vessels have been italicized, and unfamiliar abbreviations have been expanded. Curved brackets enclose Reynolds's insertions in the text, most of them apparently made months after the original composition. Square brackets enclose editorial intrusions. With these exceptions the Penguin edition reproduces the form and substance of the text as Reynolds wrote it.

The Private Journal of
William Reynolds

[CHAPTER 1: TO THE SOUTH ATLANTIC]

Saturday, August 18th, 1838

Let the day be registered & remembered; the Ships are off! *We* are "once more upon the water."

Farewell home! Welcome the stirring scenes of strange Lands. May God in his watchful care, preserve us from all dangers, and return us in safety to those, whom we love better than all the things of Earth; and *they;* oh! shield *them* from harm, give them health & peace, grant them every blessing, and in mercy to *us,* allow them *all* once more to see the wanderers from the firesides.

At Sea, Vincennes[1]
September 11th 1838

Here we are, just one half of the Squadron, with a fine fair breeze, a smooth sea & cloudless sky, the Sunny Isle of Madeira with all its charms in prospect.

The poor *Relief* was so dull a sailer, that we cast her off many days ago; I believe she is to go to Rio direct, or perhaps touch at the Capa de Verde. The *Peacock* and *Flying Fish* parted from us one night in a blow, and have not been seen since. The *Porpoise* & *Sea Gull* are with us, but we have the heels of them both.

September 13th 1838

To-day the Captain[2] *promulgates* an order from the Secretary of the Navy,[3] accompanied by some of his own remarks, to the effect that all officers are to keep daily records of occurrences, with our observations thereon, to be sent to him weekly for inspection, & at the end of the cruize transmitted to the Navy Department to be used, if they possess any merit. In obedience to which I shall commence another [journal]. I cannot think of letting this go before any ones eyes but those few at home, who will be kind enough to excuse inaccuracies of thought or expression, & who will feel an interest in the writing, because of their love for him who writes.

September 14th

That saucy little beauty the *Sea Gull* has been alongside to-day, & her commander[4] on board. Gave him the general order for his edification. Sale of contents of the lucky bag.[5]

September 15th

My forenoon watch: a glorious breeze right aft & the appearance of the ocean covered with foaming white caps so beautiful as to charm the gaze of all the Scientifics.[6] Several American Brigs in sight; the *Porpoise* spoke one of them. We sail so fast, that neither Brig nor Schooner can come near us, and have been all morning under short sail.

At noon in spreading more canvass to chase a stranger Brig, the Seaman who was loosing the lofty topgallant sail was caught around the *neck* by one of the small ropes, and swung off! A fearful spectacle! Literally hung! His form was tossed about with the roll of the Ship, and as his face blackened, our hearts were chilled with horror, for there appeared to be no chance of saving him. Should we haul upon the rope, he would be choked; did we let it go, he would be dashed to the deck. The *Vincennes* was likely to become a Gallows, and one of her own crew to be hung unto death without a hand raised to save him. Moments were passing rapidly with the unfortunate man; with us they were of terrible interest.

At length *we* could & did act. The Sail was taken in, & some of the topmen who had hastened aloft, at the risk of their own lives, got hold of their shipmate, & a sudden flap of the sail took the rope clear of his neck. God be praised, said all on deck; *he is saved!! he is dead!* came down in the husky tones of sorrow from above! Every man & boy on board was now on deck, the Doctor's men going aloft, when the cheering cry "he is coming to!" was called out.

In a few minutes George Porter[7] was in possession of his senses, which we thought had left him forever. A few bruises on his body, some chaffing about the neck, & some few moments of unpleasant feeling were the amount of the affair; but the sight was a dreadful one, one which I know will haunt me in my dreams, & be often before my waking eye. The cry & the look of the one who first saw him from the deck were wild & fearful, unearthly—the boatswain, it was he, seemed turned into a stone, inanimate, speechless, after the first cry. Well he might, the sight was most appalling.

That the man's life should be preserved was most miraculous. The rope caught around his jaws & the back of his head, and so *only* stopped his breath for the time instead of breaking his neck. He says he remembers nothing but a shaking sensation, has no recollection of swinging about, & that had he died, his death would have been most easy; he would have gone without pain. Now that he has life he feels fine. I always thought hanging & drowning were easy deaths.

Sunday, [September] 16th

All last night I was thinking & dreaming of the ghastly sight of the morning! Had the poor man been killed, I think but few of the men could have been induced to go aloft for some time to come. Their superstition would have prevented them;— innumerable tales have been going the rounds among officers & men, fearful ones, too, such as would make a volume of marvellous events; as each told his story, he could say "all of which I saw, part of which I was."[8] It is strange how much one can witness in a short lifetime; much more than many will credit to listen to.

Made Madeira at 8 A.M. & with a fine breeze came rapidly

up with the Land—performed divine Services. At sundown we anchored in Funchal Roads, the Schooner *Flying Fish* coming in at the same moment from around the Eastern end of the Island. The next morning the *Peacock* anchored—strange that we should have crossed the Ocean without seeing each other & yet have been so near. To our great joy an American Brig was at anchor and to sail in a few days for New York. We could write *home,* and our hearts were full of gladness.

We left Madeira on Saturday afternoon the 25th September, with a breeze from the West at getting under weigh, which hauled to the North East before we were clear of the Roads. We ran through a great deal of green water of the hue that the Sea has in Soundings. At 300 fathoms depth we could not find the bottom. On our coast when the water is so discolored, the depth is about 20 to 30 fathoms. When we first run into the green, the transition was so sudden and unexpected that quite a hue and cry was raised in the Ship. We were sure we would find Shoal water, and thought that such a discovery would tell well & be a propitious commencement for us.

On October 1st, Latitude 19°25' North, Longitude 20°51' West, we hove to during the night, and had the Squadron spread out abreast through the day to look for a Shoal spot whereon the Portuguese Schooner *Maria* struck & lost her rudder in 1821. We passed over the place marked on the chart, but could see nothing of shallow water. October 3d, we were looking for the Bonetta Shoal, in the same manner, and with the same ill success. As the Captain said to me at breakfast, this shoal hunting gives an excitement to navigation that makes the time pass more rapidly and more agreeably. On board all the vessels many were the eyes that were straining to catch the first glimpse of Breakers or discolored water, and many were the warnings sent through the trumpet to those aloft to be watchful & keen sighted. A spirit of ardour & liveliness was among the crew, and all listlessness forgotten.

We have disturbed immense shoals of flying fish, myriads of them, like flights of swallows leaving for a brief flight the waters of the ocean. Several were caught & drawings made by Mr. Drayton,[9] Dissections by Mr. Pickering.[10] On the 2d two

Land Birds, one a Swallow, the other Genus unknown, were flying around us.

October 5th, made the Islands of Buonvista & Mayo. On the 6th made St. Jago.[11] At Sundown stood off and on the Land, having sent the *Flying Fish* into Port Raya Roads to see if the *Relief* had been there. The sea that night presented so beautiful a sight as to keep us all long on deck wondering and admiring— the phosphorescence was so luminous, so brilliant. When our good ship parted the waters and far in her wake whereon the tiny waves broke were masses of shining spray, bright even to whiteness. Every drop that was tossed up shone from its own light, and as it fell again into the ocean, diffused around it rings & circles of the same intense glow, the night being black as Erebus. The land in the distance & the dull yet distinct booming of the surf added to the contrast and effect. Even the idlers were lured up from their haunts below.

My middle watch that night. At 7 in the morning we were all at Anchor in the Roads. The Shore is bold and can be approached nearly. We saw herds of cattle grazing on the hills, & Fishermen hauling their prey from below the rocks. A deserted battery on a rocky summit looked so forlorn & contemptible that it was a fair sample of what the town proved.

I went ashore among the first, landing on a rugged rock, the leap to which, from the boat was rather precarious. Scrambling from thence to the beach, we walked towards the Town. It stands on a sandy bluff overhanging the surf. The ascent is rough enough, and when up—oh ascent of dreariness! Such a town—not a blade of grass, but houses, streets, people looking lean, starved and miserable. *I* thought I *had* seen primitive, & wretched places *before;* but Port au Praya must now take the head of the list. One day is *too* much to spend there. God! to drag out a lifetime in such a hole.

At daylight we left the anchorage & same day spoke [a] Danish brig, 28 days from Rio de Janeiro, bound to the Baltic. Requested him to report us, right glad of the opportunity to have intelligence of the American Exploring Expedition conveyed to that quarter of the world.

On the 9th October spoke the English ship *Crusader,* 75 days from Bombay, bound to London. On the 14th, we spoke the Genoese Barque *Santa Maria* bound to Rio de Janeiro. At night lost the *Peacock* & next day began to fill up water from the rain; in my watch the first was collected. The necessity of examining some shoals lying out of the usual track will lengthen our passage & make it necessary to economize. In the afternoon spoke an English Whaler, *Narwhal*, from New Zealand, bound home; requested him to report us. We have spoken more vessels already in this Short cruize than I ever did before. Because we are in no hurry to make short passages, and we are anxious to get and to give all information possible, we run out of our own course to speak with strange sail, which is seldom practised by our lazy commanders. Let them zig-zag on. The less their sluggard comfort is disturbed, the better. *I* like the excitement of the chase & the novelty of meeting with strangers.

I have had a slight difficulty with the First Lieutenant,[12] from which, thank Heaven, I came off very well. The Captain, to whom I resorted, promised I should not be so treated again, and that *he* had *never* authorised the charge "of neglect of duty" against any officer in the Ship. I liked him for that, and true to his word he called the First Lieutenant into his Cabin. I perceive a change in the gentleman's behaviour to me already. I never expected to be at issue with him. When we sailed together before, he was uniformly so kind & so gentlemanly, that I entertained the highest opinion of him, and was rejoiced to find him on board the same ship with me. Why he began upon me I do not know.

I bore with him until forbearance ceased to be a virtue and then appealed to the Captain, whose high souled sentiments could not brook that one of his Officers, should be treated with harshness, or singled out for unjust oppression. {Bah!—he hated Craven & this was the reason he took my part. Fool that I was, not to have seen through him then.} "I understand you, Mr. Reynolds," said he, "& depend upon it, such things shall not happen again." Had I not known Captain Wilkes well and been fully aware that he was free from all petty notions, such as that my rank will permit him to inflict insult without fear of after consequences or censure, I never would have gone to him with my complaint against his first Lieutenant. {Mercy! as things have turned out, I *did not* know *him* at all. In abuses & insults, he has since exceeded any one whom I ever saw.} Most captains would have added to the insult, instead of soothing it. Captain Wilkes knows what is due one Gentleman from another, {Does he indeed? He forgot all about it soon after this} and he will have every one's feelings respected, even a Passed Midshipman's, from the ill nature of a First Lieutenant.

The row on board here has been the first & I trust will be the last during the cruize—I will try never to offend, but I *will not* be trampled on, and now to change the unwelcome subject.

Thursday Evening, October 25th

We have now been 68 days out from Hampton Roads and rather more than a month from Madeira, and 18 days from Port Praya. At Madeira I laid in fowls, fruit, potatoes, &c., for my mess and at Port Praya replenished the stock as well as I was able, but not believing that we would be so long on our way to Rio de Janeiro, I did not purchase enough, and I am witnessing the daily vanishing of Fowls & potatoes with inconceivable interest. However, we shall have plenty of Sea fare to resort to— good middlings, beef, bean soup, maccaroni, hams, tongues, bolognas, pickled oysters, preserved fruits & cranberries, pickles, cheese, fresh bread, &c. We shall do well, but if I had thought that our time would have been so lengthened at sea, I should have provided more extensively in the fresh grub line.

We have been beating against a southerly wind for some days to get in the vicinity of a supposed shoal. We have seen nothing of it as yet, and the Captain has been much disappointed in not meeting with the *Peacock,* whose cooperation he expected in the search. There is yet another shoal yet to find before we can steer away for Rio, and we may be a month out yet. Better time for working "dead horse out."[13]

We have caught 4 or 5 sharks, two of them of the Species Blue, the beautiful colour of the element which is *their* and *our* home. The largest measured 10 feet. Mr. Drayton took sketches of them, and Dr. Pickering wrote down many hard names, as he overhauled them. These Scientifics manifest much ardour in their several pursuits. At Sea on calm days they put their scoop nets into the ocean to catch the Animalculae or Verterbrae with which the water is alive. It is wonderful to observe these things through a microscope and see how nature has provided for them, and how many beauties are disclosed that were not perceptible to the naked Eye. And then on shore they collect every thing that is curious, specimens of which are preserved and drawings taken. It is part of my day's amusement, to look over the labours of the Scientifics, and I learn much that I would not otherwise have known of.

Like all landsmen they were greatly mystified at the multifarious and apparently complicated and confused operations on ship board, and were perfectly amazed to witness the nice and delicate skill displayed in the manoeuvering of the vessel. And well they might: presence of mind & promptness, under all circumstances, faultless judgement regarding the weather, a thorough knowledge of the qualities and capabilities of his ship, a keen and watchful eye to detect a wrong set to a sail, or a complaining of a spar, an infinity of resources under accident or changes, and a knowledge to apply the physical force of the crew, as well as to keep them under the necessary restraint are some of the requisites that an Officer of the Deck *must* possess and exercise every day of his life.

Long habit & severe training will often give to the dull or the naturally timid officer the qualities so essential, though it must be owned that there *are officers* who are *not Seamen*. Such an one on board Ship is well watched and but slightly trusted to. At night, particularly, the anxious commander will be vigilant when the unfortunate one may have charge of the safety of the Ship & those she contains. At other times he will slumber on in conscious security.

October 26th

I am thankful that my young years have been passed in a profession which certainly calls forth the noblest & most daring traits of man's nature—pity it could not banish all the *dross!* I think I must just be about 20 years older & wiser, if I be not better, than the quiet and simple young man who William Reynolds would have grown into had his life been passed on Shore. I can imagine how contracted would have been my ideas & how darkened my mind—and how little would I have known of the world and its ways. Not that I will say my ideas embrace the widest possible range, or that my mind is of a brilliant order, or that the insight I have had into the doings of men has made me think better of them. I mean no vanity but speak in the comparitive.

And this is Saturday the 27th of October, and we have been 70 days out from home. And this day besides being the monthly-versary of our sailing is the one on which all sailors invariably toast "Sweet hearts & wives." Disbarred almost entirely from the sweet and fascinating influence of female society, passing months on the wide ocean with the same rude forms around us, no wonder that our thoughts & memories turn "to those we've left behind."

Sunday, 28th

A few Evenings ago, the men were allowed to bathe overboard, a lower studding sail being first spread in the water so as to form a protecting basin. Some ventured beyond its limits, but no sharks came near, and all were safe.

Yesterday a Buoy fitted with a staff & having a bottle attached containing instructions for the *Peacock,* was thrown overboard and sent adrift. The Captain thinks the *Peacock* to be astern, and as she must pass over the same *ground* with ourselves, he hopes she will meet his messenger. In case of its falling into strange hands, the papers are requested to be transmitted to the Navy department. These things are often done at Sea to show the set of the currents or from utter curiosity. Today the Purser[14] and myself committed [a bottle] to the mercy of the waters. As the old Purser says, there is as much chance of my being married within the next three years as of that bottle ever being picked up. Says I, perhaps we may read of that event, when we are snug at home, with a wife and ——— by our side. Says he, *do tell.*

We have all seen the daylight and the moonlight and the

starlight. And *you* all have witnessed the green and ghastly hues thrown around by the light of the Furnace Fire,[15] but *you* have *not* seen a Blue Light burnt at Sea. The night may be utterly dark, and we wish to communicate with the others of the accompanying vessels. The blue light forms a portion of the signal. It is fired, and a blazing, brilliant illumination ensues. The suddenness is most startling, and for some moments ship and ocean are of dazzling azure. The light is most intense; it glares far above the mast heads. Sails, rigging & men are all blue, but distinct, as when the sun shines at Noon-day. The sky is hid from view, and without a small circle around the Ship, there seems a wall of blackness. A little while, and the gloom of night succeeds. Should there be one of the squadron within the range, the effect is increased, but it is grand at all times.

The blue lights are followed by rockets, false fires,[16] [and] flashes of lantherns, so that there is always much animation excited when night signals are going on. An interest is felt in the questions and replies, and we admire the ingenuity of the method by which communication can be sustained without the necessity of close proximity of position.

Monday October 29th

Last night during the first watch, which I kept most faithfully, the moon was at half full, but the scud was flying so as to obscure her at times, and there was some mistiness in the atmosphere. Yet notwithstanding these obstructions, I could read writing very easily, when I could not see the moon at all. Nights in the Tropics are always brighter than in other regions, though why I cannot tell. Our own winter moons when the snow is on the ground, do not shed so much light, at which I wonder.

I have been reading the histories of English discovery & Surveying voyages, both in the olden times & in our own days. The English have almost certainly, had vessels employed in surveying unknown seas, & the French & Russians have not been idle. The Dutch, Spanish & Portuguese, who were wont to be foremost in the search for new Lands, have now become unable to prosecute anything of the Kind, and can scarcely main-tain the possessions they have already acquired. And behold! now a nation, which but a short time ago was a discovery itself and a wilderness, is taking its place among the enlightened of the world, and endeavouring to contribute its mite in the cause of knowledge and research. For this seems the age in which all men's minds are bent to learn all about the secrets of the world which they inhabit.

Captain Wilkes is a man of great talent {great mistake, did not at this time know him}, perhaps genius. His first effort on the Sea was as a cabin boy, in which situation his Father placed him, hoping he would become disgusted, and take up with a life on Shore. It would not do, & he entered the Navy. Always of a mathematical turn, he at an early period was noted for his application to studies of that nature. He has visited at the Royal Observatories of Greenwich & Paris and worked with an Instrument maker, thus acquiring a practical as well as theoretical knowledge of the uses of different instruments. He has had much experience with them since, is an excellent astronomer {all in the wrong, all humbug—a little smattering & much boasting on his part deceived others beside myself}, & well acquainted with the mysteries of chemistry & the operations of natural philosophy. He has eighteen years of service in his profession, during which his peculiar & valuable qualities have been noted and appreciated. He speaks several tongues, and has an exquisite Skill in coloring and sketching.

While in Europe he was fortunate in meeting with the persons who have commanded the late expeditions: Captains Parry, Ross, Franklin, Beechy,[17] and others distinguished for their attainments & enthusiasm in such efforts. From them he derived much & important information that will be of service to him during the cruize. In my humble opinion {woefully changed since}, Captain Wilkes is the most proper man who could have been found in the Navy to conduct this Expedition, and I have every confidence {soon lost it} that he will accomplish all that is expected, if accidents do not interfere of a kind that cannot be avoided.

Well, who knows {*who* did know how things would change?} what will be the termination of this cruize? May it be a favorable one, say I, for the honor of America and for the credit of the humble instruments employed.

I have often remarked the change that occurs in the habits & disposition of Animals that are kept for any time on Ship board. Constant association with man and the narrow limits of Ship board effect the alteration. They come to my mind just now (i.e. at 5 hours, 20 minutes in the evening of Friday, the 2d of November) from watching the gambols of a Fox on the other side of the deck. He has become very dog-like. Though with not all the affection of the canine race, he has all the playfulness. He eat too much Shark the other day, became sick, & was brought to the Doctor. The remedy administered "vi et armis"[18] was castor oil, & in a short time Reynard had recovered his health & spirits.

A horde of huge Black Fish came swimming by the Ship last evening as my eye was fixed on the smiling seas. They were going to the Eastward, heaving their lengths out of the water & their black bodies glistening with spray.

Monday, Nov 5th South latitude.

Once more I am South of the Equator. I can recollect when passing the boundary line between "two counties" was an event with me. I thought myself a Traveller and felt as if I were then in a Strange Land. And *now,* this is the *Seventh time* I have crossed the *Meridian* line of the *great globe* itself.

This morning the Division of small arm men, to which I have the honour to belong, were exercised firing at a Target. It was well riddled. The men are well drilled, and I anticipate much of adventure in the excursions we shall make into the interior of unknown Countries. There is a rapture in the very thought!

Observing the Ocean to be thronged with living things that were of unusual brilliancy making a path of shining light on the water, we stopped the Ship's way, and fished some up. They were strange & beautiful to see. They were of the form of one's finger but longer and hollow. They became entirely dark and then suddenly changed into a bright emerald, illuminating the water in which they were confined. In a short time the chamelion-like power was destroyed, and the "Pyrosomia"[19] were dim, dull, *dead!* For they possess animation—you can see the breathings plainly, regular as those of men. And the Ocean is teeming with the like, food provided for the monsters who range the deep.

The Scientifics cut up & dissect and overhaul, and use a magnifying power the better to see, and make drawings & paintings, and search their books, and write down learned descriptions, and invent unpronounceable terms, and tell *us* all about the mysteries of organization, &c., &c. And they have dead & living lizards, and fish floating in alcohol, and shark jaws, & stuffed turtles, and verterbrata and animalculæ frisking in jars of salt water, and old shells, and many other equally interesting pieces of furniture hanging about their beds & around their state rooms—such sweet looking objects as doubtless glad scientific eyes to behold. Catch any of them in my *room*—no, no!—I'll *visit*, when I have curiosity in that way.

Tuesday Afternoon

We have run over the place where the Triton Shoal is marked down on the chart without being able to discover any traces of its existence. I have a natural liking to be aloft, and so I perched myself on the Fore Top Gallant Yard and strained my optics for a sight of discoloured water, but in vain.

Monday November 12th

Yesterday my watch was in the afternoon. We were running for "Krusenterns submarine volcanoe," said to have vented & to have been seen by Admiral Krusenstern[20] in 1806. The Russian, I believe, made it a request to our Government that the Expedition should look for it. Having every confidence in the chronometer, we ran right over the situation marked on the chart without seeing smoke or land. We had no faith in its existence, & I am surprised that the old Admiral should cling to his supposed discovery with so much pertinacity.

In calling the men up to make sail, one of the Quarter Gunners was violent & disobedient to me and of course guilty of a breach of discipline. He was confined for the night & this morning disrated—reduced in his rank, station & pay. It is unpleasant to be forced to do these things, but it is an imperative act of duty which must not be neglected. The man is a German. I hope his place will be filled by a more worthy man, and he an American. This is the 2d Petty Officer in the course of my service I have been obliged to proceed against. My feeling of regret will perhaps be not so acute as I grow used to such things. I hope they will not occur often. Two men were punished with the Cats this forenoon for drunkenness.

And now we are making a short wake for Rio. I am heartily glad of it. Few of us thought to have been more than 60 days at the utmost on the passage, & I had no idea that we should make Madeira & searching for these shoals and carrying but short sail to keep the Squadron together have been causes of delay. This is the 86th day out from Hampton Roads. We shall be near the end of 100 days ere we get in. 14 weeks! why there will be 3½ months spun out, a quarter of a year gone! April will soon come. We shall be busily employed in the intermediate time & full of happy anticipations concerning the letters we shall find at Valparaiso, & then "the Islands"—the Columbia River! New South Wales! Japan! China! and a thousand other places to go to & for. Whew! the cruize will pass rapidly—I have not had a long or heavy hour yet.

Wednesday November 14th

We have been running along famously, but not under a press of canvass. The other vessels are not able to keep up with us and we have often to reduce sail. We are anxious to get in and expect to find *late* papers from the United States, those having notices of our sailing &c. &c. *Some* will look for *letters* and perhaps receive them. I wish *I* dared hope, but I know that nothing but a fortunate accident could have occasioned the forwarding of any to me so soon, & I know *too well* that none such have occurred. I shall be sad when I see others *happy,* but I shall not be disappointed. Next April—*six months yet*—we shall be in Valparaiso, and then *all hands* will be *certain* of letters by the Store Ship that is *now,* about this time, *leaving* the United States. To be disappointed then would bring me to the very extreme of wretchedness.

The other day, when attempting to find the temperature of the Ocean at a great depth, the copper sounding line carried away, and we lost *one mile* of it & the self registering thermometer! There is yet a mile or more remaining.

Friday November 16th.

Dined with the Captain Yesterday. We have seen the Magellan Clouds for some time past. They are a phenomenon not as yet satisfactorily explained.

Whenever the Division exercises, I take my place in the ranks, and go through with the manual exercise. Run to Sea to learn a Soldier's duty. I hope to become a proficient with the Musquet and to handle it with a decided *"air militaire."* I do this from my own choice. I think it necessary I should know how to perform that which I require from the men, & having so excellent a drill officer as Mr. Johnson,[21] all hands have the best example set them in his ardor & expertness. Most sailors know how to load & fire a musket, but generally they disdain to learn more. In our instance, they have all become fond of drill, chiefly because there is hope they will have a chance for *honor* on shore.

Saturday November 17th.

This day seven years ago I was appointed as an Acting Midshipman. Of this time, I have been on duty 5 years and seven months: 2 years & 6 months in the *Boxer* & *Peacock,* 1 year & 6 months in the *Potomac* & *Delaware,*[22] 9 months at the Norfolk School and attending my Examination[23] at Baltimore & sick at the Philadelphia Hospital (in this period I made a visit home of a week or ten days), 1 month in the *Pennsylvania,*[24] 3 months at Washington[25] & 4 months on board the *Vincennes.* When I was in the Hospital, I was not on duty to be sure, but I was subject to the care & disposal of Government. One year & five months I have been on "leave of absence," mostly at home: 3 months when I returned from the East Indies, 7 months when I came from the Mediterranean, 4 months after leaving the Hospital & until I joined the *Pennsylvania,* 3 months subsequent to leaving her at the Expiration of which I went to Washington, making a trip home ere I put my foot on board the *Vincennes.* Thus, if I do not slip my cable[26] this cruize, out of 11 or most likely 10 years service, I shall have passed but the same 17 months of that time with my family.

The same average may continue while I remain in the Navy, & *what would* a wife say to have but *one* year in *ten* of her husbands company? It will *not* do—there will be *no* Mrs. *William* Reynolds. There would be but little use in registering my experience with the Ladies—at least that part of it, which has been frivolous & light. If I have had any of a serious nature—why, *mum* must be the word. But then, if I have not—well, its no matter about it, although this being Saturday evening, I have quaffed a fervent toast to "Sweethearts & Wives."

Tuesday 20th.

The weather, which for some weeks past has been delightful, yesterday changed for the worse—squally, with rain & lightning. I & all of us hoped to run quietly into Rio, to be at anchor there on Thursday. We may have still rough weather and be a longer time out. My very heart has been in my mouth, at the idea of being once more in Rio. Pleasant are my recollections of days passed there, and I yearn to be in the midst of that scenery, the sublime beauty of which, surpasses mortal power to describe. I wish that —— —— —— —— —— —— —— (fill up the blanks as you please) were by my side when the *Vincennes* shall pass through the narrow entrance & become herself a portion of the glorious picture then open to the view!

[CHAPTER 2: RIO AND THE ARGENTINE COAST]

Saturday, one week ago, or one week ago yesterday, whichever be the proper phraseology, we anchored in the harbor, no, Bay of Rio de Janeiro. 'Tis the same as ever: the same enchanting beauties, the same wondrous prospects, the same sublimity of scenery that charmed my young heart some eight years ago are now around me, fresh & unchanged. Well may you say "it is a goodly sight to see."

[A few days ago] Old Whittle[1] & I set off about 3 in the afternoon, determined on reaching the Peak [of Corcovado] if possible, though we did not know the road, nor have any idea of the difficulties that might lie in our way. We were well mounted, however, & carried some *encouragement* in our pockets.

We followed the acqueduct as our guide, and before we finally turned into the Hills, we enjoyed several glorious prospects of the City at our feet & the lively waters of the Bay. The road now led by gentle ascents up the mountain & through dense forests that afforded a grateful shade from the Sun. Now & then the trees would disappear as we passed the head of some valley and opened a magnificent vista of the distant country, the sight of which made our very hearts leap with delight. The road was smooth & green, & we galloped lightly along, the horses feet unheard on the soft turf, and the songs of birds & the murmuring of the falling water making sweet music to our ears.

The acqueduct was a noble work of masonry, entirely above ground, with grated apertures at intervals, where you could obtain a refreshing draught. When it crossed a deep valley, it was carried boldly over by a double tier of arches raised one on top of the other, & though this may be in opposition to modern methods of engineering, there is no questioning the wonderfully picturesque & airy effect, which it lends to the view. The windings of the acqueduct to preserve the most gradual rise were manifold, & we turned & turned, now losing an open prospect & plunging into a solitude of trees, & now emerging into the sunshine and gaining another glance of the far waters of the Bay until we had advanced more than half way to the summit, which at times we could discover, apparently right over our heads. So lofty & so awfully steep & isolated did it appear, that we began to admit the possibility of having to descend but little wiser than when we started.

After some sharp riding, we reached a small cleared place, where several houses were erected & were obliged to bring up suddenly, for we found ourselves on a small ridge which looked right down into a very deep valley with the Ocean rolling on to its beach. We here turned sharp to the left, & commenced the last ascent to the Peak itself. The way was very steep, & the road wound upwards in frequent "*zig zags,*" like the flights of stairs in a house. It was the toughest work the horses had to do, but fifteen minutes hard scrambling carried us above the trees and vegetation, & we emerged on to the naked rock of the summit so suddenly as to take us by surprize.

And well might we wonder at our situation. We were on an uneven mass of black rock about 30 yards in extent in one direction & 15 in another, and on every side but the one by which we had ascended, falling down in tremendous precipices for thousands of feet to the plain below, which was on the level of the Ocean. We dismounted, & fastening the horses to some iron stanchions which were soldered in the rock & had once supported a look out house, we took their saddles off & turned to view the prospect our situation commanded.

The Ocean, the Bay in all its windings, dotted with Islands & Ships, a vast extent of country & the city were spread beneath us like a map, and formed a panorama the glorious magnificence of which is not in the power of the mind to conceive or the tongue to tell. The peak we were upon projected into the plain from the ridge of mountains in the back ground like as a Cape obtrudes itself into the Sea, and as I have mentioned, it was on three sides a grand wall of granite, so steep and perpendicular that from where we stood it seemed as if we could cast a stone into the Streets of the City below, though, in reality, it was 7 or 8 miles distant from the base of the rock. The baldness of the summit contrasted strongly with the living green of the vegetation which reached so nearly to the very top, and the only objects in the view that were at all indistinct were the spirelike peaks of the Organ Mountains at the head of the bay, which in themselves were an appropriate barrier to occupy the horizon in one direction, in opposition to the Ocean in the other.

A small portion of this rocky table was separated from the rest by a wide chasm of about 20 feet in depth, the sides of which were precipitous and afforded no hold for the hands or feet. On the detatched part, a flag staff had been put up from which waved the tri colored ensign of France. I own to possessing some little of that restless disposition which prompts men to undertakings that expose them to great personal risks without affording the slightest advantages except the gratification attending the successful accomplishment of one's whims, & in the present situation, I think I must have been impelled by the desire merely to carry out Sam Patch's[2] maxim "that some things can be done as well as others," although I confess that when the idea first occurred to me, the method whereby to achieve the feat did not present itself. But it was evident that some Frenchmen had crossed over, and why should not we!

Old W[hittle] was content to let well enough alone, & thought we were well enough where we were. He could see no contrivance to aid us, and to attempt the thing with hands & feet only would be to give ourselves a very certain & gentle slide into eternity. I was bent upon putting my handkerchief above that Flag, and after puzzling a little while, went to work with the only means in our power.

We took the cruppers, stirrup leathers & girths, knotted them together, & securing one end to an Iron stanchion that stood near the brink of the fissure, hove the other down the rock. Now, to be sure, these made a very precarious rope & we had some misgivings as to the result of the adventure. If the leather did *not* break & we succeeded in the descent, we were not so certain of our ability *to get up* again, a process which was likely to resemble the crawling of a fly up a wall. However, "nick or nothing," here goes, and easing myself over the edge as gently as I could, I trusted my weight to the frail contrivance I had rigged. The instant I found myself fairly hanging by it, my confidance in its strength vanished entirely, & the thought of the 2000 feet below me was somewhat distressingly intrusive. In 3 seconds I was safely landed to my great relief, and encouraging W[hittle] to follow, I held the end of the rope for him & he joined me, safe & sound.

We here feasted ourselves upon the view beneath us, and the splendors of the mighty scene were now increased, by the golden glory of the whole Western sky when the sun was sinking in the Ocean, while in the East the full moon was whitening the Mountains, the City & the Bay. If Earth can afford another prospect like to this, I would travel for a year to see it, but I would take some one with me, who should *not* be *a man!*

We managed to ascend the rock, by the exercise of sheer strength of arm, & agility, and saddling our beasts, we commenced the descent, quite happy that we had *persevered* in all things. We chose a different route to return by, and that moonlight ride through the shadowy forest and along the shores of the glorious bay was like an excursion amid the witching scenery of fairy lands.

The *Relief* came in on Monday night, having been *one hundred days* in the passage. On leaving us, her commander struck to the South, and instead of fresh Westerly breezes, had variable and Easterly winds. Such a zig zag course I never saw. There was not the slightest occasion to explore so much of the Atlantic Ocean.

Sunday January 6th, we left our moorings & stood down the Bay with a light breeze from the Land. This ship and the *Peacock* ran into an English Slave Brig (a Prize[3] with her human cargo yet in bonds, not disposed of) but got clear without damage & with little delay. We were much mortified, because the thing *looked lubberly*, and right in the very face of every body among all the men of war. It was the first mishap of that kind that I ever witnessed occur to an American man of war. The English could not boast, however, for several of their Ships had lately gone on Shore and were days getting afloat. The Sea breeze set i[n] as we got clear, and we beat out, running clear in Shore on either tack, and obtaining the most beautiful views of the Shores and Bay. We all anchored outside, about 2 miles from the Sugar Loaf in a position which commanded a fine prospect of all the bold & strongly marked outlines of the Coast, the islands to seaward intercepting the horizon, & the grey towers of the City far in the distance.

The Altitude of the Sugar Loaf was measured, and the *Flying Fish* returned to Rio with officers to look for a Boy who had deserted from the Dingy but an hour before we sailed. Great must have been the surprise which overcame Henry Hughes when he felt the strong grasp of his officer on his shoulder at the very moment of all moments when he could have deemed himself safe & free.

At 9 P.M. on the 8th we weighed and stood to Sea. The night signals to the Squadron of rockets, blue lights, & the firing of the Guns had a fine effect.

February 7th

Time goes. I have left a wide gap, but actually I have not been able to write a line. Now I will endeavour to bring up the Lee way since leaving Rio.

Steering to the Southward & Westward. In two or three days, the wished for intelligence leaked out about our destination. We were to go to Orange Bay, adjacent to Cape Horn, where we would find the *Relief* & wood & water. On the 18th we spoke the [American whaler] *Leader*.[4] I dressed myself as spruce as possible & went on board. I wanted to show them a cleanly looking individual, a sight I knew they had not met with for months. The Captain was a hearty looking man, but rather greasy and a perfect Yankee. He gave us some Lemon juice, putting his Steward to some inconvenience to find the *third* tumbler. The Purser, who was with me, detected the smack of Rum in his glass. The old rascal indulged in something stronger than the acid antiscorbutic which he gave to us. We gave him our Letter Bag as he said he would send his Boat into Pernambuco, where he expected to be in a few weeks.

And now came out some more news—that we were to touch in at the mouth of the River Rio Negro, the boundary line between Buenos Ayres and Patagonia. This was unexpected but it was true, and before the first whispers grew loud, we were at anchor. On the 26th we came to, in a heavy squall from off the Land. The Schooners, running in Shore, grounded, and our boats were sent to their assistance. In the morning they were again afloat. Captain Ringgold,[5] several Officers & the Scientific Gentlemen went on board the *Sea Gull,* and stood in for the River. In the evening they got aground, and by a mistake in the signal we understood that the natives were attacking them. The Ship was in a commotion, & we soon had five boats full of men & Cutlasses pulling stoutly for the Shore.

I happened to be in the foremost & largest boat, and as I drew in, the other Schooner crossed my path, & I heard Captain Wilkes's voice calling me alongside. He had just left the *Sea Gull* & explained the true meaning of the Signal, but that she would not need any help. Presently the other boats came shooting out of the darkness & were also hailed. In a few minutes we were all again on board our own Ship, unstained with blood. I thought it was lucky we were called back, for the night was dark, and no one of us knew the way through the breakers. We would have been lost had we got among them.

As Events turned out, the people on Shore took us for a French Squadron and thought we had come to attack the place. The Governor withdrew all the Pilots from the mouth of the River, and the populace were in arms to resist the expected invasion. The women & children were sent to the Interior. It had entered into our heads that we might be mistaken for the French, & hence our readiness to conceive of an attack being made from the Shore.

On Sunday we had divine Services, and on Monday morning

the boats commenced the Survey. I went into the River in the *Flying Fish* to ascertain the rise and fall of the Tide and had an exceedingly tedious and uncomfortable day of it—nearly carried out to Sea by the current once, and perplexed & worried because I had not the means to go to work handily. The River was narrow but deep, and the rise & fall of the tide more than 12 feet. The Shores & Country as far as we could see were but plains of sand with now & then a slight hillock, green with long & wiry grass. Two horsemen came down mounted on noble beasts. Oh! but they were wild & picturesque in appearance as they coursed along the dark beach or dashed across the uplands, horse & rider in clear relief against the sky. How I wished for a sketch of the fierce & mobile features & graceful costume of the men, & of the Arab looking steeds.

In the Evening we returned to the Ship, and the next morning I was sent in the Dingy with the Tide Staffs[6] to Anchor off the mouth of the River and make my observations there. The weather was mild when I left the Ship, and I reached my birth & commenced operations without delay. The Whale Boats were at work all round me. At 8 I began, and until half past one all was right enough. By that time the tide had fallen considerably and was running out to Sea with great rapidity, the wind setting fresh against it and causing an unpleasant swell. Finding I could do nothing with the staffs though I had heavy shot to them, I hauled them up and lashed them along the gunwales of the boat & secured them, cutting the Shot adrift, as they would have proved too great a weight in my small boat. I trusted to the Lead line, which I had used in anticipation of the Staffs becoming useless.

Captain Wilkes had promised to pick me up at 2 with one of the Schooners, as he & I knew full well that after that time the Sea would break where I lay so as to swamp the Boat. ½ past 1 came, & a heavy squall hung over the Land, & the breakers were fast coming in. I could see the Schooners lying at their anchors, no sign of a movement there, & yet I did not like to quit my birth or relinquish my duties until the last moment, & I could see that if I remained much longer, the breakers alone, setting the squall out of the question, would prove my destruction, as my boat could not live in any sea. While I was hesitating, but at the same time all ready for a move, the welcome report of a Gun from the Ship broke on my ear, & the Cornet[7] was up, recalling all Boats. The Captain's watchful eye was upon us & the weather too.

Right gladly did I weigh my anchor & turn the Boat's head for the Ship, though in doing so I shipped a quantity of water. By keeping a bright lookout, I avoided the Breakers, passed safely between them, and aided by the Tide, in half an hour was on board, the Boat being half full of water, taken in from the tops of the Seas. The Whale Boats got off without difficulty, & all hands were rejoiced to find themselves in the safe asylum of their own good Ship. It is the most comfortable feeling in the world, when a man steps from danger into the midst of companions & security.

Next morning the Captain & myself left the ship in the Dingy to go on board the *Peacock* & then to the Schooners, he to one to Survey, I to the other to anchor in shore and make observations from her. When we got alongside the *Peacock,* the Schooners had been drifted far to leeward by the Tide, & leaving Captain W[ilkes] on board the P[*eacock*], I proceeded on to the *Porpoise* lying about two miles and a half off, thinking to come back with the turn of the Tide, which would also bring in the Schooners.

I did my errand on board the *Porpoise* & had got ½ a mile back on my return, when a Fog suddenly came on, and in a moment the *Peacock* was hid from view. I turned the Boat back, & lo! the Brig was obscured. The chance of finding her was the best, and after pulling 15 or 20 minutes, I caught sight of her and was soon on board, determined not to leave her until I could see my way. The Fog hung on till midnight, the Ship firing guns every half hour to denote her whereabouts to the absent Boats. But I held on to the Brig as there was no telling where the current might set me and the boat was not a fit one for a struggle. At Sundown, Captain Ringgold hoisted my Boat on board, declaring I should not venture from his vessel until I had a fair chance.

At 4 in the morning, the wind had shifted and was blowing

very heavily from South & South Southeast, tumbling a high Sea upon the Beach. Before 6 we were obliged to slip our cable and stand out under a press of sail to clear the Land, the whole Squadron doing the same. It was an anxious time, but the vessels behaved well, & aided by the set of the Tide, we soon gained a sufficient offing. I regretted much that Captain Wilkes could not know his Boat & crew were in safety. It was afternoon ere we came near enough to communicate by signal. I was miserably sick from the violent motion of the Brig, notwithstanding my 17 months experience in the Schooner *Boxer,* which I thought would quiet my *interior* forever. And then I missed my comforts, which are so great on board here, & I had a wretched day—the nauseous bilge water, too! oh faugh! horrid!

At Sundown the blow was over, & the Ships steering back for the Anchorage. My boat was hoisted out, and after tossing for a few minutes among the still troubled waters, I put my body once more aboard the *Vincennes,* receiving congratulations from many, who had thought of my return as a matter of some doubt. Truly I too rejoiced, and that night I slept well.

In the morning at 8 we anchored and sent two Boats in to look for 6 men that had been left on the Beach from the Boats. They had wandered into the country and could not find their way back. They were glad enough to return, as the resources of life were by no means plenty on the Shore. The tide was against the Boats as they came back, & it was midnight ere they came on board. The men were punished, for example's sake.

The Governor treated the Officers who visited him with all the generosity in his power, right glad to find friends when he expected & dreaded foes. He made presents to several of some fine Guanachoe skins and received in return such things as we had that were most acceptable to him, some cutlery, compasses &c.

Six Armadilloes & Ostriches were brought on board. The latter died; the former were killed & eaten. I have the armour like skull of one, which I hope to carry home. Game is abundant—deer & Birds. Barn door fowls were not to be had, but good Beef and Mutton were drove in for us. The Scientifics had quite a time & procured many Specimens, in their various branches.

Saturday Afternoon we weighed & went to sea with a fair wind, having made rather an unsatisfactory survey, the completion of it not being so necessary as to cause further delay.

Monday Evening the weather was threatening, and a heavy swell from the Southward & Eastward. The Schooners were directed to make the best of their way into the destined Port, and at dark they were out of sight. At 8 after one or two warning blasts, the wind increased to a half gale, and we soon had the Ship snug for the night under close reefed Topsails & Trysails. The Gale continued all Tuesday, blowing heavy, with a tremendous Sea. The Ship laboured much, damaging crockery by the wholesale & taking in oceans of water.

My bed not being in trim for a Gale, I could not lay on it and had no sleep.[*] To pass the night among such a million of noises from the tramping & voices of men, the bleating & grunting of the live stock, the workings of the Masts & guns, the creaking of the Ladders, the howling of the winds, the strong dash of the breaking waves, & the continual fetching away of some thing or other about decks is to suffer more than can be imagined, but which is well known to all who have weathered out a Gale at Sea. It is torture to sit at Meals. You are in agony for fear of broken dishes & lost mouthfulls & of becoming the recipient of your neighbour's plate, contents & all. A Mess at dinner when the Ship takes on a Gale, presents a sight ludicrous in the extreme to behold, but most horridly disagreeable to be a participator in.

Wednesday morning the Gale broke and the Sea went down. At 8 in the Evening it fell calm, and at 9 we had a breeze from the West South West which sent us on 6 & 7 knots on our course South South West. The Gale had blown us off East South East. We shook out the reefs and made sail, *Peacock* & *Porpoise* in company. To day it has been rainy, with squally appearances, & the breeze lighter.

The warm clothing has been served out to the crew, and we

[*]Lyman Gallard breaks his collarbone—groaning by my door.

all have had storm clothes prepared for the bad weather we expect—cold & rain. If I can only keep dry. It is the very devil, this getting wet on board Ship, but now, while I have my room as a sanctuary, I am better off than when in a steerage, where all was common.

Saturday February 16th

This morning at 4 A.M. in my watch, Cape Horn, was in full view, about 25 miles ahead—the weather mild, the sky clear, the sea smooth, & the Ship with all her studding sails set. This day 24 weeks ago, we left Hampton Roads!! It seems as if it were but yesterday!!

We have had several days of boisterous weather since leaving Rio Negro, and the air has been rather cool. Thermometer 40° to 50° and this in the heighth of summer *here*. My old acquaintances the Albatross have been around us for some days. And with them came some new visiters—Penguins & Shags.[8] The former dive, the latter fly much like our Ducks.

Daylight continues until after 8 P.M. and commences about 3.30 A.M., so that darkness has but a short reign. Long after the Sun sets & long ere he rises, the sky is of a bright & ruddy glow in the Western & Eastern horizons. The other night while all around was blackness & gloom, there remained in the West until 10 o'clock the fiery light left by the setting Sun.

We had a fine run through the Straits Le Maire, a passage dreaded by so many navigators, wind & tide carrying us 12 & 13 miles the hour by the Land. Both shores were bold, and with strongly marked outlines, Staten Island resembling the coast near Rio de Janeiro but infinitely more contorted & confused in its features. It seemed as if it had been thrown up by an Earthquake but the night before. The higher summits were covered with Snow while in the valleys we could discern whole forests of trees & Shrubs, though not *very* verdant in appearance. Numerous small & Rocky Islets were strewn along the Coast, detached from the Main Land and showing in the distance like vessels under sail. The Schooner *Sea Gull* came out from Good Success Bay as we passed but did not join us. She kept close in with the Shore, the wind blowing strong in Squalls, & reducing us down to close reefs more than once.

The Captain intended to hug the Southern Shore of Terra del Fuego and run into Orange Bay, passing between it & the Northern Shore of Hermit Island, the South Extremity of which is the much dreaded & much talked of promontory, Cape Horn, & had the wind held, would have done so, although the channel is imperfectly known, of narrow limits & lined with shoals. In this case we should not have doubled Cape Horn, although we should have attempted a more perilous navigation and have gone but a few miles to the Northward.

The change of wind brought us the unusual fine weather of to day, and at the time of this writing, we are a little South of the Cape, & as I have said before, with *warm* weather, a *light breeze* & a *smooth* Sea—a Good fortune which the oldest Cape Horners on board, never experienced before. How long this will continue I know not. Changes occur here, like Lightning—quick & often unexpected.

Sunday February 17th 1839

This day *Seven* years ago—I made my *debut,* on the ocean, and *now* I am off Cape *Horn.* Off Boston the weather was freezing, & here at this time it is mild & summer like. Seven years!!!

We doubled the Cape with Studding sails set, and even yet the weather continues pleasant. At Sundown last Evening, Cape Horn was to the Northward & Westward of us; we were fairly by it. This morning it was out of view. We are near the entrance of Orange Bay, but the wind being light and variable, we cannot make much head way. This Bay is the rendezvous, where we are to find the *Relief,* & wood and water. After supplying our wants, we shall leave of course, but whither none of us knows.

[CHAPTER 3: ORANGE HARBOR AND THE FAR SOUTHERN ISLANDS]

February 23rd. Saturday

During all Sunday until midnight the breeze continued light & baffling. At 6 "all hands" were called to work ship, for it was "*tack*" every 5 minutes. As darkness grew upon us, we became more anxious and were finally wound up to a high pitch of intense interest. We were in an unknown place; we knew nothing of the localities, nothing positive & certain. We had no soundings & of course could not Anchor. We were close in with the Land with but circumstances as they happened to guide us. We fired Guns & Rockets, hoping to attract the attention of the *Relief*. We strained our sight to find the Light which she was to have displayed on a high hill, and twice we mistook the twinkling stars as they rose over the Land for the revolving light of the *Relief*. At Midnight the wind freshened slightly. The Men were sent to Supper, and regaled with hot Coffee! We, the Officers, had a *lunch* below. The Topsails were reefed, and we stood off Shore & then hove too, the Land being all around us. Spliced the "*Main Brace.*"

At 4 there was light enough to read, and we stood on, the *Porpoise* close by. At 5 we descried the *Relief* at Anchor, and the Sun was rising in fiery splendor. At 6 we were anchored, and all was right. The troubles of the night were at an end. The hammocks were piped down, and until 12 there were but *two* individuals awake on board the *Vincennes*. Oh! *how sweet* was *my sleep*.

Officers came on board from the *Relief;* instead of the usual stir & bustle of a man of war's deck there was, in open daylight, the deathlike silence of sleep. All hands were at their rest, that rest which they needed so much. At noon we were aroused. All the Boats were hoisted out & the Ship Moored. The water was smooth as glass and the air of a summer warmth. Many birds were flying & swimming around us—Penguins, Ducks, Albatross & Gulls in fancied Security. I shot a Penguin from the Deck. A canoe with a Family of *Fuegians* was coming alongside. They very quietly transferred the bird to their canoe and manifested no disposition to give it up. I let them have it. They would not come on board, the man intimating by signs that he had far to go. They had, however, been on board the *Relief,* where the crew gave them old clothes. The manner they put them on was grotesque enough.

The Canoe was small, of bark, and rudely constructed. The Cargo was a living one. Father, Mother, & a half grown boy formed the active portion, and *three babes,* coiled away on beds of grass were the passive part. The little innocents were nestling close to each other and took up but small stowage. Abaft there was a fire made over a layer of mud, and in the Stern the three who used the paddles, the woman and boy working the most. The young ones were of a light yellow colour and had bright black eyes & an animated expression of countenance, unusual in children of so few years. They were not disfigured with paint. The woman was, & her mouth ran from ear to ear. The Man's face had an intelligent look and was rather a pleasant one. His tongue ran fast, and his voice was musical. He manifested no fear or distrust of us and evidently was an old visiter to Ships. After appropriating my Penguin, he paddled away and soon disappeared around a point of land. Whither he came, or where he went, we know not. His was the third canoe that had visited the harbour, two prior to our arrival.

No sooner had we cast anchor here than the veil of mystery regarding our movements was withdrawn, and all hands went to work as if Life & death depended on their exertions. The *Peacock* & *Flying Fish* were to go *South* in one Meridian, Captain Wilkes in the *Porpoise* with the *Sea Gull* to go South in a different Longitude. The *Relief* [was] to pass through Magellan

Straits, [and] the [*Vincennes*] to be laid up snug to receive on board the invalids of the active vessels [and] to supply their places with the strong of our crew. Not only this, but officers were to change their Ships & the whole domestic arrangement of the Squadron was to be overturned. And of all this we had been in utter ignorance; we did not even dream of it, and yet the effect it has produced among us has been great. We shall *not* get our letters for many months!

Busy and stirring were we. Wood and water from the Shore & provisions from this Ship and the *Relief,* were put on board the other vessels, employing all our Boats in the transportation. Every preparation was made that could promote the efficiency of the cruizing vessels & their crews. Yesterday, which was Monday February 25th, they sailed, and we gave them three hearty cheers, wishing them with all our hearts, a prosperous time and a safe return. Next year! will be our turn.

This harbour is Land Locked in all but the North East from whence the winds never blow heavily. South West is the quarter from which the gales blow; there the Shore is high & bold, and we are moored right under its lee. The Shore is hilly, rugged, broken and covered in most places with a dense growth of Birch & Beech trees. Fresh water streams are numerous, and in the interior are several Lakes. Fish are plenty and Game abundant, but troublesome to get at. The Ducks are sweet and eat well with the Red Jelly.

I have been on Shore but once as yet. I went with Mr. Drayton on the 22nd, on Washington's birth day, into a quiet cove shut in by high land, with many rivulets emptying into it from among the hills. A native hut stood at the far end of it, which Mr. Drayton wished to Sketch. It was constructed of boughs interwoven & thached with leaves, with a small opening for an entrance; form conical, well sheltered by trees, and a brook purling, close in its rear. The Muscles & limpets which had been food for the inmates or, rather, their Shells, were heaped up before the open place so as almost to shut us out. The creatures had not taken the trouble to throw them to a distance, but after eating the contents, had tossed the Shells out of the door way. I picked up several which bore the marks of Fire and shall retain them, because they were handled by such rude and singular people as the Fugeians.

The Sketch was made, and we returned on board. The Ships were dressed with American Ensigns, in honor of the day, and "the memory of the General" was the toast on board for the first time in Orange Harbour.

Cranberries grow wild, and a berry like our black berry in appearance but of a red colour and of the mingled taste of strawberry & pine apple. Celery also grows in plenty, so that this harbour affords an excellent resort for Whalers for anti-scorbutics, wood and water.

At Sea, Lat 43° 11' North.
May 3rd 1839

I am most lamentably backward in my log, but nevertheless have the satisfactory consolation of knowing the reason to be any thing else but the want of inclination to write.

Now to go back to Orange Bay. Well, all the vessels went to Sea, and the *Vincennes* was left alone. The weather became as March advanced more dreary & wintry—fierce storms of wind with rain & hail confining us to the Ship for days at a time. But one Officer on deck at one time. Oh! how tedious those watches were by day or night. Nothing to do—no one to converse with—nothing around to look at but the hills; they possessed no attractions & were most of the time hidden by the low clouds.

Oh those watches! when for the rain & hail, one dared not to expose even his nose; all he could do was to try & keep under a shelter, whiling away time by his thoughts. But too much thinking becomes burthensome, & those watches were the most weary, I ever kept.

When the Captain left, he ordered the Launch to be fitted out & prepared for a cruize among the Islands adjacent to Cape Horn. He was pleased to designate the service *"as a hazardous one!"* and gave many injunctions regarding the precautions to be observed for the safety of the Boats & Men. The Launch was rigged; I had the honor to be selected by Lieutenant Alden[1] as his 1st Lieutenant & was of course duly proud & elated. The Said Launch *was* 35 feet long, of 8 feet beam and 5 in depth.

She was to carry 10 men & 2 Officers with their clothes, cooking utensils, provisions for 30 days, instruments &c., &c. She was decked over forward as far as the masts; under this deck were two berths. Abaft she was open, but fitted with an awning of canvass to haul over the Main Boom when at Anchor.

On Monday the 11th of March the weather, which for a week previous had been boisterous in the extreme, became mild & pleasant. All the preparations were completed, and at 11 A.M we went on board the Launch and made sail from the Harbour with the hearty wishes of those we were leaving for our safe return.

We, I speak for Alden & myself, knew as well as Captain Wilkes that the service we were bound upon would be *hazardous*. We knew that our Boat *could not* weather out a gale, and we were sure that of hard gales we should have many. We were perfectly aware that if we should be caught *"out"* in a South West blow and driven off the Land, we would be *lost!* We knew that while under sail, we could have no protection from the weather; that all hands would be exposed to the rain & the washing of the Sea; that the provisions &c. would be wet by the water the boat would make; that it would be difficult to free her by baling on account of the bulky stowage.

A small, insignificant chart, which was all incorrect, & a few remarks of Captain King,[2] an English Surveyor, were to be our guide & directions. We were to grope our way like a man in the dark over dangerous ground. The chart was magnified by means of a Camera lucida[3] to a sufficient size so that we could read the names of places & trace the imperfectly laid down coast without the aid of a magnifying glass. Well, with this imperfect chart, with but a little better idea of the route in our minds, in the most stormy month of the most stormy part of the world, we set sail in our frail boat on a month's cruize to venture clear out into the South Atlantic Ocean.

Our start was most propitious. The weather was so clear & beautiful after the storm that a party of Natives came alongside the Ship just as we left, and they never quit the Shore unless they are certain of a smooth time.

I shall copy *My Log*, the Launch's Log, from my public journal, making remarks as I go along.

Monday March 11th

At 12 weighed & stood through the inland passage along the Eastern Shore of Hardy Peninsula. At 1.15 the wind failing & tide turning against us, we came to under the Western Shore, a little to the North of Schapenham Bay. The route thus far is entirely landlocked & secure for Boats, smooth water in all winds. Sent the men on Shore near a hut, to cook their dinner and also a quantity of Pork for future consumption. At 8 P.M. wind light from the South East, sky overcast with clouds. Until midnight light airs from the South.

Such is the *Log* for Monday. Our anchorage was in a narrow passage, hemmed in every where by high land. We lay but two boat's lengths from the Shore, which was thickly wooded with bold, rocky projections and many streams, fresh water tumbling over the beach. The men built their fire on a grassy bluff, & while some took the guns to kill the Geese & Ducks which were flying around in great numbers, others were felling trees for fire wood or carrying water, a few sauntering idly about, amusing themselves like boys let out from School. And there, riding quietly on the calm water, was the Launch & her tender (a small whale boat). *They* were to us the most interesting portion of the picture. In them was to be our trust, frail though it might be.

Gun in hand, I rambled several miles along the beach all alone, where most likely white man had never trod; now scrambling through the undergrowth, now over the rocks; again lying in wait, for the birds as they passed; at times forgetful of the pursuit & lost in a train of thoughts suggested by the wild & unbroken loneliness of the scene. The *Birds* & I were all that savoured of life *there*. I looked upon the giant & rugged hills, the dashing waterfall, the gloomy woods, the glimpses of Ocean in the distance & the placid, lake like water at my feet, but there was no busy City, no hum of men; only the screaming birds, my quiet self, and my noisy gun.

At length I came to where a huge rock made out far into the water, which I could neither climb over nor go around its base. The surf had worn many cavities in this rock and broken it into several parts, making summit like spires & pinnacles of every fanciful shape; immense trees grew from the loftiest points; some of them were withered & blasted, others green & fresh. *I felt as one of the small pebbles on the Shore; grim Nature humbles Man!* I turned and strayed slowly back to the Launch. Once I thought I saw some canoes coming round a far off point, but I was mistaken—the objects were rocks just even with the water.

The tea was smoking hot, the limpet soup & the stewed birds of most exquisite & Gipsy flavour. And this was our first repast. After it was over we went in the whale boat along the Shore, firing at the Birds as they passed by. Pulling close along the beach, we came to a narrow entrance, the break in the land being scarcely distinguishable except in minute examination, and only 40 feet wide. When we had gone several hundred yards from its mouth, the shores receded from either hand, and we were in a vast basin, of five or more miles in length & half a mile in width & having 90 feet of water in its middle. Its slight connexion with the Ocean is all that can prevent its being called a Lake. Darkness was fast coming on, and there was something awful & solemn in the solitary stillness of the place. A single white Goose was resting himself in the centre of the basin and did not deem it necessary to fly or even cackle at our approach. We left him undisturbed.

The two berths forward in the Launch were 6 feet in length each, but in the widest part but 20 inches. Between them was about the like space, or perhaps 2 feet. We crammed an India rubber mattress into them as well as we could. When turned in, if my nose had been as long as *some* peoples', it would have touched the deck above me. I was jammed into the smallest possible stowage and could only be on my back; my shoulders were *too* high to permit me to turn on my side. Neither Alden or myself slept well. Our black valet made *his* bed on the deck between us. The men stowed themselves over the boat where they could best find room.

Tuesday March 12th

Commences with light airs from the South. From 2 to 5.30 calm & pleasant. At daylight turned the men up and sent them on shore to prepare their breakfast. The accommodations of the Boat we found to be quite comfortable, though we had some little difficulty in berthing the men so that they could lie down without being in a cramped position.

We eat a hot breakfast of coffee, bread & butter & soup, & at 7.30 weighed the anchor & towed through the Passage into Schapenham Bay.

At the Entrance of the Bay, met a light breeze from the Northward & Eastward, took the whale Boat in tow, and made all sail, standing towards Point Lort with the intention of proceeding to Cape Weddel & examining the coast along, the weather being as yet fine. At 9, however, heavy masses of dark mackerel clouds were collecting in the South West and the scud flying rapidly from that quarter. Squally appearances also in the North West & South East.

How well we knew what was coming! Hauled by the wind immediately on the Larboard tack & stood for where the passage appeared to be between Wollaston & Hermit Islands. We hoped to get under a lee *there,* before the threatened South Wester could reach us and, for the present, abandoned the project of examining the Shores to Cape Weddel.

Most anxiously we measured the distance we had to run and watched the moving clouds. We were in the open Bay, where a South West wind had full sweep. Our only hope was to get under the other Shore before the Sea could get up. The wind alone would not be so bad, but wind & sea together, we could not withstand.

At 12 light rain fell. At 12.30 the wind ceased and hauled suddenly by North, to West. Took in all sail instantly but the Mainsail & Storm Jib, and had just done so when we jibed with the wind fresh from South West with heavy rain & a thick haze. This change of the wind caused us to alter our course once more, and we steered parralel with the land under our lee. Hermite Island was hid by the haze, but as the Launch made much lee way, we passed *within* half a mile of several low points of Land on Wollaston Island over which the surf broke tremendously. I never in my life beheld such a terrific Surf. We saw plainly what would be our fate unless we could soon find a secure anchorage, & the moments became of the most intense & harrowing interest.

The crew of the Launch were the picked men of the Ship's company: prime seamen, active, vigorous & experienced. Our situation had become one of imminent danger. The Sea had risen wonderfully in the short time, and the wind was fast increasing to a Gale. We could not discern the Land ahead where we *trusted* to find shelter, and astern & much under our lee was a long line of Iron bound coast where, as I have said, the surf broke so furiously as if it would wash the very Land away.

The rain fell in torrents with sharp dashes of hail occasionally. In this state of affairs, we allowed the men to express their opinions, having great confidence in their judgement, knowing that in the long course of their service on the Ocean they had acquired by Experience that sort of ready Knowledge which must direct the judgement, and those habits of energetic & daring skill that are so necessary when the preservation of life depends entirely on one's personal action & resources.

One only dissented from the course we were pursuing. He thought, he was *sure,* he saw indications of a harbour far, far astern, and that it would be better to turn the boat's head in *that* direction, for *ahead* of us the land was not *yet* visible, & we were utterly ignorant whether we should find shelter even *there.* A wide tract of boiling sea must be passed ere we could reach it, but yet *one look* at the breaking surf was sufficient to deter us from venturing to make the proposed alternative. We were at least certain from the trending of the land ahead that the Shore there would be less exposed & that should we not gain a harbour, we might at least run the Launch ashore with some prospect of saving our lives. No one else could discover such flattering signs astern, and the Launch was held on her course.

She was pressed with sail & bounded from Sea to Sea with a speed that astonished us, for the boat astern acted as a heavy stop water.[4] At 1.40 we could distinguish Hermit Island and were glad to find that we had brought the extreme point of it to bear almost in the winds Eye. An hour more passed. I watched the fearful rising of the Seas and endeavoured to count the chances for our safety. The heavier waves broke over the Launch, and sometimes the whale boat was near being capsized. Still we rode buoyantly on the troubled waters & hope was strong with us yet. I did not feel so bad as when in the Dingy at the Rio Negro. If *She* had been loaded with *Gold* then, I would have thrown the precious metal overboard. Death becomes mighty disagreeable on a close approach and drowning is a mode of quitting the world which I do not approve of as either dignified or satisfactory, yet I half expect to make my exit in that way. But a truce to trifling on so grave a subject; it is both irrelavent & indecent, or at least unbecoming.

At length we *thought* we could see through the mist indications of sheltered anchorage under our lee & kept away for the place. The Seas were now running so high that we felt it was high time we should be in a harbour. A little while and they would be too heavy for our Boat to live among them. I remember talking to Jim Gibson[5] about Lancaster and how Comfortable we should be, if [we] were only by his Aunt Hubley's stove, sipping a hot Punch. Presently we passed close to a rock above water about a mile from the Shore. As we advanced we became convinced that appearances had not deceived us, and that in a few minutes we should be safe. But we were in the heavy seas yet, and they swept over the Launch, deluging us fore and aft. Nearer & nearer we came to the Land. We shaved a projecting point about two boat's lengths. We came abreast the indentation of the Shore which afforded a secure asylum, the helm was put hard down, and in another moment we were in calm water, riding quietly at anchor.

There was not a heart in that boat that did not feel the relief, and we turned to congratulate one another that we had weathered the blow so well and hit upon so *snug* a cove to ride it out in. As we were running in, we observed a hut near the beach & two canoes hauled up by it. Smoke was ascending from it, and a dog barked furiously at our approach. Presently the inmates came out & went over the hills.

We went on shore to the Hut, though the rain had not ceased, & found in it an old man, very sick & shaking like one with the Palsy. Two young men returned in a short time. They had secreted the women away in the distant parts of the Island.

The smoke from the fire & the bad atmosphere of the interior of the Hut drove us out, in a few minutes. Indeed we only ventured in to gratify our curiosity & to be for once among a family party of *Fugeians*.

Some baskets made very neatly of bleached grass, two or three small buckets of bark & 20 or 30 fish were hanging up to the branches which formed the *solid* part of the Hut, and the bodies of several Shags were lying among the leaves & dirt that made the only floor.

One of the young men went off with us. He would drink nothing but water and eat only Pork & Bread. A seasoned dish that we had he would not touch; it was not to his taste. Fish & birds eaten half raw, with limpets & Muscles & perhaps the wild celery & berries, afforded the natives Subsistence, and this specimen of them turned with disgust from our delicacies. He was entirely naked and took great delight in mimicking whatever we said among us. We soon grew tired of his company and sent him ashore with a present of red flannel for himself and brethren.

The Gale continued to blow with increased violence and soon reached its heighth, but we were all snug, and as we watched the seas sweeping by the point, we felt we had good reason to be thankful for the timely shelter we had found. On the next day, Wednesday March 13th, the fury of the Gale was unabated, and there still fell heavy squalls of rain & hail. To make our moorings more secure, we let go the small anchor & our Gun[6] ahead.

Neither Alden nor myself could sleep more than half an hour at a time. The confined positions we were obliged to lie in, the noise of the rain & hail right in our ears, the sharp quick motion of the boat, the jarring of her cable against the stem, & the anxiety we felt, which we could not entirely allay, that by some accident we might get adrift caused us to start from our fitful slumbers a dozen times or more through the night. The men kept watch one at a time, and as either of us woke, our cry was, "Who has the lookout? how is the weather? has she dragged?

what time is it?" We were always disappointed to find so short
an interval had elapsed since last we had been awake and that
day break had not yet come.

And here I may as well say that during the whole time we
were in the Launch every night was passed in the same harrassing manner. We were glad when it was morning, that we
could leave our dog kennel of a place. Nevertheless *it* was as
comfortably arranged as the Boat would admit of and possessed one virtue: it was dry. The men slept better than we did,
and the accommodations for them were bad enough.

Thursday March 14

The squalls became lighter & less frequent towards daylight,
and by noon the weather had moderated. In the afternoon the
Sun Shone out, so we rolled up our tent like cover and dried all
the wet things in the Boat.

The men went on shore to cook their meal, and I took a
stroll over the Island, with my Gun. The features of the soil
were similar to the Land about Orange Bay: soft, spongy &
boggy; uneven surface, sometimes rising to high & rugged hills
& seldom level for any distance. Indeed there is not such a
thing as a plain to be seen any where. Immense Masses of rock
exist. The whole under-formation consists of strata of hard
rock which in places is covered with the watery and marshy
soil, in others breaking out in projecting ledges or rearing in
barren grandeur to a mountain's height. Again are the patches
of Forest of the densest growth, the trees growing so close to
each other & the underwood being so thick & luxuriant as to
render a passage through a grove almost impossible.

Streams of fresh water abound and they are the only things
that possess any beauty, or that one can take any gratification
in beholding in this, the most barren, wearisome & uninteresting region of the World. In many places along the coast, water-
falls come streaming down the hill sides from heights of 500 to
1000 feet above the Sea. Far above you, you see the shining fall
dashing in narrow channels from rock to rock. Now you lose
it; its course is through the Forest, and would you find it again,

you must look where it takes its last leap into the Ocean. These water courses are visible from a great distance on account of their elevation and the glistening path they make over the black & gloomy rocks. They are good land marks for Navigators.

And now to return to my ramble on Shore—After a long & toilsome walk over the yielding soil & rough hills during which I shot a couple of Ducks, I was returning towards the Boat, when I heard the barking of a dog. This betrayed at once the hiding place of the women, and the native men, who were near watching my motions & also those of some of our crew who were straying about, set up a great shouting & appeared to be alarmed & angry.

We could hear the women calling to the Dog, but the brute continued his barking most obstinately, running to & fro the mouth of a cave from whence the voices came. As we did not wish to disturb the anxiety of the men any further than we had already done so unwittingly, & not feeling the slightest inclination to make a visit to the Ladies, we turned away from that part of the Island, though we were clearly of opinion that the males need *not* have used such excessive caution & mystery, in the concealment of their women. If the *she* creatures *had* remained in the hut there would only have been collected there so much more hideousness in the human shape, so much more that would have been filthy & disgusting, that we should have cut & run the sooner for their presence.

This being but a mild & *even* favourable description of the Ladies, it will not be thought that the jealous care of the Men was necessary, yet the Fuegeans were evidently of the contrary opinion. They could not abide our discovery of the secret place wherein they had hidden their lovely ones. At Sundown we observed them preparing for departing, clearing away the stones, & making beds of kelp over which to launch their canoes. In the morning they were flown, their migratory habits rendering a change of position a matter of but little trouble to them.

Jim Gibson was one of the men I met with. The remembrance of days when we shot at Redbreasts together, happy in the boys' Saturday afternoon holiday & in waging the mimic warfare against the innocent birds, came back to our minds, and we rested on some high rocks that over looked the great ocean & talked over bygone days & the sports of fortune that had brought us both to a sailor's life, a life so different from the calm & even existence of the patriarchs of Litiz & the following of which had not entered into our boyish plans or dreams at the time when we had last met & first parted, he to go to a new home, I to remain in the old.

Years rolled on & after being "Wide as the Poles asunder," we met again; and, though in different conditions, in yet closer companionship than when we were schoolmates on the same bench!—both of us the inmates

"Of a winged & Sea Girt Citadel"—[7]

Also now, we were in the midst of a rugged scene, some 6 or 8 miles from Cape Horn!—our home! our friends! where were they!

[CHAPTER 4: BOAT DUTY OFF CAPE HORN]

On Friday the breeze had changed to the North East & a heavy squall was setting in. At daylight we attempted to get out, but not succeeding, returned to the Anchorage, which we named "Shelter Cove." On the beach we found a scrubbing brush, a boat's thwart, and a small spar. Whether they were remnants of a wreck, we could not tell.

Saturday, weighed at daylight with a fine breeze, and stood down the passage between Hermite & Wollaston towards North Westward. When we had gone 10 or 12 miles, it fell calm; towed the Boat into a Sheltered cove that was near at hand and anchored.

The crew went on shore to cook their meal & I set out with the Gun & walked myself into an appetite. This dinner, which consisted of a Fish Chowder & a delicious "Fisherman's stew" of Game & Salt pork with flour & seasoning, we eat on the Shore, and, as it is written in my log, "the change from the narrow confines of the Launch to the open air & unlimited space with clear & beautiful weather produced a happy effect upon us all." And so the change did—the remark in the log, if brief, was correct.

The bad weather and the close atmosphere of the Launch had not a tendency to make the boat an agreeable eating place for 12 grown individuals, particularly as she supplied the sleeping apartments & other conveniences for the entire gang with but little need of alteration in her interior arrangements. Bed, seat, & table were all one. Dishes were few & they of that rare & elegant metal commonly called tin-plate. But there was good humour, hungry stomachs, & tastes that under such circumstances were neither fastidious nor epicurean, but exceedingly rude & accommodating.

He who acted as the chief cook was skilful in his culinary operations, & he made as many delicious messes of as good savour as the flesh pots of Egypt,[1] or the seething cauldrons of the vagrant Gypsies.

When the meal was over, Alden, myself, & some of the crew set out to ascend a high hill near our anchorage, so that we might obtain a view of the surrounding Islands, & the channels between them. Our chart was *all wrong,* and a bird's eye view would afford us a knowledge of the run of the coast that would be of eminent service in the further prosecution of our *hazardous* cruize.

Several Geese were shot on the way from the boat, & leaving two men in her to pursue the Sport which provided us with such desirable food, the rest of us commenced the ascent, which proved to be toilsome & fatiguing in the extreme. The first step from the boat brought us into the woods, where the hillside rose abrupt & where was, as usual, the dense & almost impenetrable wilderness of undergrowth. We struggled on, though obliged to stop for rest & breath every few minutes. The spongy soil yielded beneath our feet as if it was melting away, and every effort to advance was made wearisome & half fruitless by the incessant slipping of the feet. Head, body & limbs suffered from the prickly branches, as we broke through them; and every now & then, treading unawares upon a soft spot, down we went to the knees in the mire, & to extricate ourselves required exertion enough to half kill one.

Emerging at length from this forest, we came upon more open ground, though the nature of the soil was not changed, and as we crossed the numerous water courses, we became entangled among the thickets that grew along their banks. I had some liquid in a flask which, diluted with a little of the limpid element, had a wonderfully renovating effect, and as we paused by these streams to get a little rest, we endeavoured to recuperate by the aid of some good—shall I write it?—whiskey!

As we approached the summit, we met with immense projecting ledges of rock, & millions of loose stones were strewn over the ground. These afforded us better footing, and we progressed upwards with the greater ease & rapidity. We were near the highest ridge. We were about 1300 feet above the water, but we were not quite at the summit, & the view was not satisfactory, but we saw that a storm was threatening in the South West & that we had no time to spare. Compass & Spyglass were put in requisition, and in a few minutes a sketch was completed that gave us a better idea of our whereabouts than we had previously possessed.

To aid our view, we climbed some rocks that started up like tall pillars 20 or 30 feet in height. There were many of these Giant like rocks, rearing their heads as if they were spectators of the extended view. We sunk to dwarfishness beside them. We that were so far removed from all that had life, surrounded with the grand & gloomy wildness of one of Nature's wildest scenes, felt an utter insignificance. We were awe stricken and humbled into fear & wondering, & our thoughts turned to the power that made & created all things.

That great Ocean, whose bounds are not known, the Icy barriers of which have never been passed, lay beneath us stretching away in the distance until it met the Sky, for once undisturbed, almost unruffled by the light breeze that kissed its Surface. But there was no sail to be seen on the watery waste; the vast expanse of sea upheld no moving or living thing, though starting from our feet, there was the bold & terrible promontory Cape Horn, thrusting its rugged form far into the Ocean, the last, lingering point of the great Western World.

The Storm which had threatened was now fast coming on, and we made a rapid descent to the Boat in a much shorter time than the weary hours consumed in toiling up. The pull to the Launch's anchorage was a tough one, the wind blowing strong in our teeth & greatly impeding our progress, while the hail beat in our faces with such violence that we could scarcely look up and bruised and benumbed our hands so that we could scarcely use them at the oars.

The hut on the beach was larger than any others we had met with and had evidently been erected by others than the natives. A beaten path led through the wood to the summit of a neighbouring hill, & the trees near bore marks of the axe & were in some places perforated with bullets & slugs. The rim of a Scotch Cap[2] was picked up on the beach, & we supposed that some Sealers had been there lately. Many large bones of the whale were lying around.

I know *whose* name[3] I cut on a tree at the place—on a huge beech that overhangs the brook.

The night was clear & beautiful after the squall, and we slept tolerably well.

Sunday March 17th

We cooked our breakfast on shore, and soon after daylight weighed & stood out of "Scotch Cap Cove." We were be-calmed and obliged to anchor at 9. Set the pot boiling on shore again & by the time dinner was ready a breeze had sprung up, & we made sail & beat down towards the Southern entrance to the Straits. A huge whale was gamboling near us, throwing his whole length out of the water & spouting up jets like the Spray from a Cataract. This whole strait seemed to be too limited a play *ground* for him, the great Leviathan of the deep.

We left Cape Horn away on our right & turned up a passage, that led out into the Atlantic, to the Northward & Eastward of the Cape. The weather continued fine, & at Sundown we were at anchor in another Snug cove. We were determined never to remain underweigh at night if we could avoid it by finding an-chorage, for to do so would be only exposing us to danger in many ways and cause us to suffer much anxiety & discomfort. Luckily all along the Shores were indentations affording good Shelter from the prevailing South West winds, & it was a God-send to us that the Conformation of the Land was such that the coves were so numerous & so well protected.

'Tis a poor country indeed that is destitute of *all* natural ad-vantages. Fuego has but few; such as they are, however, they seem sufficient for the rude inhabitants. The smooth water of the coves makes them good havens for their frail canoes, the hills present a defence from the violent gales, & the woods at their base afford Shelter to clusters of huts that are yet more frail than the canoes; the numerous running streams supply drink

& the ocean teems with fish. But to go on with the yarn—more
of the Fugeans anon.

We found a Hut at this anchorage also. A babbling brook
ran by it, the hills rose in its rear, wooded almost to their summits, but terminating in tremendous ridges of rock. The Fire
was soon underweigh & while our supper was preparing, I
strolled away with the Gun to procure the materials for another meal.* It was dark when I returned & the fire was blazing cheerily, casting a bright glow over the water & throwing a
strong light on the objects on the Shore.

We had a sufficient quantity of Matches when we left the
Ship, but some had been spoiled by wet & others lost. A few
nights previously to this, the man on watch fell asleep & the
light went out. Alden & myself were awake soon after, raising
a row because of the neglect, and to shame the men, we told
them we would keep the watch that night and both of us set
to work to strike a light. The tinder was expended & our only
hope lay in the virtue of a slow match.[4] This burned like a coal
but with all our puffing, we could not raise a flame, & the result was that the candle melted away from the wick. A Match
would have caught in an instant, but the wick of the candle was
as obstinate in resisting our attempts to light it, as if it had been
made of asbestos. Then we tried powder, charging both wick &
match with a few grains & applying them together, blowing
until our cheeks cracked & ached.

Our patience was wearied out, & we more than once ceased
our efforts & laughed heartily in spite of our vexation at the
ludicrous figure we made; so earnestly at work in only our
drawers; the flashes from the powder & the light from two ci-

---

*In half an hour I turned the point; the wild hills were behind me and the
Ocean at my feet. Presently I clambored up a high & rugged cliff that hung
butting over the surf, the hollow roar of which thundered in my Ears. The
Coast was lined with lofty rocks, and these were worn into a thousand Caverns by the Everlasting beating of the Seas. Seated here alone in the shades of
night fast gathering about me, at the very verge of the Western World, with a
waste of waters before me that for half the circuit of the Globe rolls on unbroken by a single Isle there was something so imposing in the sublime and
solitary nature of the scene, that it seemed to me as if I were like the last man,
looking upon Eternity.

gars (which Alden & Gibson were smoking most zealously) occasionally revealing our disturbed features & the scanty nature of our covering. We were shivering with cold, too, by this time but were so eager that we would not relax our exertions to put on more clothing. Presently we found that the powder in both wick & match was too much; the concussion put out the flame. So I cut a candle afresh & opening the wick carefully, insinuated a few grains of powder among the threads. I applied the match & to our great joy, the candle was at last fairly alight! We drew a long breath & looked significantly at one another as much as to say, "how smart we are."

But my luck was in another instant changed to dire disappointment. I have often observed that the very measures adopted to ensure success defeat the plans, & so it proved in this instance. Anxious to double the chances for preserving our hard earned treasure, I called for another candle. They gave me one with powder in the wick, & the instant I applied it to the one burning, the confounded thing exploded like a squib & the light was out again. The hour's labour was all in vain: we were once more in utter darkness. I turned in in despair and Alden consoled himself with a Segar until daylight. I came near blowing both our heads off!

Monday March 18th.

During all of this day, the wind blew in violent squalls from the South West, with much rain & hail. At 9 A.M. we shifted our berth to clear some rocks that were rather close under our lee. Let go the anchor to Seaward & made fast lines from the Bow to trees on the Shore.

Soon after we got in this new situation I heard a great chattering of Birds overhead & looking up, I saw numbers of black birds larger than crows flying about & others perched on nests that were built on dead trees. I thought we had discovered a new species of Land birds, for heretofore we had not met with any so large except the water fowl.

Although the Snow was falling at the time, I was so anxious to have a Shot at the bipeds that I got at once into the Boat &

with a couple of men pulled immediately under the nests. We could hear the cheeping of the young ones, & though the old birds kept up a horrible din, they did not fly, and as we fired, down they fell two or three at a time, and lo! & behold they were web footed! Now I thought this exceedingly strange, that water fowl should build their nests, lay their eggs & raise their young in trees at a height of 70 feet above the water. *They lit* on the branches, too, with all the ease of a claw footed bird.

Nothing would do now but cut down a tree & so procure the young ones & eggs, but this proved more difficult than I expected. The bank rose steep, and the climbing over the wet & slippery rocks & through the thick undergrowth of bushes & grass was neither pleasant nor secure, particularly as one hand had sufficient employment in holding on to the Gun. And more than once in this, as well as in many other like attempts, I came a *leetle too* near to breaking my good-for-nothing neck.

At length we got up on the hill side high enough to look down into the nests, but we found that with only a single exception, all the trees bearing nests took root midway down a precipice, the extreme perpendicularity of which, forbade all attempts either to descend from our position or to scale it from the water. The tree that was accessible we soon felled, but it lay right down the Precipice, & the nests were as much out of reach as before. We tried to climb it ere we applied the axe, but our efforts were as fruitless as those of the celebrated Jack the Giant Killer, who could not get to the top of *his* pole until he had planted the "wonderful bean" by its side. Not so fortunate as him, we had no bean, & unlike "Peter Wilkins,"[5] were without Wings.

We shot away, however, at the little things in the nests. Our zeal in the cause of Natural Science, & curiosity in regard to the Phenomena of web footed birds breeding in high trees completely quieted any compunction we might otherwise have felt in dealing such slaughter "among the innocents." But this was of no avail either; we could not jump them out of the nests.

The snow was several feet deep & streaming down as it does in Boston, & the wind howled through the trees furiously enough. So we returned to the Launch & the black web footed birds that built their nests in high trees were soon boiling in the Pot. We cooked every kind of Bird that we shot, even Hawks, & found them sweet and savory without any Exception. Indeed I never before eat so much meat—strong, juicy meat—in the same space of time, as while I was in the Launch. My appetite was always Keen. Alden & myself were well furnished with boiled hams & corn beef, Bolognas, bread, butter, cheese, pickles & various other comestibles, suitable for such an excursion. The provisions for the men were the best the Ship could afford.

Often we started a boat's crew on Shore Empty handed, or at least with only the cooking utensils, and they would return with smoking dishes of Soup, Fish & Birds; and yet they had not gone to Market! but while some were picking muscles & limpets for the Soup (which tasted as delicious as Oyster Soup at home) others would Gun & Fish, bringing plenty to the Fire ere it would be well underweigh. I never saw any thing like the abundance of Fish we met with—the water swarmed with them, and it was so clear that we could see them take the hook & hauled up two & three at once. We lived well, & our feasts possessed a peculiar zest from the manner in which they were got up & the rude but hearty way they were discussed.

We had also of Burden's choice Madeira a few bottles, and some sparkling Champaign just to keep the life within us, and if I ever sipped Nectar, it was in some draughts I swallowed while in the Launch. Neither Jupiter nor Gannymede[6] were ever near Cape Horn in an open boat that I know of.

We remained in this Anchorage 8 days without moving, the Gale blowing with tremendous fury all the while with rain & hail & snow. The hills were white from the fall of the latter, and a wintry scene was around us though the season was the middle of Summer.

We lay so close under the high Land that the wind could not reach us but swept over our mast heads, & the water was perfectly smooth for a quarter of a mile beyond us; but outside, the seas were running at an awful height & the lashing of the breakers on the opposite Shore came to our Ears with startling distinctness. Mercy! how the wind did blow. The squalls swept over us in fierce & angry gusts, as loud and violent as if an hundred Whirlwinds were in the air! Oh! the storms were terrible indeed—enough so to send a chill to the stoutest heart. We thanked God that we had a Sheltered spot to ride them out in.

There was no cessation, not even breathing time, between the blows. Blast followed blast in quick succession, & they seemed to come heavier as the Gale advanced. Rain, hail & snow poured down with but little intermission, and we had to watch a chance for a dry time to set our fire going on Shore. But we never missed having at least one hot meal every day, though that was often cooked in spite of the wet, for the men were indefatigable in their exertions & fertile & skillful in expedients.

Those 8 days were tedious, and time hung wearily on our hands. We could not walk on Shore at all & could take no more exercise in the Launch than a chicken in its Shell. We shot the Birds that came swimming or flying near the boats & had some sport fishing, but most of the hours were passed in listless inactivity both of body & mind. We had neglected to take Books with us, & conversation often flagged of course. We began to feel the effects of such close confinement on our limbs; they were becoming slightly stiff & painful, to which the continual cold & dampness of the atmosphere may have contributed.

To cheer us up, we set the men singing & spinning yarns after nightfall & thus whiled away moments that would otherwise have been dull enough. One of the men had an exceedingly fine voice & sung many of the old fashioned but most excellent songs with much taste & feeling; songs that Mother & Grandmother used to lull *us* to rest by, years ago.

And such yarns as they told, mostly of events that had happened in their own experience. I thought *I* knew some little about a roving life & considered that I had seen some strange things in my short life time but I found I was a mere child, an infant scarcely free from the pap spoon, a novice as yet, in adventure. The tales were marvellous and made truth stranger than fiction. It is really wonderful what sailors go through with in their *knockabout* life, and one can learn from their narratives how much suffering the human frame can bear, & that it is the best philosophy never to despair, to cling to Hope as long as you have breath within you.

Tuesday March 19th

We *caught* the Sun this morning for the first time, without the Land intervening and just long enough to get an altitude[7] for the correction of our time. In the forenoon 5 or 6 natives appeared on the Summit of a high & rocky hill to the North West of our anchorage. Notwithstanding the snow and the coldness of the atmosphere, which at that elevation must have been below the freezing point, they remained for some time on the loftiest ridge, dancing & shouting, their figures showing strong & clear against the Sky. When they descended the Hill, they came near to the Launch, calling out loudly "Yam Eschoona," the two words addressed to us by all the Natives we have fallen in with, but to which we have not been able to attach any definite meaning.[8]

As we landed, one of them advanced holding an otter Skin in his hand, which he offered to the foremost of our party as a token of his friendly disposition towards us, or perhaps of his desire to trade. His courtesy secured for him, however, our good graces, for in all our previous intercourse with his countrymen they had proved themselves inveterate beggars, with scarcely the least wish or intention to make any return for the presents given them.

Some pieces of red flannel, which they immediately converted into a sort of head gear, neglecting the body entirely; two or three medals bearing the Ship's name; a few brass rings & some raw pork were eagerly accepted by them, in the possession of which they appeared to be highly gratified & contented, giving us in return their only covering of otter skins, their slings, &c., &c.

They delighted like the others we have seen in exercising their talent for mimicry, repeating our words with singular exactness & joining in the songs & dances of the men with a perfect observance of note & time. Some were utterly destitute of clothing, others had but small skins slung over their shoulders, &

yet they stood the peltings of the snow storms with scarce a
Shiver. When they next came down to us, they made a fire on
the beach, but we could not learn by what means they kindled it.

These natives were all young men & boys from the ages of 6
to 20 & 25. They were not painted and were taller & better
looking than the majority of the Islanders & of better dispositions. We had a great deal of fun with them. They were very
lively, and we Skylarked among the snow together, as if we had
been old friends. They were naked & we warmly clad, & I just
thought that we presented as wide a contrast of person & habit
as could be met with any where in the world.

The inhabitants of Terra del Fuego & the adjacent Islands
are certainly as primitive & simple in their mode of life as any
other race on the Globe, & if *they* be the children of Nature, I
am thankful that I am a member of a more artificial community
& will waive forever the belief that those barbarous ones who
have the fewest wants lead a more enviable existence than the
great civilized mass, who are always wanting, & whose wants
are never sufficiently supplied.

The only weapons we observed the Fuegeians to possess
were spears with points of whalebones, bows & arrows &
slings. With these they obtain their food & the only method of
cookery they practise is roasting on coals. They neither boil,
bake or stew and would not taste any thing we had but bread
& raw pork, refusing ale, whiskey & seasoned victuals with
every symptom of disgust, horrified as much as we would have
been if they had invited us to partake of their cleanly & delicate
viands. Clothing they have none, & what they do in the wintry
Season I cannot imagine, for then the cold must be intense.

As they have nothing to take with them, their migrations
from place to place are made without difficulty, one canoe suf-
ficing for a whole family. We never found more than three huts
together; there were no villages, & the people seemed to live independent of each other, recognizing no chief & acting without
order or form, just as their inclinations led them, every man for
himself. There was no community of interests among them, no
ties, save of blood; for those who came alongside in different
canoes did not interchange a Syllable, but directed all their talk

to us, jabbering away with the greatest volubility & creating to our ears a confusion of tongues worse than a Bedlam.

The women & Boys paddled, the men rarely assisting; the squaws were as denuded as their lords, but we could not induce them to rise from their *squatted* position. They were as immoveable as if they had been glued to the bottom of the canoe. Many of them had children of a month or two old, little things not so big as a handfull & entirely unclad. The unnatural "Mammas" offered their babes for sale, asking only a bottle, broken or whole, in return, but we declined the bargain.

In Stature the Fuegeians are below the common height of men, generally large bodied with fine, expansive chests but diminutive limbs. This defect arises most probably from the cramped position they always occupy when in their huts or canoes, & is much less observable in the women than the men— the Forehead low, nose short & flat, eyes black, but devoid of much expression, teeth universally white & regular.

The adults of both Sexes, were painted or stained over the body & face, but the delineations were made without either method or accuracy, the colours, blue, black & red. A white, paste like Substance was intermixed with their long & matted hair, the forehead generally receiving a portion of it, which, from their natural indolence & the extreme filthiness of their habits, they neglected to remove.

The Fuegeans have not altered since the days of Cook.[9] They know of no other Land save their own, and perhaps they are better satisfied with its rugged face & boisterous clime than they would be with a smiling Island, rich in luxurious fruits, fertile in Soil & basking under a Tropical Sun.

Tuesday March 19th Continued.

As *this* day was *a certain monthly*versary of Alden's marriage, when night came we returned to *our Sanctum* to celebrate the occasion by discussing a bottle of Madeira. There was just space enough for us to sit on the deck with our feet together and placing the bottle, glasses, Segars & candles between our legs & having the curtain drawn, we were as exclusive & sociable as possible. And so we spun yarns until the Bottle was empty, when we turned in, but not to sleep.

We had been in bed but a few moments, when the Old Launch began to jump about with a short disagreeable motion, chaffing at her cable & kicking up such a row that we jumped up to see what was the matter, for "*all was well*," but the minute before. The wind had hauled in a heavy squall to the Eastward without any warning and was blowing us upon the rocks. The Launch was trying to swing to her anchor, which lay to the Seaward, but the lines fast to the Shore prevented her, & she was tugging and straining as if she would part every thing.

No time was to be lost; our situation was dangerous & all of us were busy and stirring at work to make the best head possible against the storm. I was too much engaged, too earnestly employed in going on with the necessary expedients, to cast around more than one glance or to allow the horrors swept in by that glance to have any other effect than to increase & keep up my exertions. No reflection was necessary to suggest what was to be done. A Seaman's instinct supplied the place of thought, & the means to be adopted were in forwardness without any delay.

Some men were sent in the Boat to cut away the lines as close to the Shore as they could get & haul themselves back by the ends fast to the Launch. The rest of us roused on the chain so as to draw the Launch as far from the rocks as possible, before we let go "the Gun," which was to Serve again as a Sheet anchor. This was accomplished, & we veered to the chain as much as we dared so as not to trip the moorings & to keep as distant from the Shore as we could. And how distant do *you* suppose our poor Boat with her precious living cargo was? Why, the whale Boat riding astern by *one fathom* of painter was just clear of the breakers. The spray from them as they broke on the rocky shore almost reached us.

And now that our exertions were over, when there was nothing more to do but to wait calmly and watch the changes & chances, I sat myself in the Stern of the Launch & began to speculate upon the probabilities of our being wrecked in the course of 15 or 30 or 45 or perhaps 60 minutes! & how it would come about! & how many of us would be saved! & *how the rest would go!* & what would become of the survivors! & all other interesting subjects that would be apt to come into one's head on such a pleasant occasion. Oh, it was extremely agreeable! delightful! charming! & I shall remember those moments as long as I live.

The more I looked to windward, the blacker the clouds seemed to become, & they rose & rolled over us in heavy masses, so low that we could almost touch them. The wind howled & stormed, the rain fell, and matters seemed bad enough. The thickness of the Kelp among which we lay prevented the Sea from breaking around us, but the huge swell set us upon the shore, each roller as it passed us threatening to snap our moorings & hurl us on the rocks, where *only one short boat's length off,* the surf was dashing with a strength that would have ground a stout Ship to atoms.

Our hope was in the fastenings that had their hold on the bottom, yet the chain might go like a thread, & the first warning we would have would be the shock of the Launch settling on the rocks. It was a stirring thought that all of us now so full of life & health might be in a moment struggling vainly & for a brief time among the raging waves. My glance went from face to face of the hardy crew, & I read there the same quiet & determined expression that each had worn when so actively at work a few minutes before. *It does one good* to see the way Sailors go on with their duty, when their lives are in imminent & terrible danger. They show no timidity, no nervous trembling, no sinking of the heart, no loss of their reason, no bewilderment of mind; but Calm, obedient & untiring, they pursue their exertions with, as I have said somewhere else, a steadiness not to be overthrown.

Towards midnight the wind moderated & hauled again to the South West. Glad to be relieved from our anxious watching, we turned in once more & were soon in that restful slumber from which we were so often aroused.

This squall was felt in Orange Harbour—the *Vincennes* dragged her anchors.

The Gale blew until Monday morning, though it began to

moderate on Sunday, attended all the while, as the Log says, "with heavy showers of rain, hail & snow." Sunday afternoon 9 of the natives came alongside, & after receiving our presents, they paddled on their way. From their unvarying clamour, we called this place "Yam Eschoona Cove."

On Monday March 25th we commenced at daylight to furl the cover & weigh the Gun & anchor. The clouds were hanging low on the hills, but believing that the Gale was expended at last, we sailed at 7 precisely. We ran through a narrow passage between some rocks & shot some fine ducks. Presently we passed a point & found ourselves in the Atlantic with an extent of Ocean on one hand that reached away to New Holland, unbroken by even a Single Isle. We kept close along the Shore, beating against a moderate breeze from the North West.

Gibson's sharp eyes espied a Seal on the rocks at the waters edge, & we steered directly for him. He was asleep, stern on, & we neared him without disturbing his rest. I had a double barrelled Gun, Alden & one of the men each a musket loaded with ball. We took good aim & fired together. The monster raised himself, howled as if with pain, & rolled clumsily off the rock into the water. We were certain we had hit him, but not in a vulnerable part & were much chagrined to lose what we had deemed a sure prize. I reserved my second barrel & pulled for his head as he exposed it, but the miserable *cap*[10] would not go off. However, it is some satisfaction to say that you have had such noble game in range. It's not every body gets a crack at a Seal close to Cape Horn!

We shot many Fowl as we sailed along & just before Sundown we found a beautiful little cove, just such a resting place as we wanted, with a growth of trees rising like a wall in the rear of a fine sandy beach that made around the head of the Cove. Here also was a hut, that was almost hidden by the creeping vines & plants around it. Our Kettle was smoking in a short time & as usual away I went with the Gun for more game.

Leaving the beach, the Shore was very rugged, and I passed deep caverns that ran far underneath the hill & clomb over the grass coated masses of rock & waded under them where arches had been worn through by the eternal battling of the Surf, &

this was the wildest walk of all. I shot two birds like our "Fly up the creeks."[11]

The Supper was excellent and done justice to by a set of as hungry mortals as ever picked a bone. Breakfast & dinner had been cold.

The night was calm & warm. The moon & stars shone with a lustre that was undimmed, and all of us sat up for some time, enjoying the unwonted balminess of the air & admiring the brilliance of the Heavens. The sparkling sky glowed with the more brightness from having been so long hidden by a murky & stormy pall.

[CHAPTER 5: THE RETURN TO ORANGE HARBOR]

At daylight on Tuesday we were off again, intending if the weather continued clear to run across the Bay for Orange Harbour, which we might reach in the course of the night. We felt it to be utterly impossible for us to venture off to Islands 60 miles away and gave up the idea, glad to believe we should so soon be on the old Ship's decks. An hour after leaving "Beach Cove," we discovered a Schooner ahead. For some little while we thought she must be a Sealer, but we made her out the *Sea Gull* by the marks a Sailor judges by, even when at more than one mile distance. The Yankee colors were flying at both our peaks, & to please the crew, Betsy Baker[1] was mounted on her carriage, and we fired away in Man of War's style, much to the amusement of every one.

We supposed that She was on her way to Orange Harbour, returning from the Southern cruize, & congratulated ourselves on the "nice tow" she could give us over. Some of the men Scouted the idea; they did not want to be towed, they had rather pull the Launch. They were sure, they were certain, they'd be d——d if the old Launch could not beat the *Sea Gull* all to pieces, and they were willing to stick by her to the last, honest Souls!

At 7 were alongside & aboard. The moment my foot was on her decks, my feelings underwent a sudden & entire change. I felt *safe once more*. I knew the craft beneath me could dare the worst, and care & anxiety, which had been weighing heavily on me for many days, now disappeared, & my mind & my mood were again light & free. Oh! the change was blessed indeed, & I was ready to leave the insignificant & unseaworthy Launch with a happy heart.

And then we met the hearty grasp of our friends, who had come with so much eagerness & ardour to search after & assist us, for the *Sea Gull* had been to Orange Harbour & was now, for a second time, on the lookout for the Launch. The continual & tremendous gale experienced at the Ship had alarmed all hands for the safety of the Launch, & the *Sea Gull* was despatched the day after her arrival from the South. She returned once, unsuccessful in her first search, to ride out the Gale then blowing. The next time, more fortunate, She found us, & there was a mutual & common rejoicing.

The contrast between the dimensions of the two craft was wonderful; the *Sea Gull* seemed a monster. I thought her almost *too* large, and her rigging looked huge enough for Giants to handle. The poor Launch & her spars & gear dwindled to a plaything's size. She was soon dismantled, most of the things removed from her & all the crew. She was then taken in tow, & we steered away before a fine breeze for those Islands which we had given up the idea of visiting in the Launch alone. In two hours the wind was blowing hard from the South West, reducing us to Short sail. In the Launch, we would have been obliged to run for an anchorage, but the *Sea Gull* flew onwards like the bird of her name. The storming of the blast & the heaving of the Seas were alike unheeded by her, and it was a glorious excitement to control the movements of so gallant a craft. The Launch followed in our wake, boiling & struggling thro' the waves at a much greater speed than she had ever gone unaided.

At 11 o'clock we anchored in Goeree Roads in a berth that was protected only from South Westers. That night we had a merry time. Alden & I, seated once more at a *Table* with all the decent appliances of eating around us & companions of social rank, felt translated into a new state of existence, and the wine cups, flowing with the rich juice of Madeira, were quaffed with an honest fervour & relished with an exquisite degree of contentment that was rather heightened as we listened to the loud raging of the Gale & the heavy pattering of the rain on the deck above us. That night I rested well—I was not disturbed, & my sleep was sweet and balmy as a child's.

The weather continued bad during Wednesday, but on the

succeeding day was clear & fine, with a light wind from the Eastward. The Schooner weighed and stood on to the Eastward. I sounded thro' a large bed of Kelp that was lying along the Shore in the Whale Boat & got on board the *Sea Gull* as the breeze freshened.

In the afternoon 4 natives came alongside from out a small cove on Lennox Island. Presently we discerned several canoes hauled up on the beach in front of a hut, and a group of 8 or 10 persons were assembled on a grassy eminence near it. The Schooner was run close in shore & hove to, and we went on shore to buy a Dog, certainly not with the least expectation of finding pleasure or interest in the Natives themselves. They were similar to the hideous beings we had fallen in with before. There were two huts here, and many paths were cut like labyrinths through the woods, shaded by the thick foliage & crossed by small streams of fresh water. The scene was soft & quiet & peaceful & rural &—& only wanting a warm sky, golden fruits, & inhabitants a few more removes from the hideous to have made it exquisite & heavenly. The features were fine, but all else was deficient.

About 30 of both sexes were jammed together in a hut, the most filthy crowd I ever mingled with. The specimens of their domestic economy that came under our eyes were revolting, & after buying a Dog for which or for *whom* we gave a Knife, we hurried to leave the sweet creatures.

Just as we were shoving off, we detected a fellow walking away with one of the rowlocks of the Boat. He gave it back when we demanded it & showed no concern in his countenance. His ideas were either extremely innocent regarding the right of property, or else he was an old offender in the pilfering way. This was the only instance of thieving that came under our notice.

That night we stretched over into a wide & beautiful bay near the entrance to the Beagle Channel & anchored close to the Shore, the approach being very bold. We heard the Natives jabbering loudly thro' the night & saw many fires along the Shore. At daylight 12 canoes came off to us, & such a Babel of tongues I never listened to before, each endeavouring to attract the attention of some one on board, holding up skins, beads & spears to tempt us to an exchange. And when these were expended, the *fond mothers* offered the *Babes from their breasts,* all of them keeping without intermission the most infernal squalling 'til our very ears ached with the din. One old rascal tried to entice our dog into his canoe, & we ordered him in an angry tone to leave us. He did not pay much heed to us but returned after paddling to a little distance and again endeavoured to get the Dog. One of the crew tied the animal, for he seemed willing enough to return to his old habits, whereupon our old friend appeared desirous to cut him loose. As he came near the Schooner, we got a bucket of water ready, and when he was close to, Mr. Johnson stepped out & hove it over him. He laughed very good humoredly, & we turned our backs to look at something else. The old man approached his canoe right alongside, so that he was within a few feet of us, & he & his companions dipped their paddles into the Sea & flung a shower of water over us, which caused much merriment among the whole gang.

The sweeping curve of the Bay was superb, and the shores possessed more of varied beauty than we had yet seen. The weather was summer like, & all of us felt a wish to linger a little longer there, so that we could explore a portion of the channel & get some knowledge of the interior, but we weighed while the canoes were alongside & stood out with a light breeze. Whittle, Bacon[2] & Myself went off in the Boat & procured a fine mess of fish for our dinner. When the canoes were leaving us, the breeze had freshened, and one of them getting across the Launch's bow, was very near capsizing. The poor devils were much alarmed & screamed with affright, but it was more from the fear of losing their treasures than from an apprehension of drowning. Two of the frail Boats came off to us from an Island when we were at least 6 miles from it, a distance greater than I should have ventured myself in one of them.

That afternoon we coasted along Lennox Island looking for anchorage, but finding none, hove to for the night. I kept the middle watch & Gibson was at the helm. As the Schooner was motionless, there was nothing to do & we had a long and cosy yarn about our schoolboy days.

We anchored in a cove the next afternoon, Saturday March 30th, Alden & myself leading the way in the Whale Boat &

having fine sport among the clouds of Ducks that took wing as we made our entrance. As usual, I went ashore Gun in hand; Reed was with me, & we strayed about to see if we could find any traces of the *Beagle*'s stay.[3] A shallow beach ran along the head of the cove, and a wall of rocks crowned with trees made out on either hand to the Sea. We shot some snipe on the Land and going a little farther, we came to a stream of water that was large enough to be termed a creek, much exceeding in size those we had before met with. It rolled merrily & brightly over the Sandy beach, where it paid its fresh water tribute to the Ocean, but we could not trace its meanderings for any distance into the forest, where all was wildness & gloom & solitude. In wandering about, I got a leg in a soft place up to above my Knee and stuck fast for some moments, nor did I get extricated without a struggle.

We could see no traces of the visits of any but the Natives, and returning on board, we weighed & made sail. In the mean while the others had procured fish & limpets in abundance.

We beat up to the Northern part of the Island, passing between several small Islets & rocks, & towards evening ran over & anchored in a cove at the North West extremity of New Island. This berth was not well protected & at 1 A.M. we left it with a light wind off shore. It was my middle watch, the night was clear & pleasant & the Natives were calling loudly to us from the Beach. My watch passed agreeably enough, for I was busy in thought & all around had become still.

Sunday March 31st.

During the forenoon the weather was fine. We stood along the Eastern shore of the Island with nothing to Leeward of us but the broad Atlantic. At 2 we came to in a small Harbour, where the Land was not so high as in other places and was entirely clear of a Forest growth. The short & bright green grass overspread the ground, and in the glancing of the sun's light, the surface seemed covered with a velvet mantle, rich, soft & luxuriant. A beautiful waterfall tumbled over a mossy bank onto the pebbly beach below, and there was a total absense of any thing harsh or rugged to offend the eye. Looking towards the

Sea, we saw indications of a storm brewing, & hastening on board, we sailed again, standing towards the Hermite Island. The threatening appearances still hung in the Heavens, & we knew that another *Sou Wester* was at hand. This was the 4th day of good weather, & the time was come for another struggle. At 8 in the evening the wind was blowing a Gale from the old quarter, & we hove the Schooner to under a reefed Foresail. We secured the Launch astern, but as she was very uneasy & wet, the men left her & came on board. We had kept four there to steer her. Now it was neither safe nor comfortable to be in her.

Monday April 1st.

I had the morning watch, & when I got on deck I found the weather thick & hazy, the Gale blowing fiercely as ever & the little craft labouring over the heavy sea, yet buoyant and dry. The Launch was plunging & tossing a short distance astern, and I thought *then, she would be short lived.* As the heavy squalls passed over & cleared the sky of clouds for a few moments at a time, I could see land ahead & astern (Barnevelt's & Evout's Islands), but mostly the darkness was intense, the waves as they rose on high, looking through the gloom like rocks in fearful proximity.

It was wonderful to me even, & I was not then a novice in storms, to watch the behaviour of the *tiny Schooner, for now in the Gale,* she too had decreased to a cock boat. She was but a *little thing* amid the raging Seas, and a Landsman, could he have woke to such a scene, would have deemed his hour come. He would have put no faith in wood & iron in such a chaos of the elements.

But so perfectly was the *Sea Gull* modelled, and so well balanced were all her qualities—qualities that fitted her to outlive the heaviest gale that might blow—so faultless was she as a sea boat, that with her helm lashed a lee & the foresheet flat aft, *without a human being to aid or control her,* she rode with her head offered to the Seas in triumph & in safety. I could scarcely believe that all was mechanical, that her nice & regular motion was merely the result of the properties bestowed on her by the skilfull builder. It seemed much more natural to think that She had a mind, an instinct, a will of her own, & that guided by it, she defied the threatening dangers of the Gale. She seemed endowed with human sagacity, with a knowledge that directed her movements—those movements, in which to have faltered in the least would have been fatal to herself & all on board.

John Sac[4] the New Zealander & myself were the sole occupants of the deck. And in those dark moments all that we could see was the immense waves heaped up as if they would cover us and a glimpse of the poor Launch every now and then, as she struggled on the top of a foaming Sea.

At length, daylight came, and we thought to get under the Land & anchor. So the helm was righted, & the Schooner feeling the impulse started on like a courser from the Spur. Her speed was too much for the Launch; she offered too great a resistance as she parted the waters, and one of her fasts snapped like a Thread. It was necessary to heave to again, & secure her afresh. To get a man aboard the Launch was an operation of extreme difficulty & danger, but after many trials, we accomplished it in safety, and made two hausers fast to her, which we thought would hold on well.

The Gale continued without abating, rain & hail falling in violent squalls. At 9 the Schooner's head was turned to the Northward & Westward, & she was allowed to forge ahead a little. At 1.30 we attempted to pass to windward of Evout's Island, but discovering breakers 2 miles from the shore, we had to bear away to run to leeward. The Schooner now had 6 or 7 knots way on her, and the Launch sheered wildly about as the Seas struck her & took in much water. In 15 minutes she was more than half full, & rising high on the crest of an enormous wave, the poor old Boat capsized as it melted away from her, and she was a wreck!

The cry of "the Launch is gone"! brought every one on deck, & the Schooner was again hove to just to Leeward of the Island. The Sea lashed furiously on the Shores & the rugged Land, thus obtruded on the Ocean, gave additional wildness to the Gale.

The Launch's fate was nigh. We knew the ropes could not hold her long, and we watched for the moment when she would go. At 3 one hauser parted, at 4.15 the other, and the Launch went adrift, a helpless wreck upon the waters. The old craft was gone, a prey to the insatiable Sea. Once or twice we saw her, rolling at the mercy of the waves, and then we lost her for ever. Fervent & sincere were the thanks we gave to God that *our* lives were spared, that we had been rescued from the unfortunate Launch in goodly season, that *we* were in safety, while *the poor boat* was as a broken reed upon the angry waters.

Now that there was no longer any impediment to the Schooner's progress, we gave her "a little sheet" and stood to the Northward for Lennox Island, intending to anchor under its Lee. At 8 we were in *smooth water* & at 9 snug at anchor.

All Tuesday & Wednesday the Weather continued bad, & we remained in the Harbour, fishing & shooting to procure us fresh meals. I made some delicious Stews in the Chaffing dish with Ducks & jelly & champaigne & Madeira Sauce. I flatter myself that the exquisite manner in which I conducted the operation would have charmed the heart of an Epicure, as much as the savory morsels would have tickled his palate.

On Thursday, the Gale had broke, & we stood out with a light breeze towards the Eastward, keeping in the track of the blow & looking out for the Launch. We went far out into the Atlantic, but the search was of no avail. In 3 days the Launch had been swept by the currents to a much greater distance than we would be warranted in going, and the Boat was but a speck, as a bubble on the face of the mighty deep. We had not the slightest hope that we would succeed, but yet it was well to make the attempt.

At Sundown we had the Straits Le Maire open & hove to. At Midnight the breeze came fresh from the Eastward, and we could not resist the temptation to bear away for Orange Harbour. Our work was done, & we were anxious to be once more among our friends. It was my watch, and most cheerfully I put the helm up. She went round like a dancing Master, & when she was fair upon her course I set the Mainsail, & the little craft was darting along, over 10 knots the hour. The moon was out bright & full & threw a glorious flood of silver light upon the Sea. Island after Island was passed—on, on, we flew, with a speed that was exhilarating. The *Sea Gull* with all her snowy wings abroad swept over the sparkling waters at a rate that almost equalled the swiftness of her namesake in the air. She had *"a bone in her mouth"*; the foam whirled under her bows, and a long bright path in her wake, glowing with the phosphoretic tints that render the Ocean so brilliant & beautiful by night, marked her rapid track over the moonlit Sea.

At 7 when I turned out & went on deck after enjoying 3 hours of delicious sleep, the *Vincennes* & *Porpoise* were plainly in Sight. We had run nearly 80 miles since midnight, from out of the Atlantic clear into the mouth of the Harbour.

We were thrilling in every nerve with a feverish & anxious excitement, for we knew that when those in the Ship would see there *was no Launch in tow of the Schooner,* they would give us up for lost. *And so it was!*—the glasses fell from their Eager Eyes; *"there is no Launch there! the poor fellows are gone!— the search was unsuccessful!"* But in a little while they discerned *our* group on the Schooner's decks, and soon *we* were in the midst of Officers & crew, almost torn to pieces by the hearty shakings of the hand & overwhelmed with innumerable questions asked in a breath but not answered quite so readily.

Thus on Friday, the 5th of April, our adventurous cruize was ended, and we were all most happy to be once more inmates of our good old Ship, after an absence from her of 25 days. Though we were in situations that were perilous, & though our accommodations were neither so elegant & comfortable, nor our fare *always* so delicate & luxurious as some people conceive to be necessary for man's Existence, I shall always remember those days in the Launch with much of interest & pleasure, and when our *new one* is sent on a cruize also, I shall be a ready Volunteer to go in *her,* but I trust not quite so far as to the bottom of the Sea.

Now to return to matters & things on board the *Vincennes.* Captain Wilkes had returned in the *Porpoise* some 10 days previous to our arrival, having found it impossible to proceed beyond 63° 30' South. They had been obliged to put into Good Success Bay in a Gale & were allowed no rest even then. A change of wind drove them out to Sea; to remain would have been destruction, and they "Slipped[5] & run" *for safety* out into the *open Sea* in such haste that a Boat's crew & several officers were left on the Shore, the heavy surf preventing them from launching their Boat, though they tried it at the imminent hazard of their lives.

The Brig was gone; the poor fellows were left alone without Shelter & without food. However, before the Brig slipped, every thing that daring could attempt or a seaman's ingenuity devise had been tried, but in vain, to rescue them. A boat manned with volunteers was nearly lost in endeavouring to land, & all the means tried to send a line ashore failed. The only resource left was to anchor a boat with a long scope of line, in which they deposited food, & this was done just as the Brig made sail. But for *four* days the Gale did not abate, & *the food though in sight could not be reached!* Hungry & wet, exhausted with the cold & exposure, worn down & weakened by the long deprivation from food, their sufferings were great, almost greater than they could bear. At length they got off to the Boat after a severe struggle, & then they had Grub in abundance. The Brig came back in a week, & taking the unfortunate ones on board, reached Orange Harbour without further incident.

There had been many of the natives to visit the *Vincennes* while I was absent. One of them lived on board for 10 days. The men washed him clean with warm water, shaved him & trimmed his hair & clothed him decently. He soon became at his ease & took his meals with the Officers & men, behaving with perfect propriety, for he imitated the manners of those around him without an effort. He was a great glutton and eat to repletion of all the dishes that pleased his taste. He was greatly mystified at many things & could not understand the working of a Boat under Sail seemingly without the aid of hands. He delighted in sleeping by the fire, and in mimicry of all kinds was an adept. The men dubbed him "Jim Orange," but he left one day without any show of ceremony or affection & never showed himself again—of his individual traits there was an opportunity to judge, but no information could be gleaned from [him] regarding the habits & customs of his race.

On showing a woman her face in a Glass, she burst into tears at the reflection of her own ugliness in contrast with a white Countenance by its side, & could not be prevailed upon to look into it again.

Whales frequented Orange Harbour in numbers. In the calm nights they would come close alongside the Ship, so near that I was afraid they would capsize the boats lying at the booms. They must have had rare sport in their midnight revels; the harbour resounded with their breathings, which were loud & shrill as the Whistling of a tempest. And in the clear moonlight, one could see their huge black forms heaving out of the water, & the jets of spray that they flung aloft!

On the 11th of April, the *Flying Fish* came in. She had reached 70° of South latitude & had experienced tremendous weather. I told Walker[6] when I boarded him that he had "the feather in his Cap" this cruize, for he had been more fortunate than either of the vessels.

We were employed surveying the Harbour & waiting for the *Relief* until the 17th, the weather becoming much milder than it had been in March. Filled up the Ship with wood.

The observatory had been in full swing, all the time. There was quite a colony there. A wharf had been built, & huts were peeping from the woods. The portable Houses containing the Instruments stood on a low & level Neck that terminated just beyond them in a rocky hill crowned with trees, and the waters washed close by them on either side. Men & Officers lived there, & there was always a busy air around the place, which in all likelihood had never before known the presence of civilized man.

Game was plenty there, & 9 wolves were shot that came down fearlessly in search of a meal from among the live stock; but the leaden morsels disagreed with them. The beasts heeded not the approach of the men; as savage as the country they inhabited, they had never before come in contact with any of the human race. They gave battle without turning to flee & were shot down without trouble, because they had not the instinct to run away.

The *Relief* did not come. It was time for us to be on our way—the days were becoming short & winter was approaching when there would be almost eternal night. Defend me from *such* a *summer*; *it* was sufficiently dreadful. On the 17th we left Orange Harbour without regret, just *two months* after we had entered it.

[CHAPTER 6: TO VALPARAISO]

We anchored that same evening, indeed after an hours run only, in Schapenham Bay. We had fondly thought that we were on our way for Valparaiso, but there was to be delay still, & as usual the most perfect mystery had been preserved regarding it. Captain Wilkes took up a berth so close to a rock above water as to cause us some uneasiness. The *Flying Fish* returned to Orange Harbour to remain there with the *Sea Gull* for some days longer. On the next day, we were obliged to leave the anchorage as a Gale was blowing, so we went back to the mouth of Orange Harbour and remained there until the 20th, when we actually started for Sea. The wind was light & baffling, & we drifted lazily between the Hermite Islands & the Shores of Terra del Fuego.

The Land was all around us, thrown up against the Sky, in a thousand varied & contorted Shapes, & possessing interest in its extreme ruggedness & gloom. Away in the distance were ranges of snow clad mountains that were of intense & dazzling whiteness.

"All hands" were called that night to work ship. Sunday Morning was clear & fine & Divine Service was performed. Cape Horn was in sight most of the time until Monday afternoon, when we bade the timeworn & weatherbeaten promontory a welcome farewell. We made the Ildefonsos, a group of Islands lying to the South & West & much frequented by Sealers.

On Tuesday the wind freshened to a Gale & the Sea rose & the rain & hail & snow fell. We knew that the struggle was come, that now we should have to contend with the Elements in their wildest fury, but our good Ship was prepared, & in all that was requisite on our parts to force her on her way despite the Gale we were satisfied that nothing would be wanting. The first night we lost sight of the Brig. She was obliged to heave to, while our Ship, more staunch, still had her canvass spread to urge her onwards.

To *"lie to"* long, for two days, for even one day, would have been fatal to the passage. We should have drifted far to lee-ward, & in the transient lulls, which were now becoming yet more rare & brief, we could not have recovered the lost ground ere the gale would have again overtaken us & again driven us back, and so again & again wearing out Ship & men by the continual & wearisome toils & the severe exposure to the bit-ing weather & drenching seas of such a high Latitude. Scurvy, diseases of other natures, and a long train of ills, to say nothing of the chance of Shipwreck, or the possibility of being obliged to run back to Brazil, would also have been among the pleasant consequences attendant on "heaving to," or carrying but Short sail on the Ship. To crowd on her & drive her on was the only course to pursue, and *sail was* carried to such a degree that we often seemed to be running at a maddening rate towards de-struction.

The heighth of the Gale cannot be exaggerated. Landsmen may not be able to conceive of its fury, but Seamen well know how the Wind blows off Cape Horn! The Seas were awful, & if they were not so lofty as mountains, they were pretty re-spectable as hills.

I have been in Gales before, & I have heard of Gales; and I have heard of carrying sail, & I have witnessed it before, but *this* was the *great grandfather* of *all* Gales; and *this carrying sail* threw all my previous Experience into the Shade.

The Ship trembled and shook under the mighty blasts and yielded to them at times, as if she would disappear altogether beneath the waves, but, true as Steel, the old craft would re-cover herself, and as if with tremendous effort again force her way through the Seas. The small portion of canvass that we could Show, was confined to the lower yards & masts. The up-per ones were bare and as the Ship rolled, swept in huge circles against the Sky. Often & often even this little spread of sail was too much to expose to the fury of the squalls, & "all hands" would be called to get it in in time & to Set it again the moment it was possible. The work was hard, killing. Men & Officers had but scanty rest. All had to be "up & doing," exerting themselves to the utmost in the Midst of the beating hail & rain.

It was startling even to the oldest hands to see the way in which the Captain pressed his Ship with Sail. He carried on her at a fearful rate, & the poor craft's frame shook like an aspen leaf in the violent encounters with the Seas.

A wondrous degree of nerve was requisite, tempered with a judgement correct & unfailing, to urge such a strenuous opposition to the Gale & be successful. It was well for us that in this there was no want, & we battled throughout that long blow with but one little accident occurring, the loss of the Jib boom. That night I was a volunteer in the Fore Top (the midshipman was sea sick), & Gibson & I had an everlasting job in sending down the Fore Top Gallant Yard, but it did get to the deck at last, & I got wet to the Skin in the endeavour.

The Moon was at her full. Sometimes, though rarely, the clouds would break away, and the glorious planet throw her radiant over the troubled Sea. I never before had seen her in a Storm, and the play of her placid beams upon the bursting waves & the foamy track of the Ship was beautiful indeed. The Gale at night during the hours of blackness was terrific & gloomy enough, but when the moon shone forth, there was an inconceivable grandeur & Sublimity in the aspect of the Ocean & in the motions of the tempest tossed Ship that awakened new feelings of admiration, while the degree of awe was lessened in every heart.

For 6 days the Gale blew without any cessation, and the ship was extremely uncomfortable from her violent motion & the continual wet. The snow & hail cut our faces & hands, and whenever we were for a little while free from duty on deck, the only way we could make ourselves comfortable, was to turn in—go to bed & between the blankets seek the comfort which was not to be found elsewhere, and the rest that we stood so much in need of. 90 of the crew were on the Sick list, & the few remaining were but half able to do their duty.

Those were tough times, but next winter! Ice bergs!!!—*then* will come the rub—*then* we must *do or die!!* and, so help me Heaven, I do believe that not one of us will ever return from the Antarctic Ocean! Or if one *should* be *so* extremely fortunate as to get out of *that* scrape, why, notwithstanding, there is a strong voice at my heart that tells me we shall never see home again!! Let me drive it away as often as I will, the withering, blighting thought comes back like a knell of death to my soul.

May God in his Mercy shield us from such a fate! I know it is worse than madness to have such thoughts, but they come without bidding, and I cannot drive them away! Yet I think I have acquired Philosophy enough to bear with my fate, if I cannot conquer it. But Death has been near me often; I have been accustomed to look him in his skeleton face; and I have thought & thought on those two principles, Life & Death until I have become bewildered and—but why write thus? It is almost silly.

On the 7th day of the Gale, the Wind hauled to the Southward, strong & steady. We had made sufficient Westing & were in 59° South, so we set the Studding sails, though at a tremendous risk to the spars & canvass, and stood away North North West, the good old Ship going over 12 Knots by the log. We made 270 & odd miles that day, a wondrous speed through an Element that offers so much resistance. It was a ravishing excitement to see the old craft walking off at such a gate, & the Seas, though no longer alarming in their heighth, still kept the Ocean alive with foam—oh! this was glorious sailing, and would have woke a dying man to a sense of extatic joy. We had none such on board, however, but all of us, who were mere living Seamen, were in a perfect thrill of rapturous delight from the blessed & wonder working change.

We thought to have a rapid passage, but on the 3rd of May the wind hauled to North & drove us off West. On the next day William Johnson fell overboard.[1] Until the 13th the wind continued mostly strong & unfavourable with disagreeable rainy weather. We despaired of ever more enjoying a Sunshiny day, & the Ship was as cheerless & uncomfortable as—I am at a loss for a comparison.

On the 10th of May we made the Island of Mocha, & on the 13th we discovered the Land to the South of Valparaiso, and on the same day, the Weather became clear & pleasant, much to our satisfaction. Once more there were dry decks, dry clothes, & smiling faces. The sick ones, even, brightened up amazingly. 14th painted Ship. 15th anchored in the Bay of Valparaiso—the *Peacock* was already there.

It was somewhere about 8 o'clock in the morning when we came to. Captain Hudson[2] came alongside & was saluted with manifold scoldings for not bringing *our letters* with him. However, he had sent his boat on shore for them, and in a few minutes the treasured bag was on board. I left my station on deck & ran down to the cabin without leave, trusting to the occasion for an excuse should one be asked for. Letters & papers were thrown over the deck & table, and after a little search, I found three that I recognized at a glance and a bundle of newspapers. 9 months had passed by without any word from Home, & with an eager hand I broke the Seals & read away as fast as I could. *All was well*—and I was happy.

The *Relief* had been here and gone. She was nearly wrecked about the Straits of Magellan—lost all her anchors, & all hands had given themselves *up as gone, without a hope to be saved!! & they were saved, by a hair's breadth only.* She was now at Callao with the Store Ship *Mari Posa.*

Four months amid storms & dangers had well prepared us for the comforts and luxuries of a Seaport town, and the feeling of getting ashore after such a siege, though not new, was never more joyous than when I first set my foot in Valparaiso!

Valparaiso Bay makes a huge sweep & is very open to the Sea. The town runs along the beach for miles in two streets. The rest of it is scattered over the massy & broken hills that rise immediately from the water. Over these first hills are piled others that reach to the height of 1000 feet and more above the level of the Sea. There are no trees to be seen; a little grass & a stunted growth of shrubs constitute the only approach to verdure that meets the Eye in the widest view. The innumerable ravines & gorges worn by the waters give to the whole Country the appearance of *one of our mine hills,* only on a much grander scale.

The roads winding up the ascents & the bridges across the

deep valleys are completely bare & exposed, and it was a curious sight from the Ship to watch the varied groups & corteges
passing along them—Soldiers & peasants, cavaliers & senori-
tas *"a pied"*—some gallantly mounted, scampering like mad,
and others on the slow but easy ambling mules.

Well, I thought I *had* seen places possessing *some* singularity
in their Situation; that I *had* been, where the habitations of men
were seated amidst the wonders of Nature, and that I *had*
looked & wondered my fill at such things, but *here* was the climax! Nature in her most whimsical & rugged & contorted
mood was not proof against the Encroachments of men, and in
her almost inaccessible places were perched the dwellings of
the two legged bipeds, looking about as airy & comfortable &
secure for abiding homes as we might suppose an Eagle's nest
to be in its perilous & giddy height.

Imagine a number of dark hills thrown up confusedly & ir-
regularly along the Sea Shore. They are rocky & ragged &
sandy, all three. They seem only to offer a foothold sufficient
for that best of climbers, the goat, and yet there are paths cut
over them (such as they are). Excavations have been made, &
there are houses *stuck* hither & thither that seem to have been
placed purposely with a view to afford the inmates a chance for
a *slide* to the bottom, which chance might occur from an hundred causes about once in every hour in the twenty four. The
handful of earth dug away leaves a *sort of a level* spot where
the house is built. The hill overtops its roof, and a flight of
steep stairs gives access to & fro it, the landing place being in
the path far below, & the termination of the steps, in the doorway. By removing these, all communication could be cut off,
and in such plight are most of the dwellings of the majority of
the inhabitants of Valparaiso.

So they line the side of the ravines, and so they cling to the
shelving & precipitous portions of the hills, scattered about in
the wildest manner in places that are terribly precarious. You
become amazed as you look & can scarcely credit your senses
that such are the dwellings of beings like yourselves, that men
can trust themselves, their wives & children in such perilous,
break-neck residences, where a single slip would cause a loss of

life or limb. And yet accidents are rare, & the people are contented with their seemingly treacherous homes.

On a rainy day, it is the very devil to pedestrianize about Valparaiso. I would not have given two-pence for my neck the morning I was cruizing over the *Fore Top* for deserters, or Liberty Men who had overstood their time. This hill is made of about a million precipices, and the houses are squeezed & stuck wherever there is a yard of Earth or rock that will permit of their Erection, rising from Each other's roof, helter Skelter, one story in the front, no story in the rear, the hill side serving for the back wall with shed roofs & "Jacobs ladder" stairs.

One day a wild Bull came tearing through the streets, driving every one in fear from his path. He reached the Water! Some jumped overboard, and others hid beneath the wharfs. One of the Men, who kept his wits about him & had seen too much of angry seas to be nervous on slight occasions, took up a position behind a huge post, and as the Bull rushed past him, he caught the end of a rope which was trailing from the animals horns, & quick as thought, had a turn with it around the post. The sudden jerk threw the Bull on his side, & he was secured without further difficulty.

A pleasant cottage, charmingly situated on one of the most elevated hills, was rented for our observatory, and the instruments were in full operation. From thence we overlooked the whole Town and could see right *onto* the decks of the Shipping in the Bay. The duty at the Observatory was most harrassing & uninteresting. The house was the grand gathering place for swarms of the most vicious fleas in the world, and the blood thirsty insects, glad of the chance at fresh blood, showed us no mercy and nearly dried our veins. Some nights that I passed there, I was in perfect agony, tortured until I almost went mad.

There were some pretty girls living near, and an occasional glimpse of them had an electric effect on my poor nerves. Think of the contrast between a blushing beauty of sweet 17 among her Birds & books & flowers and one of the dames of Fuego in her filthy hut. Heavens! I was enchanted. The unconscious girl appeared to me like an Angel of Loveliness, and I could scarcely turn my eyes away from the gaze that had become *too fixed* on her youthful, blooming face.

The weather was disagreeable & rainy during the most of our stay. The *Porpoise* & *Flying Fish* arrived a few days after us, but the *Sea Gull* came not, & terrible suspicions crept into our minds as to her fate. Mr. Craven was ordered on Shore to await her coming & take command of her, but I am afraid the poor *Sea Gull* will never more need a Captain.

The English frigate *President* (once our own)[3] lay alongside of us, & the Sloop of War *Fly*, Captain the Hon. Mr. Locke, was anchored farther in Shore. On Queen Victoria's birth day they made a great rejoicing, and every Englishman that had any kind of a chance got loyally drunk, as in duty bound.

One misty day during my watch on deck, a Brig was observed becalmed near the breakers on the Northern side of the Bay, some 6 miles distant. The Captain directed two Boats to be sent to her assistance, & I volunteered to go in charge. Two were also despatched from the *Peacock*, & we all pulled lustily so that we might arrive in time to save life & property. Sailors *will* work like Devils when others' lives are at stake as well as their own. Only show them an Example, stimulate them a little & there are no bounds to their Efforts. Poor fellows! they are themselves so often at the mercy of a mere chance, that they can feel for others, and particularly for brother Seamen, when they see them in danger.

As we neared the Brig we could see that she was quite unmanageable and much too close to the Surf beaten shore. She had English colors hoisted, & 4 shore boats, sent off by the Captain of the Port, were towing lazily ahead without any effect. I jumped on board. There was no one to receive me; the crew was grouped idly about the decks, not one of them doing a hand's turn to help themselves. The mate was engaged on the Poop with the Captain of the Port, & to him I made my way, perfectly astonished & disgusted to witness such unaccountable, lubberly inactivity instead of the stir & bustle of men working for their own preservation. After hurrying my men, too, to unusual & overstrained exertion, that we might not be too late, I was astounded & indignant.

The Mate told me *that the Captain was below sleeping;* that he had been up all night, watching and anxious; that worn out with excitement & fatigue, he had had a fit and was now sleeping it off. This was all very plausible, and, as I thought, true. My squad of Boats were soon ahead, towing with all their might & shaming the crews of the Shore boats into increased exertion. *I threw chips overboard;* now they floated alongside for a moment, but presently the united force of the Boats drew the Brig ahead, and with great pleasure & relief I saw the pieces of wood left slowly astern. Satisfied that we were leaving the Land, I took the bearings of two points by Compass to ascertain if we had any drift, trimmed the Sails, roused about the crew & put some life in them, holloa'd encouragingly to my own men, cast a contented glance on the boiling surf now that we were going away from it, & then turned to renew my talk with the Mate.

The vessel in whose destiny there had been such a change wrought in a few minutes was the *Superior,* of & from London via Santos, & was deep loaded with Sugar. Her original Captain had fallen overboard two days out from London & was drowned. The now Commander was the then 1st Mate, & the present Mate, a young man of 20, had been the 2nd Officer. Their passage round the Cape had been long & stormy. They had made the land in the evening, & overshooting the Harbour, had fallen close in Shore and drifted parrellel to the breakers for 10 or 12 miles, expecting every moment to be thrown among them. They were bewildered & did not know what to do! 14 great big sailors, and they had not moved a rope yarn toward getting their own boat out, which should have been the first thing for them to attempt. Oh! the rascals; I had no compassion for them. They almost deserved to be wrecked.

The Captain of the Port was pretty much of the same opinion as myself, which he communicated to me by a whole series of confidential grimaces & expressions in the best English he could Muster. "The Capitan sleepe! dam bad! no good! bah!" and the accompanying shrug of the shoulders & contortion of the features had a grand effect in expressing his indignation. Then he wondered, "*Why the Englishmen* had not sent assistance?" and complimented the American character most highly; he had often known it honorably displayed.

An hour & a half passed during which we made a gradual

progress, drawing slowly off the Land, when at last came one small boat from the *Fly,* a tardy succorer to a countryman in distress. A faint breeze came over the waters & aided us slightly but not sufficiently to cast off the Boats.

I had soon observed that the Mate was but a new Seaman, and he seemed to wish that I should take the whole charge & responsibility upon my shoulders. This I could not think of— the Captain was on board, & how could I usurp *his* place, who was alone accountable for the safety of his vessel? Besides, I had not seen him yet, but supposed he would awake in time to anchor his vessel, and there would be no farther trouble. So I told the Mate that I would not interfere with him any more, now that all was right.

Presently he went below. I heard a scuffling in the Cabin immediately afterwards, voices in loud & angry dispute, and a tumbling about as if two men were clinched in a violent struggle. The voices became more passionate in their tones, more abusive in their terms, and the parties seemed to be engaged at regular built fisticuffs. At first I thought the Captain was still in his fit, & in his insane state, unconscious of what he was about. The suspicion that he might be in liquor had occurred to me some time before this, & I had questioned the Mate upon it. He denied that such was the Case, and kept to his first story. Now, however, I was almost convinced the voice was that of a drunken Man.

The uproar increased, and I could hear them dealing blows and dragging each other about the Cabin. I hesitated whether I should go among them. The cabin boy, an extremely handsome lad, came to me to request that I would step down & part them; that they were actually fighting & that most brutally. Not caring to mix in such an encounter, I sent the Carpenter below, who succeeded in separating the Captain & his Mate. The latter came on deck in rather a bad plight, uttering a most blasphemous tirade of invective & abuse against the Captain, & he told me in plain terms that the fit was the effect of both habitual & recent intoxication; that the Captain had been drunk during the night & forenoon [and] was now only in a partial & stupid state of recovery.

I felt vexed at having been deceived and expressed myself so to the Mate, telling him that if I had known at once that the proper Commander of the vessel had rendered himself *incapable of his duty at such a time as this* by a beastly indulgence in liquor, I should have pursued a different course & should have deemed it *my duty* to assume the charge & direction of the vessel. He excused his prevarication by saying that he did not like to tell me the truth—he was ashamed to do so. His motive may pass for good, but his shame was falsely placed.

Soon after the Captain appeared on deck, & I was first aware of it by hearing a number of needless orders given accompanied with curses & angry threats at the crew. The miserable brute had been totally unconscious for many hours. He was not aware that our Boats were ahead; that he had been visited by the Health officers; that he & his vessel had run so near to destruction, all this while he had been in a drunken stupor and knew no more about the condition of his vessel than if he had been in the other world. This was fulfilling his trust; this was guarding the precious lives of his crew & the property, perhaps the all, of his owners.

I went up to him & addressed him. He merely answered me with a vacant stare and was evidently unconscious of who I was, or what I was doing on his decks.

I was again in a dilemma. Here was the Captain on deck, giving orders to his crew. To have allowed him his sway would not answer at all, and yet how could I, a foreign officer, deprive him of it or even request him to deliver up the control which was his alone by might & right? I did not know in what manner he might be disposed to receive such an application. I could not decide how to act, and yet it was necessary to do something quickly. However, I thought it would be best to defer interference until the last moment and then appeal to his fears & his ignorance of the harbour, offering at the same time my services to anchor the vessel. For I felt that my reputation would be touched if harm came to that Brig; not that I would be liable to the *Law,* but that my conduct would be canvassed by every officer in the harbour.

A Merchant from the Town came on board, and after explaining to him the state of things, he agreed to make the proposal to the Captain. And I was satisfied to have a Civilian to back me, one who was altogether disinterested.

The Captain had brought up his chart & compass and was vainly trying to comprehend the situation of the Anchorage, frequently breaking out in oaths & orders to the crew which were so contrary that I had to countermand them quietly to keep the Brig under command. When he referred to the Chart, he became confused and finally sat down in despair. His intellects were not yet clear enough; his faculties were still bewildered. The effects of his intoxication still disordered & killed his mind so that he was perfectly helpless, and I could not help pitying his evident distress, though it was manifested in the most incoherent & hysterical manner & though it had its origin from such an inexcusable cause.

Now it was, that the Merchant said to him, "Let this officer who has already done much for you anchor your Brig. Give her up to him, & all will be well." "I will! I will!" he cried; "I give up the Brig to you, Sir!" And from that time, he said not another word. Indeed, he went below in a few minutes & slept again.

And *I was Captain* of the English Brig in the face of two of their own men of war. The breeze came ahead, & I furled the Sails, the crew of the vessel obeying all my orders readily & cheerfully. They foresaw a speedy end to their toils & dangers. Most of my own men were on board. I had cast off all of the Boats but two as we were immediately among the vessels, and the whole of them towing only created confusion.

I felt strange: for the first time in my life, I was unexpectedly placed in this entirely novel situation—a Captain—Mercy—and to anchor my craft in the face of a whole squadron. I had to be cool, and I succeeded. Praise be to Neptune, whose humble votary I am! Slowly we swept by my own Ship, the *Vincennes*. I was standing on the night heads,[4] the most conspicuous individual on board the Brig, conning her and giving the necessary mandates in the most assured & off hand manner that I could assume. I knew that I was a mark for many, but I stood fire to my perfect satisfaction, and all went well.

The Boat from the *Fly* was the first one that I had directed to cast off from the tow line, and by this time she was alongside & the Midshipman on board. I certainly did not present in my dress any striking marks of the uniform of an American officer, for I had on a coarse pilot cloth suit & a most uncouth though Serviceable Sou'Wester. Therefore I was not very much surprised when this English reefer made his way to me and interrupted me in the midst of an order with the question, "Pray, Captain, will you tell me where *you* are from?" "Sir," cried I, & I could not help smiling, "*this Brig is last from Santos, but I am from the American Sloop of War* Vincennes"! And as there was no leisure to parley any more, I referred him to the Mate for further information, saying that I should wish to speak to him before he shoved off.

I had my Eye on a good berth near to the *Vincennes,* and though I may say it myself, the Brig *Superior* of London was brought to anchor in a style that could throw no discredit on my Seamanship. I gave her the requisite scope of cable, added some hints to the Mate about Sundry necessary precautions to be observed against breaking adrift, and then felt happily relieved to resign my brief Command after having contributed my mite in bringing the *Superior,* after her long & hazardous passage, to a secure & quiet resting place.

The English reefer (who by the by, was a very handsome & gentlemanlike youth, and for aught I know, a Lord or an embryo Duke, for there were several precocious specimens of Nobility on board the *Fly*) was awaiting my Leisure as I had requested him. He did not now allow me to commence until he had apologized for his mistake, which seemed so ludicrous to both of us that we could not avoid a hearty laugh! And was it not a good joke? indeed it was! *Me! this child!!* who am but a miserable Yankee Passed Midshipman, to be accosted as the Captain of an English Merchantman by one of the Royal officers of Royal Victoria's Royal Navy!

I wished the Midshipman to tell the Honorable Captain Locke the condition the Brig was & had been in, so that he might be perfectly aware of the Captain's Conduct. I thought it was both right and necessary to do so. In all likelihood no one else would expose him, & he might again be trusted with his all important charge and again abuse the confidence reposed in him. Unpleasant as it was, I could not spare him. His offence—too mild a term by far, his crime—was too heinous for a Sailor to pardon, and therefore I recommended the miserable man & his vessel to the especial care of the Commander of the *Fly*.

Our ship was fairly disgraced while we lay in the roads. We fouled the *Peacock* twice, once when the swell was very heavy. Dire confusion—our decks were in an uproar, spars crashing & ropes going. 'Twas an angry sight, & I could not help thinking that the Ships were possessed of animation and engaging each other in bitter strife like as if they were Gladiators of the Sea. Then we must foul a Dane, the *Canton,* a ship as large as ourselves. This was all Captain Wilkes's fault & arose from his mismanagement & obstinacy. What a time we had of it to get clear. We were a spectacle for every one in the Harbour. While all the other vessels were riding securely, we were dragging about & swinging into those who happened to be near us. I was crazy with shame & vexation, that our seamanship would be so disgraced.

Time wore on—no *Sea Gull* came!

[CHAPTER 7: THE PACIFIC ISLANDS]

On the 6th June, we sailed [for Callao, Peru]. For three days we had hot & misty weather with strong winds & a heavy sea. We were in despair! We had heard so much of the balmy Pacific yet we had scarcely seen the Sun since we entered it. However, the weather cleared off, & then indeed it was fine enough! 4 months of rough weather had fully prepared us to enjoy the change.

On June 20th, we made the Island of San Lorenzo. I had the morning watch, & we stretched far into a Bay as we were beating up from whence we could see the City of Lima spread over the plain. 'Twas dark when we run through the Boqueroon passage. Captain Hudson came on board as we neared the Anchorage, & soon afterwards we anchored amidst the other vessels of the Squadron, all of us together once more save the poor *Sea Gull,* and I am afraid that she has anchored forever.[1]

We were to lie under the Island until our provisions & all were stowed, as we had the whole place to ourselves & nothing to bother us. Callao, the port of Lima, crowded with shipping, was seven miles distant. All hands were busy at work, & the instruments were put up on shore. The Island is about 5 miles long, 3 or 400 feet high & composed of nothing but Sand, the most barren spot I ever saw. I abhorred the duty there. It was killing—but little sleep, and that on the thwarts of a broken boat, & all day the heat was intolerable. Besides, my poor eyes suffered from the intense accuracy required in the observing. I thought the balls would split. I never want to acquire a reputation as a scientific man or as a surveyor, if I am to do so at the expense of my sight. There was some little interest in the scene at night, when all was quiet & the moon at her full poured her brilliant light upon the sandy wastes, the tents, the ships & the ocean—a slight stretch of the imagination, & I was in Arabia & my thoughts were every where.

On the 2nd July, we moved the Ship over to Callao, and that night, I was sent upon the beach to observe with the instruments. I expected to wake up & find my throat cut, for such a villianous neighbourhood I never was quartered in.

The *Falmouth* came in. Captain McKeever gave us his Launch, 1st Cutter and his Nephew, which latter was heartily wished at the d——l by us all.[2] The *Relief* was to be sent Home, dismissed from the Squadron. Much difficulty & diplomacy there was in quieting Captain Long. Three Lieutenants sent in her from *Porpoise* & other changes made in the Squadron.[3] We all wrote by a Mr. Foster, whose passage we paid by a subscription among the Squadron. I hope he had a safe & speedy journey, for I trusted in his getting home in November.

On the 13th July we sailed.

Thursday August 15th 1839—

After a quiet & some what monotonous passage of 30 days, we made the Island of Clermont Tonnere and are now fairly entered among the tempting Edens of the South Pacific.

This Island is not over a dozen miles in length. The shores are low & *narrow.* Where the white beach terminates, there is a beautiful fringe of Trees & Shrubbery hiding from view the Lagoon within, but from aloft you can look over the quiet lake, the Isles that stud its bosom, and the green strip that encompasses it round about. We ran close in with the Ship, and I spent more than an hour on the Royal Yard, entranced with the Singular & picturesque loneliness of that gem of the Ocean.

We only saw a few of the Natives. They opposed our landing by throwing stones & clubs at those in the Boats, though they did not do any serious injury. A few charges of mustard shot sent scattering about their posteriors drove them among the bushes, and the party landed to procure specimens without further interruption.

Friday morning we made Serle Island, 20 miles to the Northward & Westward of Clermont Tonnere, & surveyed it before

Night. Alden & myself were in a Boat coasting along the shore. We anchored just abreast of a group of Natives who were collected on the beach and soon induced them to swim off to us. They manifested all the signs of peace & desire for intercourse— sent their weapons away & threw presents out towards us, trying to bring us to them. But we did not wish to land, and it was no inconvenience to them to make an excursion in the water— no unrobing, or any thing of that sort. While some were coming off, one fellow ran at full speed to the huts & returned in an instant with two Cocoa Nuts, which he threw to us, & now we commenced to trade. They gave us cloth made of bark, feather plumes, & fish hooks. In return we offered knives, handkerchiefs, &c., for we were not provided with a trading stock. I sacrificed one of my snuff brown kerchiefs for a hook, which, please the pigs, I shall carry home instead of adding it to the collection of the Expedition.

The villains tried to steal, but we watched them too sharp. They showed no concern when detected, & immediately repeated their attempts. They were all well formed, fine looking men with bright intelligent countenances; dark brown in colour; hair wavy, long, black & glossy, gathered at the back of the head & tied so as to droop in a graceful crest; teeth white & even. The women we could see in the distance under the trees. They had only a modest covering around the loins. They did not come near the beach.

We regretted exceedingly that we could not land, particularly because the other Islanders had been so hostile. I forgot to say that *those* rascals gave to our people in the Boat the gratifying information that if they *would* come ashore, they would certainly be made a meal of. When the Shot struck them, they brushed away at the spot as if a fly had bitten them, manifesting the utmost unconcern & contempt for us & our weapons, & exhibiting more of the cannibal in their faces & gestures tha[n] was agreeable to witness. However, they withdrew after the second volley, moving with deliberate dignity.

At another Island, when several managed to land, the natives met them upon the beach & gently but firmly resisted all their attempts to penetrate into the woods. It was quite amusing, as related. Dr. Pickering accidentally falling overboard from the reef, the fellows jumped after him & picked him safely up with much concern. Passing vessels must have left a bad character among them.

Sunday August 18th 1839.

A year to day since we sailed—Heavens!! I have had some correspondence with the Captain this same day of no very pleasant nature. All I have to say on this Era is, that as great a revulsion has taken place in *my* feelings in regard to the domestic part of this first grand National Expedition, as has *actually occurred* in the *family* arrangement. Look back—see the changes in our brief twelvemonth: officers dismissed, sent home with hopes blighted & prospects blasted, for no offence but to gratify the malignant propensities of a *nameless man,* but he will have to answer for it *yet!* His day of reckoning must come. And if he expects to produce great results from this cruize, he must not use the beings under him as if they were so many stones.

Sunday August 22nd.

There has been more correspondence between the worshipful Skipper of this craft, and his Officers. He has received a bitter dose, & he almost choked in the swallowing.[4] The gentle creature! how I am learning to love him! He has become crazed with the power conferred on him by his Situation, and he has forgotten how to use it. He imagined that he could bend us all to follow the arbitrary & absurd notions of *his* will; that he could introduce among us *his* rules for our conduct in matters that are beyond his interference; that he could break up the sociability that is so happily existing between his officers, because He was getting out of odour himself.

But the instant he outraged his power, so soon as he stepped without the protection of Law, there was a strong & a stirring spirit of resistance aroused among those to whom he had appealed with so much confidence. He, even He! the mighty and awful Commander of this first great National Expedition, found *his will disputed* & his insults & sarcasms flung back in his teeth by his Subordinates, whom he thought would have bared their necks to his Knife as unresistingly as the sheep in the fold submit to the Murderous Butcher.

Conscious of our own innocence, we could not brook the foul nature of his charges; with law, the "iron customs of the Service," & good sense & feeling on our side, we expressed our indignant resentment of his scandalous interference in terms that must have been bitter as gall to him, but to which he could take no official exception. He had thrown aside the armour of his station, and our weapons of defence were sent rankling to his heart. The wound will fester, for the man's passions are vile as Satan's & as ungovernable as the winds.

But enough of this! I had intended never to introduce such themes, among these pages. Once, I fondly dreamed, hoped, believed that I never would have occasion, but like most of the hopes of life, the vision was false and has been rudely dissipated long, long, ago! The occurrences would furnish inexhaustible subjects for the pen, but I will keep them in my memory, and if it pleases God to restore me to my own Home, I can tell of the Alpha & Omega to those whose love I trust I shall never lose.

Yesterday we were off a lovely Isle. It was uninhabited and had in all likelihood never known the presence of man, the destroyer! The vegetation was rich & luxuriant, and the groves of trees were beautiful as the leafy bowers of the fairies. The air was darkened with clouds of Sea birds on the wing, and the whole Island swarmed with myriads of all varieties of the feathered tribe.

I did not get ashore at this Paradise though I should have liked it above all things. The Skipper has been showing his teeth, manifesting his spite on every occasion that offers, a mighty dirty way of proceeding. He would not let us land, neither did he afford the Scientifics an opportunity for a research that would have afforded a rare collection of curious things.

Sharks abound without the Surf. They were thick around the Boat, hundreds in a drove, the agreeable creatures; it was pleasant to see them so familiar. Some fine Turtles were brought on board weighing over 237 lbs. We had a delicious meal from them yesterday & might have had an hundred others, if the Captain had been disposed.

August 24th

Off another Island to day. We were close in Shore, and these Natives, unlike the others, came alongside the Ship without hesitation, but they would not venture on board. The Ship being underweigh, they could not trust themselves on her decks, for fear they would be carried away. Had it been possible to anchor, they would have swarmed up.

The natives were collected to the number of several hundred on the beach, some lying in groups under the Trees, others walking along the waters edge, spear in hand, singing and dancing. Some were constantly retiring among the woods, and others stepping out from their protecting shades. One single Stride from the beach sufficed to hide them entirely from our view, and their appearing was equally as sudden. The trees were as a screen, a drop curtain, & we could not see what was going on in the sylvan recesses of their midst. But from aloft, the transparent blue of the lagoon and its rich green frame lay beneath the Eye, looking as if it could have been created for no impurer use than to yield up the Pearls* that abound in its depths, a fitting home indeed for those precious things that possess so much of poetry in their appearance & in their use.

Sunday Afternoon, I was in one of several Boats coasting along the Western shore of the Island. We could not find an Entrance to the Lagoon, which we regretted exceedingly, for our only hope of landing was in the existence of a passage between the reefs.

We had a traffic with the Natives, & they danced & sung for us, while up to their knees in water, and swam off to our boats & rubbed noses with us in a manner that was truly amicable & delightful, when we consider that their great white teeth might

*The Pearl fishery in many of these Lagoons is extremely valuable.

have just been unfastened from a human bone. They received our presents with a singular mixture of fear & boldness, if two such compounds can be agglommerated, and it was evident to us that that they had had but little intercourse with white men and did not know whether to regard us as beings like themselves or not. The experience of a life time on their Island with no other mode of locomotion but their Shanks & their slight canoes could give them but little idea of the strange beings who came in huge things that moved through the water without visible help, who covered their whole body, & who had thunder & lightning at their command. This is too much for the simple minded Islanders, & it is not to be wondered that they regard us with some awe.[*]

Those fellows at Tonnere Island must have been visited & badly treated by the Whites to account for their conduct towards us. There is no mention of this Island having been touched at, for several centuries.

These Islands, are in many places just even with the water's edge or merely showing above it. It is curious to observe them from the deck: as the Ship sinks with the Swells, you lose the Land altogether, & as she rises again, you catch the faint outlines in the Sky. The trees give the appearance of any elevation to the Islands, and when there were any straggling ones, at first sight they resembled a squadron of vessels underweigh.

At the Island of Carlshoff I went on shore for water with one of the Natives for a guide. We cut & scrambled through the woods for a quarter of a mile to the edge of the Lagoon, where we found two pools of water accumulated in the hollows from the rain. It was *rather* brackish, but then we must not stand upon any fastidious notions of taste, when the choice lies between *bad* Water *or None.* The manner in which we filled our water bags may have had some slight tendency to purify the

---

[*]A singular contrast strikes one here: reared as we are to the daily & almost indispensable use of innumerable things that the whole world is ransacked to supply, we are surprised, pleased & interested to see a people, whose wants are satisfied by the scanty productions of their small & sea girt home, and who never quit their narrow & solitary Shores.

pool & sweeten the whole collection. A dozen men & three or four greasy skinned natives were up to their middle, dipping away as if they would drain the pond. If I had not by long use become accustomed to such things & *far more revolting*, I should scarcely have credited my eyes, that drink for men should be procured in that way.

Ah's Me! the running stream *at the back door*, & the crystal Springs among the Hills came into my mind. The fairy Island, with all its beauty, had no treasures like to those. It would have done my heart good to have seen a dancing, bubbling rill, but my eyes only rested on the shallow & slimy water that was almost boiling under the fierce rays of the Sun.

It is in situations such as this that recollection of the luxuries & comforts of one's Home crowd upon us & almost make us regret th[at] we ever left it & them. But the mind, without effort, soon resumes its natural tone, and we are satisfied to purchase the pleasures of roaming, at any price.

[CHAPTER 8: THE SOCIETY ISLANDS AND SAMOA]

On the 10 of September we anchored off Point Venus in the Island of Otaheite, or, as the Natives call it, Tahita. It was a peaceful evening when we came to in this place, so famous in the eyes of all Navigators.[1] The Natives were soon alongside in swarms, & had we permitted them to come on board, our decks would have been alive. Some few chiefs only were allowed to board us, & we soon became on terms of the most familiar acquaintance with them, exchanging names & going through all the ceremonies of an Otaheitian introduction.

The high & towering peaks, the rich valleys, the groves of Cocoa Nut trees along the beach—the golden Oranges, the clusters of huts, the groups of people—*the dogs, the cows,* were all in strong contrast to the low Islands we had been among for the past month. The sight was cheerful, & we were right glad to find ourselves once more among people who had some pretensions to civilization. As we had been on Sea fare for some weeks, our appetites were marvellously regaled by the quantities of delicious fruits that we destroyed. The oranges in particular were the very best I ever met with—and the cocoa nut!

The *Porpoise* was already at anchor, & we learned with great satisfaction that a Ship was to sail in a few days for the United States. This was as gratifying as it was unexpected, and we all embraced the opportunity of writing to our Homes.

The observatory was erected on the same spot occupied by Cook & subsequent Navigators for the like purpose, & a Hospital was established close by in the Queen's houses, where all the sick of the Squadron were accommodated. The Forge was also put up for the Armourers, & they & the Carpenters were busy at work, side by side. Tents were pitched for the Officers, and there was all the bustle & stir of a colony on the usually quiet point. Cook called this place Point Venus, because it was here he observed the transit of that Planet. It is a low, level, narrow tongue of Land making the head of the Harbour, covered with Cocoa Nut trees & divided by a considerable fresh water Stream that here empties into the Sea. It is a lovely place, of such delicious beauty that we were all sorry when the time came for our establishment to be broken up.

Hundreds of the Natives of all ages & of both Sexes were continually on the point, thronging around our temporary abodes. The whole people are extremely indolent, & most of them do nothing more than to pluck the fruit, which grows & ripens without the aid of man. These seemed to have nothing in the world to do but to gratify their curiosity by mingling with us. New faces appeared every day coming from distant parts of the Island to look at the white men, the rich white men of the Men of War. They slept on the Earth with no covering save the Trees, & during the day, they were always ready to assist us in any thing we might require. They hovered about us as if it was actually necessary to their happiness to be always near us, & never quitted the Point so long as we remained. Some had things to Sell—Pigs, fruit, fowls, shells, tappa, &c. In most cases they demanded money, for they have been taught the value of that by the Missionaries. Cloth they would take some times & made up clothes, but they were not so simple & primitive as to prefer gewgaws & trifles.

On entering their Houses, which we did without any ceremony, we were always welcomed. They were happy to have us come. Whole families seemed to live together in the most promiscuous manner, & the numbers of young & old who followed in our wake also made themselves at home within doors, as though they possessed a natural right to do so. The Houses are of light & exceedingly airy construction & of only one apartment, there being no division of the interior into rooms. Leaves are strewn over the ground & form the floors; when green & fresh they are pleasant enough, but when allowed to remain too long they become exceedingly dirty & disagreeable. The inmates lie about on mats or rude benches, & we generally saw two or three sea chests in each hut wherein the women keep their Sunday finery. The Keys of these chests are carried with much ostentation, hanging to a string from the waist as an evidence of the wealth of the owner. Poor creatures, they are so proud that they have any thing to lock up. There was a day among them when bars & bolts were not known.

The most prominent traits exhibited by both sexes in their intercourse with us were a rapacious desire for money & the most open & profligate display of the most extreme & wanton licentiousness. Money is valuable, because it is demanded as a fine for various offences. Otherwise, it is not in the least degree necessary to the comfort or importance of the Islanders.

There is no longer any worshipping of wooden Gods, but the only worship which has succeeded this consists in a fear of the Missionaries and the complying with the prescribed forms of the church. It is idle to say that there exists on any of the Islands a dozen Natives, who may be called intelligent, devout & sincere Christians—there are none, not one!

The observance of the Sabbath by all classes is strict in the extreme & would seem wonderful to one unacquainted with the cause. No work is done, nothing is bought or sold, no journeys are made. From daylight until dark the people are crowding to the churches, where religious exercises are performed in their own language. They are not remarkably attentive to the service but this is no wonder, for where *is there* a congregation who are wholly wrapt in attention to the words from the Pulpit? I have never seen them! As to the keeping of the Sabbath as a day of rest, the measures adopted are such as would produce a startling change among our own people. The Laws devised by the Missionaries & sanctioned by the King inflict a severe punishment upon every one who shall violate the decorum & sanctity of the holy day.

On week days they are unrestrained in a great measure in the indulgence of their own propensities. When they wished to sin against the Laws, they have the Sense to do so secretly & thereby avoid the fines. The horrid & revolting association of the *Arreay*[2] has been abolished for many years, but one of its terrible laws has been succeeded by a practise equally odious, though it is carried on in Secret to escape the inflictions of the new code of justice. They have no sense of Shame or impropriety in the indulgence of their passions. They are as open as the day & more promiscuous than the beasts in the fields.

Who can judge one nation by another? What man can say, this people shall be my standard, by them I will judge all others? Custom of more ancient date, perhaps, than any among us, has formed the habits of the Otaheitians. They differ from us widely, but they are unconscious that *they* are wrong. That, which we would point at with the finger of Shame & condemn as obscene & sinful, they deem of no harm, but as worthy of commendation & observance. Principles different from ours as night from day are deeply engrafted in their natures, & human efforts have failed to subdue them. Here I must draw the veil! The moral condition of the people passes description.

I was interrupted this moment by seeing a shark dragged past the port I am writing at. The rascal had taken the bait, & the men with much exultation were hauling their prize on board. I had to drop my pen & run to be in at the death, for "all hands" collect & have a sort of jubilee over the dying throes of their common enemy. It is impossible to convey the least idea of the degree of savage satisfaction that sailors enjoy in the capture & destruction of one of these monsters. While they are torturing him with all the means their ingenuity can supply, they are as merry over his floundering as if they were contributing to his pleasure. They jest & laugh & talk to the victim as if *he* possessed understanding, though there is as much of hearty spite in their tone as there is of positive happiness.

When he is cut to pieces & completely overhauled, his heart receiving particular notice (as if there was some doubt about a shark's being the possessor of *such an attribute*), the carcass is contemplated with infinite complaisance & then hove into the Sea to become food in *its* turn. The voracious creature meets with, after death, the same fate to which it had consigned so many living things while in life itself, for it is generally devoured by those of its own species.

After the Spectacle was over, I returned to my writing, but first I emptied a cocoa Nut of its milk, drinking from the cup which nature has furnished to the fruit. The draught was cool, sweet & delicious & oh! how grateful to the palate. While at sea I drink a dozen in a day, & when I turn out to my watch at night, I am reconciled to the disturbance of my sleep by the opportunity afforded of quaffing this nectar of the Tropics. This is Thursday October 10th, A.M. 10.

Peacock, *November 18th*

We removed our Anchorage to Papahite to have a meeting of the Chiefs on board relating to the affairs of the consul Mr. Blackler,[3] a person unfortunately not qualified to do credit to his station. The Chiefs assembled on board. I was director of the Squad of Boats sent to bring them, and after starting the oddly dressed Patriarchs of Tahita, I escorted the two Princesses of the blood Royal to my own boat & pulled on board. The girls, forgive me, ye aristocrats, for the term, were young & not at all repulsive in feature, but they were huge in frame & not at all deficient in flesh! They were dressed alike in loose white muslin frocks with ruffs around the neck, full bosoms & slack at the waist. A belt would have stood no chance, & a draw string sufficed for the slight pressure their figures allowed. Shoes & stockings on feet that had rarely worn them, & straw bonnets of a fly-a-way description, perched on the summit of a huge mound of hair, completed their attire. Their movements were awkward & constrained & totally devoid of grace, while in their native dress, with bare ancles & unshod feet, they really were attractive.

The assemblage of chiefs was composed of the most important in rank on the Island. They were monsters in size, all of them—a well known fact which is not easily accounted for. In costume they presented a singular & ludicrous mixture of European & Savage garments & *nakedness,* all of them. They were delighted with the exercise of the Marines. One old gentleman could not constrain himself, his joy was so great—he jumped & skipped about the decks, pulling every one by the arms to tell them, *"Maitie, Maitie."*

I landed one set & sent the Boat back to the Ship, intending to return myself in another about half a mile farther from the vessel. I walked to where she lay on the beach, & we had just shoved off when we heard some one hailing us from shore. The cry of distress came from one of the most portly chiefs whom I had just left & who was now toiling along the beach with as much rapidity as he could exert, his shoes already off to facilitate his progress. I waited for him & found that he had left his handkerchief on board & was in dreadful agony lest he should lose it. I assured him that there was no danger on that score, but he was uneasy until we reached the Ship & received his property from his brother, who had not yet left. I mention this, to show the value they attach to European goods.

Many of the girls were really beautiful & of such soft & simple & winning manners that a charm was thrown around them, more than I can Express—teeth like pearls, unmasked by smiles sweet & irresistable—the garland of wild flowers in the raven hair, & the dark Eye that was burning in its force—the fawns of Otaheite—the Sylphs of the forest, the wood nymphs. I shall ever remember them with delight.

Many of the girls at Point Venus have learned the chorus songs common with sailors in heaving up the Anchor & other work. We frequently amused ourselves by collecting a group & getting them to sing for us. It was so singular to hear them pouring forth in song English words of which they knew not the meaning, nor could they pronounce them in a speaking tone. Their voices were good, and the ditties of "So early in the morning the Sailor loves his bottle oh," "Round the corner, Sally," "Tally Ho, you know" & a dozen others were often heard along the beach for half the night.

We left Otaheite on the 24th [of September] and anchored in the harbour of Eimeo the same afternoon. The Scenery here was sublime. Our Ship lay immediately under & between two towering hills that formed the entrance of a Bay which ran far into the Land. A plain made along the head of Bay for some 10 miles, & in the back ground there rose ridge after ridge of high mountains, shooting up against the Sky in peaks of every wild & fanciful form. Some were wooded to the summits, while others displayed the barren grandeur of naked Rock. On one of the loftiest heights a natural bridge threw its arch upon the mountain's side, affording by the passage of clear & vivid light a strong contrast to the gloomy shades around it. One isolated peak bore a strong resemblance to a Gothic Spire & terminated in a point fine as a needle to the view. On the left the shores continued ruggedly high, while to the right they were less abrupt, & villages were scattered along the Beach.

Five of our men deserted in the night; mustered the crew at quarters as soon as it was discovered & sent Boats & officers in pursuit, offering a tremendous reward to the natives ($150) for their apprehension. The next morning we descried them on the summit of a high ridge immediately over the Ship, & natives in pursuit. The fellows had tracked them like blood hounds & escape was impossible. I brought them on board & thought they had paid rather dear for their whistle.[4] $150.00—'twas 10 times too much for the men to pay, or the natives to receive.

At Tahita we were in the habit of pulling ourselves to a quiet part of the beach after Sundown and enjoying an hour's bath in the Sea, and refreshing were those immersions after a sweltering day. Pursuing the custom, we landed abreast a small white House on the beach near the Ship. An American was the occupier of it, and in a few moments' conversation, I found that he was from *Chester County—Coates by name*. He had often been in Lancaster & we were soon underweigh in a yarn about the old place & such of the people as he had known. Fancy the interest of this scene, at night, on the Shores of an Island in the midst of the Pacific, as unexpected, as it was curious. We were to sail at daylight. I begged him to come on board, & I would endeavour to give him some things he stood in need of. He pressed upon me a cane of Whalebone & two mats, & as he would not hear of a refusal, I told him to bring them with him.

I had the morning watch, & daylight brought the Pilot & Mr. Coates on board. I gave him a Hatchet, some plane Irons, files, &c., & a Suit of clothes from Stem to Stern, with which he went his way rejoicing. His presents will I trust find a place in my extensive Museum at Home.

While we were weighing, a black sow, huge & fierce, forgetting the dignity proper to herself, set off on a most violent crusade about the decks, overturning every one in her way. Finally, scrambling over the Purser in his bed, scenting his Sheets & bemiring his person, she leaped into the Sea & struck out for the Shore. After a hard chase she was captured & brought on board. I laughed, every body laughed, at the condition of the Purser—who could help it? But while I was in the midst of my mirth, the same individual swine came up behind me, & making a wonderful spring, took the whole of my leg into her mouth & amused herself for some moments by grinding away with her tusks & shaking me as she would a corn cob. The attack coming from the rear, I was not in a favorable position for defence; however, I slued round as well as I could, & taking a fair aim at her head with a Hatchet I had in my hand, I was about to spoil her fun forever, when one of the Men came to the rescue & belaboured her with a club until she let go. Mem.—never to laugh, when a sow skylarks with a Purser.

Had the satisfaction to eat a piece of her next day.

Leaving Eimeo, on the 27th September, we made & passed the Islands Saunders, Huaheine, Bora Bora, Raiatea & Motorita and as there were no vessels in company, for the first time in the cruize our men had some rest & the decks were unusually quiet. The *Peacock* had remained at Tahita to repair the *Flying Fish,* & the *Porpoise* was to meet us in a few days.

We hove to off Bellinghausen's Island, & I with others went on shore to make Magnetic observations. Coral formation & Lagoon—birds innumerable in the woods—no inhabitants. Afterwards made Rose Island—same description—Birds in black millions.

On October 8th made Manua, the Easternmost of the Navigator group. This Island is high & wooded to the summit, and oh! the beautiful beaches sweeping between the headlands, with the enchanting groves & the clusters of Huts, and the dark skinned people moving to & fro—so sweet, looking so cool, so airy, so free (so different from a Ship). The mere view gave us intense enjoyment; just to gaze on the panorama as the Ship swept by filled our hearts with glad feelings & dreamy fancies.

I was rejoiced to find myself ordered on shore in charge of a Boat. We landed in an inlet guarded by rocky projections from the wind, though the passage over the reef was so narrow that there was barely room for the Boat to pass between the breakers. A level place that did not extend back more than a quarter of a mile from the water's edge & was perhaps for two miles along it formed the site of a village, & a wall of rock rose perpendicularly in its rear to the heighth of several hundred feet.

A noble array of Bread fruit & other trees sheltered the village from the Sun, & the huts were pitched without much order, though in the most picturesque confusion. It was a pleasant morning that I spent among these people, & I almost wished that all my days were to be passed there.

There were 8 or 10 Englishmen loitering about, some naked as the natives. Several applied for a passage to Sydney, which our gentlemanly Skipper refused with curses & drove them from his ship—such a pleasant disposition has he.

One of the girls on the beach, was beautiful—European features, with the blood struggling through her cheeks. She had, like the others, nothing on but a tappa around her loins. She was like a Princess in the Land, & capricious as the winds.

We could not but admire the athletic & vigorous frames of the men, and some of them had extraordinary fine faces. They were without clothing save an apron of colored grass girdled around the waist & dropping to the thigh. It answered the purposes of decency & was highly graceful & ornamental. They were all tatooed from the waist to the Knee in such a manner that they seemed clad in *"open work" breeches*. The lines were drawn with Extreme accuracy, & the coloring looked so well that I almost wished my breech in a similar condition. This tatooing is upon every adult male upon the Island of the group; the women are free from it.

On the 10th we made Tutuilla, where we were to anchor for

some days. Alden & Dr. Pickering were sent in the *Porpoise* to a neighbouring Island, Savaii.

As we approached the Land a Canoe came off to us, from whence *a White Man*[5] stepped on our decks. He seemed to have been recently very ill & bore on his face the traces of disease. His costume had evidently been long suffering from want of acquaintance with the wash tub & the needle, but still in neither of these two circumstances, as the man's address was civil & humble enough, could we see sufficient reason for the cruel coarseness & bitter insult of the Captain's opening words. All who heard were shocked, mortified, disgusted, & I could not help cursing the unfeeling, brutal disposition of him who could thus treat one so far beneath him, & who was for the present seeking the hospitality of the Ship. If Captain Wilkes ever reflected upon this piece of his conduct, he must have felt a voice of condemnation at his Heart, but, like other of his atrocities, it doubtless never troubled his callous & stony conscience. However, the man's character soon became apparent, & it was necessary to employ & confide in him the whole time of our stay.

As we neared the Harbour [of Pago Pago], an Englishman came off as Pilot, and after an anxious time beating in through a channel dangerous from the existence of sunken rocks, we dropped our anchors in a quiet & beautiful Bay with high hills tumbling in all around us, villages at their base & the ocean shut from view. The night proved warm & I made a couch of a *soft* plank on the Spar deck & lay me down to Sleep. The anxiety & toils of the day were over, & I had but few moments of consciousness ere I was wrapped in a most refreshing slumber.

The next day was Saturday, the Sunday among the Islands. At an early hour mine was the morning watch. I saw many groups wending their way towards the church. Some were afoot; others I noticed coming forth from their huts, lifting their light canoes from the shore & launching them into the Bay, paddle noiselessly onwards.

On board we were all agog. The observatory was to be set up, Instruments landed, a Boat was to be built, & two Boats were to be got ready for a Surveying cruize around the Island. I was to have charge of one, & I was busy through the day in making arrangements, delighted with the prospect of novelty & adventure before me. On our Sunday we rested & there was worship. In the evening we visited a small village, & bathed.

Monday morning dawned fair, but the breeze was so fresh that we were in some doubt whether to set forth, or remain. However, we agreed to run our chances, & the Boats were called away. Arms, provisions, articles for trade, Instruments, &c. were all stowed & arranged, & we shoved off, pulling directly out to Sea in the face of a strong breeze & heavy swell.

When we were clear of the land, we found so much sea that it was difficult in the extreme to make the observations. The Compass whirled like a top from the jumping motion of the Boat, & the Seas that broke over us drenched all hands & were sure to come as I was putting pencil to paper. We did the best we could, & reefing the sails, stood away along the coast. If you can imagine yourself upon the back of a wild Horse, tearing madly over a broken & stony causeway, with precipices on either hand & the fall & roar of torrents almost stupefying your senses, you can have some idea of the critical chances of a Whale Boat in a sea way & of the feelings of her crew.

My nerves were fairly tried this time; I was thankful that they had been tolerably well strung by previous experience. The *Greyhound* fairly leaped out of the Seas as she felt the pressure of the reduced canvass we could show, but so low was she in the water that we were shipping seas all the while & one hand was continually baling. The *Leopard,* a large boat & more staunch, outsailed us & weathered a reef of breakers to which I had to douse my sail & pull again out to sea.

We would have gone back, if that had been possible, for we felt that our situation was precarious, but now it was impossible to return, and I once more spread my rag to the breeze. Two hours of anxiety passed slowly away, but our progress by the Land was rapid, & it was a relief to me to know that soon we would be in smooth water. We rounded a point, Kept off before the wind. The Boat rolled deeply and took on water over both gunwales, and God help me, we were exceedingly uncomfortable to say the least—wet to the Skin & sore & ever wearied from the quick, jumping motions of the Boat. We could scarce preserve our equilibrium on our Seats—it is damnable! a Boat in a Sea way!

In a short time, we got the Land between us & the direction of the wind & were in smooth water. Sailing thus a little while longer, we came abreast of Leone village, where we ran in through a narrow passage & landed on the Beach amidst the whole population of the Village. We were made known to the Chief, a man of 50, stout in frame & of a strongly marked & intelligent countenance. He welcomed us to his town & was made quite happy by learning that we would be his guests for the remainder of the day & night.

He spoke loudly & authoritatively to the men of the village who were around us and directed them to assist us hauling up our Boats, a command which they instantly prepared to obey with a hearty good will. Those who could not obtain a place at the gunwales of the Boats grasped the others by the shoulders, & raising a song, they walked away with the burthen & deposited her high & dry on the sands. This done the Chief drove them away from us, that we might not be crowded nor experience any obstruction in our operations of unloading the Boats. We had a small tent with us in which we intended to stow our things, & as we were rather ignorant of the amount of confidence to be reposed in the honesty of the natives, we were watchful & careful as if we had been surrounded by arrant thieves.

Lieutenant Underwood[6] & myself were to lodge in the house of a white man who was employed as interpreter on board Ship, & thither we removed with some few of our things. I walked there with two young girls, having a hand of each. One was the Chief's daughter of about 15, with an extremely handsome & rather European face & long hair; the other was younger still. I had given them a looking glass, & as we strayed along in this manner, my two sweethearts were the Envy of the Village.

I noticed in the men a fondness & care displayed towards their children which I had not expected to find. While on the beach many huge fellows had infants & babbling youngsters in their arms, & some of them were now those accompanying me.

There was deep quiet in the Village, & the little scene around me, in the grove of magnificent Bread Fruits, was so simply innocent that my soul was touched. My pride as a white man melted away, & I thought in my heart, *these people have more claim to be called good, than we.* Strangers as we were, we were at once in their confidence, & they seemed to look upon us as if we were too sacred to be approached with irreverence or levity. Every passer by extended his hand & his kindly greeting, & my little brown skinned fawns, happy in the distinguished honor they were enjoying, looked into my face as if they had known & loved me for years. I could not help thinking, what would be the reception of these people in *our Land?*

The Chief directed Hogs to be killed & prepared for all hands. The Pigs were baked in the Native manner whole, in ovens formed of heated stones. Bread fruit, & taro & cocoanuts, with some luxuries of our own made the accompaniments. We sat upon the Mats that were spread over the pebbly floor, the Edibles were served up in the leaves they had been baked in, table & seat were alike & we fell to with our knives & fingers much to the delight of the group around us.

A piece of biscuit thrown to them was received with the greatest joy & devoured with a Keen relish. Whenever we gave them any of our food, the portion was shared by all without the least display of Selfishness.

After our meal we strolled about; visited the native Missionary's wife, he being absent. She was much pleased to see us & gave me a very fine water melon. She was a fine looking woman & wore a long robe of calico. In return for her present I bestowed upon her treasures more valuable in her eyes than gold—a shawl, scissors, needles thread &c., &c. The men, we found, had made themselves perfectly at Home among the people, had chosen friends, & Exchanged Names, & were privileged characters wherever they went.

We observed that nearly every one we met in the village—men, women & children—had books in their hands & were either going or returning from lessons. We had seen nothing of this at Tahita, & this was the first evidence we had of the wide difference in the character of the people of the Islands, & of the more moral & improved condition of those we were now among. About Sundown the voice of men in prayer & the music of several hymns broke forth from every hut. Surprised, pleased & wondering, we sat ourselves down to listen & to reflect.

After dark Tuetila, the chief, some of his family & others came to sit with us for an hour or two. The old chief offered a long prayer in which he made frequent mention of his guests, & when he concluded, those assembled sang a Hymn. It was a Scene of no common interest & the emotions excited by [it] were singular & intense. The hut, the group, were worthy of a Painter's touch. The light from the rude taper was but faint, so as scarcely to illumine the Space occupied by the worshippers. The roof of bark & the Sides of the hut were indistinctly seen. All were kneeling—the natives with their faces bowed to the Earth, the white men after their own fashion, with the body erect, & head drooping—while the chief poured forth his petition to the God he had but lately learned to adore. There was solemn, touching & impressive eloquence in this, more than I shall learn in a lifetime from the religion of the Schools! Our presence there was in strong contrast to the rude Structure of the hut & to the dusky skins & naked busts & limbs of the Islanders.

I exhibited to Tuetila the contents of our box of Trade. To be the owner of all that was there would have made him rich beyond measure, & the promise of a Hatchet set him wild with joy. When I told him how numerous such things were in America & of the quantities we had on board the Ship, he took various methods to express his astonishment, & I received some embraces that were as vigorous as they were sincere. I invited him to visit me, telling him in 5 days I would be on board & that I would dress him as a Papalangi[7] from head to foot & make him other presents, for I was pleased with the character of the old man. He promised to come, & I had to show his Wife & others who dropped in the beautiful Hatchets & the abundance of Scissors &c., &c.

I slept on the mats, with a tappa screen over me to keep off the Mosquitos, & at daylight I turned out, & our breakfast was soon ready, as we were to make an early Start. Our own men cooked this meal from the fragments of the day before.

We made the promised presents to the Chief & to the women of the house, & some few indiscriminately. We also bought shells, mats, cocoa nuts &c. from the people, paying with fish hooks, needles & scissors, for in all this group of Islands the use of money is unknown. Since leaving Otaheiti I have not seen the colour of a coin. All our barter has been with cotton goods and Knicknacks—a hook, a knife, a needle, would procure what a golden guinea could not. Dollars & cents have as yet no existence in the minds of the people of Samoa, though they will soon be as grasping as the Tahitians—the white men, with all their ideas of good & evil, carry their own vices with them wherever they go, & the thirst for ardent spirits & the love of money to an excess soon becomes part & portion of those who were innocent of either.

One may well pause and ponder deeply on the fate of these people, now that the influence of the white man is beginning to be felt among them. With all his faith & confidence in those of his own colour, with all his pity & commiseration for the benighted savage, he will find there is a black train of consequences attending the footsteps of the one which degrade & dishonor him, as much as it oppresses & ruins the other.

The more I see, the more I think, the more problematical does the matter become in my mind. It *is* a problem with me whether the Example & sway of the whites will in the end better the condition of this portion of the human race. I should like to see them left to themselves, if that were possible, but to make them as good & wise & learned as we is the great object. Before this result is attained, the people must struggle through difficulties & evils of all kinds: discord, war, domestic strife. But still the change must be effected at any cost. They must be redeemed from their barbarism, though the half of them perish in the attempt. There will still remain a portion to be added to the fold, & for the sake of these, father must battle against son, wife turn against husband, neighbour war with neighbour until all those who cling to the old predjudices & resist the new are destroyed, & peace comes once more. But the original nature of the people will have left them forever.

[CHAPTER 9: TUTUILA, UPOLU, AND AUSTRALIA]

We parted from our friends of Leone with warm & affectionate farewells on both sides, and steered along the Shore to the Westward. A white man[1] had been missing for 7 days, & it was the general belief that he had been murdered, but all efforts to find his body or trace the perpetrators of the foul deed had as yet been in vain. The arrival of our Ship just at this time had produced a strong effect upon the whole people. They were extremely alarmed, fearful that we would adopt strong measures, yet they all denied that the man had been killed, though they could not account for his disappearance.

The unfortunate man whose fate had been so recent was on a visit to the Island, from the neighbouring one of Upolu & had been living in a Village about 8 miles from Leone. Our purpose was to land there, if practicable, & to gather what information we could upon the Spot. On reaching *Murderers' Bay*, we found the Surf so heavy & the passage so narrow that we could not venture ashore.

In leaving this place, the *Leopard* was a short distance ahead of me, & while I was getting the Boat's sail properly set, I observed some confusion on board her & her sail taken in by the run. They were waving to us to alter our course. Before I could think what the matter could be, I had a warning close at hand. The boat sunk with the swell, & high above us, as if it were coming right aboard, broke a tremendous sea with a roar that told us it fell upon a rock. We rose, just clear of its influence, but our danger had been great. I felt rather bad for a few moments, for a sunken rock is an ugly thing, & no sailor has any *inclination* to loiter near one. I did not know that this was the only rock—there might be others. However, I steered right for the *Leopard,* and after a few moments' pull, we rounded a huge rock that stood out clear of the main land, overgrown with trees & thickets, & were in smooth water & in Safety.

We proceeded on for the village of Fungisaá, where Midshipman Henry[2] was residing for the purpose of making Tidal & other observations. The squalls were sharp from off the high land. They came off so fresh & quick that for a moment or more we would lose all control over the boat, & once the men's oars were blown quite out of their hands. The water was smooth, & "giving way" during the "lulls", we reached the village just before dark, happy that the time for rest was at hand.

Our first business was to purchase a Pig, for which we gave a Hatchet. The men dispatched the grunter in a very summary manner, & he was soon over the fire. The Natives looked on this operation with much curiosity & Wonder. They choke the animals & disembowelling them, bake them whole; so their method is tedious & we preferred our own. The boats were hauled up, & all the things removed to the Hut occupied by Mr. Henry, where we were to establish ourselves.

The Hospitality of the people is simple, but it answers every purpose & prevents any inconvenience. In each village there is erected a large hut called by way of distinction the "big house"—some villages contain two or three of them. These huts are supplied with mats, the only furniture they need, & are for the sole purpose of affording accommodation to strangers of whatever class or colour. If the travellers bring no food with them, they are supplied from the abundance that springs up in the very path.

This big house is kept in order by the single people of the Village, who also occupy it when they are inclined. On the night of our arrival at Fungisaa, the big house was thronged. We created an unusual sensation, & every body was agog to see us. I was tired, & was glad to lay me down to sleep. Our couches were merely mats laid over the pebbly floor. I put my jacket under my head for a pillow & was soon in a Slumber.

When I awoke at an early hour in the morning & raised myself to look about me, I found I was the only one stirring in the

"Big House." The mats were pretty well filled with sleepers, & my nearest neighbours were two or three young girls, who were dozing away in all the confidence of simple innocence. I sought my pillow again to indulge in thoughts about the singular beings with whom I was thus intimately associated, & of the wide difference between them & my own race.

When I was ready to rise, the others were moving. Accustomed as I am to a "knockabout" life amongst all varieties of people, my modesty (of which I have but little left, I am afraid) was somewhat tried when I essayed to make my toilette in the midst of bright eyes & pretty faces. However, I summoned sufficient brass to proceed; & why not? when there were bare bosoms & glancing ancles about me! Half rigged, bare headed & unshod I left the Hut & took a glorious wash in the clear stream that ran bubbling into the Sea. Oh! what a change from the little *state* room on board. The magnificent cocoas waved over the brook, flowers grew on its banks, velvety grass lined its sides, birds twittered about & opened their tuneful throats, natives were lingering near & there was a dewy & balmy freshness in the morning air & a brightness in the whole scene that set my heart dancing for joy!

The sunshine turned into rain, & we were confined to the "big house" all day. We had the whole population for visiters, old men & young, mothers & babes, & daughters in the bloom of youth—all made themselves quite at home. We were as a family party & passed the time in observing & commenting upon each others peculiarities. We were closely watched in every thing we did, however trifling. Their sharp, prying eyes were always upon us, and in the remarks they made, they evinced much shrewdness of observation & ingenuity of conjecture.

The complicated nature of our dress was altogether at variance with their slight & simple costume. *Two* shirts, *two* trowsers, a waistcoat, stockings & shoes, & *a hat,* and an eye glass that must always be hung round the neck, & a kerchief for the throat & one for the pocket, and a toothpick & penknife, and a *toothbrush* and towels—all used & resorted to, as if they were absolutely necessary for an existence—threw these people into a perfect fever of mystification & curiosity. They thought we took unnecessary care of the body—that we wrapped it in too many folds. When *they* went among white men, they were always offered clothing & sometimes persuaded to wear it. Why did not we, when we came to their towns, off with every thing & appear *Sans any thing* save the girdle of Colored grass? We would be much more comfortable & only need to take a bath of cocoa nut oil to save the Skin from Sun & Musquitoes.

Whenever we sat down to a meal, a circle was immediately formed around us. They gazed with the interest of people witnessing a tragedy, & were eternally whispering in tones of wonder about habits that seemed so strange to them. It was rather irksome to me at first to endure this assemblage, but we soon became used to it, and I took especial delight in giving choice morsels to the prettiest damsels I could Select.

Melayta was my favorite, but there were also *Cyáfa* & *Tantuli* equally beautiful. They were the very emblems of purity & innocence, & although not so reserved in manner as their fairer Sisters, a prude could not have censured the innocent freedoms they permitted. I was delighted with their native grace, & the simple & winning confidence which they reposed in us almost cheated me of my heart. My trinkets went; I enriched them with ornaments & presented them with articles of more homely utility. I taught them to play upon the Jew's Harp & they soon surpassed the teacher. I learned them the infantile practice of "sawing, with a string," and in such pastime whiled away the day. I do not believe I have been so good or so happy in a long while as I was during this day. I could not be evil minded in the midst of primeval innocence; I was happy, because the virtuous thought I was all excellence, & because I could contribute so much to their pleasure, amusement & perhaps instruction.

There were several deformed children, from disease of the spine—poor, pitiful objects to look at; men & women afflicted with Elephantiasis, horrible to the sight. And one man had only a stump of an arm; a shark had made free with the rest.

The next morning we Surveyed the Harbour & returning about noon to the Village. After lunching we shoved off & proceeded on to the Eastward. The afternoon proved rainy, & we were thoroughly drenched.

The Coxcomb rocks off the Eastern point of the Island form a natural breakwater for ⅛th of a mile from the Shore. Viewed from to leeward, [they] present a likeness to that particular appendange of Chanticleer, after which they have received their name. The whole mass is separated from the Island by a narrow chasm clear down to the Water's Edge, and presents a stern & majestic contrast to the lovely verdure of the Shores.

We had to pull around these Rocks, & we lost our lee at once. There was a heavy swell & a fresh breeze, & the poor Boats were nearly swamped ere we could get into the village immediately to windward. Once or twice I thought we should have to take to the Life preservers & trust to the mercy of the Sharks, but our time was not over yet, and after a terrible struggle, we forced our boats into the smooth water of the Bay of Vetee.

We marched at once to the Big House & established ourselves without any ceremony. The people met us on the beach as usual, & we were as much the objects of curiosity as at the other places. We got the fire going, & taking off as much of our wet clothing as we could decently dispense with, the scanty remnant was allowed to dry upon the body.

I slept as if I would never wake, but *never* came soon & I was roused Early to breakfast. A bath in the Sea & a race along the beach set me all in a glow, & I did ample justice to our meal. We left Vetee about 8 and had a heavy pull all day, wet again from the drenching of the Seas. We put into several villages for rest & Cocoa Nuts. I drank about 30 of them every day. They kept me from fainting in the heat, & I would not have changed them for the most costly liquor in the world.

Towards Sundown we ran into the village of Awa for the night. This was a night of torments—the musquitoes & sand flies gave us no rest, & we almost went mad with agony. I was wearied to death & would have given the world to sleep, but sleep came not, & I tossed & tumbled until I could bear it no longer, & rushing from the "Big House" in utter despair, I threw off my clothes & plunged into the Sea. This was about midnight—the men were suffering also. Some were almost in the fire! Others were wrapped up in the Boats' sails, & they swore the musquitoes bit thro' the canvass—faith & I believe them.

We were a miserable set, & loud were the complaints & murmerings of our hard fate. I rolled in the Salt Water & raced along the beach until I was tired, & I returned to the Hut to try sleep once more! I wrapped myself up in divers articles— American Ensigns, tappa, &c.—& did all I could to doze, but it was of no avail. Curses loud & deep were frequent from all quarters. An Enemy was waging cruel war against us, & we could neither Escape or resist. Human patience since the days of Job, that man of many afflictions, could not have borne with such bloodthirsty attacks & remain peaceful in spirit. I could not rest, & after a little while I went again into the water, & while the irritation was something, I thought of *Home,* & I laughed loud & long at the Situation I was in.

The moon was up & there was a clear & brilliant light over the Sea & Shore. Determined not to enter the Hut again, I wandered through the groves, forgot the musquitoes & dreamed I was in Fairy Land. There was an unearthly witchery in the Stillness of the morn, and alone amidst the solemn trees, I gave myself up to rhapsodies until the day dawned.

By the unanimous voice, the place was called Musquito Cove, & as soon as we swallowed our breakfast, we were off. The tide was low, & we had the aid of half the people to carry our boats over the reef. When we had got clear, we heard some one singing out & turning back, there [were] two fellows coming to us through the natives, as if their lives depended on their speed. Oh! rare spirit of Honesty!—they brought an axe & Powder flask that we had left, valuable to them as diamonds to a white man.

This day was the toughest of all. There were more Seas, & from loss of rest, the men were done up. Poor fellows, they went to sleep over their oars, and the Coxswain went into such a desperate state of somnolency that in pity to him I did not wake him but performed the duty myself. The others I encouraged by choosing words, & they did their best. I thought the Boat in more danger than any time previous. Rounding the headlands, the swell was tremendous & we progressed by mere inches.

This was the 5th day that we had passed in the Boat hard at work, & even *my* bones were sore from the short, quick motion, the hardness of the thwarts & the cramped & uneasy position that I was obliged to remain in. To quail or shrink or tire would not do, & we struggled on, I taking notes & observations whenever necessary.

In weathering a small Island off the South East point, I nearly swamped, & when I did get around it, I came nearer within an ace of capsizing in the rollers. One big fellow came on us & reared on high over the Boat, curling its monstrous head. It broke, just missed us, & I rather think that we hurried away before the next one reached the same spot.

Rejoining the *Leopard* in the passage, we now sailed before the wind, & the motion of the Boat became pleasant. The men went to Sleep—poor fellows! they were worn out. On this account we put into the Village of Fungisua about 2 in the afternoon although we were but 6 miles from the Ships in the Harbour.

When we landed & the things were removed from the Boats, I could hold out no longer, & dropping upon a sail under the Cocoa Nut trees, I was gone in a moment, fast asleep. I awoke refreshed; the men, who have their own ways of doing a kindness, had spread an awning over me & driven the natives off so that I should not be disturbed! The dinner was underweigh & the usual crowd around. Two or three young girls were dancing, & the men were as merry as if they had never known suffering.

This place is a "Devil town." They cling to their old customs & resist all the applications of the Missionaries. The Chief & all the young men & women were absent on a visit to the Neighbouring Island of Upolu, & there was none but old people & children in the Village. The people determined to entertain us with a dance, but they regretted the absence of the men & women which prevented them from conducting it on a grand scale. Accordingly, the whole population assembled in the big house about 9 o'clock, and 5 young girls from 11 to 13 years of age appeared as the dancers, the only force that could be mustered! The boys were not expert enough.

The Hut was brilliantly illuminated by many torches of dry cocoa nut leaves held by the lookers on. They cast a strong glare over the half naked group & the front part of the Hut, leaving the rear in darkness. The audience were down upon their haunches, & we reclined upon the Mats that were placed for us immediately in front of the juvenile performers. The music was made by 5 or 6 women beating with long wands upon a log of wood covered with mats to deaden the Sound. They accompanied their thumping with a Song. The time was perfect, the result of much practice.

The dancing nymphs were naked save the short girdle of grass or leaves around the waist. They placed themselves in a line & went through an infinite variety of motions & gestures without quitting their places. There was much of method in the performance, and it was evident that study was necessary to attain the least perfection. The changes were rapid but were always made together. Commencing slow, the motions became violent by degrees, until the dance terminated from the exhaustion of the artistes. After a little rest it was renewed again & so kept up until a late hour of the night.

To say the least of it, the dance was highly immodest & indecent; nay, it might be safely termed wanton and lascivious.* It seemed doubly so to us from the Extreme youth of those engaged in it. The old people who were the Spectators applauded with all their might the Efforts of the precocious crew, & turned to see if we were elated in the like degree. They seemed to take great pride in the Exhibition, though they much lamented the absence of the young men. Whether the latter would have mended the matter by their presence was rather doubtful in our minds.

The next morning was Sunday, & after a pleasant Sail of an hour or more, we got on board. I was not the most interesting or picturesque individual in appearance, neither was I very clean. I was horrified on stepping over the gangway to see a Lady there, or rather that the Lady should put her eyes on me in such a pickle! My old White Hat (which has served me well, and is still good), my blue sailor trowsers, my soiled shirt & Jacket, that were *once* White, were in pretty good keeping with my sun burnt face & hands and my disordered hair. But I reflected that I had been suffering for my country, & that the

---

*I have not ventured to describe it fully. It will not do, to tell it all afore folks.

Lady in question would make all allowances. She was quite young & had followed her husband to be a participater in his labours. They were the only Whites on the Island except the sailors who lived in the villages & had native wives.

I was glad to find myself in my room once more, notwithstanding the invidious comparison I have recorded a few pages back. I experienced absolute enjoyment while I was abluting & changing my apparel with all my old comforts about me, and the valuable attendance of my black valet, *David Smith*.[3] Few people know the real luxury of feeling clean, because they have never experienced its opposite. If Grandmother could only have seen me then, or an hundred other times, she would have wept for my condition, and Peggy, of odious nursery memory, she who scrubbed me so faithfully & so unmercifully, she would have been appalled & lost to utter despair.

Tuetila, chief of Leone, faithful to his promise passed the Mountains & came to see the Ship. Mr. Underwood mentioned his arrival to the Captain & represented the attentions he had shown to us. Captain Wilkes refused to receive him, much to our surprise & mortification. Why, we could not tell! 'Twas not politic & was rude & insulting. The old man was one of the Seven principal chiefs of the Island. However, we did the best we could & gave him & his Son many presents, so that they parted from us with expressions of affection & returned to their home rich & happy & with a high opinion of our generosity.

On the 23rd [of October] we weighed to beat out of the Harbour. It was smooth as glass within. In the first attempt we missed stays,[4] but this was not to be wondered at. Our first Luff[5] had disgraced himself often before. The Pilot recovered her, & we got along pretty well until we were near the mouth of the Harbour & in Some Swell. Now the greatest care & the nicest skill & judgement were required. The Ship was to be watched & tended, for she had a critical chance to play. We approached the Western point of the bay, a high bluff called Tower Rock. Says Captain Wilkes, "I think we'll weather it,[6] Pilot?" "I do not know yet, Sir, no," the reply, & in a few seconds the latter ordered the Ship to be stayed.[7] The Captain repeated the order, & the 1st Lieutenant proceeded to execute the Manoeuvre. Had we gone round then, all would have been right, but the Ship refused stays, nothing was done to help her, she lost her way, gathered Sternboard & finally fell off with her head right on the rocks.

During this time the man with the trumpet[8] was standing amidships, his arms akimbo, looking at the sails in utter ignorance what to do. Several of us were looking over the gangway,[9] watching when she would gather Sternboard. Presently the Captain inquired if she was going astern. The one who should have been ready with his answer, the 1st Lieutenant, was unable to give one, & Lieutenant Underwood & myself did so for him. This was the last the Captain said! The Pilot knew his business, and it was well for the poor Ship that he did. He raised his voice now, & by his manoeuvering the old craft came to the wind once more! Now was the tug—"*do* old Ship, or die you must!*"

It was fairly left to the Ship herself to get clear if she could— God! how I watched her; life hung on her bottom! We were within the influence of the rollers. The Surf dashed & broke upon the rocks a few boat's lengths under the lee, & looking down beneath the Ship, the rocks *there,* were staring you in the face. We could not anchor, & if the *Vincennes* failed to claw off, she'd have but a rough bed to lie her bones in.

We watched, with a suspense that was harrowing. She moved—she went ahead—she drew past the rocks—but it was with a sidelong drift that seemed to carry her nearer to destruction. We thought *we must go,* and there was the Stillness of death about the decks! The Officers & many of the crew lined the lee gangway, looking fixedly on the foaming breakers that were so close—time to try the nerves! I turned to look for the Captain. He was in the weather gangway, leaning on the booms,[10] with his face hidden in his hands.

He had not the courage to look up & count the chances for the safety of the Ship, and instead of standing erect, observing the drift & progress of the Craft he commanded, inch by inch, he made the shameful spectacle I have mentioned to the utter surprise of all who noticed it & to his own deep disgrace. A few

minutes decided it—the breeze freshened opportunely, & the
Ship just cleared the danger, with nothing to spare!

When the Pilot wished to leave us, Captain Wilkes would
not heave to for his Boat, but ran away out to Sea. The Pilot
told him his mind about it plain enough, & when he did get
into his Boat at last, he turned & said with the most provoking
coolness & some little impudence, "You may fill away now, sir!
fill away as soon as you like." A wave of the hand & he was
gone. Captain Wilkes could have eaten him.

When we got fairly clear of the Land, it was "pipe down" for
a little while. I was below, dressing some hurts upon my feet
that were painful. I could scarcely bear my shoes on. Presently
"all hands" were called again to "in boats" (the *Leopard*, a
light 10 oared whale boat & the dingy were to be got in, an operation of five minutes work & requiring but few men). I received the usual summons & hurried with what I was about, so
that I might repair to my station.

In a few minutes time I received another call, & directly after, another saying that the Captain was waiting for me! In less
than 5 minutes from the first call, I was upon deck. I went up
prepared to make an Explanation of the cause of my delay,
whether one should be required or not, & certain that it would
be received as satisfactory. I was not known in the Ship, as a
Skulker from duty of any kind, & I thought upon such a trifling
occasion as this, my absence would be attributed to a proper
cause.

I appeared on deck in a perfectly quiet & officer like manner
& went at once to my station, barely casting a glance aft. Captain Wilkes was standing a little abaft the gangway. Ere I had
time to look about me, I received an order from Captain Wilkes
"to consider myself suspended," not accompanied with the
customary expression of "to go below." I was surprised at this
sudden mode of procedure & took a turn or two to leeward,
endeavouring to account for it. Then came an order "to confine
myself to my apartment." Upon receiving it, I went below. I inquired of Lieutenant Case[11] & Mr. Knox,[12] who were on the
Forecastle when I came up, how long in their opinion I had
kept all hands waiting? "Not five minutes," they said. I made

the inquiry because I could not lay my suspension to any other cause.

As I had been sentenced to punishment in this public manner before the whole Ship's company without being offered the least chance for explanation, I did not deem it proper to volunteer one, and therefore waited until I should hear further from Captain Wilkes. Conversing with Captain Wilkes's secretary upon the singular injustice of such a mode of punishment, he remarked that it was Captain Wilkes's way "to punish first & inquire afterwards."

For 6 days I remained below, with the range of an apartment 12 feet square & devoid of daylight, the thermometer standing at 80+. On the 6th day Captain Wilkes sent for me in his cabin to say that he was about to restore me to duty, & to inform me why I had been suspended. I told him, "I should be glad to know the reason for I had been entirely at a loss as yet to account for it!" Much to my astonishment he said that it was *not* because of the delay, but because I had come on deck in an improper & disrespectful manner & set a bad example to the crew.

I knew in my very heart that I was innocent of this, & I denied it in the strongest terms. Captain Wilkes persisted in his accusation & said he hoped it would not happen again. I replied that I could not amend, while I was not conscious of any impropriety, & that I must again positively deny there had been any thing in my manner to justify his proceedings. He said he would restore me to duty, as he was *now* convinced that I had not been conscious of any thing singular in my demeanour (how easily he might have ascertained this, on the instant, by one simple inquiry). I insisted that not only was I unconscious of this very serious charge, but I wondered how any thing in my manner could have been twisted into the least approach to disrespect or insubordination. With more conversation to the same purpose, the interview terminated.

When I was graciously permitted to appear on deck, the Ship was at anchor in Apia Bay. I was so happy to snuff fresh air again that I remained for a long time looking upon the scenery around me. The Skies wore a brighter face & the Shores seemed doubly beautiful. God! to be blind or shut in a dungeon for life!—terrible.

It was not intended to run into the Harbour, but to bring out the *Peacock* & *Porpoise* & proceed on to the Fegees, we thought. Head winds keeping us off the Land, Captain Wilkes went in with his Gig. Under the able management of Mr. Carr the ship drifted to leeward & did not regain her position for several days. Captain Wilkes came on board, & on the 29th October we ran in & anchored.

I was gone four days on a surveying cruize in the same Boat that carried me round Tutuilla. The first night we remained at a large Village called *Avenga Alofa,* or "the Seat of Mercy." This was the most lovely place of any that I had seen in all Samoa. Here dwelled old Manituoa, the Prince of the group, a venerable, silvery headed patriarch, who received us with all kindness and hospitality. The people welcomed us in crowds, aided us to draw up the boats, & were in a perfect extacy of joy to find that we would remain with them during the night. The little children ran wild & capered about us, happy when they got a look from any of us, and a small present, whew! they went crazy. My Eye was soon attracted by the extraordinary grace & beauty of a young girl who was standing rather apart from the rest. She was about 15 & was the very emblem of innocent girlhood.

She was the youngest & the favorite daughter of old Maneitoa. I paid my homage to her at once, for I am early to render tribute to beauty in any corner of the earth. There was a sweet fascination about my Princess that was irresistable. If I had been 5 years younger, I should have been in love with her to distraction. As it was—but no matter! She had a companion with her of a more humble caste in life, younger than herself, but with a remarkably intelligent face. With these two, hand in hand, I strolled thro' the village, meeting happy looks every where, until we came to the Big House. Here I undid my bundle & made my two companions presents of the most *valuable* things I had with me.

I could not help thinking of a life in this Eden—a half wish came in to my head, that I could free myself from my Ship, & under the shade of the delicious groves, form the mind of sweet Emma—ripen the bud into the full bloom of maturity—cherish the flower, & wear it for ever! What a dream!—yet it was natural. Do not call it silly, until you have tried yourself.

[On returning to the *Vincennes*,] I had the whole family on board the Ship. The younger midshipmen, who were perfectly frantic in their adoration of Emma, attended on her, & I supported the old Chief, for he was decrepit in his limbs. He was very grateful for our attentions, & we went frequently to see him, *en famille*. One night we remained rather late & he sent us off in his great war Canoe. His son, a very fine looking & spirited fellow, accompanied us. At our request he set the crew singing, & we paddled in great state around every body in the harbour. We passed close to the *Peacock,* & we could see her bulwarks crowded with heads. They thought there was some grand turn out. There was great excitement, & we found our own decks alive with the crew, who were expecting to see a grand procession. I enjoyed it much!

On Sunday November 10th, the Squadron sailed. On the following day, I was transfered to the *Peacock* under the following circumstances. An India rubber frock, loaned to me from the Ship, was found upon the gun deck. On inquiry, the 1st Lieutenant ascertained that it belonged to me & ordered it to be put in the *Lucky Bag*. Now, be it known, this "lucky bag" is the receptacle of all the old & dirty clothes, blankets, soap &c., &c., that may be kicking about the decks! It is *not* the custom to consign Officers' apparel to this accumulation of rags. I felt indignant that any thing of mine should be thus disposed of. I had not been questioned about it, & there had never been an instance of any neglect of the kind on my part. In this case, the frock in question had been worn by some one in my absence. I knew not that it was out of my locker, but even under the most aggravated circumstances of neglect or carelessness, this improper procedure would not have been justifiable.

Feeling this keenly, I addressed the 1st Lieutenant by asking him if he had ordered a frock with my name upon it, to be put in the lucky bag? Yes, he had! I requested him to let me take it out as soon as possible? The reply was delivered in a short & peculiarly snappish tone, "You shan't have it, Sir!" I answered that I could not conceive why he ordered Officers' clothing to be put among the filth & scum of the decks. "I shall tell you, Sir!" I observed I felt it necessary to appeal to the Captain, for

I could not bear that any thing belonging to me, should remain for an instant among so much that was foul, & that my frock *must* be taken out! The 1st Lieutenant said he would report me to the Captain. I told him I would save him the trouble, for I should report the matter myself.

Accordingly, I laid the case before him, detailing the above conversation. The reply of Captain Wilkes was that he entirely approved of the 1st Lieutenant's conduct, & that such were the orders of the Ship! I mentioned that there was no *written order* to that effect. Well, it was his order, & if his own coat was found, it would share the same fate! A Captain's coat in the lucky bag!—laughable—oh! no, no.

I represented to Captain Wilkes that of late I had been away from the Ship upon duty & that this particular garment had been used by some other person. Now was I to be subjected to highly disagreeable & offensive treatment, & shamed in the eyes of the Ship's company without having been in the least culpable? His answer was that I must suffer unless I could find out who had made use of the frock! I did not consider that this individual, whoever he might happen to be, should suffer at all, much less myself.

Now, on board the *Vincennes* the contents of the lucky bag are disposed of at *public auction* to the highest bidder, & I had the pleasant prospect before me of seeing the frock put up for any one to take a chance at. I asked Captain Wilkes finally if he would order my frock to be restored to me? No—all clothing once in the lucky bag was forfeited to the Ship.

In ten minutes after I left the cabin, I received a written order to report to Captain Hudson for duty on board the *Peacock*. There was great hubbub in the Ship, and God knows, I fairly cried to leave those whom I had learned to love so well. May[13] & I made perfect babes of ourselves. 'Twas like the parting of man & wife, like the dissolution of a household! 15 months companionship had drawn many of us together by the strong tie of real friendship, & to be parted in this rude manner was a shock that we could not bear unmoved. Pshaw! I am mad anew when I think about it.

I felt horribly—not that I deemed myself disgraced, for I well knew the feelings of most every one in the Ship were with me, & this was a proud satisfaction. Gibson came to me in not much better plight than I was in myself, & helped me to pack up—poor fellow, I was sorry to leave him, too.

The Ship was hove to, & the transfers made. Bag & baggage was soon on board the *Peacock,* & I was once again an inmate of my old Ship[14]—sent to her for the good of the Service, I suppose.

I was received very kindly, but I could not feel comfortable for many days. Used to change as I am, it was some time before I became reconciled to this. For nearly a week, I had no duty assigned me, but leisure was worse than activity. Owing to the illness of one of the Officers, I was given charge of the Deck, & whenever we came within hail of the *Vincennes* during my watch, I took great delight in shaking my trumpet & displaying myself in a most conspicuous manner. Sent away as a convict, banished for punishment, I was well pleased to show that in my new Ship I occupied a post of honour!

On the 29th [we] discovered the high land of New Holland on the larboard bow & beam! Sydney was near at last, the place that had been so often in our minds. We looked forward to our arrival there with much of curious interest, and after our sojourn among the Islands, we were full of schemes for enjoyment in all the modes practicable in an English Town. Visions of Beef Steaks & sundry other substantial meats were floating thro' my imagination, to be discussed in a comfortable inn, with a friend one side & a well filled decanter on the other! For the true & luxurious appreciation of all such things among a people speaking our own tongue, we were fully prepared.

The breeze carried us rapidly along the Land. At Sundown we were between 30 & 40 miles distant from Sydney, & the shore about there was not yet in sight. The Ship was going 10 or 11 Knots, but we gave up all hope of getting in until the next day, and were sorrowed to think of the breakfast we should miss. Contrary to our anticipations, the *Vincennes* crowded sail—at 8 we made the Light, right ahead. On, on we went, &

undertaking rather a critical chance, Captain Wilkes ran his Ship clear up into the Harbour, & we followed, anchoring off the Town at 11. A Boat came alongside & those in her, asked most earnestly, "What Ship we were?" But we were determined to let daylight solve the mystery, & we chuckled at the way in which the people of Sydney would be astounded in seeing the Yankee flag flying in their very faces!

And greatly they were astonished—never had such a thing been heard of. They could not credit their eyes, & the Pilots who were looking out for us were mortified to death. Of course we had not been seen from the Coast & the surprise was complete. In time of war, such an *Entree* would be a glorious boarding of the Enemy—take them in their beds, & they not dreaming of a foe within a thousand miles of them! The papers were full of jokes about it, and thus we had a notoriety at once, highly flattering to our nautical skill & daring. I am always glad of a chance to stir up an Englishman, & I & all of us were perfectly elated that the first visit of an American squadron to the place had been in a manner so well calculated to excite their jealousy & to give us so much *Eclat*.

The beef steaks & fresh bread & butter & milk—oh! *what a breakfast!* Pork was execrated! No more of that! I had not looked for a letter here & was most happily surprised to have one handed to me, though the date was 10 months before. All were well!

Early in the forenoon a party of us were off for the shore. We did not walk about much, but we ordered a sumptuous dinner, and when 5 o'clock came, we sat down to it & had a most uproarious time. Why should we not enjoy ourselves after months of hard work & deprivation?

I did not go into any other society, save that of the Military Men. The social circles in Sydney are rather peculiar, & those who did mingle with the people, in some instances, felt unpleasantly. There are a few, a very few, honest people there, but you must be cautious in your mode of speech. It is dangerous to whisper *transportation* in the street. You cannot ask a question of him who may be your host about the condition of the colony, for fear you touch *him* in a vulnerable point. I saw a fellow dashing by, driving tandem. He was wealthy, but *his term* had just been out *three weeks*. One man built a palace on the ground where the gallows had been erected for him, & from which he had been reprieved when the rope was around his neck! (3 times as the story goes.)

Transportation, however, is about to be abolished, as far as New South Wales is concerned. The System is to be changed; it has failed entirely. With every chance for reformation, the majority of convicts only become the greater villains, abuse their liberty & have to be hunted down like dogs & shot & hung at last. The Natives, who sometimes assist them & commit depredations on their own account, also are pursued by the Mounted Military and sabred without mercy. And yet some Englishmen have the conscience to talk about with abuse & slander the conduct of *our Government to our Indians*. Let such men look at home and excuse the atrocities perpetrated in the name of the British government, *if they can!*—India, Cape of Good Hope, New Holland! *What right have Britains to butcher these?*

There was much difficulty between Captain Wilkes & the Officers while here originating in the returning the civilities we had received. He was unreasonable & proposed measures that no one could think of adopting—refused the Ship, on the ground that "the People at Home would not approve of the [out]lay," insulted the whole body of his Officers, & made himself despised & contemptible; finally said he was glad the difficulty had occurred, for he was not dependent on us, &c., &c., &c. The foul scamp—he should be hung. I have not patience to speak of him with decency, neither does he deserve I should. Mercy, how he is hated. *Four sycophants cling to him*—the rest abhor him!

[CHAPTER 10: ANTARCTICA]

[The day after Christmas] we were underweigh & standing out, ere I was up. For six days we were much delayed by the tedious manouevering of sailing in Company, which in this Squadron keeps us back & retards all our passages. Now, when time was every thing to us, & *want of time,* the most likely reason for abandoning the Southern regions, this dilly dallying was maddening. 'Twas too trifling & evidently with some object in view, of which I flatter myself I have very shrewd suspicions. The first fog we separated from the *Vincennes,* Captain & all hands happy to be clear of her. *Why* we should keep together, no one could imagine. The field explored was certainly not enlarged by it. We were detained nearly a week making a place of rendezvous, Maquaries Island, which, as we afterwards learned, the *Vincennes* had taken care to keep clear of & so get the advance. Another we passed by accident, thus saving us more delay! As it was, we reached the barrier of Ice to windward of the flag Ship.

I shall never forget the first Ice berg we met with & passed close by. There is no such thing as describing its appearance. I cannot tell either of the feelings excited or of the wondrous beauty of the floating mass—of the wildest forms, & weathered into the most fanciful shapes—& cold & Icy as they were, glowing with the most vivid & brilliant hues; blue as azure, green as emerald, and, oh! the contrast, whiteness like unto the raiment of an Angel. We all came on deck, and we all gazed till our very vision ached on the dazzling Ice that we were passing slowly by, and that which we were looking on was neither earth nor sea!

Soon after passing the 60th degree of Latitude, the stormy weather left us entirely, & we had a smooth sea & a mild breeze. Some days were misty, with snow & quite cold, but mostly the weather was clear & pleasant as in the Trades. Our hopes were at the highest. Though we passed Ice bergs every day, we saw no signs of a barrier, & from the extreme & unexpected mildness of the season, we were sure that none could exist but in a very high Southern Latitude. We contemplated with much satisfaction the prospect of an uninterrupted run for at least 10° of Latitude, & 75° South was the most moderate stopping place proposed.

On the 15th January at noon, there was no Ice in sight from the mast head. We were in 65° 25' South, the wind was fresh & fair, & we were steering directly South! On the morrow, we would be farther South than the Ship had reached last year. Soon we would pass 70°, eclipse Cook, & distance the pretender Weddell.[1] No one hazarded an unfavorable opinion, & we were all in a perfect fever of excitement! I shall never forget that day!

At 4 in the afternoon, the weather had thickened a little, & presently, we made the Brig *Porpoise* & the Barrier at the same time. There was the low & continuous field of Ice running East & West, broken by many Bays & Islands, but effectually stopping any farther progress South. Like men awakening from a dream, we could scarcely credit our senses, but it was too true. *Our dreams* were at once destroyed! A Boat from the Brig soon came alongside. They had met the barrier farther to the Eastward, and had beat along it for several days, before we met.

Chilled but not disheartened, we commenced working to windward in the hope of finding a passage farther to the West. We kept the Ice in sight, so that we might not miss any passage. We passed many Ice bergs, & on the 17th at 5.30 in my morning watch we discovered the *Vincennes* to leeward. I remember she passed behind an Ice berg, & there was an immense discrepancy between its height & that of the Ship.

Towards noon {of the day previous} we were very close in with the barrier, & Mr. Eld[2] & myself, from a motive of curiosity, went to the masthead. We wanted to obtain a good view of the field of Ice that spread away beneath us, & the sight was grand & singularly imposing. We tried to talk to each other, but we had no words. To look over such a vast expanse of the frozen sea upon which human eye nor foot had ever rested, & which, formed from the Ocean, now resisted its waves & presented an impassable boundary to the mysterious regions beyond, filled us with feelings which we were powerless to utter.

Presently we observed what we were certain *must be Land*. At a great distance over the barrier were several peaks showing very distinctly, & other summits were hidden in the clouds. They rose to an immense height. We looked for half an hour at least & procured a glass to satisfy ourselves that we were not mistaken. We were convinced that our judgement was correct & that we actually beheld the long sought for Terra Firma of the Antarctic continent. When we returned to the deck, by joint inclination & as a matter of duty too important to be neglected Mr. Eld reported the matter to Captain Hudson. We tacked soon afterward, as we were beating to windward at the time, & stood directly away from the quarter where the Land was sighted. I will never give up my belief that this was no deception & am perfectly willing to abide by the researches of any future navigators, confident that our discovery will be verified![3]

In the afternoon {of the 17th} at 4 spoke the *Vincennes*. Captain Hudson had a long yarn with "Kill Biscuit,"[4] & I had the pleasure of seeing all the faces of those whom I like so much.

Next Sunday 19th entered an extensive Bay & sailed along many hours ere we discerned Ice at the head of it. The swell of the ocean was shut out, there was no motion of the water, & we were encompassed on all sides by Ice save the one small passage by which we had come in. 'Twas like a Bay running into the Land, but the borders were not the green of Earth! Towards the head of the Bay, we passed among millions of pieces of floating Ice that were drifting slowly out to sea. The edges of the field were strewn with the like kind & presenting a strong resemblance to the ruins of a City with its towers & buildings tumbling from decay. Several penguins that were about with solemn aspect might have been taken for the melancholy remnant of the inhabitants, contemplating the approach of strangers to their deserted Homes.

This afternoon Clark[5] & I were at the Fore Top Gallant Masthead. I was higher up than him, & spectacles on nose of course. No sooner was I settled on my perch & looked around than I saw Land as plain as possible & sang out to Clark, "Do you see that?" I pointed & he agreed with me that it must be Land. It was of great height, of rounded, uneven summit, & broken sides. We looked at it for some time, & returning to the deck, I reported it to the Officer of the Watch. He agreed with me, & soon Captain & all hands were up to look for themselves. Well, it was Land! but we could not reach it to get ashore & had to content ourselves with the mere view. We gave names, however, in jest to certain points, & one cape was honored with the cognomen of the discoverer. The *Vincennes* saw the same land! & as it Happened, this was the same day that the Frenchman[6] in another longitude also saw land for the first time. Eld & myself have saved the Squadron, though we little thought our discovery of so much immediate importance.

Continued beating until the 23rd. We had now become convinced that the barrier of Ice was aground & that the Land was all along behind it. So that we gave up the idea of getting far South, & reposed our hopes in tracing the Land at different points, landing if possible, getting soundings &c., &c. On the 22nd saw many whales, & about 7 P.M we witnessed a terrible fight between a large Whale & a *"Killer,"* a fish nearly as big. They were close to the Ship, & this combat of the monsters of the deep was a wonderful display of the immense power & strength which they possess and of the incredible size to which they attain!

It was absolutely frightful to look upon. The Killer would open wide his jaws, showing an awful mouth flaming in a red & yellow lining, & bear down upon the Whale. The shock of coming together was great, & the Whale from its heaving & writhing, seemed to suffer the most. The water became dyed with blood & was lashed into foam by the evolutions of the combatants. Now both would sink, apparently fighting as they went down. Then they rose in a flurry, fighting still. This continued for half an hour, when they moved off, grappling with each other as they went. 'Twas a grand encounter, & every soul on board was on deck to witness it. I shall never forget this Battle of the Leviathans.

At 5 two Boats were sent away from the Ship. Soundings

were tried & *bottom* found at 350 fathoms, mud & pebbles coming up on the Lead. Great was the joy & Excitement throughout the Ship, for this was a certain indication of the proximity of Land, & now we were sanguine that ere long we should discover "terra firma," & the prize would be our own. As the Boats were returning, the crew were sent in the rigging to give three cheers, and they did this, so heartily, that the old Ice rang with the Sound.

All was bustle about the decks. Below some were playing shuffleboard. On the gun deck we were *rolling ten pins,* and on the spar deck the men were running away cheerily with the lead line to the music of the fiddle, occasionally bursting into the songs & hurrahs common among them when at any exciting work. "All hands" was called to splice the main brace, & we were a merry ship. Little did any one think of the change that a few short hours would bring about!

The Sun set at 10 in all the splendor of a warmer clime, leaving a ruddy glow on the horizon which vanished not, but chamelion like, changed its hues from bright to brighter. 'Twas my middle watch, & when I came on deck there was a deep peace all around. But a breath of air was stirring, & the ship was quiet and motionless as if she had been moored in a sheltered lake. The full Moon was high in the heavens, but She threw no light abroad. This Eternal day puts her to shame & blots out the Stars altogether. The East was illuminated with those soft & blended tints that form the glory of an Italian Sky at Eve, and the reflection of these colours upon the Ice produced a splendid Effect. To heighten the Scene, in the North to West the clouds were black & hung in gloomy contrast over the stainless field of White beneath them. Never have I looked on so much sublime & wondrous beauty as this Sun rise presented amidst the Icy Sea.

At 4 I turned in, dreading no evil & confident that we would succeed in finding Land ere we were many days older. True! even in a few hours we came nigh to finding it, but—at the bottom of the Ocean.

At 8 o clock I found that the Captain had run the Ship among the drift Ice with the intention of forcing on towards the barrier, as there was a strong resemblance of high land in the rear of it, & he needed to be certain about it. At 8.40 it was evident that we could go no farther with any safety and that we had best get out as speedily as possible. We were entirely surrounded by loose Ice. Some pieces were larger than the Ship, & they were packed so closely together, that we had no room to proceed or to manoeuvre in. Here and there a small place of clear water occurred, but these filled up & changed continually from the drift.

In endeavouring to tack, the Ship got Sternboard & went Stern on to a huge lump of Ice, splitting the rudder head & carrying away the wheel ropes. This shock sent her ahead for a moment against all her sails (and it brought all hands on deck), but she gathered sternway once more & this time coming in contact with the same piece of Ice, the rudder was shattered & the head of it carried away entirely. Two of the pintles & two of the gudgeons[7] were broke, & the rudder freed from the Sternpost entirely.

This was a terrible disaster alone, but it was merely the *commencement* of our troubles. Our situation was evident at a glance: we must get clear of the Ice at once—if we could; repair the rudder—if we could; and get back to Sydney—if we could! All of which was problematical in the highest degree. We failed in the first attempt & were obliged to run farther into the Ice to reach a clear space that we noticed near a large Island of Ice. We were obliged to steer the Ship by the Sails, & of course her movements were awkward & slow. We could not avoid the Ice in our way & thumped heavily several times, carrying away part of the Fore Foot, the Larboard Bill Port, & the Shackle of the palm lashing[8] of the Larboard Anchor.

We now lowered a boat & carried out an Ice anchor to the largest piece of Ice near us, hoping to ride by it until we could hoist in the rudder. The Sails were furled, but the Wind freshening, the Anchor broke its hold notwithstanding the Exertions of the men to Keep it in its bed. The Ship got rapid Sternboard, & ere we could help her, she went on to the Ice Island with a tremendous crash. This Island was many miles in Extent. From the Mast head I could see over its flat top a long ways but could not discern its termination. It rose from the Water, bluff as the

Side of a House, & while we were under it, it towered above the Main topmast head.

It was the weakest part of a Ship's frame that was in contact with this Mass, & the Shock & crash & splintering of the riven Spars & upper works were any thing but agreeable. For an instant I thought that the Whole Stern *must* be stove, & that a few minutes would send us to the bottom without a hope. I thought any struggle for life would only be in vain. To reach a piece of Ice, would only be to die a more horrible death, and I settled in my mind that it would be best to go down with the Ship. I may safely say I felt neither fear nor dread, though there was that quickening rush of the blood towards the heart, and sensations indescribable in themselves but which must come over every one at the startling approach of Sudden death. Of course, no one felt unconcerned or at ease, but there were no Shrieks, no Exhibitions of bewilderment, & I verily believe that *had* the old ship settled in the Water, she would have gone down with three as hearty cheers as ever came from an hundred throats.

There was prompt action though, for there was no time to lose. To Strike a second time, would be to ensure destruction. Sail was made at once, & the Ship's head paid slowly off from the danger—I had been almost immediately relieved from the apprehension of the Ship's sinking! The Spanker boom[9] & Stern boat went to splinters, the Boats' davits, Taffrel,[10] & all the Starboard Side of the upper works were Started as far forward as the gangway. These, receiving the heaviest of the Shock, saved the Ship. I shall never forget the look of the old craft as she lay beneath that ridge of Ice, trembling from the blow, & Ice—Ice piled around her, so that we could see nothing Else from the Deck. The dark figures of the men & boats were the only relief to the dreary Whiteness.

Now that we were freed from this peril, it was determined to struggle again for the clear sea. It was about 11 o clock. We thumped, thumped until about 3 in the afternoon, making but little progress, & drifting to leeward all the while with the Ice, while the distance between us & the clear Sea was increasing Every moment from the quantity of Ice brought down by the wind. The men were Kept incessantly at work, but all our efforts to get into places where the Ice was thinnest were in vain. We were so jammed & the Ship so unmanageable that we missed Every chance & became more involved. An hundred times we thought we should surely succeed, but the Ice crowded upon us the more, & the Ship struck as if she would knock herself to pieces. Labour was not slackened, however unfavourable appearances. All the responses that ingenuity suggested were tried, & the men did their duty, as sailors always do, when working for their lives, occasionally giving a cheer as we advanced.

At 3 the Wind died away, & it came up thick with snow. We made fast again with the Ice Anchors & hoisted the rudder in. It came in two pieces, & all of us were relieved to see *it* safe upon the deck. The Carpenters went immediately to work upon it. Soon after, the breeze sprang up. Again the anchor would not hold, & we made sail to try once more to force her out. It was the same thing over & with the same ill success. We became more & more shut in, & the chances of getting out seemed to grow more remote than ever.

To dwell at all upon our situation, while in a measure free from instant risk, afforded but little that was consoling. The Ship was helpless as an Infant, without her rudder. Allowing that we did escape the Ice, until we could get command of the Ship once more we could not choose our course, and after that would be accomplished in the imperfect manner that was alone practicable, we had a long tract of Stormy Sea to pass over Ere we could gain our Port. I did not allow these anticipations to usurp my attention, but I could not help their intruding at times. How wearily the time wore, and oh! how vexatious, Killing, it was to miss chance after chance for Escape, when we had struggled for dear life to obtain them!

We toiled & toiled on. "Never say die!" was the word. We used the Boats to plant the anchors for warping by, and when we could no longer use them, the men went upon the Ice & crossing from piece to piece by planks laid across the chasms, transported the anchors to different positions. We had spars over the bow, also, pushing with all our might! In this way by 6 o'clock, our exertions had brought us to within 100 yards of the open Sea, but there we were wedged immoveable. We could

neither advance or recede, & we had the cruel mortification of
seeing the place of comparative Safety so close at hand, & yet
be in as much & more peril than we experienced through the
day. We could all have *walked* to the Edge of the Ice, but the
Masses surrounding the Ship were so huge that all our thumping only did her injury, while it did not budge them an inch.

Now was the time, when the anxiety became almost terrible.
Hitherto the weather though thick, had not been threatening.
The wind had been moderate & there was but little swell. Consequently, the Ice had but a slight Motion, not sufficient to
throw *it* with any force against *us*—the *Ship* had been forced
upon it. Now it seemed the tables were to be turned. Black
clouds were gathering in the West. They were rolled & curled
together in windy looking wreaths, & they had all the appearance of a coming storm. I went up aloft & I fixed my gaze upon
that portentous Sky. I watched until I saw the *clouds move*—I
saw their *shadow coming over the water*, & now I thought in
sad earnest, *"our time has come at last!"*

While I was in the rigging returning to the deck, where (as I
thought) the last grand scene in the Drama of Life was so soon
to be enacted, there was Something spoke at my heart, & with
a few words, I reccommended my soul to the mercy & Keeping
of God! *I gave up all hope of Life.* The approach of the squall
seemed so evident & certain that I saw no prospect of escape,
and I thought tha[t] in less than an hour there would not be a
vestige left of the *Peacock* or her crew. Here were two hundred
of us, in the full vigour of health & strength; in a few moments
not one would be left to tell the tale of our destruction. All
must go, without the hope of *even* a *struggle* for life. When the
crush came, we should be swept away like the spars & timbers
of the Ship.

Every one was watching the clouds, & the symptoms which
had influenced my judgement directed that of others. Every rag
was taken in, & now, as we could do no more, we awaited our
fate. The little breeze which had been blowing from another
quarter died away entirely, & that sort of breathless calm succeeded which is generally ominous of the wrath & tempest
about to follow. With nothing to do, you could read anxiety in
many a face. You could tell of the trouble within by the quiver-

ing lip & the unsettled eye, but there was neither the voice of murmur or of fright.

Nearer & nearer came the funeral Cloud. Suddenly its appearance changed—it Spread wide & broke away. It lost its stormy aspect, the windy wreaths were dissolved in Mist, and with *that change* our sense of danger passed away. With the Keenness of judgement common to Seamen, every one knew that the crisis had passed, and that we might once more deem ourselves in *Comparative* Safety. The spell was broken—we breathed freely.

Heavens! what a hideous death we escaped! The poor old Ship was lying with her whole broadside exposed to the Ice, pressed, strained, groaning in Every part of her frame. Her strong build alone enabled her to hold together. The *Vincennes* could not have borne it even with the little breeze & swell.

Cold & weary, some of us now went below to solace ourselves with some hot compound & something more substantial. We enjoyed the lunch with a relish and returned on deck to participate in the toil that was renewed. Instead of a storm of wind from the cloud, we had a thick snow squall that blinded us & shut both Ice & Sea from our view. Presently a light breeze sprang up again, & sail was made once more. The Ice still came drifting down, & as before, when we had got the Ship nearly in a channel, it would close up & we had to try another. Disappointment met us at Every Step. In this way the time wore heavily & wearily away. At 1 o'clock in the morning, we had all been up 17 hours hard at work, and as it was *labour in vain,* one watch's hammocks were piped down, & the Officers & crew, save the watch on deck, were allowed to sleep—if they could.

I turned in to my cot at once to make the best of 3 hours below, for I had the morning watch to keep. I suffered horrible tortures during my troubled sleep. All the feelings I had mastered during the day haunted me in dreams. I was buried under the Ice; & the whole terrible catastrophe of a wreck from the first moment of the Ice striking the deck to the last drowning gasp occurred with a vividness that I shall never forget. God Keep me from ever feeling so, when awake. Those 3 hours in my cot were worse than all the others on deck with real danger to look upon. I was glad when they were past & turned out willingly to renew my watch. Just at this time, aided by a light breeze & a fortunate opening of the Ice, the Ship slid in to the clear water, free from the rough & cold embraces that had held her so long.

The weather was thick & chill & the wind light, but we managed to steer our disabled craft tolerably well, and without further accident reached the middle of the Bay we had entered with so much confidence, and where our hopes had been raised so high. Towards 8 the mist cleared a little. All around as far as Eye could see the Icy barrier Extended, the slightness of its Elevation above the water relieved in many places by towering Ice bergs of every form & hue & by immense Islands that arose like mountains from amidst the frozen plains.

My Eyes were red & smarting from the loss of rest, & I was fairly *used up,* done over, by Anxiety & Exertion. I swallowed an uncomfortable breakfast & wrapping myself up in my robe of Skins, I dozed for a little while until the rudder was about to be shipped. The Carpenters had worked all the night upon it, & at 10 o'clock it was ready to be launched. This was too important an operation not to be witnessed by every soul on board, & so foregoing the chance for sleep, we all assembled to see it completed. The precarious manoeuvre was accomplished with a seaman's skill, & at 11.30 we were on our way again, heading for the only passage that existed leading to the Ocean.

I lay me down again until dinner time, but it was not until after this meal, that I could get any refreshing Sleep. From 3 to 6 I slept like one of the dead, & when I had to rise to my watch again, I felt fresh as ever, and the change was blessed indeed. The winds were light during the night & much to my joy, I had the Sleep in—no watch to Keep.

On a Sunday, after service, the Commissioned Officers were called to a consultation in the Cabin, & the result was that we should make the best of our way to Sydney for repairs. The passage was long & stormy. We had tremendous gales & heavy seas, and we were anxious about the rudder for fear the shocks it received from the waves would carry it away.

On the 27th the first gale commenced, fair at first, but soon hauling ahead—weather thick, with much snow & hail. We were continually on the lookout for Ice bergs. To have run foul of one in such a Sea would have sunk us at once, & we could not see half a Ship's length before us. Many a weary four hours did I stand on the lookout with my eyes fixed on the misty space ahead, snow, hail & seas coming over me unchecked. My poor feet—how they suffered; a tread-mill process of stamping was all I could do to warm them. In these uncomfortable hours of most uncertain safety visions of *Home* & a winter fireside & all the out & indoor enjoyments of a snowy season *there* were floating through my head with a tantalizing vividness. It was consoling to reflect that the season was the summer here.

When passing through the patches of floe Ice, great care & quickness of judgement & action were necessary to avoid striking them. "Touch and go" would *not* be a good Pilot.

On the 2nd February, we saw the last Iceberg. It was of considerable height, as we run 20 miles before we came up with it. On the 4th we made Maquaries Island for the second time. On the 7th & 8th the Heavens were most splendidly illuminated with the Aurora Australis. From a crown of brilliant hues in the zenith, rays of all colours darted in every direction towards the horizon. These wavered, quivered, & changed in tint continually, and in the South West a glorious rainbow spanned the sky with its mighty arch. The Sunset amongst the Ice & this painting of the sky at night were spectacles such as are rarely beheld. It was impossible to look at either & not exclaim, "In this is the finger of God!"

On the 11th, we got into mild weather. On the 17th we made high Land to the North of Sydney. On the 20th we stood in towards the shore with a full breeze, but not making the light by 8 P.M. wore & hove to. Made Land next day at 3 P.M., & at 7 saw the Light ahead. Ran in & anchored at 11. Thought of the breakfast on the morrow. Next morning beat up to the Town & moored. I was on shore soon afterwards, & we capered over the grass & among the flowers like so many children, mad with joy at a holiday. 'Twas such a change from the Ice!—grass, flowers, houses, men, women & children!

And so ended our attempt South! So vanished our bright hopes, and all that was left for us was to wish the others better fortunes! True we had seen the Land afar off & had touched the bottom with our lead! But this was a Lame tale to tell, &

though we had so much cause to be thankful for our preservation, we could not help feeling that so far as our Ship was concerned, the result would be small, not sufficient to satisfy the world, or to gain for us the enviable distinction we had so much coveted, that we should be the first to satisfactorily prove the existence of continuous Land around the Southern Pole. True we had done all we could and had nearly become martyrs to our zeal, but disasters never tell much when productive of defeat, & we were mortified to the very heart's core.

But the *Vincennes* redeemed it all. The splendid success which attended her in her run of 1500 miles along the Land was more than even our most sanguine expectations had led us to expect. The great question was set at rest; never before had there been such an immense extent of Land explored in this Latitude. And in the present instance, a rival squadron had made the attempt and ended it by mere child's play. Monsieur Jules D'Urville may truly say, "Comparisons are odious."

This is the 17th April 1840. I have recorded that Eld & myself saw Land on the 16th [of January]. When we came down from the mast head, Eld made the report to Captain Hudson. There was not much attention paid to it. No one else was sent aloft, & presently we tacked Ship & stood directly away from the quarter where the Land lay. There was no mention made of it in the Log book. Why the Captain treated this so lightly, we did not know. Perhaps he was fearful to make a Statement on such Slight ground as a distant view. So it was on the 19th. He would hardly call *that* Land, because it was white! So in his report to the Secretary he made no mention of the discovery on the 16th.

Well, when he heard of the *Vincennes'* run & saw that on the 19th they had put the Land down on the chart which Clark & I first saw, he was quite ready to believe that Eld & I had not been deceived. But how to remedy it? We took care to spread the circumstance, & it was known through both ships. Captain Hudson would *now* give his head had he paid more attention to the thing. How to get out of the dilemma, he does not know. *His* judgement must be sacrificed & his neglect must be censured, if he now *asserts* that we saw Land on the 16th. Yet he is convinced that we did see it & would give any thing could he have it credited to his ship.

[CHAPTER 11: SYDNEY AGAIN AND THE PASSAGE TO FIJI]

On Wednesday we moved the Ship over to a very retired cove, and hauling into the Wharf, commenced discharging her of every thing. We had mechanics employed from Sydney, & gangs were busy at work upon the rudder, bulwarks, &c., &c. By means of an India rubber diving machine, we ascertained that all the damage could be repaired without "heaving down," an operation that we much dreaded, as we should have been obliged to live ashore during the tedious while.

By running the Ship stem on to a Sand bank at high water, the injured part was left bare when the tide fell so that the Carpenters could work on it without trouble. The destruction had been much greater than we supposed. With all our sense of the risk & danger, we had not known its true extent, and it was absolutely with a thrill of horror & fright that I looked upon the shattered wood & saw *"that one little inch more, & the Ship would have split in two."* A few more thumps & there would have been an end of us. Several feet of solid timber had been knocked away and there remained but a finger's breadth to protect the planking of the sides. Ugh! I felt worse than when in the danger, & shudder now at the thought.

The *Vincennes* came in one day very unexpectedly to us, & they were as much surprised to find our Ship in such condition. From an English Officer, Captain Andrews, we heard of the *Porpoise* being at Hobart Town, & by the Frigate *Herald,* of the *Flying Fish* at New Zealand! Thus, much to our joy, *we knew that all were safe!*

The country is dreadfully dreary all about Sydney. There are no walks, no drives, & Town & all together is enough to sicken any one. Save me from ever seeing it again, though had it not been for its existence, we should have had a long road to go for our repairs.

Snakes are numerous & very venomous—kill in 30 minutes. Walking on Sunday on the Hill above the Ship with Eld, we were speaking of the Snakes & yet forgetting entirely to look out for them. Suddenly, I know not why, I cast my eyes on the ground, and I was in the very act of putting my foot upon one of the most poisonous kind. The foot was arrested in its descent, & I sprang away on the other leg. Turning to look for the Snake, he was just disappearing in the bushes. It was only as thick as my finger, about 18 inches long, black back & silver belly. During the rest of the walk, you may be sure that we kept our eyes about us.

Time passed very slowly & wearily at the Cove, but on the whole we got along with the work better than we had expected, or we hoped for.

Captain Hudson was indiscreet enough to make some remarks unfavorable to the Catholics at a meeting of the Wesleyan Society. These came with a very bad grace from *an American* in a foreign land, where many were of the creed that he was abusing. The Papers gave him a most severe castigation, which he admitted he deserved. 'Tis strange that Religion, politics, almost always run away with a man's common sense. Now, what could have been more improper than Captain Hudson's preaching a tirade against the poor Catholics in such a far corner of the world, when men of all beliefs had joined to welcome him & us, and of all others, the warm hearted Irishmen who so kindly invited us to St Patrick's ball, even after the publication of our Captain's speech.

It was a matter of the deepest regret to us that the Commander should travel so far out of his line of duty in expressing sentiments which he might utter in welcome at his own fireside, but which it was the height of imprudence & folly to express before an assemblage of Sectarians, who gave them a conspicuous notoriety at once to *favour their cause!* Religion is tortured into curious shapes in this world, and it is a melancholy truth, which ought to shame us to remember, that men's blood has been shed in its name, & more tortures inflicted & borne for its sake, than we ever hear of among the Heathens for any cause.

[Sydney] is the dearest place I ever was in—eggs a shilling a piece; chickens two dollars a piece and every thing else in proportion. I was $50 in debt when we first arrived, & when we left the Port the second time, I was $500—& that was doing well! There is a fair chance now to pay it off, however. We shall not be in a civilized port save at the Sandwich Islands for at least 9 or 10 months. I was glad to get into Sydney as a change, disgusted when we had to return to it, and now am perfectly contented to be among Savages once more.

I must not forget to say that many of our Officers pursued an entirely different course from myself & mingled freely with the Society of Sydney. I never knew such an *excess* of feeling and sentiment manifested between persons so lately known, & so soon to be left. Notes, presents & parties going on continually. As we were leaving the Harbour, a number of Ladies were collected on one of the points "to take a last fond look," and there was a waving of kerchiefs which exceeded the display on the ramparts of Fortress Monroe when the Squadron sailed from Hampton Roads. The Midshipmen answered from the Top Gallant Yards & from the Tops—though one Youth's symbol was any thing but white—and from the deck there was a universal fluttering of rags kept up until the Captain could stand it no longer. So when the Ship, in one of her tacks, approached near to the fair disconsolates, he sent the crew into the rigging & gave them three cheers. The white 'kerchiefs waved more violently than ever. A Reefer became seized with a Poetical phrenzy, and hastening down from aloft, he perpetrated an imitation of the "Soldiers Tear" and sent it back by the Pilot. All that I can remember is, "And the Sailor, leant against the Mast & wiped away a Tear"—Oh my!

To day is the 18th of April 1840, Saturday—just *twenty months* since we sailed from Norfolk! I can scarcely credit it. The time has seemed so short to me that I can hardly believe so much of the three years has passed away. We are on the *down hill* of the cruize, & overjoyed am I to know it. Every 18th day that comes, I record with a feeling of intense satisfaction. I never miss one—when the *last* shall come, I will be fairly crazed with happiness!

Thursday April 30th

After a very long and tedious passage we have at last made Tonga Taboo. Light & contrary winds have lengthened our run, to twice the time we gave her, & we are very much afraid that we will gain but a slight glance at the Island, which possesses so much that is interesting.

Owing to the wind coming ahead, we did not get in as speedily as we had expected & passed another night at Sea. The next afternoon we had a fair wind & ran in through a very narrow & intricate passage for the anchorage. We had hoped to find the place deserted by our squadron, for we knew that so soon as Captain Wilkes would see us coming in, that he would not permit us to anchor at all. We thought it very likely that they had gone, as we had been ordered *to leave* the Island on the 23d April. I was aloft, looking out as an amateur, & much to my chagrin, had the mortification to discover the squadron at anchor! In another minute the *Vincennes* had set her Topsails at the mast head & was underweigh, standing out. Our fears were confirmed. We should see nothing of Tonga Taboo, and this was as cruel a mischief as ever befel my miserable self. "Signal from the *Vincennes*—Join Company!" and join it we did. The *Porpoise* passed us & gave us three cheers!

We sailed by the Town & could see the groups of people on the shore, but, alas! we were not to land and were in despair. We anchored together about 12 miles from the Land, & some had the pleasure of shaking hands with those whom we had not seen for months. May, Johnson, Simon,[1] Whittle & a host of others came on board & with kindly forethought brought with them all the fresh grub they had to spare. Captain Hudson had gone to the *Vincennes,* & in our joy at meeting, we soon got up a noisy jollification all about the house.

As was natural, we had expected to hear of fresh troubles on coming once more athwart the *Vincennes,* but the amount & extent of new outrages exceeded all our anticipations: Pinckney,[2] broke, suspended, confined to his vessel, obliged to pay the Public bills of his vessel at New Zealand & to be sent Home from the Sandwich Islands—Alden turned out of his room for Dr. Fox[3]—Steerage Rooms knocked down—the old room wherein I had enjoyed so much comfort & in the embellishment of which May & myself had spent $150.00, *made a stow hole of* to gratify the malignant spite of Mr. Wilkes—Thompson,[4] a poor little midshipman, persecuted until every one felt ashamed, & disgusted—and a thousand other instances of falsehoods, and outrageous acts that I shall not take the trouble to write down here.

When these things will cease, I do not know, nor can any one imagine what will come next; but if the day of retribution does not arrive, I am very much mistaken. Mr. Wilkes will have a fearful array of charges to meet and will have to answer for the atrocities he has committed with such impunity when the day of his power shall be passed. And if he escapes the honest vengeance of those whom he has so trampled upon, it must be by a miracle.

I have not recorded the dark doings in the domestic annals of this Expedition, because I have no wish to fill these pages with angry accounts of such a system of villainy as was never before practised by a commander, but all will be unfolded at one day. I have forgotten nothing and nothing will I forgive.

The next day was a Saturday, but Sunday on board the *Vincennes,* as they had not changed their reckoning. I breakfasted with May on board the *Flying Fish* & tasted chicken, the first time [in] 7 months; afterwards went on board *Vincennes* to church.

About midnight two women came on board & claimed our protection & a passage to the Fegee Islands. They said they would be killed & eaten if they could not get away from Tonga Taboo. They implored in vain. The Captain would not receive them & hurried them away. They had thrown away their paddles when they came alongside in the vain expectation that they would not have to use them again. Others were made by one of the Carpenters, who was "turned out" for the purpose. Captain Hudson said, "No matter who they were, he would not have them on board his Ship, one night, for a thousand dollars!" Such is the charity of a man who proffesses religion.

Well, the poor fugitives paddled towards the Schooner, and when they came near her, jumped overboard from the canoe & swimming alongside, clambered on board her. They were allowed to rest in quiet for the night, but in the morning were sent to the *Vincennes*. Captain Wilkes put them on a small Island about 10 miles from the land, which was destitute of water & had but few Cocoa Nuts on it. Oh, rare humanity!

In the afternoon, I went with Old Emmons[5] to a small Island merely to have it to say, that I had landed on the Tonga Group.

For some time passed, we have been very busy in making preparations for active duty among the Fegees—boarding nettings[6] for the Ship; arms, & all the conveniencies for stowing them in the boats, provision boxes & a hundred other things necessary in boat work among a treacherous people. You cannot move about the decks without stumbling over some arrangement of aspect most ominous.

This group of Islands has a hard name with navigators. The people are generally believed to be ferocious cannibals, & the numerous reefs & shoals & labyrinths of rocky passages among the cluster are so many snares, for the seaman's destruction. The difficulties presented both by the nature of the inhabitants and by the dangers of the navigation have prevented any thing like an accurate survey by which the perils could be lessened. And the imperfect chart in our possession, in addition to the frightful display of rocks & reefs, is garnished here & there with notices such as "Brig *Eliza* lost," "American brig lost," &c., &c., &c., &c. This was procured at Tonga Taboo from the Master of a small English vessel.

The *Vincennes* took a Pilot[7] on board there also, a white man. Captain Wilkes said to him, with his usual assumption of superior knowledge, "You will find when we get to the Islands, that I know as much about them as you do." The fellow had spirit and sense enough to reply, "You may know all about them on paper, but when you come to the goings in & comings out, you will see who knows best, you or myself."

This was just like old Kill biscuit. He has said many such things before. He does not allow there is any body in the world but himself & sneers at whatever any one has done or said that does not exactly tally with the notions he has formed. He has endeavoured, seperately, to convince each of the Scientifics that he knew more about their particular & favorite branch than they themselves.

May 16th. 1840

Well, we are among the Feegees, & have not been killed, nor eaten, nor wrecked yet. The Schooner, however, has been on a reef & nearly lost, but as the accident occurred during the night, the natives did not see her in so tempting a predicament, & those on board were spared a visit which would have proved any thing but pleasant in its consequences. As she did not appear for four days after we had reached our anchorages, we were really very seriously alarmed for our friends, and some of us volunteered to go & look after them. Captain Hudson refused to mention any thing of the kind to Captain Wilkes, "because he would be highly displeased & think it a presumptuous interference with his plans." 'Tis true; so he would! Comment is needless.

It was on May the 8th that we anchored within the reef at the Island of Ovelow. The appearance of the shore as we approached was very beautiful. The Island is high. There were many valleys sweeping from the hill tops to the shore, bounded by bold projecting points of rock, and affording all the finest contrasts that can well exist in scenery. There was a cry of joy from a reefer as with his glass he descried a *cow* whisking her tail among the bushes & feeding just as quietly as our own cows at Home. This was a domestic feature which we had not expected to find at Feegee and was one of those sights which carry the mind directly away to Home & childhood.

All was still & quiet on the shore when we anchored, and there were but few natives visible, although we were only a stone's throw from the beach. When we had been at anchor a little while and communication taken place with the Chief through the medium of the white men living under his protection, the natives began to appear upon the beach, and we took our first look at a group of Fegees. The survey was unsatisfactory, for they were ill looking beyond conception. By & by canoes ventured off, & a nearer view settled the matter. Excepting the Fuegians & the New Hollanders,[8] they were the ugliest in physiognomy of any race we had seen.

Tall in stature, well made, of athletic & vigorous forms, they were fine specimens of men, but black in color, Negro in features, begrimmed with dirt, daubed with red paint & soot, the ear slit & hanging down to the shoulder with a bone or shell thrust in the hole, hair frizzled out to a most grotesque extent from the head, dyed of various hues & teeming with life, naked save a girdle of Tappa around the loins, they presented a spectacle of mingled hideousness & ferocity that well becomes the character they have earned for themselves, & which, as we have since fatally experienced, they well deserve. May they be smitten from the Earth!

During the afternoon a signal was made by the *Vincennes* that officers could go on shore, armed, until sundown, but not to pass the bounds of the Chief of the Village. All who could availed themselves of the permission. Duty detained me on board, but at sunset I went in the Boat merely to put my Foot on a new Land. The next day, Guillou[9] & I equipped ourselves with small articles to trade and arms according to law, for a visit on shore. We took with us Little Jack Williams, an intelligent boy who shipped in Sydney & had been among these Islands before. He spoke a few words of Fegee & carried our bundles for us.

The singular construction of the Huts first attracted our attention, for they were totally unlike the living residences of the Tahitians or the Samoans, & the Village lacked the pleasant & cleanly appearance which was always found in those of the latter people. The huts were mostly high with peaked roofs & gables, the perpendicular sides being cut about 4 feet from the ground, where the roof commenced with projecting eaves & of course formed the most considerable portion of the structure. The sides were of close cane-work covered with mats, the roof of very thick thatch put on in a manner that shames such work at Home. One or two small doors, just admitting a single person at a time by crawling on all fours, were the only openings for air, or inmates. And in the matter of ventilation, therefore, the habitations of the Fegees are essentially deficient. At a little distance they look like so many haycocks.

The village was upon uneven ground, & Mounds & walls of

stoney earth intersected it in all directions, serving as covers & lines of defence in time of war. A stream of water ran through it & was the most cheerful feature in the scene. Another portion of the Village occupied a rocky hill that rose immediately over the houses on the plain, & this was resorted to as a stronghold in war, if they should be driven from the more exposed position below.

The people were differently employed, but most of them suspended their work and followed the Papalangies about with curious eyes. Some huge fellows were very busy cooking a sort of pudding with sugar & cocoanuts, simmering the mixture in large earthenware pots of their own manufacture. And these were the first Islanders we had seen who practised any of the culinary arts save baking & roasting. It seemed unnatural to see men of this calibre engaged in such a peaceful occupation, but they were adepts, and the Fegees seldom employ their women to do all the cooking.

The labour of the women mostly consists in making mats, tappa &c. & bringing water, but they sometimes aid in fishing & rarely in agriculture. The men are fond of nursing, & you often meet with gigantic figures dandling infants with all the tenderness imaginable. Strange as it may seem, I—even myself, a peaceful looking, mild & quiet individual—have been as much an object of terror & fright to a Fegee babe, and on my approach caused as much screaming on the part of the child & vain attempts at soothing on the Mother's as could possibly happen were the reverse the case, and a great black Cannibal with murder in his looks to draw near to a group of our feminines. So it is: a *good* Catholic thinks his neighbour of another creed to be worse tha[n] the devil himself, & the Chinese delight in terming *us* Barbarians. And we, who can easily conjure up fright at the sight of a Savage, do not so readily understand, why a Savage (even if it be a Baby) should be terrified by us.

Some were building a canoe by the water side, and this is still a most important, tedious & troublesome operation to the Natives. With the aid of iron tools, they progress more rapidly than when their implements were but shell & bone, but still the event of completing one, is made a matter of celebration.

The women we saw were all ugly, save one, the wife of the Pilot Tom & daughter of a white man. She was of very fair complexion, and in another generation, her descendants will have but little resemblance to the Fegee. None of the women wear long hair. As soon as they are married, they are cropped & generally shave a portion of the head bare. They daub & mix in with their wool a wet paste of mud to change the colour from the original black to a foxy red & are filthy looking and any thing but attractive. I saw old hags who would have made unexceptionable witches for a German romancer to describe, or for an olden Judge to have burnt.

We left the Village & walked along the stream, which wound through a beautiful valley with bold & striking scenery encompassing it, until we came to a fitting spot to bathe. We selected a basin formed among the rocks & into which the water fell in a gentle cascade & tall trees threw a shade over the spot, & we enjoyed the luxury of a fresh water bath to the full—a thing unknown to us since leaving the ever to be remembered waterfall in sweet Upolu. The wash was delicious & refreshing—we felt like new men. The natives were looking at us & observing with curious eyes the whiteness of our skins.

After the bath we started leisurely back to the Village, attended by many Natives wherever we went—purchased a few trifles, shot off our Fire Arms to awake the People, got the white men spinning yarns & so passed the time until Sundown summoned us on board, and such was my first day in Fegee.

The next day Captain Wilkes & a large party of Officers ascended the highest ridge of the Island for the purpose of obtaining a plane table sketch of the adjacent Islands, so that some idea could be formed of the nature of the survey now about to be commenced. The chief accompanied them for protection & many of his people to carry the instruments, &c.

The observatory was erected on a small hill not far from the Ships on a very pretty & pleasant site, & several Officers were detailed for duty there. I was glad to get clear, for I have no fancy for work that is so hard upon my eyes. The Natives were employed to build a fence around the tents, and this they did with incredible celerity. Sentries were posted, & the hill, which had been quiet for ages, was now all alive. From the Ship's deck it presented a beautiful picture & was a singular contrast to the village close by.*

Four days after our arrival, the Schooner came in. We were relieved from the anxiety we had felt for her safety, & Captain Wilkes could now fix his plans.

This was the day that "Old Snuff," the most potent Chief among the group, was received on board the *Vincennes* with all the ceremonies befitting the remarkable occasion. His Majesty was naked as his subjects & had no external marks of rank or authority about him save a breast ornament made of pearl & whale's teeth & which was sacred to his Kingly person alone. He was old, tall, thin & black, face hidden by his hair & a beard which fell to his middle, & was grisly from age. A Turban of white tappa was wound about his brows, and a narrow strip of the same encircled his loins, the ends of which dropped to his feet & trailed for some length upon the ground, or deck, which you will. His train was allowed to follow their chief on board, & the decks were full of black heads.

The Ship was dressed off with flags, and all her wonders were displayed in turn to the Monarch, whose presence did her so much honour. The immensity of space between decks, the many men, the great guns, the number of Musquets & other arms, the operations of the Turning lathe, the Armourer at work, the groups of Officers, and the respect & attention shown to himself, fairly amazed the King. He spoke of the difference between these Ships & the Traders that had been among his Islands for many years, & he was satisfied that a man of war was in reality all that he had been told. The Guns were fired with round shot & grape, & the natives burst into loud shouts as they saw the water dashed up in a succession of jets at the distance of a mile & more. The Marines were paraded and exercised, & this is a sight that always pleases a Savage. The tune they marched to was "The King of the Cannibal Islands."[10]

---

*When the *Vincennes* left Ovelau, Lebooca immediately commenced building a Spirit house where the observation hut had stood. He had been mystified by the star gazing, &c., and thought it had something to do with the worship of our spirits, so that his superstition determined him to keep the place sacred forever.

Snuff was remarkably fond of liquor, when he could get it, and in deference to his distinguished taste, he was treated with whiskey, which he swallowed with the air & relish of an old toper. Presents were made to him and the principal chiefs, the most valuable of which was a patent rifle,[11] the like of which had never been seen in all Fegee, & fairly turned Old Snuff's head.

Snuff was the title most irreverently applied to this despot by the white men whom he protected—his native name[12] is too much for my orthography. He had been a great & successful warrior in his day & had reduced many places to his sway, so that he became the most dreaded chief among the Islands, owned the most property & the greatest number of slaves, men & women, the fruits of his victories. As he was always assisted by white men in his wars, he became the patron & protector of the Papalangies who resided within the limits of his authority, and in several cases of wreck, he took care of the survivors & sent them away in safety when opportunity offered.

Snuff was said to have had strong cannibal propensities in his youth & to have indulged freely in repasts that seem to us so horrid & unnatural. It was supposed that he still retained the taste & eat in private, but none of the white men had ever caught him in the act. Snuff was not amiable among his subjects, & his principal pastimes were running down canoes & shooting & spearing people, just by way of amusement.

Snuff came on board the *Peacock* the day after his visit to the *Vincennes,* & received presents again. It was really interesting to attend these people about the Ship, explaining or trying to do so the uses of the different things & listening to their expressions of wonder & delight. Snuff did me the favour to hug me in his arms & call me his son, but this was after he had taken his second glass of whiskey. The idea that those arms had slain so many men made me feel quite strange.

But let me get on about the Ship. The boats were preparing for surveying cruizes. The Schooner was to be actively employed, & our Ship was to have a cruize, all alone, by herself. Alden & Whittle, Knox & Elliott[13] went in the *Vincennes'* Launch & Cutter, & Emmons & the Parson,[14] & Blunt & J. W. W. Dyes[15] in our boats to survey the large Island of Bete Leb.

On the 15th May we sailed in the *Peacock,* & the next day

anchored in the harbour of Rahwa, on the "big land" of Bete Leb. We had an American on board as Pilot who had been living for 11 years, among the Islands—his name, Cunningham.[16] Our boats came in soon after us on their way along the Coast, and also a small sloop tender to the *Leonidas,* an American Ship at present fishing for Bich la Mar[17] near Sandal Wood Bay & the only vessel among the Islands at this time. She had not long before lost a man on the Island of Veuna Leb, murdered by the natives.

We commenced the survey of the harbour that same afternoon, & I had the pleasure of a yarn with Simon Blunt, who remained on board for the night & slept in my cot. A Boat was despatched to the Town, which was two miles distant up the River. She returned at Sunset, bringing a Chief named Philips, brother to the King. This chief had been to Tahiti in an American Ship & could speak English very well. He owned the Sloop I have mentioned & had hired her to the *Leonidas.* She was built for him by white men & named the *Who'd Have Thought It!* He remained on board all night & promised to accompany our boats that were to survey the River. All hands of us bothered him with questions that we could not resist asking, for to us it was the very height of novelty to converse with a Fegee in our own tongue.

The next day was Sunday. I went off surveying, a duty which, though arduous in the extreme, always interests me in its performance. I landed on a muddy flat & had to wade some distance over very bad bottom to get to the station, and in doing which I cut my feet badly. After angling[18] at this point, I walked along shore for a mile or more to the next position, sending the boat to meet me as near to it, as the depth of water would allow it to approach. Two men I took with me to carry Sextant, &c.

This station was near a village, and on our appearance, out came the whole population, curious to see what we were going to do. They swarmed around us like bees & burst into their peculiar shout betokening wonder & delight at every thing we did. Wild & savage as they were, they looked upon us with reverence & amazement, as if we were spirits of another world. They did not know what I was doing with the Sun, & I thought of Columbus & the Eclipse.[19] Finally, they were confounded on seeing one of the men *unship four of his teeth,* toss them from hand to hand, & then replace them in his mouth, firm as ever. This frightened them & they cried out, "Whoo! Whoo! Whoo! Venaca! Venaca!" louder than ever.

Leaving them, we had to wade up to our middles for some distance to get to the Boat, & then I pulled across to another point, where I placed a flag in a high tree. There was more wading, & the sun was scorching. From here I had a long pull & had to drag the boat over a reef, in which operation my weight had to come out of her & my strength added to the exertions of the crew—or rather *my exertions* added to *their strength.* Before we could reach the shore, it came on to rain in torrents & we had nothing to do, but stand & take it. I went under the Trees for a time, but thick as the Shade was, it could not stop the deluge, & I returned to the Boat. Two Canoes came in, & the people tried to persuade us to go to their village, but this was impossible for several reasons, & much as I wished to go, I refused them. We had much fun, notwithstanding the rain, in capturing a huge crab & in astonishing the natives.

After wasting an hour at least, & no signs of clearing up, I pulled for the Ship & got on board about 6, wet, soaked & shivering & with an appetite for my dinner that was ravenous. Such is about the amount of comfort found in a day's surveying, to which add the wear & tear of eyesight, & vexation enough to spoil the temper of a Job. To crown this, I had to keep the morning watch, preparatory to another siege, which was owing to the excellent arrangements of the First Lieutenant for carrying on the duty of the Ship.

The Ship was made ready, for the reception of the King of the place, & the Captain detained us on board to await his arrival. Between 9 & 10 a large double canoe was seen coming out of the river, and all hands of us were mustered on the Quarter Deck in long togs & swords to salute the King, who was naked. As he came over the Side he was honored with one roll and a half of the drum, instead of three, the black steward of my mess, who flourished the sticks, breaking down in the middle of the second, so that this part of the show terminated in several abortive squeaks of the fife breathed by the Ship's Cook. The Marine guard consisting of the privates, two Corporals, &

one Seargeant, presented arms, and assumed the most imposing & martial appearance that can be imagined, barring the
fact that none of them had whiskers & all were pale faced.

Tuindrecate, the King of Rawha, was over 6 feet high with
good features & a noble form. His hair was cut short, & his
tappa trailed behind him after the manner of old Snuff's. His
walk was majestic. Captain Hudson took him by the hand & led
him to the after part of the deck, where a mat was placed for the
Royal personage & chairs for ourselves. He was unattended by
the greater part of his retinue, who were coming in other canoes.

When his brother Garangia came alongside, the party were
conducted through the Ship & just the same scenes enacted as at
the reception of his relative, Snuff. As we had so few Marines, the
Captain paraded the small arms men & made a great show of
muskets. He also told some hard yarns of the dreadful power
of our arms: how every man & boy could use them, & that *one
of the latter* was a match for 6 Fegees, with clubs. However, he
had a motive in thus drawing the longbow, but whether his
Fegee Majesty swallowed it at all is rather dubious. The Captain
wanted to impress him with a terrible idea of our terrible power
in war, for there was a play to be acted in a day or two. The big
guns were fired, the shot tore up the water & the Fegees were
astounded. "Whoo! Whoo! Venaca!" echoed about the decks.

When the first hubbub subsided, the Boats left Surveying.
Owing to the want of regulation in such matters, I was obliged
to supply the crew of my boat with grub from my own mess, or
let them go hungry all day. I do not intend to record all the vex-
ations that harrass me so much, for indeed it would not be
possible—my book is not large enough, but just a few every
now & then, for variety.

The Captain of this Ship, the second in command of the first
great American Exploring & Surveying Expedition, is a perfect
Seaman & a very good man generally speaking, but he knows
nothing of Surveying and he is too old to learn. Of course we
are without a system, and things are done in the most confused
disorder, when they are done at all. It is damnable! You are ordered to prepare yourself for a day's surveying. Well, there are
many articles required for your Boat, none of which can be dis-

pensed with. You must pick up what you can, & after begging
for articles which should be *seen* in the Boat by the *Executive
Officer himself* & being *refused* them, at that—after trusting to
the ingenuity of the crew to procure what *they* can *on the sly*—
after wearying yourself to death in running all over the Ship for
this & that, you shove off at last, half supplied, for as tough
day's work, as men could well be set at.

This day it rained again, & it was dark when I got on board.
Rain for two days. Surveying & morning watch as usual. One
of the Flags that we had put up was missing, & the Captain requested the King to recover it & punish the Offender, at the
same time giving him a lecture upon the iniquity of stealing
& the horror white men had of persons guilty of theft. His
Majesty felt that it became him as a monarch to show his newly
found, generous & powerful friends, how much he regarded
their interests, & how deeply their principles had already taken
root within his breast, as well, as to exhibit the despotic &
summary authority which he exercised over his subjects.

Accordingly, he ordered his brother Garrangia, who was of a
fierce & sanguinary disposition, to take the matter in hand &
when he had found the Thief, to bring him before the King.
Such a Police Officer was not long in ferreting out the culprit,
who proved to be the Chief of a Village on the river & a man
of wealth & consequence among the people. He said the flag
looked so pretty that he could not help taking it, & this was
the only reason he had, thinking there was no great harm in so
doing.

The King called a council of his Chiefs. The Offender was
deprived of his rank & property, his wives & children taken
from him & made slaves, & then he was held at our disposal.
The King asked if we wished to kill him, and on being answered in the negative, offered to kill the man himself & was so
intent upon this that the Captain had to intercede for the fellow's life. The severity of the punishment exceeded any thing
that we had thought of, but the King would not abate a jot of
it, nor will [the offender] ever again become a chief or regain
the wives or property that he lost, for they were portioned
among those who condemned him according to Fegee law!

[CHAPTER 12: FIJI]

Now appeared upon the stage the most remarkable character that I have ever had the fortune to meet with, & whose history, could it be written, would far exceed in interest & wonderful adventure, the imaginary life of Crusoe, or any other tale of the marvellous, true or false. And this will be evident, when I mention that for Forty years, he has lived among the Cannibal Islanders & never been absent from them a single day. Pat Connell, called Berry among the Islands, came on board at Rahwah, very unexpectedly, & his coming was the prelude of an occurrence of some interest, the result of which must be looked for at a later day.

Some 3 or 4 years ago, the mate & crew of the American Brig *Charles Dagget* were massacred at the Island of Cantab by the natives, but the deed was planned & directed by a brother of Tuindrecate, who also bore a prominent part in its execution. While the Brig laid at Rahwah, this chief, Vendobi, was frequently on board of her, and as was customary, engaged to accompany her to Cantab (of which Island he was Chief, by his Mother), & get her a supply of Bich la Mar. As he was the brother of Phillips & the King & had always behaved in the most friendly manner, no suspicions were entertained of his harbouring any evil design, and the Captain took him into the Cabin as his guest. But the sight of the riches on board the Brig, so temptingly strewn before him in his daily visits, had been too much for the Cupidity of the Savage to withstand, & before they sailed, he had formed the plan by which he was to capture her & so become the possessor of property enough to buy all Fegee. Some of his men went also in the Brig & the others in canoes. This man Pat was on board as Interpreter.

The vessel anchored at Cantab, & operations were commenced. The Bich la mar house was put up, and all went on swimmingly for some days, when the work of death was commenced on shore,* and all of the crew who were absent from the Brig were killed. In the attempt on the vessel, the natives were repulsed, & she got clear of the Harbour with only one or two hands left. Pat had warned the Captain that there was murder & treachery going on, but he, intent upon his Cargo & relying on the good faith of the Chief, never heeded the old man, & like others, found out his error only when too late. Vendobi was disappointed in his object of getting all the property. The Boat of the Brig was the sole acquisition the murderer attained, & for this, the blood of so many white men was shed without mercy or remorse.

Pat had seen the [*Vincennes*] passing by the Island upon which he lived, & as he said, he thought they were too large & taunt[1] for Bich la mar traders, & he must needs go & see all about them. So he went to Lebooca in a Canoe, & Captain Wilkes sent him to us at Raywah that he might identify Vendobi and serve as an Interpreter on our cruize.

The Captain & officers had gone up to the Town with the King & passed a night there, & there was utmost confidence in our intercourse with the people, so that the King & all others were delighted & thought we were the best people they had ever seen. Accordingly, on the Friday after his first visit, the King came again on board the Ship bringing with him his Wives & household, his brothers Garrangia & Phillips, his principal Chiefs and a horde of common people, in all more than a hundred. The royal party were feasted in the Cabin & their happiness was at its height, when suddenly the scene changed, & from the condition of illustrious guests, they at once became prisoners without a blow and for as much as they knew, without a cause. We were to take Vendobi, if we could, but that personage had kept aloof from us, evidently not to be caught without stratagem or force.

---

*Vendobi commenced the work of death by catching the mate, whom he was walking with, by the hands and so held him until he was dispatched with clubs—his men were killing the others all about.

Well, all of a sudden the drum beat to Quarters, the men went to their Guns & Sentries were placed at the Cabin door. The Royal party were separated from their attendants, & they had nothing to do but submit without resistance. Man to Man, the natives on our decks exceeded in number all of our crew, & if they had made fight, there would have been many lives lost on both sides. But the Surprise was too complete, & they had such an awe of us as effectually checked any idea of resistance upon our own decks.

When the momentary hubbub had subsided, the Captain told the King that he meant no harm to him & that he [and] all now there might feel perfectly safe, *but he wished to have Vendobi.* He had expected to find him in the King's train, but he supposed that the knowledge of his crimes & the fear of consequences had kept him away. *They all knew the guilt of Vendobi; that as they avenged such things among themselves, so also did we, & we must have the man who had killed our countrymen.* If he had come on board, we should have seized him & let the others go, but now the only way was to keep them Prisoners until the King should cause his bad brother to be given up.

The King listened to all this with impatience, & when the Captain ceased, he broke out in angry reproach. Why had he been thus trapped like a bird? Why had not the Captain asked him for his Brother, when he was free? He should have given him up! *His blood was up,* and it was as much as he could do, to keep his passions from breaking out, in some act of violence, but he *did* restrain, and went on with his indignant inquiries. How could he get his brother now?—was he not a Prisoner?—would not Vendobi soon know this & fly? It was not fair, for he had trusted to the Captain, & he thought that White Chiefs never lied, nor deceived.

The Captain endeavoured to pacify him & told him again that he had not intended to touch him if Vendobi had come on board; that if he had whispered any thing of the matter before, or even if he had required him of the King's hand, there would have been much more trouble, than there need be now; and that if he, the King, would send to Town & have his brother brought on board, all the rest should be set free the moment

Vendobi was put in our power. There was much more said on both sides, & finally the King directed his brother Garangia to go to the Town & take Vendobi, *alive* if he could, but if he resisted, to *kill him* & bring the body.

In the mean time, the natives had been cleared out of the Ship & sent in their Canoes, which were made fast astern, but none were allowed to shove off to prevent the news of what was going on being carried ashore. One fellow made the attempt but was brought back by a shot from a musquet & the threat of another from the big gun. Old Paddy was in a perfect fever when this Canoe shoved off, & jumping on the arm chest, he begged leave to have the musket, so that he might shoot the man at once, & he was very much disappointed when the aim was directed over the native's head. Paddy had some self interest at stake, and he was anxious that the plot should succeed without any unnecessary trouble.

Captain Hudson was quite willing that Garrangia should again be selected as the Constable, for there was strife between the two brothers & of course no compunction of feeling to stay his hand in the somewhat unnatural duty which he so willingly undertook. His large double Canoe, highly ornamented with a profusion of white shells & having as many streamers as Cleopatra's barge, was got ready, & Garrangia left the Ship, promising to return, with the first of the tide in the morning.

As it was blowing fresh & raining, the natives were allowed to come on board again, though a few remained in their Canoes all night. Seventy of them Slept on a sail on the Gun deck, while the Royal party were still confined to the Cabin. They were no longer gay or happy. The Queen took off her feathers & her gaudy robe, & they maintained a sullen silence, which none of us were inclined to break. Our men were kept on deck all night, sleeping together abaft, with their arms close at hand.

I had the morning watch, & the weather was still disagreeable & wet. The natives in the Canoes were shivering with cold & had to bale continually to keep themselves afloat. The larger canoes had fires burning in them, and the naked devils huddled by them looked wild enough. At daylight those who had slept on board roused up & came on the Spar deck, where the Quarter Master, myself & a man kept to lookout on the Canoes were the only persons moving about. The rogues eyed us very closely, & I could not help thinking that they were charging themselves with having remained too quiet during the night. I knew that the slumbers of the crew were but light, & while the dusky crowd were around me, I stamped my feet upon the deck & called to the men "to heave out there, every one of you!" Much to my gratification &, as I could perceive, to the surprise of our prisoners, every man was on his feet in an instant. The effect was Magical, & the sable crowd dispersed about the decks, satisfied, perhaps, that in submitting so easily, they had followed the wisest course.

Old Paddy came on deck, & I had a sociable yarn with him about his life & adventures, for at this time he did not know how long he would be with us, & every one was at him. By & by Phillips came up, anxious to see if the Canoe was out of the River yet. By & by she appeared, and at 7 she was alongside. Garrangia did not come on board at once but sent the King's head man, "the Old Governor," to say to the Captain that Vendobi was in the Canoe, & he was ready to deliver him up.

The Captain asked him to come on board & to bring Vendobi also. I drove the men away from the gangway, where curiosity had brought many of them to stare at the miserable captive as they would at a wild beast. The Captain led Garrangia below, complimenting him upon his promptness, & Vendobi was put in Irons at once. He was then taken into the Cabin, where by this time the Missionaries, who had followed in their own canoe, & most of the Officers were assembled in a sort of council to question Vendobi, & to announce to him that he was to be taken to America, for it seemed that the King & all of them could hardly believe our object to [be] any thing else than to kill him at once.

The King & Phillips said that we were doing what was right in taking their Brother away, that they did not blame us, and that now they were satisfied that the thing had been accomplished in the easiest manner. They were quite reconciled to the Captain, & while they expressed much sorrow at losing Vendobi, they were no longer angry, but very sad.

Vendobi's face was painted black, not according to any custom for such an unfortunate occasion, but merely after the every day fashions of the Islands. He was very much dejected, and this additional gloom threw a more mournful cast over his countenance, so that he looked as solemn & woe begone as the most sensitive observer could have desired. He did not deny his crime nor disown the motives which had led him to it. All that he had to say was that he had only followed the Fegee customs & done what his people had often done before!

The Captain assured the King, that no harm would befal Vendobi, even in America, but after keeping him there for some years & showing him every thing, he would be brought back to his Home, a better man and with the Knowledge that to kill a white person was the very worst thing a Fegee man could do; that he would be taught to speak our language & learned our ways & that in the end, he would be a great benefit to his own people by being able to tell them all about us, how rich & great a people we were, & how, by a peaceful & honest intercourse, every thing that a Fegee man wanted would be brought to their shores, &c. &c.

They would scarcely believe that such mercy & kindness would be extended to one who had killed so many of our countrymen in cold blood. They thought that the *"big chief"* at home would not be so disposed but would want *life for life*. The King & Phillips asked every one of us about this, & though they were told over & over again that the killing of Vendobi in America would be of no possible satisfaction to any body, but that the keeping him alive & endeavouring to make him good might produce the best results, they were in some doubt to the last moment they remained on board. We told them that if he had been taken soon after the massacre, he would have been hung or shot as an example, but that now we would try the milder & more merciful plan of sparing his life.

They exhibited a great deal of feeling when about to part, and we actually beheld the singular spectacle of a group of savages in Tears. The old Governor sobbed aloud & made such a fuss & display of his weeping as to create a doubt whether his sorrow was real or feigned. I suspect that like a true courtier, he looked to effect. But there was something manly & dignified in the grief of the King, which no one could sneer at or disturb, & the scene was one which certainly made *me* feel queer & the singular interest of which I shall never forget.

The King promised Vendobi that his wives & property should be kept for him, until he came back. And the Monarch also gave his fallen brother much excellent advice & a little reproof. He exhorted him to conduct himself properly, to keep his heart big with the thought of his return, to learn all that he could among the Papalangis & much more to the same purpose. He also said that he had often warned him to let the White people alone & do them no harm, but his words had not been heeded, but now all could see their truth.

And thus Vendobi, who but yesterday was a chief of the blood royal of Fegee, with 55 wives & scores of children, with whole Islands & many villages under his sway, became a solitary prisoner with Irons on his limbs to a people of whose ways he had the most superstitious & confused ideas, natural to one of his race.

The Royal party received more presents, but they took them with a listless air, and as soon as the farewells were over, they hurried to leave the Ship they had approached with so much delight.

When we first came to the Islands, we made particular inquiries about the existence & prevalence of Cannibalism among the people. We knew they had the credit of indulging their tastes in that way but were anxious to have the thing settled, without a doubt. I remember reading in some book of travels the assertion of the author that he considered all the accounts of such a practice among any people, to be fabulous, the bug bear stories of voyagers who delighted in tales of the marvellous; that he did not believe mankind could be so vile, or human nature so degraded; in short, that there was no such thing as a People who fed upon men for the love of it. If this gentleman, who had such exceeding faith in the goodness of human kind, had been killed in Fegee, *his ghost* would have corrected his notions with a vengeance.

The white men told us that the eating of men, women & children was common all over the Islands; that prisoners & the slain in war were so disposed of; that they had seldom seen anything of the kind, because the natives did it in secret, knowing the horror the Papalangis entertained of the practice, but it was a well known fact, beyond dispute; and that in all likelihood we could judge for ourselves ere we left the Islands.

One story they told of this same Tuindrecate, whom they considered a Cannibal of the first order, was that he was out in his Canoe & saw an old woman fishing on the reef. Saying that he should like a meal of that kind, he ran his Canoe on the reef, killed the woman & cooked her at once. Mr. Wynn, the mate of the *Leonidas,* told me that he was sleeping at Rahwah one night in Phillips' house when a meal of this kind was preparing & that he waited until he saw the pieces of the body taken from the oven, when he quit the spot.

The D[octo]r,[2] who is writing a very full history of the cruize, & several others were at Vendobi & Paddy all day long, drawing from them the legends & wonders of Fegee. And indeed there was a singular interest & charm in listening to the tales of that strange old man. I have sat down by him for hours & never was aweary, & he often said that if all he had seen & thought & gone through with could be put in a book, it would be fit for the Queen to read & would be very curious to every body. It is time you were introduced to him, & so I'll tell you all that I know about him.

Pat Connel was at this time about 75 or 7 years old. He was born in the "County Cavin, Sir," Ireland, & joined the French troops when they came over; was taken & put to jail; was sent on board a convict Ship for Botany Bay *by mistake,* & when he landed there his name was not on the roll, nor was there any evidence of any crime against him! He was allowed the range & shipped aboard a French Vessel mounting guns & carrying a large crew. When they got to Sea, they did not like the way things went on aboard her & suspected she was a Pirate. So in passing between the Fegee Islands, 30 of the crew left the Ship with their arms to try their fortunes on shore.

They landed at Old Snuff's town, who was then at war with his neighbours, & was much rejoiced to find this body of white men so opportunely thrown on his shores. He received them well. They went with him on his expeditions & contributed greatly to their success. It was in the year 1800 that this little army of whites turned Crusaders in Fegee, at which time there were no others of their colour on the Islands. They soon dispersed when Snuff's combats ceased for a time. Many left the Islands in passing Ships, & the rest scattered over the group. Pat remained with Snuff, who gave him many wives & slaves, & they fought together in more battles than Pat could remember.

Pat was short in stature, below the common height. He was not stout, nor was there anything singular in his appearance except his long gray beard, which was his mark as a warrior & which he regarded as the apple of his eye. He tied the end in a knot, & at one time when he had not cut it for 20 years, he carried it round his body in two parts & knotted them in front at his waist, so that it was long enough to trail on the ground & was *fiery red,* to the great envy of all the Fegee men. He had been very healthy all his life & now was hale & active; his eye was remarkably clear & bright. Pat said he had in all 150 wives, as well as he could recollect, and only 45 *"childer."* At present he had 3 wives. He wished he could live to be 100 years old & fill up the number of his children to 50.

He had also 2 or 3 muskets that had never been properly used yet, & if he could kill a few Fegees with them, he would feel ready to die. He had no wish to go home. He had outlived, he supposed, all his kin, & no one would know the old man, if he was to return. No, he had a name among the Fegees, he would die there & there he would be buried, but he should like to have a little out of the "Book" read over him, if there would be any body to do it.

Pat had all the richness of the brogue upon his tongue and possessed a great deal of the humour which is so common a characteristic of his countrymen. His mode of expressing himself was amusing & very interesting, for the flowery & metaphorical style of the people with whom he had lived so long was strangely mingled with his original fancy; & his speech was always ready & unconstrained. We suspected him of *romancing* a little, but we never detected him in a falsehood, & if he did colour any transactions of his own too highly or exaggerate in his accounts of the Customs of the Natives, there were no witnesses against him, & we could not separate the truth from the fable. So that what I learnt from him, I shall record, but it is impossible to attach to any narrative the like charm which it possesses, when heard from the lips of Sinbad himself. Some of his yarns were of subjects entirely excluded from these pages, but which are matters of discourse among men.

I one day overheard him singing to himself a line or two of "Sa vour nan Deelish"[3]—something about "escaped from the Slaughter." It struck my ear at once. He said he remembered it was part of a song he had often heard in the *"ould country,"* but he could not think what it was called, until I told him, when he recollected it at once, & asked me to get him a copy of the verses. 'Twas strange that through those long, long years of absence from his country & of absolute banishment from even the sight of any of his race, the old man's memory had preserved the words of the air which had been music to him in his childhood.

Pat had a Cutlass with him of excellent metal with which, he said, he had killed seven men, and he would never move from the Ship without his old Cheese Knife. With musquets he had shot 200 Fegees at least. He always told the natives that *his* God did not like *his* people to eat the flesh of men, & they, in their superstition, regarded the anger of his god, & he was excused from their feasts. He never allowed his Children to partake either of this diet, and once, when one of his sons, *by mistake,* did swallow some, he was sick for a month & brought his Father presents to offer to his God that he might be forgiven.

As we sailed along in the Ship, we were to *"fix in"* the Islands, reefs, &c., as accurately as we could by a running Survey. And all hands of us were on deck a dozen times a day with Sextants & chronometers & patent logs.[4] Vendobi was allowed to take the air on deck, attended by the Sentry, & he used to watch our operations with a surprise that he could not contain. He was told that we were making pictures of the Land, so that other ships would know where to go as well as the natives, who lived on the Islands. But it was all mysterious to him; and when he looked at the Chronometer & heard the tick, regular & unceasing, & saw the motion of the hands, he said aloud "that we must be spirits & not men, for here was something moving & speaking to us, while no one touched it." He said "that the Ship was like the Fegee land of Spirits—so clean & quiet, so many Chiefs, and all behaving so well!"

On the evening of the 26th, we entered a passage in the reef & anchored near the shore. Our way was now to lay close by the Land & inside the reef. The natives all along the Coast where we were anchored had a bad character for treachery & hatred of whites, insomuch that none of the White men who lived among the Islands ever ventured on shore in this neighbourhood. We fired a Gun at 8 in the evening & at daylight & sent up rockets, which are objects of much dread to all savages all the while we were cruising about, to let the folks know that the Man of War was at hand. I had the first watch that night, & though we had no idea that our ship would be approached, there was no lack of vigilance or caution on my part. We saw many fires along the Shore & could hear the people hollowing all night long.

The next morning we weighed & stood along the Island, surveying as we went along, the Pilot looking out from the Topsail Yard for shoals & rocks, which lined the way. About 4 in the afternoon we struck on a coral lump, the sun light upon the water preventing it from being seen in time to avoid it. We kedged off without any difficulty and anchored for the night.

Next morning the Launch & 1st Cutter came in sight and alongside. They had surveyed up to a point some miles ahead, & where a Bich la mar house belonging to the *Leonidas* was standing. The wind was dead ahead, the passage narrow, & we had a tedious beat of it all day long; our advance was so slight that we could hardly perceive it. At 4 P.M. the Launch capsized & sunk with two men in her, so that we hove to & anchored at once. The men were saved & some of the things that floated from the Launch, but she was gone to the bottom & not to be found. We only made one or two miles in all this day.

Next morning was calm & hot. 4 boats were sweeping for the Launch, with lines & sinkers let down to the bottom and dragged about. I was in one, but we had no success, and as *we thought* we had no time to lose, we weighed at 11 & commenced looking to windward leaving Emmons & Simon with the Boats to try and get a hold of the Launch & then buoy their line. At Sundown we had scratched up to the Bich la mar house and came to for the night. I had the first watch, & it was late when Simon came on board. Their attempts had been in vain.

Early in the morning our surviving boats were sent in shore to bring off the wood which had been cut for the drying of the Bich le Mar, but not used. When the Boats returned, we up anchor & had to beat all day in very short tacks, & surveying as we proceeded. We had near views of the shores to be sure, but they were not very interesting, & the progress was slow & weary in the extreme. The next day was Sunday the 31st May. The Captain read his sermon as usual, though he chose a short one, and as soon as he finished, it was up anchor, & try it again, the wind still being dead ahead & the passage narrow as ever. June 1st, the same—weighed at daylight—obliged to anchor at 8—tried again at 10—lost ground & came to, at 12.

Here a party of us went ashore, as the Natives were not bad, although we took care to be well armed & to keep together. Indeed, all over Fegee it is necessary to have your weapons with you, and the Natives themselves never move without their spear or club. They are divided into many parties & are so continually at war that they are always on their guard against surprise & never enjoy the indolent & careless repose of a peaceful people.

We had a long pull, and were obliged to land on a mud flat some distance from the Mangroves. The Village was not visible, being in the rear of these Mangroves & completely screened by them from the view from seaward. The only approach was by a narrow path, to which we were guided by the people. We went to the Chief's house at once. The old man received us very kindly, & we made him some presents. He said he had been off near the Ship the night before, but seeing so many men start up to furl sail, he got frightened & would not venture on board. The Village was small, & we saw that our party was a match for all the men in it, so that we rambled about with more confidence.

In the rear of the town the land had a gentle ascent to the foot of the hills, & several sluggish streams wound along towards the sea, by means of which the Natives irrigated the Tarro patches & which served as hiding places for their Canoes. The girls all ran back among the trees & grass & we had some fun chasing them. On making a few presents, they came in for their share at once. Simon Blunt & I bought a few pearls of small size, but which I had rather have in a ring than more precious ones obtained by mere purchase from a Jeweller.

[The next day] we weighed, as usual, as soon as it was light enough to see our way. The passage here was so very constricted that the Ship had scarcely room to turn round, & we tacked with our Jib boom almost touching the bushes. When the Tide changed and came against us, we had to anchor, having only made 2 miles.

As we were safe for the day, Guillou, Simon, & I with several others went up to the top of [an] Island from whence we had an extended view, the prettiest portions of which were the shining rivers curling like silver serpents through the country at our feet. On the very summit we made a fire round a Pandanus tree & soon had a blaze that might have been seen for miles. The natives often set fire to the long grass to clear the land for their yam patches, & some times we would see miles of the shore in a Conflagration, sending up smoke enough to darken the sky. By night their fires had a fine effect.

Next day June 3rd, we weighed again with the same everlasting head wind. After working into a narrow channel, had to run back & try another—got through it & kept away with a fair wind, intending to run over to Sandal Wood Bay, on the large Island called Veuna Leb. The Patent log was put over, & we congratulated ourselves upon getting sea room once more after the seven days of tedious & harassing beating that had annoyed us so much.

Well we were spanking it off 7 knots, and all hands ready for angling, when, smacko! the ship brought up on a shoal, all standing, and stuck fast. I & some others were seated on the

Taffrail, sextants in hand, and at first we did not get down to mingle in the duty that was going on in endeavouring to get the Ship off, thinking that she would go clear in a minute, & our observations be resumed, for we did not anticipate any stoppage until we let go our anchor in Sandal Wood bay. But "there's many a slip, &c." She did swing off this shoal but struck another, again & again. This was becoming too hot, & we put our sextants away & went to work. With some trouble & delay, we at last got extricated from the labyrinth of shoals in which we had become jammed, but 'twas then too late in the day to run on, & we had to come to near an uninhabited Island for the night.

June 4th: had to remain all day at this anchorage. The men swear that there is a Jonah on board, and that the said Jonah is the Rev. Mr. E[lliot]t.[5]

June 5th—Weather thick, but wind fair—get underweigh & have an anxious time running over. Find the passage without much difficulty, & anchor in Sandal Wood Bay. See a Boat off the harbour, which I recognize to be the *Vincennes'*. Expect to hear news, and so we *do,* with a vengeance. Underwood comes alongside & delivers his budget—Captain Belcher[6] of the English navy had anchored in Rahwah just after we left it, with the loss of his rudder. He was from the North West coast of America via Sandwich Islands, Marquesas & Otaheite. He had surveyed about the Columbia River & all along the coast & gave a terrible account of the difficulties & dangers of the place; said that it was absolutely impossible to remain there after October.

This upset our plans, or at least we conjectured that it would, & we at once supposed that we would continue among this group for several months & give up the North West coast until next Spring; that we would be employed there until August at least, which would make us *three years out,* & then we would be *nine months longer* in *getting Home.* All this came at once, and was consoling indeed! We did stay 3 months at the Fegees, & the rest is still to us mystery & conjecture.

The object of Underwood's coming was to get our spare rudder braces[7] for the repair of Belcher's vessel. Captain Wilkes had gone to Rahwah in the *Flying Fish* to see him, and a pretty pair of scamps they were. But Belcher has an astonishing mind & a vast genius. His Officers, who hated him, said that his varied acquirements & his energy & perseverance in every thing he undertook were really marvellous, but that he had no feeling for any human being in the world. *Our* Sweet Master, we are completely persuaded, is a grand humbug & a consummate fool.

[CHAPTER 13: PORTENTS]

[Returning from another exhausting tour of boat duty, we] saw a Ship at anchor close to Rock Island. First thought it must be Captain Belcher—then the *Vincennes*—but at last made her out *Peacock*. Continued our work until sundown, & the 1st Cutter getting jammed among shoals, we did not get on board until 7. This was the 3rd of July, and our 12th day out.

I felt the most curious sensations on stepping on the Ship's deck. The little motion which she had at her anchor was so different from the quick & irregular jumping of the boats that I tottered, lost my balance & staggered as a drunken man. We had a hearty welcome from all hands & were quite glad to be back. The Ship, we learned, was on her way to Sandal Wood Bay again to meet the *Vincennes* there.

But we had the most horrible tales to listen to. The mate of the *Leonidas*[1] had been blown almost to pieces while firing the guns of that ship to measure a base[2] for our boats. He had the Cartridge containing several pounds of powder in *the Bosom* of his Shirt. A spark from the touch hole caught it & the whole exploded, burning him like a cinder. He was brought 20 miles in a boat to the Ship, and at this time was lying in a cot on the open deck, the most ghastly & sickening sight, that ever met my eyes and so offensive that no one but Dr. G[uillou] could bear to be near him.

He was a very tall, thin man with prominent features & large bones. They had him completely covered with large patches of linen steeped in oil—face, limbs & all, so that he looked like a loathsome image of stained marble. Oh! 'twas piteous to see him so, & know that he was living. Death then would have been a mercy to the miserable suffering man, but he lingered on in the most intense pain & groaning continually, so that no one could rest in the Ship. And this was one yarn.

This same morning of the 3rd July, while the Ship was off Tavia, [the young chief] Nadembi, his Wife & 3 canoes full of natives came on board. They said they had taken three prisoners, belonging to the town on Wylea Rock, & had roasted them & eaten part! Nadembi's Wife was the first to speak of it, & she said that two of the bodies had been sent over to Noloa Island, where there was to be a grand feast, and that part of the third was in the Canoe, wrapped up in plantain leaves.

The infernal devils were eager to show their Hellish food, and they held up the flesh in the Canoe alongside, that it might be seen. Not content with this, they brought a skull on board, all raw & bloody, with the marks of their teeth where they had torn away strips of flesh, and one of their Epicures was crunching *an Eye,* to which was hanging some of the fat & muscles of the face & cheek. This scull & Eye were bought, and then they were cleared out of the Ship in all haste, for every body turned from them in utter disgust. And this was the second yarn.

Every body in the Ship seemed oppressed with a weight of horror, & there was a crushing & awfully nervous feeling came over me, which I could not shake off.

It was well we were hungry. We had eat nothing all day, and now, there was seen a Table set out for us, which we fell upon tooth & nail. I cracked a bottle of good wine, & we tried to get gay in spite of the general gloom. We could not help speaking & dwelling upon *those* things, but my appetite prevailed & I eat on through it all, but never wish to be so fixed again. A sensitive man would have gone into hystericks.

While at the table, Budd[3] came to me to say that we were to start at daylight again for 8 days' time. So I soon turned in to my cot, but I did not rest well. I was dreaming all night, and Home was strangely mingled with the occurrences of the previous day.

I was up at early dawn. The first thing that caught my eye was the ashy white figure of the Mate. I went forward & looked at the Skull. God! to think that *this* had but a day or two ago contained a cunning brain!

I had some Coffee made for me & sat down to sip it, sad because I should miss the turtle steaks that were cooking for breakfast. The quarter master came with a message from the Captain to hurry and be off, and the men commenced tramping around the Capstan in the first operation of getting the Ship underweigh. All at once there was a shriek, a smothered cry of anguish & pain, and then many voices cried out that a man's head was smashed between the Capstan bars & bulkhead. I set the cup down, crossed over to the Doctor's room, called him from his sleep, told him, that a man's head had been crushed on deck and seated myself to my coffee again. The Doctor was on deck in a twinkling in his ———. The shrieks still continued, but rather strong, as I thought, to come from a man with a broken skull, and as it turned out, it was his ribs that suffered not his head.

I am not destitute of feeling, not without that strange sort of curiosity that attracts men to look upon such spectacles, but on board ship one learns to subdue his feelings & not to run his nose where he can be of no service. If I had gone on deck, I should have lost my coffee, which I needed; I would have been in the way; and my boat would not have been ready as soon as she was. It did require an effort to remain below with such cries in my ear & the idea that the man was in such agony and in the last throes of life, but one learns to make such efforts in the course of a few years amid the vicissitudes of a sea life.

That there was a Jonas on board the Ship was now the open belief of the men, & they swore we should never have luck until *he* left her decks. Just before we got into Mudwater the first time in the Ship, there was a bloody accident on board which I have not mentioned. There was something wrong about the Anchor when it was hove up, & it was necessary to slack it down a little. In the absence of the Lieutenants, I was fighting Captain of the Forecastle[4] and made the necessary report to the 1st Luff, who gave the orders to those on the Gun deck, so that they might let the Chain run out.

The ponderous Anchor started and descended slowly, when it was suddenly arrested & cries of a person[5] in an agony of pain gave us warning that some poor fellow was suffering in some of his limbs. A man in lifting up the Iron lid of the Compressor[6] let it fall upon his hand, which became instantly jammed by the Chain with the whole weight of the Anchor to it. The Anchor was stopped from moving, but it was not until the men were sent to the bars & could heave around again that he was extricated, & then three of his fingers were dangling by parts of the skin! He was given to the Doctors, & the duty went on as before.

In addition to these disasters, head winds, & thumping on shoals, John Williams shot his fore finger in two, & Jim Hughes cut his leg almost off. So that the men had fair reason to think the Ship bewitched, & they abused the Parson more than ever.

So on this 4th of July, we shoved off from the Ship to work up to Mudwater & join her in Sandal Wood bay. She was already underweigh when we left. We had Mr. Wynn with us this time as Pilot & interpreter. I was in a singular mood. The little relaxation from duty & watch, the yarns & sights on board, the sleep in the cot—all seemed to me as a dream which had never been reality. The "Main brace" had been spliced on board before we left, by way of celebrating the day, & my coxswain was most patriotically fuddled already.

It was 10 o'clock before our breakfast was ready, & until then, I was in the most vindictive humour imaginable, growling "like a Bear with a sore head," according to the elegant phraseology of Jack nasty face.[7] I could not help thinking of the fun that was going on at Home, and was very disgusted with my present situation.

We often talked in very sadness of the good things in Season at Home. The early vegetables of Spring, the fruits of Summer, the cool room, the siesta after dinner, and the walk at evening with the girls. Oh! the miserable contrasts in Fegee. In open boats exposed to sun, wind, rain & seas; living on the coarsest food & in the rudest manner; and with no company save our own wretched selves. I have sometimes felt so lonely, so entirely cut off from any human being that I could communicate with, as almost to think myself destitute of all earthly ties. Solitude would never suit me.

We anchored that night close to a small Island near Mudwater. My Boat leaked so badly again, that this night I had to bale her out to keep my bed dry. So early in the morning we hauled her on the beach to nail lead over the leak. I planted a Sentry over the things which were strewn about the grass & to keep a lookout on the bushes, for I knew that the natives about here were very suspicious that we intended them mischief, & perhaps they might be disposed to begin the fun themselves. However, it was necessary to have some one watch while the rest worked, & John Theodore Beaton[8] & myself, armed to the teeth, were vigilant, all for nothing. We saw no people, & the houses were all cleaned out & deserted.

Presently a canoe came along from the main shore, & after Mr. Wynn told them what we were about & asked them to come ashore, they ventured to land. There were only 5 or 6 men in her. The first who approached was a young man of 22, & the Chief of the Island. He knew Mr. Wynn & lost all fear at once. He said that last night, when his people saw the boats coming to the Island, they were very much frightened & thought we were going to destroy the Town. So they packed up all their things & left in their Canoes for the Main land, where they hid themselves. He had remained until Midnight, when he could not stand it any longer & left also. As he saw us haul the boat up from where he was, he thought there would be no harm in coming over to see what we were about.

We soon became quite sociable, & I showed him all the wonders we had with us. He made his men throw down Cocoa Nuts for us & sent his Canoe to tell his people to come back & bring some Pigs. Some of them came over, among them being pretty damsels with whom we had a grand romp. We bought their pig & some trifles—I got a Fegee comb with one tooth.

After the boat was finished, we surveyed a small harbour & then went to some shoals, after which beat up to Mudwater against a fresh breeze & strong flaws—men all down in the bottom of the boat.

We anchored a little before Sundown. Budd, Mr. Wynn & myself went ashore by way of amusement. Had to wade over the flat, which was monstrous bad, as we were carrying arms & the mud was soft & sticky & the water over our knees. Going to the King's [house], we saw an immense pile of yams enclosed with posts & wicker works, which was taubood for a grand feast to be given to the Somi Somi people, whom the King's son had gone to invite.

We paid a visit to his Majesty, & he promised we should have a Pig & some yams in the morning, for as these people are so continually at war, they have not the greatest profusion of live stock & do not part with it readily. Captain Eagleston[9] told me he had been two months without getting even a Pig. As to Chickens, you *hear* one sometimes, & you may possibly have the luck to buy a straggler. Of other birds, there are none.

From the King's, we went to his Fegee Wife's house—an old fat woman, who shared the honors of Queen with Henrietta, the Rotomah woman. This old creature was very curious to know if we were Chiefs in America? Why we carried arms? Said we were tall, good looking men, and overhauled us from stem to stern. Next we called on Henrietta, & had a chat with her.

She had been the Wife of a Tahiti man, who was on board Captain Eagleston's Ship at that time, 8 or 11 years ago, & had gone to Tahiti, but not liking to live there, her husband humoured her, & they set out to return to Rotumah with Captain Eagleston. At Mudwater, an old & villianous countryman of her own, who was in high favor with the King, persuaded her to stop ashore, and her husband pleased her in this also, though Captain Eagleston advised both to the contrary. Very soon this old Rotumah man had the Tahitian put to death, & Henrietta became the King's wife. I never saw a more rascally face than the old Devil's. Villiany was written in every feature, & the expression was so malignant & fiendish that you could not look at him without wishing to shoot him.

We strolled about the Town a little by the bright moon light, but met with no adventures & returned to the boats with a good appetite for Supper. In the morning Budd & Hudson went ashore, and I laid myself out most luxuriously in the stern sheets of the Cutter, & thought of *Home*. It was delicious!

After breakfast, we went over to Mudwater Island & there waited to get the Latitude with a great crowd round. Budd bought a club with 40 notches in it, each one for a man killed by it. Some of these Natives were very tall & powerful. I would scarcely have made a meal for one of them. One big gentleman

& myself chopped up a piece of wood together with mutual compliments in pantomime, & I skylarked with some old women to their infinite delight.

We anchored that night under Bonsai Island again. In the morning all the people were gone, not one to be seen. They did not like our movements. At Mudwater they said, "We were like birds, continually going & coming."

Next day we went to Rab Rab Island, starting at daylight. We did not cook any breakfast and it was 12 o'clock before we stopped to eat. We had to save the tide, but such fasting was very disagreeable—a man cannot work on an empty stomach. After our meal we ascended Rab Rab Island to make a Sketch of the Shoals that lay all about, as thick as the sands on the Shore. The men soon had a fire underweigh in a place that was sheltered from the strong gusts of wind by a high wall of rocks. The Mudwater Pig was killed & made ready for the Pot in the evening.

We left Rab Rab Island after 3 & beat round into a Bay that was close by, where we anchored close to the shore. There was a Village here, & the natives soon showed them selves on the beach—at first three, one with a Musket. I pointed the Spy glass toward them, & away they scampered in to the Man-groves. By & by more appeared & the Cutter coming in, Mr. Wynn struck up a conversation with them. Now the yams were cut up, the salt pork & pig all ready for the Pot, & we were all thinking of our supper, when the man who was giving our Iron Cauldron a reach overboard let it slip from his hands, & down it went—gone beyond redemption. With it went all our hopes. We had nothing else except a frying pan, & that was only use-ful as an auxiliary, but would not serve for us all.

Terror & dismay sat on every face—hope fled. The Supper was lost, we could have no more of our favorite Stews & we were wretched, for two minutes at least. However, we lashed a Boat hook to a long staff and tried to fish it up without success, when the thought occurred to get a native to dive for it. This was caught at, at once, & hope revived.

Mr. Wynn went with me in the Boat, and we pulled into the beach, where we found the Chief & made known our distress and our want, promising a reward to the diver, whether he recovered the treasure or not. After some little noise & talk, the Chief himself & one other got into the boat & went off with us. Never were persons more anxious than we. The Chief himself went down by the pole that we had touching the pot, but he came to the surface empty handed. It was nearly dark, & he said he could not see—but he might have felt, we thought. He went down once more but with the like ill luck & then gave up the attempt, to the infinite predjudice of our appetites & to our utter disappointment. However, he promised to bring a Diver who understood the art early in the morning, & he would get our pot without any trouble at all. With sorrowful hearts, we set the frying pan on the fire, & were obliged to be content with a scanty meal.

The chief, whose name was Dowdina, was young & very lively & good natured. He told us that he had a very fine Village, that he liked the white men, & that his people had always liked the white men; that when the Ship* was wrecked here, *"None of the crew were killed."* This was a singular but excellent recommendation & intended to have weight. He wanted us to go ashore & see his town. He remained in the Boat as hostage & we landed. And this was the most singular nocturnal adventure that ever I engaged in. When we returned, we set Dowdina on shore, reminding him about the Diver in the morning, and we also told him to have a Pig baked for us after his own fashion.

At day light, I went in the boat & brought off the Diver, who made no hesitation & brought up the Pot, at the first trial. Great was the joy, and the stew was set on at once. As soon as this was happily over, I went to the head of the harbour in the *Polly* to fill the water breakers. I shouldered a cutlass & followed the men. We had to go over a narrow, winding & rough path for ½ a mile back in the country, before we came to the Spring. The grass was up to our heads & wet with the dew of the morning. The natives were with us, & we got them to carry the breakers when they were filled. The larger ones were so

*The *Glyde* went ashore in a Gale—property taken, lives spared. Her Guns were mounted round the Booruia house at Mudwater—one in Henrietta's yard.

heavy that they had to be lashed to poles. As we had no rope, the Natives used a vine, which answered just as well.

When all were down at the beach & ready to go off to the boat, I observed that one of the men was missing, and on enquiring, ascertained that he had carried a small breaker to the spring among the foremost, set it down, & cleared out without a word, I did not think any body would be fool enough to desert in Fegee, even at a place where never had a White Man been killed. But supposing he had lost his way, I sent the Natives to find him, & show him the way to the boats, along the beach. After which I shoved off, & breakfast was waiting, when we got to the Cutter. No signs of McBride,[10] the absentee, during the meal, so we offered a reward to Dowdina for his apprehension, & the Natives darted off like so many bloodhounds. Dowdina brought us the baked Pig, and then we commenced to survey the harbour, which we finished by meridian, but still no sign of our runaway.

We determined to wait until 2 o'clock and to go ashore in the mean while to see the Village. Here again were the huge trees, with the spreading branches: the stately Cocoas, the wide leafed bannana, the winding paths; the green sward steeped in the sunshine; the groups of brown skinned people; the scattered huts; the background of hills in luxuriant verdure & the clear blue sky over all!

Every thing was clean here. There was neither mud nor dust; the houses were neat; the very pigs were free from earthy incrustations. We were so enchanted that we almost determined to stay all day and take our rest amid the groves, where there was so much to admire, & which I was reluctant to leave so soon. I did wish, from my very heart, that it might come on to blow hard & detain us, for the people seemed to have more of the milk of human kindness than any we had been among before, & they were eager to have us stop with them, that they might show us how good they were.

Although the town was screened from the water by the mangroves, so that you could not see a house even when close to the beach, openings were so arranged as to afford a view of the Sea & all along the Coast to those on shore, while they were invisible from without. A deep ditch ran along the inner edges of the mangroves by which the path led that took us to the heart of the Village. There were many low walls of stone grown over with grass & moss, and on one of these, leaning against the trunk of one of those huge trees that reminded me so much of our oaks, was the Old Chief, Dowdina's father, surrounded by a dusky crowd of both sexes & all ages. He bid us welcome & told us, in the words of his son, that white men had never been harmed in his town! He had always liked the Whites & had always taken care of them. When the Ship was wrecked, he would not let one be touched, but sent them away in Safety. He admired our arms very much, & my mysterious gun was the wonder of all. It loaded at the breech, without ramming, & at his request I shot it off & charged it again in a second without rising from my seat. It had a long bayonet, & they thought with such a weapon a man ought to be invincible.

He set the young girls dancing for us. 10 or 12 of them got up in two files: motions slow & regular as machinery, gestures decent & very graceful. The performers were all in full dress, which was *no dress at all* except the slight *"hlígoó,"*[11] & they added their fine voices to those of a horde of children, who were also beating the ground with sticks & making a hollow noise by clapping their hands. The dancing continued until we were ready to go, & we enriched the nymphs with beads, so that their eyes sparkled with joy. But there were none like the sweet Emma of Upolu. I shall never see her like again.

Dowdina was gone to his yam planting, & the men who were in search of McBride had not returned, so we left the Village with most unwilling steps, the Old Chief promising that McBride should be sent to Sandal Wood Bay as soon as he was caught.

We made sail for the small sandy Island, where we had tarried for a night before, & anchored there after dark, when we made a finish of the baked Pig & turned in as we were accustomed to, before 8 o'clock. Long before this I altered the awning, so that we could haul it close over the boat, with a ridge, tent fashion. This kept us warm, but we could not move about, &c. I was the only one who could sit upright.

We had had no rain as yet to incommode us—once or twice
a light sprinkling, & no more. So that in this respect we were
very fortunate & very thankful. We were always ready to go to
roost as soon as our evening meal was ended, & the covers
were hauled over forthwith—my boat moored astern of the
Cutter; the lanthorn lit; arms all ready; the watch set; and every
man to his pillow. We managed to Sleep, but a good night's rest
I never knew until, after 20 days of absence, I found myself in
my good old Cot.

As we had only a little work to do to day, & that down about
the everlasting Monkey face passage,[12] we roused up at 4 o'clock
& got underweigh with a light breeze to save the tide. We expected to get to the Ship by night, though she was nearly 40
miles distant. The Sun rose with a misty look & soon the
breeze freshened to as much as we could carry to. But it was
right aft; the boats flew, and after a ticklish time, we got thro'
the passage once more & stopped to breakfast at 9, having
managed to keep up a fire notwithstanding a sharp rain-squall
& the spray from the seas that broke over the boat.

After breakfast, we pushed on. The rain fell again, the wind
blew strong in squalls, & was now from the trending of the
land no longer favorable. We stopped at a Point in Rooka
Rook bay to get the Latitude, but the rain continuing, we
missed it, and made sail again across the mouth of the Bay, just
able to head for the other point. Now every thing got wet in the
Boat. She almost went under in the short Seas, & it was truly
pleasant to sit still & take it all.

When we passed the farther point of the bay, matters grew
worse. The Seas had a fairer sweep at us, & the Squalls were
harder than ever. I put my mark on a snug cove as we went by
it & thought it most likely, that we should pass the night *there*
& not on board the Ship, though she was only 5 or 6 miles off.
I carried the whole sail on the boat, and she tore through the
Seas in a way that was frightful. Presently we saw a Boat coming round a point ahead before the wind, with her sail *reefed*. I
gave up now all hope of getting to the Ship, for if that boat had
to carry a reef in her sail with the wind aft, we could do nothing with a head wind after we got to the point.

We thought she had orders for us to remain out longer & were anxious with the expectation until we met. Case & Simon were in the boat, bound to Somi Somi, for yams. They had a Missionary, Cunningham & two natives, besides the crew, so that they were deep & had no room to stow at night. The boat was most imperfectly fitted out but was thus sent off by Captain Wilkes in the very height of a Gale of Wind. She soon passed us, & not long afterwards, they carried away every thing & were indebted to the *Leonidas* for the necessary repairs, which had been denied them aboard our own Ships.

Very soon after we spoke them, I saw that it would be madness to risk the Boat any more, for she could not win an inch, & the Seas were frightful. So I tacked & stood in Shore to meet Budd & tell him I could stand it no longer, but must seek a Shelter. We had not been about 3 minutes before a heavy flaw struck us, the mast snapped like glass & down came sail & all. We hauled in the wreck & took to the oars. The Cutter saw us, & we both kept away together & stood for the very cove I had picked out, & in which we anchored soon after.

No village here—quiet & solitary as if just created. I landed on a fine beach: climbed the Cocoa Nut trees, bathed, raced along the beach, basked in the Sun, shot off all the arms, cracked lizards' eggs to see the infant reptiles skip away, perfect at their birth, and was merry as a lark now that my condition was so changed. The Sky cleared off; there was no more rain, but the blow continued hard as ever.

When I was tired of the Shore, we went alongside the Cutter, and one of the men had just hooked a tremendous Rock Cod. The water was clear, & he could see him very plainly. It required much care & skill to secure him, & while my mouth watered at the thought of a chowder for supper, my heart was sore afraid that I would be disappointed, but the lucky fisherman was no novice. He took a short boat hook & when his prize floundered to the Surface, with a quick & sudden thrust he sent the Iron through its jaw & hauled it in in a trice.

We had killed a Pig, but it was voted to keep him & cook the fish at once. That scouse with Lemon juice was delicious— finished the Whiskey; much to the universal sorrow it was gone.

In the mean time, the mast had been fished, as well as the means we had allowed.

Rain fell during the night, & we did not sleep well. Early in the morning we got underweigh to try again, & I rigged an oar for an outrigger to aid in supporting the mast, but the wind proved too fresh—had to douse the mast & take to the oars. Soon found we could make no progress—kept away & run back to Dillon's Island in Nuco Murray Bay to get Latitude—now got in breakfast—Sun obscured & rain—no observation—left & went into our cove again for the night—rain & blowing hard as ever.

Next morning, July 11th, we made an early start again. Heard the Ship's Gun at daylight—take to the oars—1st Cutter, both sail & oars—get along very well—tremendous swell, but less wind—open the Ships. Pull for 4 hours ere we get alongside—much as the Boat could do, to swim, the seas were so short & high, & the wind blew again in fresh squalls. Encourage the men—they pull all they know—at last get on board after a 20 days' cruize. The Cutter was a long distance astern.

There were only two or three officers on board, the rest absent hard at work. Old Emmons was making his chart in the Cabin, & after he welcomed me back, he showed me "Reynolds Bay," so named in honor of my own worthy self. But this was but fleeting fame—Captain Wilkes ordered all such baptisms to be erased, & scores of us were at once scratched into oblivion.

My head, neck, arms, & feet were of a darker hue than James Thomas Gauntt,[13] and as my toilette had been so seldom made in these three weeks, I was in excellent condition to appreciate the luxuries of a complete renovation, from top to toe. I called into instant requisition the Services of Thomas Mizer,[14] my "valet d'state room," & of John Minnie,[15] the barber, & while I was being shaved & dressed & perfumed, I experienced the enjoyment of being cleansed to the very excess. No one can know this, until he has tried, but I would not recommend anyone to go dirty, by way of finding out. Breakfast was made & some hot chocolate, for we had not eaten before we started.

Thus ended this cruize, which was originally limited to 6 days but lasted twenty. Though we did not meet with any perilous adventures, there was some novelty in this way of living, and we got through without much difficulty, & in strong & perfect health. But I am inclined to think that we were away from the Ship quite long enough & that two months passed in such a manner would shorten one's life a year or two at least.

Simon & old Emmons were 40 or 50 days in boats altogether, Perry,[16] Walker, Blair[17] the same, & others two or three weeks. Those who were out so long as 40 days were very much pulled down. They had not fared so well in the grub line as we did, & on this duty one wants just twice as much food as he requires on board. I was very much afraid of getting the Rheumatism from my damp bed, but as it was but with salt water, I never was troubled with any twinges, though every morning I felt cramped up & sore, as if I had been beaten with cudgels.

The 1st Cutter came alongside sometime afterwards, & as soon as Budd rigged himself & got something comfortable in his belly (forgive the word, any whom it offends, for it slipped from my pen, ere I knew, & I will not scratch it out, but leave it to mark how coarse I have become), we went on board the *Vincennes,* & I had the pleasure to meet Alden, Whittle & May, friends whom I esteem as much as I shall ever love my Wife. I dined aboard, & Alden told me he had named an Island after me, one that I was the first to see while we were in the Launch near Cape Horn. It lies between Herschel & Wollaston Islands, so that I am in good company, only with such names Sir Joshua [Reynolds][18] may be thought of, or even Mr. J[eremiah] N. R[eynolds][19] before myself. Captain Wilkes approved of this, for a wonder, & I saw Reynolds Island in all the majesty of large black letters, cheek by jowl with old Cape Horn himself.

We were all conjecturing about our letters at the Sandwich Islands, North West Coast, & all such matters of interest until dark came, & each went to his own ship. I did not sleep well this first night, but was very restless.

[CHAPTER 14: CRIME AND PUNISHMENT]

The next day was Sunday 12th [of July]. We had church on board, as it was blowing too fresh for boats to pass to the *Vincennes,* where the Chaplain of this fleet, (umquhile[1] *Jonas* on board this Ship) was holding forth. If I have mentioned this personage disrespectfully, it is not because he is a clergyman, but because he is any thing but an honor to the cloth he wears— *he is too miserable to despise.*

We saw the *Vincennes'* launch standing into the Bay alone, when she ought to have been attended by her 1st Cutter, & were very anxious to learn what had happened. She went alongside of the *Vincennes,* & some one who came from there brought the news that now spread like wild fire.

"The Cutter had been taken by the Natives of a place only 20 miles distant, & so late as yesterday—no lives lost." We knew that our Expedition would go to recover her and were in a fever of excitement. The two boats had been embayed for several days, unable to beat out of the narrow passage between the reefs, which was the only outlet to the Sea. The natives were watching them, & their stay became so unsafe that on Saturday they made a trial to get out. The Cutter missed stays & went on the reef. Immediately, hundreds of the people poured down from the mangrove bushes, behind which they were following the Boats, & seized her, putting it out of the power of the crew to resist. Indeed, they had only two muskets in the boat, & these with the Pistols were all wet. 6 or 7 cutlasses were nothing among so many Fegees. The blunderbusses which were shipped on the gunwhale were pointed towards the crowd, but they were wet also, & this was only done to gain a little time & secure a retreat.

The Chief said it was "Faca bete" fashion,[2] & he must keep the boat, & he waved his hand for our people to be off without delay. So they had to desert, & they made out to carry with them all the arms except the Musquets, the chronometer, & one sextant—clothes, &c., all left. They tramped along the reef to the Launch unmolested, the Natives being too busy in securing their prize. All got safe aboard the Launch, & then commenced a fire upon the natives with the howitzers & musquets, but the shot fell among them without effect.

It was found impossible to work the Launch out of the passage, and they were obliged to anchor again where the Natives were swarming the reefs on both sides & close aboard. Two Chiefs came off, pretending that they would restore the Boat, if our people would help to launch her, but this was only a decoy, and their artifice failed. They now wanted to go ashore themselves, but this was not permitted. They were made prisoners, and a man by each of them with a Pistol ready cocked. It is most likely that having possession of these Chiefs saved the whole party from massacre.

The next day, Sunday, the Launch was again got underweigh, though the prospect of getting out seemed hopeless. The natives followed them along the reefs, and the least accident would have thrown our poor fellows ashore, only to be murdered. The Launch, loaded down with the extra men, made but slow progress, & they had to carry sail so, that the Seas swept her fore & aft. She just weathered the edge of the reef & was then so full of water & so burthened with sail, that every thing had to be let fly, and all hands go to bailing with Hats, Shoes & buckets to keep her from swamping—5 minutes more, to beat, would have lost her! 'Twas an imminent risk, and none of them breathed freely until they were fairly before the wind.

It was about noon when they got alongside the *Vincennes*. The Sunday was disregarded, and all the boats were hauled up on the beach at once to be repaired, while the Arms were got in readiness. Captain Wilkes intended to Survey this Bay over again & had ordered me to put up signals where we had placed them before. At 2 I shoved off to do this, & at that time, the boats were high & dry, with the Carpenters busy at them. I thought I should surely be back in season to go on the expedition & made all the haste I could, but the wind was so fresh & the distance so far, that I only could get to two stations by Sundown. When I got alongside, Baldwin[3] received me with the most melancholy face in the world & told me that the Boats had been off more than two hours & every body sent but Budd, himself & *me*. I felt as bad as if I had been whipped, & heartily wished Captain Wilkes & his *re*surveying at the ——.

'Twas promptly done though—11 boats & the Schooner— 80 men—Wilkes & Hudson, both in their Gigs—all gone with a celerity that was surprising when it is considered that when the news came, there were only two boats that did not need repairs. But on such occasions, no sailor needs a spur to work. They tear things to pieces.

The white men who lived among the Islands could not account for the natives contenting themselves with merely taking the boat. It was the first time life had ever been spared by the Fegees on such an occasion. It is a superstition among them to kill their own people if they are wrecked, and there are many instances of the murder of Boats' crews who escaped from a wreck only to meet a more horrid death on the shore, where they expected refuge & safety. It was supposed that they could not resist their habits & desire for plunder but obeyed their first impulses when the Boat struck & seized her. The dread of the Man of War kept them from striking a blow, although in their scheme for Capturing the Launch by getting part of her crew on shore, murder must have been done, for there would have been resistance.

The two chiefs were taken in the Schooner. They were overheard on board the Ship laying a plan to escape but were put in Irons, & kept confined until the row was over. In less than 24 hours from the time the Launch made her final escape, the boats were before the Town for the restitution of the Cutter & for the punishment of the theft. The 11 boats were anchored together close to the shore, & the Schooner off a little, rather out of Gun shot but as near as she could get.

A few of the natives appeared, & by means of the interpreters & the chiefs who were held prisoners, the principal chief came down & held a parley. The Cutter was demanded at once, but he artfully eluded this & mentioned that one of the boats was aground in a Bay, some few miles off. This was at once considered as a lie, & that it was done in the hope that some of the boats would be sent off, or the Schooner withdrawn on this false scent, & our force be weakened. The demand was again repeated, with peremptory threats.

It was a novel position for a Fegee warrior to find himself placed in, for never in the annals of his people had so large a body of white men appeared in arms, offering fight upon the very shores where the numbers were against them & where they could have no advantages of position, but must trust entirely to their superior skill in war. There was something so bold & audacious in this sudden & unlooked for appearance of our little force, and there was so much haughty confidence assumed in the tone of demand, that the Chief was dismayed, & however differently he might have acted towards a war party of his own countrymen, his heart was not big enough to risk a battle with so many whites of the Man of War Ship.

He promised to return the Boat, & his men launched her uninjured, so that she was picked up by our boats. Some few trifles were not restored, & these they said were broken up & could not be got. It was determined to burn the towns & destroy the yams, canoes & all the property that could be found, but as the men had *pulled all night,* they all went off to the Schooner & took some rest & dinner so that they went to work much refreshed.

This time they landed without hesitation & took up their march towards the two villages. The natives were in numbers in the rear of the first town, covered by a valley. A broadside from the leading division of our men sent them off, & a few rockets[4] fired after them quickened their pace until they reached a hill, on the top of which they stood looking at the scene of fire & devastation going on among their dwellings below. They had carried off all the moveables from their houses so that there was nothing but the huts to burn. Their yams, which were collected in great quantities, were all destroyed, the pigs killed, & a fine large double canoe, the only one seen, was set fire to & stove to pieces. The Seargent of Marines shot one male, who was the only one killed. More might have been shot, but it was too much like murder to fire at men who made no resistance.

So our men embarked again unmolested, but as soon as they were fairly pulling out, the Natives came down to the water side & fired from behind the shelter of the mangroves, though without effect. Two or three balls whistled over the heads of May, Davis[5] & some others rather closer than was agreeable, but no one was hit.

About 10 o'clock that evening we heard a firing of muskets one after the other in the direction we were looking out for the boats, & after being for some time in anxious expectation to know the result, the Gig got alongside & we heard the whole yarn; the boats followed. Vexed as I was, Perry was served still worse. He was in the Launch and did not get to the Scene of action until it was over & the boats on their return.

The two Chiefs were brought back & kept in Irons still. This punishment of burning the Towns was effective without being severe. The Natives certainly gained nothing, & their loss was of some consequence but not enough to put them in great distress. They had the worst of the bargain & will be careful how they meddle with man of war boats again.[*]

Some time after this, Case stopped at a village not far distant for the night, not knowing any thing about the affair until the Chief of the town told him of it, & addressed his men to this effect, that they should not touch a man or a thing belonging to the boat, or they would have their town burnt before they could turn round! He feasted Case, gave him Pigs to take with him, & was glad when he went away for fear that some accident might happen for which he would be punished!

In a day or two the *Flying Fish* sailed with Captain Wilkes on board—3 boats in company, understood to be bound on a surveying cruize, but no one knew whither. I volunteered to go & was refused—could not be spared! though I was of not the least

[*] The two chiefs who were Prisoners & had witnessed the burning of their Town were dismissed with good advice & presents, notwithstanding that they were so strongly suspected of treachery in going to our Boats. We were obliged to Land them seven miles down the Coast, as the land hereabouts belonged to their Enemies, & if they attempted to pass through it, they would be killed.

use on board. These boats left our Ship together; we parted from them with jests, whom we were never to see again!

I was kept busy surveying the Bay, much to my discomfort, & made to keep watch every night. The burnt mate was all this while on shore in a Tent, attended by Guillou with a devotion that few would have practised, for the atmosphere about him was tainted beyond my endurance, yet Guillou nursed him night & day & slept in the same tent. At last he died. Guillou opened him. He was buried on shore, close by the hut; he said he had not a friend on earth! There was not a soul who cared for him.

At this time, the allowance of provisions was reduced ¼—& the men were served but one tot of grog a day.[6] This was hard commons for hard work.

On the 22nd July we left Sandal Wood Bay, to proceed to Mudwater, & once again passed thro' Monkey face passage— was indeed for the last time. Dana[7] & I were aloft all the while to overlook the shoals & get a more correct idea of the way they were situated than we had been able to do in the Boats. It was broiling hot on the Royal Yard, but I bore it for my country's sake. *On the 24th,* we anchored at Mudwater, & Captain Hudson went back to bring the *Vincennes.*

I was obliged to *go on the list*[8] for a cut that I got on my ancle while scrambling over a coral reef. It had bothered me much, & Guillou told me I must submit to a poultice & rest for some days, or the joint would be injured. Nothing loath to lie by now that there was nothing doing, I put my foot under his kind care, and in six days I was about again. I am not unmindful of the great blessing that I enjoy, in the gift of health. With the exception of one day in Sydney, I have not known a moment's illness, which makes me think my constitution has entirely recovered from the siege it sustained in the East Indies.[9]

There was not much to attract us on shore at Mudwater. The people were mostly absent fishing for the *Leonidas,* and the place wore a deserted look. There was no life nor stir—no dances, nor feasts. We went occasionally to bathe in a fresh water stream & rambled some little distance into the country for exercise, but this was quiet & monotonous, & there was no excitement at all. We were pining for the day to come when we should leave Fegee.

I had some tatooing put on my arm by Rotomah Jack, the brother of Henrietta. He had followed his sister from Rotumah to Tahiti & from Tahiti to Fegee until he found her, and he did not intend to quit her until they both got safe Home. Henrietta was very much afraid she would be strangled when the old King died, according to the Fegee custom, but she had no relish for premature immortality. Such was not the fashion of her Country, & she wished to go away in our Ship. She had no love for the Old King.

It is the universal practise to strangle a Chief's wifes at his Death, that they may be with him among the Spirits. Most women submit willingly, for having enjoyed the honors of their station in this world, they do not wish to be deprived of them in the next. So they seat themselves in another woman's lap, & two men choke them by drawing a piece of tappa round their necks. Sometimes instances occur, when a young girl is wife to an old chief, that she runs away to her relatives to be saved, but they are seldom permitted to live. Superstitious custom demands the Sacrifice, & they are given up to be dealt with.

Poor Pat had been quite unwell while we were at Sandal Wood bay, & he lived on shore with the Doctor, who restored him pretty near to his usual good health. The change of diet, the whiskey & want of exercise had very likely caused his illness, for old age had not yet made much impression on him. Time used him gently. Pat left us at Sandal Wood Bay to go home in the *Who'd A Thought It,* & I bid good bye to the old man with regret, for I had been accustomed to talk with him daily & never failed to be interested & amused. May he have his wish to complete his century, & may there be some one to read the book over his Island grave.

Perry was busy surveying the harbour of Mudwater & had put up seven or 8 flags of the same kind as the one which was so fatally attractive to the Chief of Rahwah. These were nearly all stolen by night & when replaced, the others disappeared. Complaints were made to the King, with the threat to burn the town if he did not send in all the signals that had been taken away. The old man promised to do all he could, & he sent out messengers to take or to *buy* them, wherever they could find them, but old & imbecilic as he was, he could not use the energetic measures adopted by Phillips & Garrangea & he only procured a few patches without securing any of the offenders. The threat of burning his Town was an idle one, but he was much alarmed, & he twice sent in several thousand yams & pigs by the dozen to ask pardon for the thefts & to pay for their loss. These were accepted, as we were much in want of such food, but he was given presents in return.

He continued in a state of trepidation as long as we remained & was never at ease in his mind for fear that he would lose his town. When the *Vincennes* came, I was on shore, & he was wandering from House to house, so much disturbed that he could not content himself in any one place. I wound a turban of flaming calico around his head & assured him there would be no harm done. He was much pleased & said he believed we were good people after all, but he wished we would go away.

On Friday July 31st, I went on board the *Vincennes* with young Elliott to dine. They had fresh Pig, *we* salt. May was at work on the harbours of Tutuilla, surveyed by Underwood & myself, and we naturally got to talking of him & wondering when they would return. Sandford[10] offered to lend one of his books, saying that *Joe* would have no objection at all, & little did we think that he of whom we spoke was past all earthly concerns. Saw the boats coming in, as we were speaking and were glad beyond measure, for their arrival was to be the signal for our preparing to quit the group.

I was seated by the stern window in the cabin, trying an angle on the chart of Sandal Wood bay, when the headmost boat came under the Counter. I looked out & saw Case, very much burned & looking worn out & dejected, but I did not get up & went on with my work. Presently, May rushes into the Cabin & says, *"Oh! Reynolds, Underwood & Henry are killed, murdered by the Natives"* & out he went again. I heard him distinctly but mechanically went on adjusting the tracing paper until I finished, for I knew that if *I stopped to think,* I should not be able to touch the work again.

This done, the paper fell from my hands, & the horrible nature of the affair came over my mind, so that I was stupefied: two murdered—two butchered—& oh so young. Oh! the widowed mother & the widowed wife. *We* were dumb with grief, stricken to the very soul with an anguish that was sore indeed. I would not witness the breaking of the sad news to those whose homes have thus been made desolate, for any thing in the world. 'Twas enough to hearken to it, when it was told to me.

Case had not been with them at the time of the accident but had fallen in with the boats the day before this & then came on in Company. The rest were coming up slowly with their Ensigns half mast, & the news was through the Ship, so that every one had suspended their employments & hurried on deck to be in the way of learning the particulars. Alden got alongside next—he could not say a word. Indeed, no one went near him but the 1st Lieutenant, & he went down in the Cabin to see Captain Hudson & deliver his account to him. When he finished, he went into the Wardroom, & May & Simon & I went down to hear the story.

On the 24 July they were at *Mololo* with the three boats. The Schooner & Brig were out of sight but not far off. Underwood landed to purchase some pigs & yams which the Natives said they had to sell. Some of his boat's crew were with him, & the rest remained in the boat a little distance off but as near as the depth of water would allow. Alden with the larger boat was farther out, but coming in as the tide rose, & Emmons was round a point, taking some sights. There was a great crowd around our men. Underwood sent a hostage, the son of a Chief, off to Alden, & Midshipman Henry got permission & went ashore. Alden put the Cap on his pistol & jested with him about it, the last words he ever spoke to him.

Underwood did not succeed in his bargaining & sent to Alden for a Hatchet, but Alden sent him word to come off. Alden was keeping a lookout with his glass but could only see the crowd, & thought as he had the hostage all would be right enough, but presently this fellow jumped overboard & fled. Alden lifted his rifle & was on the point of firing, when he stayed his hand, thinking that they might not have shed any blood & that if he shot this man, it might cause the massacre of those on shore, but alas! the work was done already.

Just at this instant Emmons came in with his Boat, & Midshipman Clark was going to shoot the hostage, when Alden told him to fire over his head. Shots were heard on the beach, & the cry then rose from the Men that Mr. Underwood was killed. And now Alden & all his crew jumped overboard & made for the beach, for it instantly struck them *what* would be *done with the bodies, if the Natives carried them away.*

They were already retiring *en masse,* with the exception of a few stragglers. Midshipman Clark shot at the flying hostage again & wounded him in the leg, & then had time to kill a Fegee who was following up one of the boat's crew named Clark. The man was staggering in the water, crazy from wounds with Clubs, & the fellow shot behind him was coming with uplifted club to give him a finishing stroke. Emmons let fly both blunderbusses at the retreating Crowd, & killed several.

When Alden reached the beach there was not a Native to be seen. They had gone off to the bushes, bearing all their dead with them except two. Where the waters met the sand, Alden found Henry lying partly afloat with a dead Fegee close beside him, & this was the first that he knew of the poor boy's fate. He raised him up & had him carried to the boat, & going a few steps, there was the body of Underwood stripped & bloody, & the last gasp just quivering from his lips. Alden lifted his head upon his arm, but the skull was soft & mashed in, & the breath of life had gone forever. Alden said aloud & almost unconsciously, "your poor, poor Wife, Joe! little is she thinking of this!"

But there was no time for delay. The natives were close by. They had carried off the clothing & arms of the dead officers & the little trade which had been the inducement to this murder, and there was no reason to suppose that they would allow the rest to retreat unmolested, when they had suffered so severely themselves. The Corpse of Underwood was borne to the boats & they shoved off to clear the Island with all the haste they could.

As well as could be gathered from the crew of the *Leopard,* the attack was commenced the instant the hostage jumped overboard. Underwood discharged two pistols with effect, it was thought, and ordered the *boat's crew to save themselves* ere he fell. Henry *did shoot one* man & cut another's face open before he fell. The Natives have always undervalued Pistols & probably did not anticipate such a deadly resistance. Added to this, the blunderbusses & Clark's fire, & one fatal shot from one of the boat's crew, the loss of the Natives must have been nine or ten. The Seamen were excited to fury & could with difficulty be restrained. They wanted to go after the Natives & fight them at once. One fellow, a negro who sailed in the *Potomac* with me, cut off the head of one of the dead Fegees to make sure of him & would have carried his ghastly prize with him, if he had been permitted.

One of the *Leopard*'s crew, in running to the boat, was struck in the back by a small club thrown at him. His Cartridge box took & broke the blow, & he got safe aboard. The whole was so instantaneous & unexpected, & there was so much pell mell confusion, that no one could give a very distinct relation of the affray, which had terminated almost as soon as begun.

The boats stood down for an Island about 8 miles off, where the Schooner was with Captain Wilkes. Alden had both the bodies in the Stern Sheets of his boat covered over with Jackets. Emmons had opened a vein in Henry's arm. One jet of blood spurted, & the life fluid was stilled for ever. Poor fellows! they had died fighting & commenced the goodly work of avenging themselves! There was not a word spoken in the boats, & Alden's feelings cannot be told. To be thus situated, with the lifeless clay of those who had so recently left him full of life & hope—it was terrible. Poor Underwood's leg fell from the thwart & hung down. Alas! there was no power in the body it belonged to, to lift it up, and to do this cost Alden a pang that wrung his heart.

As the boat approached the Schooner, Captain Wilkes was pulling off to her from a small Island, where he had been taking sights. Eld was with him & saw that the boats had their Ensigns half mast. This he remarked to Captain Wilkes, who, with his usual habit of contradiction, answered, "Oh! No, you are mistaken." Directly Eld looked again & said, "They are not only half mast, but they are Union down, & something must have happened." "No, Sir—it can't be, you are mistaken." But Eld was convinced & repeated it again as peremptorily as he could.

Wilkes said no more until they got alongside the Schooner. The boats were very close to. Wilkes essayed to hail them, but his voice failed. Alden came close & said, "Two of us are gone, Sir—killed, murdered by the Natives & here they are! Mr. Underwood & Mr. Henry are dead." Captain Wilkes fell as if the life had left him, & had to be carried below. The one was his nephew, the only child of his widowed Sister.

The bodies were passed on board & laid out. When Wilkes recovered, he bent over them, kissed them & patted them with his hands, moaning over them, so that it was piteous to see him. But he soon recovered from this state of extreme & unavailing distress & was able to listen to the tragical tale & give orders as to what was to be done.

The Schooner was beat up and anchored under the Island by Sundown; and all that night the boats rowed guard around the shores to prevent canoes from leaving. The Natives taunted them to come on shore on fight: "Why don't the papalangis come ashore? If they did, they would be eaten"—& various other exclamations to the like agreeable effect. The next morning the Schooner left her berth & went to a group of low Islands perhaps 10 miles off, in the center one of which the two bodies were buried in the same grave. The blood came from them so, as to stain the Sand in which they were laid. The Isle was thickly grown with trees, and in the heart of a lovely grove the last prayers were said over the resting place of those whose Homes were so far away. The Volleys of Musquetry broke the Silence, which perhaps had been never before been so disturbed, & myriads of birds took wing affrighted at the unusual sound.

While the Schooner was employed on this melancholy duty, the Brig came in sight, & one of the boats boarded her to tell the bloody tale. At the same time a Canoe full of men, but belonging to the Big land & innocent of any participation in or knowledge of the murder, ran alongside the *Porpoise*. It was thought advisable to secure them, & they were put in Irons, much to their amazement & much against their will. They were sure they were to be killed, and would not heed any thing that was told them to the contrary.

This night the Brig & Schooner anchored near the scene of

the murder & made ready for an attack early in the morning. The Boats had been rowing guard all day & continued so during the night. The natives were following them & taunting them to come on shore & fight. Whenever the boats got in towards the reef, the natives who had muskets fired at them, but their shots were always wide. The men in the boats had great fun, laughing & joking as the balls fell in shore of them, & paid no more serious attention to the unlucky marksmen than to damn their eyes & their impudence. One Native rested on a large stone & snapped 3 times before his piece went off, with a deliberate aim. The men watched him, saying, "Well I guess he'll get it to go presently," perfectly heedless, that the weapon was pointed at them.

When there were any shots fired from the Boats, the Natives dodged behind rocks or threw themselves among the grass. They took care of No. 1, so that none of them were touched. If they had been expert with the musket, they might have picked off many of our men.

On the morning of the 26th, the second day after the murders, between 70 & 80 men were landed from the Brig & all the officers that could be spared. Indeed there was but one left on board the *Porpoise,* & the Schooner was in charge of Dr. Fox and Tom, the Pilot. The crew of Underwood's boat were to act with the shore party, which was commanded by Captain Ringgold; & Captain Wilkes in his Gig, Alden & Emmons in the two Cutters & Midshipman Clark in the Schooner's boat were to burn the other town on the Island & cut off any who took to the water.

The shore party proceeded immediately to surround the Village which was the nearest to the scene of murder & to which the principal of the perpetrators belonged. It was entrenched & barricadoed after the most approved fashion of Fegee fortification & had the reputation of being impregnable. The inhabitants were a set of Pirates who owned no sway except of their own chiefs. They were at war with every body & were generally so ferocious & successful in their battles that they were the terror of all their neighbours on the big land. The Island of Mololo, lying off the main shore, was right in the passage for either Ships or Canoes going from the one large Island to the other, & these villains would pounce upon stragglers & then retreat to their Isolated & fortified abode, where they had withstood repeated attacks & repulsed the assailants with much loss. But the day was at last come when their strong hold was to be destroyed & their invincibility put to the test.

There were some few huts outside the barrier & some Cocoa nut trees. Under shelter of these our men were drawn up at close Pistol shot & commenced their fire whenever they saw a native at any of the appertures. This fire was tolerably effectual, & several of the Officers walked right up to the loop holes & discharged both barrels of their Guns & then their pistols, with true aim at the crowd within. The Natives kept up a continual fire of musketry & arrows, but strange to tell, none of their shots took effect.

Eld told me that he was sometimes clear of his tree & at others as well stowed behind it as he could. He saw the natives come up & take deliberate aim at himself & others & yet always miss. Our party aimed for the eyes with truer sight, & it is supposed the Natives, besides overcharging their Muskets with bad powder, became frightened when they found themselves actually in combat with so many white people, although they had boasted so much. Eld went clear up to the pallisades to shoot a fellow who was just getting ready to aim, & with some trouble he managed to shoot another who had fired at him three times. Johnson proposed to Captain Ringgold to force the barricades & enter the Town, but Captain Ringgold would not permit it, as those who entered first would be killed, & he did not wish to lose a life.

In the mean while Rockets were shot among the Houses, and in a few minutes the Town was in a blaze. A man ascended the thatch of one to extinguish the flames, but he fell with a dozen balls in a moment. This the natives had not dreamed off, & they could in no manner conjecture how it had taken place. They were struck with superstitious fear & became utterly unnerved. They could no longer resist such foes, and there were only a few who continued to fire with the same determination as before. Our interpreters called to them to send their Women & Children away, & this was at once complied with. Many men it is supposed went with them. The women had been seen dragging the dead bodies away when they fell, for these people are scrupulous in carrying off their own slain to prevent their enemies from eating them & to enjoy that pleasure themselves.

Eld saw a little child walking amidst the smoking houses & called to the men not to shoot towards her, & presently as the fire from within slackened where he was, he entered through one of the sally ports, which he forced open. The flames were now so fierce in the Town as to render it impossible to remain in it, & all who were left alive, fled to the Shelter of the bushes. Some were shot & dropped as they ran, but pursuit was not allowed.

The first objects that met Eld's eye were two dead Fegees lying by a small loophole into which he had fired himself 3 or 4 times. They were both shot through the brain. One was Eld's friend who had so pertinaciously tried to hit him. This man had a musket by him with *an 8 finger load in it, for a big man,* and as Eld is very tall, the Fegee thought to make his *fourth shot* effectual. A little farther on were two children, burnt & dead. Eld did not stay to see if they had been shot or not, but it is possible the fire killed them. In one house he found Underwood's Cap, all mashed by the blows which had felled him, a handkerchief & some of the trade. These, some spears & clubs, some women's aprons, & the two muskets he took away with him as spoils of the fight, & he saw two more dead men, also shot through the head.

This done so well & speedily without any loss or damage but a few arrow wounds among the men, the party did not wait until the town would burn down so that they could enter, but set out immediately for the other end of the Island to aid those who were engaged at the village there. They did not see any body on their way, although they had 5 miles to go except a wounded man, who was found in the grass a little ways from the Town—Lemont, one of the *Leopard*'s crew, bayonetted him without a word—& one man who started to run but was shot by a dozen.

The boats soon after they left the Schooner fell in with 3 canoes to which they gave chase. Emmons, on coming up with two that kept together, hailed and asked them if they belonged to Mololo. They answered yes, when without more ado, he let fly both blunderbusses & then all his muskets. Those who were not killed jumped overboard & were shot in the water, with the exception of two girls, a baby, a woman & one man & a boy who were hauled in the boats & the two latter tied. One woman was shot in the water by mistake, and another, who swam out to sea, must have drowned. Clark with his small boat came up & shot a man who was just crawling up on the reef. Clark picked up a girl also, & as the women were naked, he took some aprons out of the canoes & gave them to put on. The women & girls were put on shore at once with the baby & directed how to avoid the path taken by our men. The Canoes were towed to the Brig for Fire wood, & the Boats went on to the town where Captain Wilkes was.

Alden, in the mean while, had pursued the other of the three Canoes, & on his coming up with her, every one jumped overboard. He determined to make them prisoners, as it was mere slaughter to kill them unresistingly, & he hoped they would be of Service as go betweens. So he ordered his men to put down their arms & haul them in the boat, but so bent were they upon having blood that this black Townsend, who cut the man's head off on the beach to be sure he was not "playing possum," raised his cutlass, twined his hands in the hair of the first person come up with & was going to strike, when Alden caught up a Pistol & told him to stop or he would shoot him. The Creature, who had been in such jeopardy, turned round & showed the breasts of a woman! They were all secured in this way & the men tied, in the bottom of the Boat.

After this, the Boats met at the town & landed to attack, but there was only a cat to be seen, & she was purring very quietly about. The people had all gone to make their grand stand at their favorite fighting place, where they had so often been the victors, but where they were now to meet with the[ir] defeat. This town was fired & burned ere the shore party got to it, so that they took up their march back across the Island, but the Natives were hid in their retreats, & none were seen.

Emmons in his boat now went after 5 Canoes that were seen in a bight of the reef, & the other boats rowed along the shores to prevent any one from leaving the Island. The odds were greatly against Emmons, who had only 8 men in his boat. As he closed with the canoes, he manoueuvred to get to windward & then commenced with the blunderbusses & musquetry. The first fire did much havock. Each of the blunderbusses had a handful of musket balls in it, & these were sent full among the canoes. One of the canoes took to flight & the remainder fought it [out] with spears & arrows as long as they could, but they were thrown into confusion from the destructive fire of the boat, & many jumped overboard & were killed in the water.[*] One huge fellow hove three spears at Emmons, who dodged them all & jumping into the Canoe jerked a fourth out of his hand, when Whahoo Jack killed him with a hatchet.

Another who was overboard was using a spear, & Oahu Jack was dancing around him on the outrigger, watching a chance to strike him. The edge of his cutlass turned on the Fegee's head, & Jack got a hatchet, & hauling his victim by the hair against the poles of the [outrigger], began to demolish it with this weapon, as if he was chopping a log of hard wood. Every blow he gave he looked up to Emmons, saying, "He very tough man to kill this, Sir; very tough," & then went on with his blows until this Cat of the Fegees was dead at last.

30 natives were killed here. Of the four canoes taken possession of, they were provided with Clubs, arrows, spears, but they were in such a Panic that they could not fight. Thus ended this day's tradgedy. One hundred natives were killed outright, and many others wounded. It was bloody work, but all the lives in Fegee would not pay for the two we lost. The Boats rowed guard all this night, & the other party returned to the Brig. The flames continued at the burning houses until Midnight, & the Natives were seen stalking among the ruins, but all was quiet, & there were no more taunting threats nor cries of "loca my," "papalangi!" nor invitations to come ashore & be made a meal of.

---

[*] The natives when shot at in the water always dove at the flash. One of the men very cooly said, "We must take these fellows as they rise," and suiting the action to the word, he scattered the brains of a Feegee who was just coming to the Surface after a successful dodge! Emmons had a percussion Rifle that fixed them at once.

[CHAPTER 15: AFTERMATH]

It is scarcely possible to form any idea of the distress & despair in which the natives who were still unhurt must have passed this night. Their situation was woefully changed since the morning: towns burnt to ashes, canoes destroyed, their taro patches laid waste, and the dead, wounded & dying every where about them. *They had slain none of the whites. All the lifeless bodies* were of *their own colour & blood,* and to the number of 60, these made a funeral heap such as they had never known before.

Early in the morning *a Woman* came down to the edge of the reef, close to the Schooner, to beg for peace & mercy. Two of the prisoners taken by Alden were sent on shore to say that all the people on the Island must be on a certain hill by noon, where the White Chief would meet them & grant them terms. Accordingly, the men were armed & went on shore to the summit of this hill, which they occupied so that they could easily defend the position if the natives should attempt an attack.

When the sun was high overhead, the natives had not yet appeared, and an hour passed most impatiently, when a large body of them were seen coming over the distant hills. As they approached, the wailing voices of women were heard in chorus, but all else was still. They halted in the valley below & hesitated to advance. Two white men, Carter[1] & Tom, were sent down to them to hurry their movements & to learn the state of feeling among them. Carter told me that they were frightened & bewildered so that they knew not what to do. He would prevail on them to advance a few steps & then overcome with fear & irresolute, they would run back again. Treachery is so universal among themselves that they would not believe the white men would be satisfied with the revenge they had already taken, but were waiting to surprise & murder them when they were unprepared.

The Chief told Carter that he would give 2 virgins—then 4—then 6—then 10 to the White Chief to beg for mercy. This though the Custom in Fegee, Carter assured him, would not do with the whites; that the White Chief wanted all the people to come up before him that he might talk to them himself; that none of them would be harmed. It was not white man's fashion to eat their words or to kill their enemies except in fair fight, but that if the Chief did not take his people & ascend the hill at once, there would not be a life spared on the Island. Before Sundown they would all be killed. Thus urged, & with the remembrance of yesterday's carnage & the apparent invulnerability of his opposers, the Chief prepared to approach them without more delay.

So himself with most of the men & some women walked to the foot of the hill, & then crouching down on their hands & knees, they began to crawl up towards the group of whites who were waiting on the Summit & looking on with astonishment on the abject & humiliating manner of this singular procession. The natives knocked their heads to the ground & crept along slowly, the chief in advance, making the most doleful wail, to which all the others added a hoarse chorus, & in this way they advanced to within 10 or 12 paces of our party, when all of them bent their faces to the earth & remained motionless & silent.

The Chief now began a supplicatory address begging for mercy, & expressing his sorrow for the crime of his people. He said that the punishment they had met with was just, but that it was also so severe that they now wanted peace. They knew that we had too much power for them to fight with us, & that they were in the utmost distress—their houses burned, their fighting men killed, & much of their food destroyed. All this time the Chief remained with his head bent, casting his eyes upwards as he paused to have his words interpreted.

Captain Wilkes promised him mercy on certain conditions. Every man, woman & child were to be down on the beach on the ensuing morning with a certain quantity of provisions, & to water the Brig & Schooner with bags that would be there in readiness, & they were to restore every thing they had taken from the murdered officers. This was instantly agreed to, and now in despite of what they had been told to the contrary, or perhaps forgetful of it, the Chief spoke to one of his men, who rose to his feet & taking a virgin daughter of the Chief in either hand, advanced toward Captain Wilkes, & all then crouching down, the man began a speech offering them as gifts of peace, but he was instantly silenced & was told to take the girls away. Their feelings may be more readily imagined than described.

Captain Wilkes went on to tell them of the power that white men possessed in battle, & of the horrid enormity they had been guilty of in treacherously murdering those who had never done them harm, & only for the sake of a few firearms & hatchets, & that they might be sure that the same fearful vengeance would be taken if any white man should be killed hereafter. All the while they had continued without changing their position, although every little while some would look up to see if our men were at their arms, & in evident dread that they were there only to be slaughtered. The Seamen were drawn up in the rear of the Officers with their Muskets & Cutlasses on the ground beside them, but they did not handle the weapons, as the natives had been directed to come unarmed & had no clubs nor spears among them. The Natives were now dismissed, thankful that they had got off so well on this day.

At daylight, they were at the appointed place, true to their promise; part of the provisions, such as Pigs, yams & tarro, were already brought down, & persons were coming & going, busy as possible in collecting the remainder. The leathern bags of the Brig & the breakers of the boats were on the beach. Numbers of the Natives were set to work filling them, & they had to carry them some distance to the spring, so that they were much fatigued & complained of the toil, for they are never given to working hard or long. But it was no avail to them, that they were tired. Our men kept them busy, & as soon as one full bag or breaker was deposited, they had empty ones ready & started the Natives right back. The fellows were in too much fear to hesitate or refuse, & it was nearly night ere they were permitted to cease. They must have felt all this bitterly.

Underwood's watch, all burned & broken, his pistols & carbine & Henry's Bowie Knife Pistol,[2] with some strips of clothing, hatchets & plane irons were brought & delivered up, as all that could be found of the things taken at the murder.

When all this was over, the boats filled up with cocoa nuts at a grove that had been long taubooed & was loaded with fruit. The Chief & his family who had been taken by Alden were not permitted to land. They had been kept on board the Brig in Irons on the opposite side of the deck from the others who belonged to the Big land & were their enemies. The Mololo people were in fear of death & would not believe they were to be spared, until they were set free.

The Chief from the Big Land said that as soon as he got home, he would raise his fighting men & cross over to Mololo at once. They had often harmed him, & now that they had no town to retreat to & their best warriors were killed, he would come against them, put all the men to death & take the women & children as slaves. Doubtless by this time, he has fulfilled his threat, & the long dreaded Pirates of Mololo are no longer in existence.

Our boats were now ordered to return direct to the Ships, & the Schooner & Brig proceeded to Cantab. They all made sail at once, & soon Mololo & the low Isles which for the past few days had been the scene of such terrible & thrilling interest were dropped below the horizon, in all likelihood never to be seen again by those who have such cause to remember them.

The place of the murder on Mololo was called "Murderers' Bay." Poor Underwood had once given the same significant name to the bay on Tutuilla, where the white man had been killed. Little, little did I think then that *his* end would have to be so, in like manner, perpetuated. Yet it is a fate that we all have had in our minds, & we may still go on the same bloody & sudden path in which our lamented brothers have so recently preceded us. *They* were as full of life & health & hope, as *we*.

The Isle on which they were buried was called "Henry's Island," & with those around it included in "Underwood's

Group." When the bodies were covered up, the sand was smoothed over so as to leave no traces of its having been disturbed, & the footsteps were obliterated so that no marks made by the living would show the retreat of the Dead. There was a fearful & hideous need for this.

The Ship's Ensigns were worn half mast during the remainder of Friday & the whole of Saturday, and an order read directing the Officers to wear crepe for 30 days. Sunday August 2nd, there was church on board the *Vincennes,* to which all of us went. The faces were wanting that had so often been among our group.

This night, I was ordered to stand by to go away in the Cutter for 6 days on another surveying cruize. [When I at last returned to the ship, Captain Hudson was] just setting down to his table. Welcomes me back & asks me to take my chance with him. I told him I was not in very fit condition, but he said never mind, set down as I was. I could not think of this & run out to wash myself & comb my hair. My ablutions had been made altogether with salt water, which is horrid for the complexion & smarts as if your skin was peeling off. I had not shaved, my clothes were not clean, & altogether I was as unpromising a candidate for a dinner table as can be imagined.

So I plunged my head in to a bowl of fresh water, donned a better jacket, twisted a nec[k]erchief round my neck, smoothed my hair, & then placed myself opposite the Captain's decanter, ready to do justice to meat & drink. He helped me bountifully, & for a time I was too busy to talk, so he very considerately kept up the conversation himself. He thinks Boat service is the very Devil, having had 3 days' experience himself, just enough to form his taste.

That night all the Officers met in Captain Hudson's Cabin to adopt resolutions expressive of their regret, &c., at the loss we had sustained, & $2000 was subscribed to erect a monument to their memory at Mount Auburn Cemetery near Boston. Mount Auburn was selected for several reasons: it was neither too public nor too retired—and the Widow of Underwood was close by.

Underwood possessed a remarkable mind. He had a strong

genius for Mathematics, & he was completing a wonderful tabular & mechanical invention, which involved much that was curious & useful, but which, now that *his* brain is forever quieted, will never be known. Oh! that the club of a Savage should in one instant destroy the cunning of so gifted an intellect & crush in a bloody death the hopes, prosperity & benefits which would have attended its existence. His own industry had rendered him acquainted with several of the modern tongues, and once his ready & skilful pencil had aided him in sustaining a Mother & Sisters. He was upright & independent in his conduct, & there was an honest sincerity about him which nothing could overthrow & which was equally exhibited in his intercourse with friend or foe. He was temperate & frugal in his habits, & was never known to indulge in any improper excess. I was long associated with him in his watch & many a weary night have we wiled away, in converse of the Homes we had left & of the happiness of a return. He has gone to his God, & I am still left to buffet the storms & accidents of life.

Henry was young, but nineteen. His character was manly far beyond his years, & under circumstances of peculiar embarassment & delicacy his conduct was so correct as to secure for him universal esteem and to give good promise of a manhood that would be an honor to himself & to the Service to which he belonged.

On this Afternoon of Sunday the 9th August we got underweigh for Mudwater to proceed to Marli, where Captain Wilkes was to meet us in the Schooner, & then we were to leave the Islands. The anchor was soon run up. The Merchant Ships had gone in the morning, & soon the harbour of Mudwater was deserted as ever, to the great joy of the King.

We had a head wind much as usual & were obliged to beat. At dusk the Schooner came in hail, & Captain Wilkes went on board the *Vincennes*. The next day, Monday, saw all our Squadron, once more collected, off Marli Island. Advantage was taken of this, & we delayed all day so that the Chaplain should preach the Funeral Sermon of those who had entered the group with us, full of life & hope, but whose bodies were now mouldering on this sandy Isle in the lasting sleep of Death.

The next day Tuesday, the 11th, we sailed at last from the Fegees, after a stay among them of rather more than three months. I look back upon the occurrences of our sojourn among these devils incarnate with the same feelings that oppress one in recalling to memory some hideous dream. It seems to me as if *all* could *not* have been real, but rather that the murdering cannibals & their habits that make their Isles a Hell upon this fair earth were the creations of a wild fancy, told to me as a tale, and riding me like the nightmare does in sleep!

Three months among a people who butcher men as a favorite pastime, & whose epicurean taste is never so highly indulged as when they have men, women or children for their food! The Divine command to all men, "to love one another," has been substituted by one too horrible to have originated with the Devil himself—"Kill & eat each other," is the religious maxim in Feegee, and it is much more rigidly observed among them than the one I have above quoted is in the Christian World.

Those three months I shall never forget. It often came in to my thoughts as something strange & unnatural, that the sun should shine as brightly & the rain fall the same as it in other lands. *Yet it was so,* & the face of nature was beautiful as Eden, & the little children had the innocent look of the babes that are fondled among us. Yet I never saw the child at the mother's breast without thinking *what it* was drinking *in* with the milk, or without shuddering to dwell upon *what it was to become.*

Ye who read or hear of Cannibals in your quiet Homes can have but a faint idea of the absolute & nervous horror & the loathsome disgust that oppresses one who has been among them & witnessed the foul traits that place them below the beasts. I never imagined *my* feelings would have been so acutely, so fearfully touched. I thought I would be proof even against this and be able to look on even *a feast itself* with simply curiosity & indifference. Never was I more mistaken, and I am glad for the sake of my humanity that my nature was not so coarse or unsusceptible as to bear with a hardened & savage calmness some of the sights I saw among the Feegees.

[CHAPTER 16: HONOLULU]

At last, on Tuesday the 11th of August 1840, as I have said before, we finally sailed away from the Fegees with provisions enough to last until the 1st October at the reduced allowance. It was *understood* that we were to make a direct course for the Sandwich Islands, although we did not know but that we would touch at the Navigators on the way. As this was a track that has seldom if ever been followed, there was some chance that we might make some little discoveries, & it was thought of course that we would separate, leaving each ship to make the best of her way without any detention beyond that of the winds, & thus exploring two different meridians, but no such thing. We went on as usual: close company—Ships hove to half a dozen times a day—Boats continually passing—more transfers of officers—multiplied orders about surveying work & such like things, to the great loss of time & to the exceeding vexation of all hands.

Three days out, Captain Wilkes found that he had neglected fixing a certain Island upon which much of the survey depended, & the Schooner was sent back to remedy this defect, and so those poor fellows were blasted in their hopes of a speedy passage to Oahu. Soon after, Captain Wilkes ascertained that all his changes of Officers, & his orders about surveying notes, & his verification of the survey by his Officers would not produce the desired effect. He could not complete his Chart of the Fegees prior to our arrival in Port. So he flew back to [charting] the Navigator Islands & ordered *them* to be plotted over again. But the work [containing the data of the survey] was not to be found, & thereupon ensued a very ani-

mated dialogue between him & our Captain as to which of
them had the said work last in possession, which ended like little boys' squabbles in each telling the other, "I know nothing
about it, except that I sent it to you."

On the night of the [blank], when it was bright moonlight,
we managed in the most unaccountable manner to lose sight of
the *Vincennes,* notwithstanding she had been close aboard &
had the Commodore's light in the Main top full in view. I had
the middle watch, & the word was passed to me that the *Vincennes* was ahead but not to be seen for the last half hour. By
the end of my watch, she must have increased her distance
wonderfully. I did *not* tell the lookout men to keep awake, nor
did I order the man at the Wheel to mind his helm & steer
steady. I did not say a word all the four hours. Every body
seemed to be unusually drowsy, & I had no wish to arouse
them in the least. At daylight, there was no *Vincennes* to be
seen, much to the relief & joy of every body on board, & as the
Captain never so much as enquired *how* she was lost, it was
fairly inferred that he was as well pleased as the rest of us. We
have not seen her since, thanks be to anybody.

When we sailed, we expected to have a forty days' passage,
for we knew we should have the North East trade against us
for the best part of the way, but we were grievously disappointed. This is the 37th day out, & now there is scarcely a
chance for us to get in, in less than 3 weeks or at least two. The
winds have been very unfavourable, & the Ship is so light that
she is out of trim & will not sail at all.

This is vexatious beyond bearing. We have nothing to eat—
no coffee—no sugar—no tea—no flour—Bread that is all shell
& dust, the nutriment having been all abstracted by fat worms
& weevils, who now fall victims to their unlawful appetites &
to our revenge by being masticated with the remnants they
have left. Ugh—this bread! it is abominable & makes one so
thirsty that even the bad water is palatable. Beef 5 days in the
week that has the most offensive odour & the utmost saltish-
ness of taste; that is close grained & hard as mahogany & is actually susceptible of polish, in addition to which virtues, the
bone forms the biggest part of the allowance. Pork twice a

week with beans that are unexceptionable & furnish good meals, & a pound of yams a man per day—[these] are the staples furnished us by the Ship for our subsistence.

We had 4 hens & 4 pigs when we left Mudwater, but these, even with the gentlest usage, have long since melted away. We have now a few boxes of preserved beef, which we regale upon on two of the beef days & thus manage to get four dinners a week that are barely passable. When we are thrown solely upon the mahogany, it is "bite & cry" in sadness. We have no breakfast but the wormy bread & the smallest portion of yam, which sometimes is mashed up with the beef that could not be eaten the day before in the most marvellous manner, & in this Shape, with the aid of mustard, pepper vinegar, & Cayenne, we manage to bolt it as a mixture, although we could not accomplish this desirable end when it was spread before us in all the tempting luxury of thin slices, hot from the coppers. A cup of water washes down this meal. For supper, a cup of water & the wormy bread, which we bake in the oven so that the things may be killed before we eat them & thus save us the pain of swallowing them alive, or in agonized & writhing pieces.

I am so hungry at times, that I could bite my flesh, yet this starvation is so universal throughout the Ship, that nowhere could I get a morsel for love or money. I shall be charitable to all hungry people as long as I live—*that* will be a plea that will open my purse strings in an instant.

This living so entirely with strange men is horrid, and though I have warm friends about me, I long to see someone that is bound to me by the ties of blood. The mere intercourse of the world is not sufficient for my heart, and I would give any thing just now for a glimpse at the Home I have left. We do not know where we shall go or what is to be done when we are ready to leave the Sandwich Islands. We shall get there Despatches from the Government, & there are some who indulge the hope that Captain Wilkes will receive peremptory orders to return home at the expiration of three years, but I am not one of them. *He* will prolong his command, if it be in his power, & he has no wish to make a speedy appearance in our own waters, where he will have to answer for his deeds.

Friday September 25th: 46 days out & the port still far distant. We have for nearly two weeks been standing to the Southward in order to make Easting & have been blessed with bad, rainy & uncomfortable weather during most of that time. We cannot hope to reach Oahu before the 1st October, & most likely it will be the 5th ere we get in—10 days yet. Oh! our letters—this delay is tantalizing beyond conception.

No change in the victuals, except that two barrels of flour were found by accident, & we have had *fresh bread* for our evening repast twice. The yams, by dint of the most scrupulous & jealous care, have held out 'till now, but to morrow we make the last dinner off them. With nothing for a stimulus to the unwholesome trash we feed upon, the digestion suffers, and the animal man feels wretchedly. I think of a tea equipage, with *Ladies* around the board! of smoking coffee, & *cream*! of champaigne and Ice! I reflect upon what is to be my evening fare, & I am a victim to disgust. It sickens me. I do not wonder Esau sold his birth right.[1] Hunger is hard to bear, and as to thirst, I would give a Kingdom for a draught of foaming Ale, this very minute.

"Those nasty roaches," as the girls call them, are as thick in this Ship as the Locusts were in Egypt,[2] & they are the plague & terror of our existence. They swarm every where in black clusters, & every thing suffers from them in sight, taste & smell. They drop on our table & cross over the edibles with the most audacious assurance. We fish them out of every dish that comes before us, roasted or boiled. Worse than all, they are decidedly cannibalistic and have eaten the toes of Gentlemen who sleep below, so that the blood ran. They are obliged to keep their stockings on to save themselves from utter consumption.

It is impossible to rid the Ship of them. As long as the Molasses held out, we daily hove overboard such numbers as to make a black train over the Sea, but now, we [are] destitute of any means to capture them & are deprived of the satisfaction of such extensive burials, although it never was apparent that there was any diminution in their ranks. The men have kept two small chickens as pets & taught them to catch these abominable pests. This they do with great glee, but the food is not fattening, for they look as if they were starved. If an unlucky roach should venture on an excursion on the deck, you may see a half a dozen jump to kill him, & when this is accomplished by an awful stamping of feet, the murderers look around in savage exultation & rejoice in the deed they have done.

The few shirts I have saved to appear in when we shall at last get into Port are peppered most awfully, & I know not what to do. They overrun one with the familiarity of flies & often travel from my neck to my heels. Yesterday I was amused for some minutes in watching one fellow double up his feelers & pick his teeth preparatory to a visit which he contemplated paying me. I did *not* slay him, but I *fled!* I went to my locker where I keep this veritable journal and was thrown into fright & consternation by a huge mouse that jumped nearly into my face. I set a trap and had the felicity to cage four full grown ones, who were committed to the deep without any unnecessary delay.

At last, on the last day of September, we made the Island of Oahu, having met unexpectedly & most fortunately been favored with a fair wind for several days before. I had the morning watch & as day cleared away and showed us the long wished for Land, an hundred eager eyes were fixed on its outline, & as many voices proclaimed the joyful tidings aloud. But alas, it was dead calm, & the Ship was flying all round the compass, though not moving an inch towards the shore. We hoped & prayed, & whistled for a wind with an untiring solicitude that ought to have been effectual. All was in vain, however, and when I went hungry to my breakfast, the ship was still in the doldrums, & the clouds gave no sign of a breeze.

I shall remember that breakfast—it was with Emmons, in the ward room. By some extraordinary good fortune they had found some luxuries, the existence of which had been unknown, and I surfeited myself with corn cakes, preserves & coffee, much to the comfort of my interior. It was the last, though—coffee, sugar & all were now gone, and on the morrow, it was terrible to think, we might still be at sea.

The anxious faces that were about decks that morning, the conjectures that were hazarded, the doubts that were reluctantly expressed, and the feverish impatience with which every one was fretting made us a very sad & wretched set. The morning wore heavily away & no mind—*no letters & nothing to eat to night* was the gloomy conviction of every one.

At 1 a breeze came but so light as not to raise our hopes. Presently it freshened. The sails were trimmed with a promptitude & skill worthy of the cause. All hands collected on deck, Idlers & all, & we had the satisfaction to see the Ship racing in for the Land. *More wind!*—as much as we could carry to. *Hold on every thing! Let her go!* and she was making nine mile the hour, *pointed fair for the little bay!* Wondrous change—no one in the sulks *now.* See the houses, the Shipping—*letters in an hour!* Boats coming out!—*letters in 5 minutes!* No one able to keep still—boat alongside—Pilot!—another—*and the letters are on deck!* Immense bags—how they are eyed, as they are lugged below. "All hands bring Ship to an anchor!" No time to pick out, or read a line yet. "The letters will be delivered, when we are snug, not sooner." Captain as much concerned as any body.

Now, moments seemed heavy. At last we anchored. It seemed as if the men *never would finish furling the sails,* though they were working with all their might. I was stamping at the delay, & I hollowed to the men till I was hoarse. Three boys came forward—*What is it*—"pipe down" *yet?* No Sir! The deck was swept; ropes coiled away—*all done!* "Pipe down" *surely now; no, not yet!* 5 long minutes & then came "pipe down"—*I dived!* & was in the Cabin in a second.

The letters were assorted & ready. With a precious armful, I sallied below & was two minutes finding a place where I could trust myself to. Settled in Guillou's room—turned the letters over & over—*Which shall* I open first? Could'nt tell— Went haphazard—got *half through one.* Quarter Master at my elbow—"You're wanted, Sir, on deck." Go on deck in despair— 6 o'clock—my watch till 8—pleasant, very. Every one else reading away—no, not every one—See Davis—he tells me, *he has no letters to read*—poor fellow. I give *him* the *Deck* to keep & once more betake myself to my news.

About 10, I finished & was happy to learn that all was well at Home & that my dates were as late almost as any one's.

Now the papers were to be read. Conversation was permitted
& intelligence bandied about. Any thing of interest was
screamed out for the benefit of all, and we had great & glorious rejoicing. I turned in at 12, but not to sleep; the excitement
had been too great, & there was loud talking at my ear & all
over the Ship. All that I had learned was floating through my
head, and it was near 3 before I fell asleep—Oh! this was a
memorable night.

There were many vessels in the Harbour, and the American
Flag was the most conspicuous. There were rude Wharves,
where Cargoes were discharging; there was a Ship Yard, where
the *Flying Fish* was hove down & being repaired. Numerous
boats were plying to & fro, & on the water were most of the
symptoms of a busy & thriving port. On the Shore there was
the Fort, with its harmless Guns & the Hawaiian Ensign floating from its staff, & the town, an immense concourse of low
mud & grass houses with here and there more substantial &
prominent edifices of stone & wood, & the spires of a Church
& School house rising over all. In the rear of this rose the hills
of bare red earth, looking as bleak & sterile as the State of
Maine in Winter, but relieved by vallies of the richest verdure
that swept in beautiful contrast down to the water's edge. But
there were no forests, & you looked for the luxuriant foliage &
the lovely groves of the Tropics in vain. A few straggling Cocoa
Nuts on a sandy point, looking like skeletons of their kind,
were all that told you, you were within the Limits of the sun's
path in the Heavens. The elevation of the Land was not great,
& the summit was flat & tame, without a single peak to remind
one of Tahiti. Such was the picture of Honolulu that met my
eyes on the morning of the 1st of October 1840.

Our men were all sent on liberty, and the Ship was left deserted to the rule of the Carpenters & Caulkers from the shore,
and a pretty mess they made here for several weeks. The Sailors
had command of the Town, and nowhere else in the world
could they have found recreations more suited to *their* tastes
than those that tempted them in Honolulu. Fiddles were going
in the many dance houses from morn till night & from night to
morn again with scarcely any cessation, and there were plenty

of girls who were ready & willing partners. It was most amusing to look at them—such a shuffling of feet I never saw. Then there were lots of Horses, & you might see the most comical feats of Horsemanship performed, all through the streets. Then there were ten pin alleys, where the balls were never idle, and drinking shops, where liquor was always in demand.

There was nothing to interrupt the men in their rude & noisy enjoyments. The good natured people looked on with quiet amazement at the mad pranks of the reckless seamen, as much astonished as amused. The "harum scarum" fellows straggled about & did just as they listed. Some of them became very patriotic, & procuring a large American Ensign, they marched over the Town in procession, some mounted, some on foot, with all the Music they could muster & attended by crowds of natives as admiring lookers on.

At the corners of the streets, at the Consul's, at the observatory & at the officers' houses, they would stop, have a grand "roll off"[3] from the music, give three boisterous cheers, defy the whole world to harm the flag, & then go on amidst the most uproarious merriment & in the most extreme disorder that can be imagined. They kept this up by night, torches, flag, music & all, and in their own way, they were perfectly happy. It was glorious fun for them: two weeks liberty, plenty of money & their own masters—no wonder they went into such half-crazy excesses to find pleasure in the extreme of excitement.

And I & the rest of us also found that there were many sources of enjoyment of which we could avail ourselves. The Gentlemen on shore were kind & hospitable in the extreme, & we enjoyed their society very much indeed. We hired houses & horses by the month and endeavoured to make the most of the comforts about us, as a recompense for the hard times in Feegee. A House cost but a trifle, a Horse only $15.00 a month, so that our purses did not suffer much, and the advantages we gained were worth ten times the money. Fresh water baths, good food, and a gallop on a fine horse gave us new life & vigour, & never in my life did I feel more joyously the exhilerating influence of strong & perfect health.

We did not have any too much idle time, however, but were kept busy continually with the duties of the Ship & observatory. Generally at 4 P.M. we were free, and then it was "to Horse." Such merry cavalcades as set forth—& we came back, with as much hilarity & noise as we started with. Down the plain & along the beach to "Diamond hill"; up the valley to "Pierce's";[4] or away to the magnificent spectacle of the "Parri"; or through the "Vale of Manoa;" or over the country to Pearl River, 'twas all the same, & on the excursions my heart was light as a child's.

A case of poisoning occurred about the time of our arrival. The actors were a chief of middling rank & a man of the common order, who was an adept at the art, & the sufferer was the wife of the former, who had no other reason for taking her life except that he could not live with her, & there was no other way to get rid of her. The murderers were tried, condemned & *hung*. The execution was conducted with much ceremony & decorum. I perched myself in the Topmast cross trees with my glass & looked right down upon the whole scene with a bird's eye view that took in every thing.

The Gallows was erected on a platform over the gates of the Fort. The few *"Regulars"* were in arms & uniform, & the mass of Militia were also under arms & drawn up in the center of the fort. The Prisoners were dressed in white, their arms bound, & were seated in chairs beneath a balcony from whence the Governor & the clergymen addressed them. They were attended by a Guard. When this had continued for some time, rather prolonging, as I thought, the uncomfortable situation of the condemned men, they were marched to the ramparts & placed upon the spot where they were to die. The soldiers were marched & counter marched until they had taken up their proper positions. The ropes were adjusted round the necks of the two victims to the law, and after an interval of prayer, the drop was sprung, and the stout men who but the minute before had been walking, ay, walking, though to their grave, were "soon changed into dangling heaps of clothes."[5]

There was an immense crowd assembled, and the foremost spectators were immediately under the Scaffold. At the instant the men were turned off, there was a rush among those in front, as if they were terror stricken. The panic was communicated to those in the rear, the crowd wavered, the sea of human forms swayed to & fro, and finally there was a break in the multitude, and many turned & fled, casting hurried & frightened looks behind them as if they were pursued by some terrible foe. I have been told that this is a common occurrence at executions. The strange & morbid curiosity that attracts men by thousands to witness such spectacles gives way when the actual horror of the scene commences, & the dying agonies of the writhing forms, in which consists the thrilling interest of the tragedy & to look upon which, it may be supposed, the people chiefly attend, become too much for the nerves of many to withstand. They turn their heads & flee.

My gaze was steady & fixed, though some very curious sensations were crossing through my mind. I could see that some of those who ran away never stopped until they got clear to the outskirts of the Town. Others, when they had gained some little distance, halted & looked on, & now there broke out from a thousand voices the melancholy wail which these people always chant for the dead, & long after the life had left the bodies, I remained aloft, watching the crowd as it dispersed & listening to the solemn cadences of the dirge, until all were gone, & all sounds hushed. The bodies swung about in the wind for several hours & were then taken down for burial. The gallows were removed, and thus terminated an affair which I had viewed with feelings of singular interest, & which was well calculated to excite reflections equally strange in the minds of all who beheld it, whites and natives, young & old.

Amongst the intelligence from Home that met us here came the very disagreeable information that our *extra pay* had been stopped & that Mr. Secretary Paulding had denied his having authorized it. This denial is an absolute & wilful falsehood, for we have his written order granting to us the pay allowed to Officers on the Coast Survey. The news destroyed the castle building we had indulged in, and we became aware that instead of having a nice little sum of ready money at the expiration of the cruize, we should be utterly bankrupt & poverty stricken. We have hopes, however, that it will be given to us in the end, and that the mean duplicity of Mr. Paulding will be fully exposed. I don't care very much either way. I did not come on the Expedition for money. I would take it if they offer it, for we have earned it, but if they choose to withold it, they may do so & be —— & much good may it do them to think how *we* were cheated & deceived by the highest functionary, the head of the Service.

Captain Wilkes, instead of ceasing in his insane career, went on to greater outrages & excesses—dismissed Couthouy[6] & Pinkney, & endeavoured to rid himself of Guillou. His every day conduct still continued as unreasonable as ever, & he is hated & despised with a venom such as we would bestow *only* on the vilest of the vile. I wish, almost, that the plea of insanity could be advanced for him, for his acts proclaim him to be either crazy beyond redemption, or to be a rascally tyrant & a liar black-hearted enough to be the Devil's brother. I incline strongly to the latter belief myself, & hope & trust, that the day will come, when stripped of his present authority, he will be shown up to the scorn & loathsome contempt which he so richly deserves from all honorable men.

It has been our peculiar good fortune to be free from dissentions among ourselves with scarce an exception. The intimacy of the Officers has been unbroken in its confidence & happy in its effects. If strife *had* ever crept into our circle—and once *he* tried to produce it—*his* design would have been complete, and we would have been in a very Hell.

Various causes delayed us in Honolulu for two months. By the last of November we were ready for Sea. The *Peacock's* launch was built & hoisted in, and this was the last cause of our detention. The Charts of the Feegees were nearly finished, the Observatory was broken up, & the *Vincennes* was preparing to leave for Owhyhee, where pendular experiments[7] were to be made on the summit of Mouna Roa, 12,000 feet above the Sea.

I still belonged to the *Peacock,* was Caterer of the Mess & had been busy as a bee in procuring stores for a long siege at sea. In Callao, I had written to New York for $500 worth of stores for the *Vincennes* steerage mess, not deeming that I was to be ousted out of *her,* and these had duly arrived in Oahu. I had a liberal share allowed me, and after a great deal of trouble I had got my portion on board the *Peacock,* congratulating myself at having obtained, as the reward of my foresight, a supply of good things such as could not be found in Oahu. Bills were paid, & I had crammed every stow hole full & felt that I had no more to do, when on the last day of November, I was thrown into despair by receiving orders to the *Flying Fish,* & she to sail the next morning.

In a very few minutes, I bundled my traps aboard & found myself in a mess utterly destitute of any stocks, whatsoever. Here was a change, with a vengeance, & of course, without any warning. Luckily the Schooner needed repairs, & I had a part of two days to transfer a few things from the *Peacock* and to purchase some others on shore, but I regarded with a sad stomach the very scanty supply upon which I was to depend, while others were feasting on the bountiful store which I had taken so much trouble to procure. This was another lesson for my philosophy, but I stood it well, & made myself as contented as was possible.

Old Knox was again in Command of the Schooner, and I knew that we should agree much better than 3 in a bed, but two men form a poor society, and we were to be alone to our twa selves. Besides, I had not much fancy for Schooner Sailing, having had a prior taste of it that was not so pleasant in my recollections, and despite of some disagreeable duties on board Ship, I felt that I would prefer the *Peacock,* with the comforts & the companionship of 20 fellows, to the tiny schooner and a solitary associate, amiable as he might be. Guillou remained in the *Peacock,* & Dr. Whittle had been sent to her also. As these are two for whom I have a special regard, I had counted upon the solace of friendly intercourse with them in the unrestrained familiarity which so happily exists between messmates *who can be intimate,* & which far surpasses such a feeling among persons on shore, at least as far as my experience goes.

[CHAPTER 17: RETURN TO SAMOA]

On the 2nd of December we sailed from Honolulu in company with the *Peacock*—next day saw the *Vincennes* coming out—soon after got a breeze & made sail to the Southward. Knox now got his orders from Captain Hudson, & we found to our infinite astonishment that we were bound for Upolu once more, a destination welcome enough, but one we had not dreamed of. We were also to look at some Islands & shoals on the way.

My birth day passed quietly, but I drank a bumper of Champaigne to all hands at home. "25 years old—was 9 years in the Service & a miserable Midshipman still!" There, *that* is as good as a chapter; I need say nothing more, but I shall die soon if prospects do not mend. I cannot bear this being kept back, this wallowing in the mire, this horrible degradation of being kept to duties & in a station beneath my years. My pride if not all gone has received a cruel blow, and my zeal is fast vanishing away. What hopes have I? to be what I am now at 30—the thought is enough to drive me frantic. It is not the miserable & trifling ambition to be called a Lieutenant & to decorate my shoulder with the golden insignia of rank that disturbs me, but it is the all absorbing desire to be trusted with duties & responsibilities that are becoming to mankind, & I want to be rid of the insulting arrogance of *some, who are called my superiors.*

January [23d?] 1841

Who does not know old Knox? old Sam Knox! the present Captain of this vessel, and the only companion I have, or am likely to have, for a year to come? To answer my own question, I opine that none of the favoured ones who will even glance at this wondrous book have any idea of old Sam Nox! Yet from one end of the Pacific to the other, Sam Nox is known to every man, woman & child. In the Navy, Sam Nox is a familiar name to all hands from Captains to Midshipmen. Sam Nox is at this moment 2½ feet distant from me; that is, he is writing at one side of our round table, & I am at the other. It is not often that we are farther apart. The reason is obvious—this Schooner has not much more than 6 feet width, abaft.

Sam Knox is between 4 & 5 years my senior in years. He is of the same date as myself in the Service, though he entered 3 years before I did. Sam Knox is not 30 yet, but he has the bald head of a man of 60. Sam Nox has led a life of exposure, & his face shows it, as well as his hands. He looks old enough to be a Grandfather—I am afraid he will never be even a Papa!

Sam Knox, is one of the very best old fellows in the world, & he has a heap of shrewd sense. Sam Nox is an excellent Sailor and is worth his weight in gold most any time. Sam Nox has a good & a kind heart. Sam Nox & I cannot quarrel, though we are left all alone and are subject to daily annoyances that are very trying to the temper. Sam Nox & I never become cross at each other. Sam Nox has been at sea all his life almost, as were his father & Grandfather before him & as are all his Brothers now. But Sam has some very queer fancies at times. He is old fashioned; he belongs to a race of sailors that are fast disappearing.

Sam Nox & I have often nothing to do from morn till night, but to stare at each other, & to talk about any and every thing, but we get weary staring, & we can't talk for ever. Then we are puzzled. We can't read—we have no books (they are too stingy to lend us any from the *Peacock,* though I paid $3.60 in Oahu for a lot of new ones, just come out, & bought by subscription for the Ship—now I can't have any—*that* is provoking). We can't write—we have nothing to write about, or else the Cabin is too wet. Though to be sure, they *did repair* our Hatch on board the *Peacock* the other day. It used to be like a sieve; now it is like a shower bath. Let there be the least sea on, and our table is useless.

So *what* have we to do? What can we do? Nothing. We can't walk—oh, no, there is no space *here* for a promenade, & what's worse we can't even stand up unless we have something to hold on to. *There is nothing to hold on to;* we must squat down. No exercise, & I, who require it so much, suffer most horribly from the want of it and am pining for a run among the woods.

Old Nox & I are in a very small cage, & like the unfortunate Starling, "We can't get out! We can't get out!"[1] 53 days have we been tossed about on the vasty deep since leaving Oahu, & I have not seen the outside of the Schooner. Three or four small, uninhabited Islands that cost us a great deal of search & trouble to find and that were of no interest have been the only variations of the passage as yet.

Now do you know Old Sam Knox, or as he is familiarly called, Old Hard Nox? And have you any idea of the space & comfort to be found in this magnificent vessel of 70 whole tons & three sails? And what do you think of the intense degree of intellectual enjoyment that falls to *our* daily lot, that is Nox aforesaid & myself. As to our food! why name it? Why tell of the three staples that we poor sailors have to live on—Beef, Pork & Bread, in our case, increased by Potatoes? Why! yes, why growl about this? Well, I do not know, but I must vent my abhorrence of this sort of fare once more. I am disgusted with it, yet if you had seen me eat my dinner to day, you would have thought that *Salt horse*[2] was my particular delight! You would have been mistaken though. I hate it, as the bad man does the holy water; but nevertheless, nature's cravings must be satisfied, & I long ago learnt to make my meal off what ever I could get.

So we go on, and although we growl, growl, we keep going on, though we know that things will not mend. I ought to be used to such things now—and so I am—but the most patient Horse will kick sometimes. Well, now perhaps you know how I am fixed at present, and that is what I wanted, so will have a change.

Yesterday, no, the day before, which was the 26th day of January 1841, we made an Island marked on the Chart as Duke of York Island and as uninhabited by the *Pandora,* when she was in search of the Mutineers of the *Bounty*.[3] We had no accounts of its having been seen or visited since. Not expecting to find any people, though we remarked that there were but few birds about & that the Cocoa Nuts were thick on the Island, we were surprised as we ran along the shores by the sight of three or four huts peeping from a grove on the inner shore of the lagoon.

As we got under the lee of the Island in smooth water, the *Peacock*'s boats were about landing, & we could see the people moving among the trees. Presently, as we drew closer in, we observed five or six canoes full of persons paddling off to the farther end of the lagoon. Some there were on the beach, however, assisting the boats in landing, & now we were right among the folks ourselves, for the sea was smooth as glass, and we had shoved the Schooner almost ashore.

So, I began to complain aloud—"Well, this is too bad. Here we are, ordered to keep close in, & bring off the boats & we can't go ashore ourselves. There are the fellows on shore among the trees, surrounded by people & enjoying themselves, and we are to be satisfied with looking on"—So I went on, scolding & grumbling & feeling discontented & wretched, until Old Knox got weary listening, I suppose, for all of a sudden he said, "Well, you shall go ashore if the Boat will float—out with her, boys."

Whether the Boat *would* float was a matter of extreme doubt. She was old, chancy & leaky; she had no rudder; her gunnel was stove & she could only pull three oars. We had never ventured her in the water since leaving Oahu, so that even now my getting ashore was problematical in the greatest degree. However, the experiment *was* made—the boat was launched. She did not leak alarmingly, & provided with a *bailer* & some few trifles to trade, I pulled alongside of Old Emmons' boat & veering in, jumped on the reef & waded to dry land. I was ashore at last!

I felt like a bird let out of its cage, & my tread upon the grass was light as a feather. Oh! but it was gladsome to be once more under the shade of Trees, to hear the breeze rustling amid the foliage, and to breathe the untainted & fragrant air of the Land so pure & sweet as the first kiss of first love—hem!

[After surveying a number of other small islands], we steered for Upolu, where we hoped to rest & refresh, & whence our knowledge of our plan of proceedings ceased. We cannot guess whither we will turn, in leaving it.

Saturday February 6th, that is, yesterday, we made the high Land, at sight of which our eyes & stomachs were exceeding glad. We killed our last Pig, though we were loath to do so, for it was quite a Pet and skylarked so merrily with our Dog, "Fanny Squeers." The two gambolled about the deck, chasing one another like boys at "hide & seek," but conscience & mercy vanished before hunger, and old Nox & I were keen for some fresh food. So we eat the pig, & horrible to tell, Fanny partook largely of her quondam playmate. So we were in a very good humour, and we looked for a quiet time in the harbour of Apia & counted with certainty on having a mess of Pigeons for breakfast, a bath at the waterfall, and a roll on the grass beneath the Trees.

At Noon the *Peacock* hove to. Her Boats came to us. Imagine our distress, amazement, disgust, on learning *that we were not to go into Port at all,* but to commence a survey of the Island at once, & carry it all around. There was rank mutiny in our breasts, but it was no use, & by a most tremendous effort, Old Knox & I became resigned to our cruel fate—chiefly because we could not help it. But I leave it to you! 66 days at Sea!—right off the Harbour, full of the idea of entering, and suddenly forbid, & ordered on hard duty. Was it not *too* bad?

Besides this, the Island had been perfectly Surveyed when we were here before. This same Schooner had circumnavigated it, the *Peacock*'s boats had worked all around it, & Judge, Chase[4] & my humble self were fried to death for 4 or 5 days in "fixing in" the reefs & shores for 20 miles to the West of Apia. Captain Wilkes pretends to have lost this work. I never thought that that conversation would lead to this infernal resurvey that we were now to undertake. I no more believe that Captain Wilkes has lost that survey than I believe in Mahomet—and to answer his abominably malicious designs against a certain Lieutenant,[5] he will produce it when his purpose requires it, & comparing it with the second one, endeavour to substantiate the false charge he made. Time will show.

Well, in no very amiable mood, we received from the *Peacock* 80 Gallons of stinking, muddy water, & prepared to obey our instructions upon empty stomachs, for the Pig was all gone. However, we stood in for the Harbour, after the *Peacock,* & as the Wind was light, and the afternoon almost gone, Old Nox & I began to think that we could do nothing before night & that it would be much better to be at anchor until morning than to be crawling off the reefs. We became desperate and resolved to make an effort. Accordingly, we run up a signal, "asking permission to anchor," calculating that Captain Hudson would be rather taken aback, and in his surprise at our assurance, say yes! instead of no! He *did* say yes, & in a short time, we were riding quietly within a stone's throw of the beach.

It was Sunday on shore, and all was quiet & still. Not a canoe was launched, & the groups of dusky people that were collected under the trees to see the Man of War preserved the rigid silence which they have been taught to consider as due to the day of the Lord. The Natives met us on the beach, and we had so much shaking of hands, as we could attend to. Old & young crowded about us, and the welcome of "Calofa! Calofa!" was echoed by every tongue.

We had Fanny with us, intending to give her a run among the grass and a good scrubbing, but the creature was so frightened on touching the shore that she ran howling into the surf & had to be taken back in the boat. She was but a few weeks old when she came on board the Schooner, so that she has no recollection of the Land—the Schooner is her world. Alas! as will be seen, she was to be ours, too, for a while!

Old Knox returned to the Schooner, but I determined to have a look round, got a Native to paddle me over the river in a most diminutive Canoe and pursued the path to the Village, my ear delighted with the melody of the tiny birds that flittered from every branch. The old Chief of the town met me with a friendly recognition. [He] carried me to the big house, which had a young village under its roof, and offered me food. Water I accepted, and the draught, pure and cool from the spring, was more delicious than I can tell and more grateful than *you* can conceive of, as you have never been two months on foul water

at sea. I took a passage in the *Peacock*'s boat, went on board
her to see the folks, took old Whittle back to the Schooner with
me & after a swim alongside, spun yarns until late in the night.

Early in the morning we sent our boat for water, and the natives came alongside with Pigs, yams, cocoa nuts, chickens,
eggs & Taro, so that we very soon had a fair supply of fresh
grub. Eggs, boiled & fried for breakfast, were relished keenly.
We procured 200 Gallons water and at 9 went to sea better prepared for work than we had been the day before. A good looking young native was so anxious to have a cruize in a big canoe
that he begged to go with us, and we sailed with him aboard as
a cabin passenger & guest of our owner.

The weather proved very bad and prevented any thing like
surveying—calms, squalls & thick weather with a heavy swell
that knocked the Schooner about to the great prejudice of our
Samoa friend's bowels, who was horribly sea sick all the while
and did nothing else but lay on his back and sleep. We split our
sails, parted the rigging, and to keep from going to pieces altogether in a storm that we saw brewing, we went back and
anchored in Apia to wait for better weather.

As we neared the place, our *"flen,"* as he called himself,
began to revive a little, but he had still a squeamish feeling, and
he said he would go ashore and sleep. When we got fairly in,
however, his nausea left him, and his pride kept him on board
while he related to the folks that came off all the perils he had
gone through. He put on airs, too, and was very supercilious in
his behaviour to them & paraded his importance in a variety of
ways that afforded us much amusement.

The next day it came on to blow hard. Knox was on board
the *Peacock*. The Schooner dragged, & we had to let go the
second anchor. The rain came down in torrents, and the wind
blew so fiercely that we could not look up, for it battered the
drops into our faces like sharp hail. We dragged into two fathoms close to the beach & brought up just when we had no
more room to spare. I had to be on deck several hours, and for
the 999th time, I received additional & more convincing proof,
"that I could not melt," and this was all the satisfaction the
rain left me, for I was soaked *through the skin!*

In the heighth of the squall, our boat, with only two men in her, got adrift from the *Peacock,* and missing the Schooner, would have got into the surf had not our smart little *Kanaka,* "George Wash," done precisely what no one else would have attempted. He jumped overboard, swam to the boat, and by his help, they got safe alongside. I hoisted her in at once.

Towards the morning the wind lulled, but the thick & rainy weather kept us at anchor & confined the Schooner for 5 days. Our *"flen"* still hung on to the Cabin, & we became tired of him, so we devised ways and means to clear him out. We knew he was waiting for presents—he did not wait long. He asked for Trowsers. I gave him a pair of mine. He tried them on; they fitted to his perfect satisfaction and his limbs, for the first time, were cased in tights. Then he asked for a shirt. Now though I was disposed to gratify him to the extent of his wishes, my shirts were articles too sacred in my eyes to be lightly thrown away. Shirts do not grow on the trees, hereabouts, nor are shirts to be met with every day at sea. No, I could not part with a shirt, but I gave him a sheet instead. Was he contented? No! "Jacket" was his next cry.

Now, I was not yielding to his begging, because I had any particular regard for him, for neither Knox or myself liked him at all. He was foolish, greedy & selfish, but for amusement['s] sake, and to see how far he would go, I determined to humour him. Of Jackets, like shirts, I had none to give away—2 fathoms of Calico, supplied this demand. Then he wanted a hatchet—I gave him a handkerchief; a knife, I handed him one; a pair of scissors, he got them; tobacco, tobacco swelled his pile; pipe! "Go to the devil!" said I, my patience and generosity at an end, and I bundled him out of the Cabin and out of the Schooner with his easily gotten treasures, right glad to be rid of him and firmly set against having any more Samoa *"flens"* of his calibre.

I went on shore one morning, between the squalls & remained for a couple of hours, but the walking was so bad, that I could not see the waterfall, but had to remain in the Village. I was quite shocked to learn that Emma Malietoa, the Rose of the Islands, was married to a man old enough for her father.

We sailed again, with a good supply of food and water. The second day, spoke an American Whaler, the *John Howland*.[6] They had a Whale alongside and were "cutting in," a sight I had always been most curious to see, and it was strange to look at those huge strips of blubber and blood as they were cut from the carcass & hoisted on deck. Two of her boats were some distance off, each towing a whale, making three captures in one day.

That night it was calm, and in my watch I had to sweep the Schooner[7] clear of the breakers. It was not until the afternoon of the next day that we got a breeze and commenced the survey. We hated the work and were as cross as men ought ever to be. Our instructions were a perfect curiosity. It was impossible to fulfil them at all, and yet we were expected to execute all they required in 3 or 4 days. So much for having a Commander, who has no idea of surveying. We concluded to do as our reason told us and to let the orders go to the dogs. Sea soundings, Latitude & Longitude, best anchorages, harbours, sailing directions & all—bah!

So we worked slowly along the Island, eating Fresh Pig every day, the only consolation we had. One evening it fell calm, and we anchored off a very picturesque & romantic part of the shore, with a bold, bluff rock overgrown with trees and vines and moss & flowers immediately over our decks. A white man came off and many natives with things to sell. I went ashore with the white man in his Canoe to refresh myself with a walk. The unwonted exercise was quite exciting. I strode on most vigorously and felt so delightfully buoyant that it seemed to me as if I had never known the charms of pedestrianism before. My whole frame was in a glow and thrill, and I almost fancied I was on wings. I felt as if I could step out for ever. It was just sunset. Have you any idea of the Garden of Eden as it was, fresh & glorious from the hands of the Creator? Eden could not have been more beautiful than the scene amid which my path led.

We continued knocking about until the 24th, when, on rounding the East end of the Island, we saw the *Peacock* outside the reef and under all sails. We supposed that, tired of waiting for us, Captain Hudson had determined to meet us and proceed on his cruize. We thought we were clear of Upolu at last. Not so, however—the *Peacock* stood in for the Land and anchored in the harbor of Salufato, and at 8 that night we came to alongside her, having learned that the Town was to be attacked and burned the first thing in the morning.

This was news to us. We had not anticipated any thing of the kind, and full of the expectation of a tremendous conflagration and of great deeds to be done, I could scarcely sleep a wink. I was up at the first peep of dawn, roused out the Rifles & Pistols, put fresh flints in them & loaded them all myself, while Old Knox got the shot up & the 12 pounders ready for action. Next I gave my long sword a rub on the Whetstone, and then I was ready to try it on the first native, who might give me a chance. I was in a perfect fever. It was rumoured that the people would show fight, and burning for the fray, I scarce could contain myself within sober bounds.

All my valourous longings were destined, however, to be nipt in the bud. There were no signs of haste & scarcely any of preparation to be observed on board the *Peacock*, and 9 o'clock came before they began in earnest to make ready. As the schooner was to be idle, I went on board the Ship, to try and squeeze myself in with the shore party, but Captain Hudson sent me back, took all the Schooner's crew from her, and left none but Knox, myself, one white man & four Kanakas on board.

There was not a breath of air stirring on the water, and the shore seemed wrapt in deep repose. Occasionally and but very seldom a native was to be seen for an instant, moving amid the trees. The boats were manned and dropt clear of the Ship, and the first gun was fired, loaded with round shot & grape. We were within a stone's throw of the shore, and we watched the shot as they made destruction about the houses & trees, for this fire was merely intended as a preliminary thing to cover the advance of the boats. Before the smoke cleared away, we saw about a dozen people run from a sheltered spot where they had been stowed and make a strait wake for the Hills.

After a short interval, a second gun was fired, and so on, very deliberately, until some dozen shots had been sent, when the

Boats pushed for the beach. They landed & set fire to the houses of three Villages without seeing a soul. The people had become panic stricken & fled, and there was nothing to war against that had life. When this was done, the Boats repaired to another part of the Bay & burned and destroyed two other towns without any opposition. The blaze was bright among the trees, the smoke rolled upward over the green hills, and the only sound that reached our ears was the crackling of the light wood amid the flames. The boats returned, & during the rest of the day, we saw no signs of life upon the shore.

[An American seaman had been] killed by two brothers who lived in the town of Salufato, one of those now laid waste. To secure these two culprits had been Captain Hudson's object, & he had demanded them of their Chief without success. Failing in getting them, he resorted to the means of burning all the towns belonging to their Chief as a punishment which the whole community would feel & by which all would suffer inconvenience, though not the extreme of distress.

Next day [one of the *Peacock*'s boats], with Emmons & Harrison,[8] came alongside of us to be employed on Secret Service. We were to go to the small Island of Monono and endeavor to secure as prisoner a Chief, who was a relative of "Popotuná,"[one of the fugitive brothers,] in the hope that by holding him, we might cause the murderous Popotuna to be delivered up to us. Next morning was Sunday on shore, and we anchored close to the Island. After breakfast, Emmons, Harrison & myself pulled to the beach. The Natives met us, and the very first moment asked us what we have come ashore on Monono for?—a question very unusual, and indeed one never asked us before. They also inquired about *Salufato*, the news having reached them already. We told them we were come to survey the Island, which was the pretext assigned in the orders of Captain Hudson. Emmons, after making a show of obtaining some observations, proceeded on with the boat, while I started to walk around the Island & gather any information I could pick up.

I was soon alone in the path. The people were at Church, for the sounding of the "hollow log" was summoning them as we landed, and I pursued my way, charmed with the music of the birds and lost in wondering admiration of the lovely prospects that every step disclosed. After I had walked some time, I met Mr. Heath's congregation[9] returning from Church. Like the others, they asked why the man of war boats were come on shore on Monono? and I marvelled at their anxiety. One man dressed in a black frock coat and no trowsers demanded of me if I had been at Salufato? I told him, yes—he replied [that] I was no good, and looking at me, as if I had been a common hangman, he passed on his way in great disgust. Many of the men looked doubtingly on me. Some would not salute me, and others would not answer my "Calafa!"

I thought this strange but could not attribute it entirely to the affair at the other Island. The women were free from this, and I had to shake hands with them all—a very serious task. Their hideous bonnets were quite a deformity to them. More uncouth things could not have been invented, and they were but a sorry substitute for the green leaf wreathed around the brow & the wild flowers in the raven hair! The Missionaries have no poetry in *them,* or they would not be so.

As I came near to Mr. Heath's house, an elderly native, whose countenance had an expression nearer the divine than I ever saw on human face, came from his hut, all smiles & joy, and after hugging me in a most affectionate embrace, he walked on with me arm in arm, repeating the words "Man of war," & looking into my face with so much reverence that I could scarcely bear his gaze. He left me at Mr. Heath's door, where the Reverend gentleman met me & ushered me in.

After a little conversation, I was completely taken aback by Mr. Heath's saying, "Three or four days ago news was sent here from Apia that you were coming to Monono to take the Old Chief of the Island away in order to get Popotuna, and that he should look out for himself!" Now, I had been considering in what way *to pump* Mr. Heath, without the least idea that the object of our visit was suspected, and I had been somewhat puzzled how to proceed without creating suspicions in the mind of one so shrewd. My intended manoeuvering was knocked on the head, and diplomacy had to go on the other tack. *Pump* Mr. Heath indeed! Keep him from suspicion, when he & every one on the Island had known for four days all about the affair!

Mr. Heath continued, "The natives have heard that you have burned Salufato. They have been greatly frightened and are much alarmed about the Old Chief, who is beloved by them all. They have come here since you entered the house & begged me to ask you, whether you have really come to take him away." I was at no loss, now, to account for the singular conduct of the Natives I had met, & I saw at once that we could not hope for success.

I *had* to give Mr. Heath a reply, and in the course of the next few minutes, I told him such a complicated mass of falsehoods and discussed all the pros & cons of the affair with so much coolness, treating it altogether as an improbability, that I saw he believed *me,* and that his uneasiness had vanished. *I have a conscience,* I know, and this was not the first time I have felt its twinge. There was a very disagreeable sensation in my throat that came nigh choking me at the outset, and altogether it was very unpleasant to tell so many lies.

I was half inclined to say nothing to the discredit of the rumour, but rather lead him to put some faith in it, for in my own mind I viewed the measure as extremely absurd, and was fully impressed that if we did capture Pare, it would only raise a tremendous outcry against us through the group, without aiding us in the least to secure Popotuna. Pare is Popotuna's Uncle, & Pare has influence on Monono, but Pare could not, as Tuindricate did at Rawah, say to any one, "Go & bring my brother here & kill him, if he resists!" Neither would Popotuna's people deliver him up, even if we were to threaten to kill Pare. Pare is nobody, on Savie—Popotuna is dreaded by all & liked by many.

The project seemed to me so silly and to be fraught with nothing but evil, that I was completely disgusted with the part I was necessitated to play. I knew that to get Popotuna was made a great point of by the Commander of the Expedition. I knew that his former attempts to Capture him had failed. I was fully aware of the orders of my superiors. My sense of duty would not allow me to mar their plans by any scruples of my own, and I made up my mind to the only course I saw open for me, and that was to deceive Mr. Heath by telling him a lie.

Having led him to believe that the rumour was false and told him that we merely came to survey the reef around the Island & the passage, that the Ship was not coming near, & that we should only remain one day more, I ascertained in the most artful manner the residence of Pare. After some more talk, I prepared to leave and continue my walk. At the door, Mr. Heath said, "Well, I suppose I may as well tell Pare's friends that they need not be alarmed any more about him, that you have not come to do him harm. They are still waiting and very anxious to know." The effect that such an assurance might have & the probable chance it *might* give me to capture our man by removing his fears flashed through my mind in an instant, but to give it so directly and explicitly was what I was unprepared for. There was a very hard jerk somewhere between my heart & mouth. I could not help it, however, and I capped the climax by telling a bigger lie than I had told before! My cheeks burned as I went my way; I was ashamed, and I felt an inward consciousness of wrong! It was of no use to worry myself, however, & I dismissed the matter from my mind [and returned to the schooner].

Next morning, Emmons shoved off to land again, and we got the Schooner underweigh to cruize around the Island. Canoes now came off to us with yams & Pigs. Every canoe had clubs in it, and this we had never seen before. The natives would hold up these clubs & pretend as if they wished to sell them and had brought them for no other purpose; then they dropt them down in the bottom of the canoes and turned to other things.

In the evening Old Emmons came off, loaded with Pigs & yams, so that we had a good supply, notwithstanding our loss at Apia. He had not been able to take a single measure towards the object of his visit. The jealous fears of the Natives had been too keenly awakened. Pare was not to be seen and to have but breathed his name or hung about his house would have aroused young and old to arms. The orders were express, not to capture Pare by force, but stratagem. All attempts of the latter were frustrated by the timely warning that had reached the

Island, & I was not at all sorry that the Expedition was now to be abandoned.

In the morning watch (mine) we stood over for Savie to find the harbour where we were to meet the *Peacock,* but we had no idea of its position, and could only hope to discover it by strict search. The weather looked bad, & that night it came on to blow quite hard. The *Peacock*'s boat had to be hoisted in, and we stood off shore under short sail. The rain came down as it did when Noah launched his ark, and the mist prevented a sight of the land. Those watches were very disagreeable, and while I kept them, I vowed for the 10,000th time that I would never go to sea again.

For 5 days did we "battle the Watch" around the Island without success. Still *we had hopes,* and we expected to have a quiet spell at anchor for several days to repair damages and take a run ashore. At last we discovered the *Peacock* at anchor and run in. Disappointment met us again. The harbour was nothing but a most unsafe roadstead that no one would think of remaining in at this season, and the first salutation we got was, "Be ready to go to Sea, in four hours!" The *Peacock* had got in the night before, only, and three of her boats were stove already by the swell as they were landing for water.

We lay about twice our length from the breakers that came rolling over the reef in all the grandeur of Ocean spending his might upon the rocks, and the Schooner tossed like an eggshell, just without the foam. We got some wood & water from the *Peacock* & went to Sea in the afternoon with our minds made up to any fate.

[CHAPTER 18: RETURN TO OAHU]

It was March 6th that we sailed from Savie. On the 13th we made Elliss Island. We have been conjecturing about out arrival on the Nor West Coast & endeavouring to judge from our manner of navigation what Captain Hudson's ideas are, but every thing is so unsatisfactory that we puzzle ourselves in vain. We thought that if there was any hurry (and why the greatest expedition should *not* be used, we cannot imagine), we would only fix the positions of such Islands as lay in our way and not delay to survey them, more particularly the low Islands that are entirely without harbours or anchoring places and destitute of every thing save people & cocoa nuts. Why these should be surveyed at all is an incomprehensible mystery to me. Some are even without tree or inhabitants.

Elliss Island was to be surveyed, and we set about it. We had a fresh breeze, but a number of canoes came off in the hope of catching us, and we hove to to pick one up so that we could see what kind of people they were. They were a new race, differing from any we have seen—light of colour as the Navigators but with sharper features and with beards. We allowed one keen eyed fellow with "as Eagle a Nose" as Mr. John Effingham[1] to come on board, and he was in an extacy of joy. He took a fancy to me at once—we rubbed noses in a most loving manner, and he hugged me to his bare breast. Now he would let me go and pat me all over with his hands, mumbling the while as if I were his dearest child, and then he would catch me in his arms again and caper about, like one frantic.

I was highly amused, and I felt a great deal of regret that I could not go ashore among a people evidently so new to white men. My friend gave me his neck ornament, and we got all the mats & cocoa nuts in his canoe for a few fishhooks. As we had no time to delay, we had to use some gentle force to get rid of our visitor, who left us in sorrow & despair.

Other canoes were near us, paddling in vain & waving & shouting to us to stop. We passed by one in which were an old man with a silvery beard and two boys of such extraordinary & noble beauty that I shall never forget their looks, though we saw them for but a moment. They must have been twin brothers, they were so much alike—both with a profusion of shining hair that fell in luxuriant & wavy curls below their waists, and with faces of so mild & fascinating an expression that I felt miserable because I should not see them again.

It is curious to me that we spend months among people who have been visited for centuries, and when we come amid those who know so little of white men as to think they come from the clouds, we cannot spare a day to land on their shores. It is most outrageously tantalizing, & the journal of the cruize is robbed of that which would give the most interest to its pages.

[After several days of stormy weather, we came upon a low island] & surveyed it. We hove to alongside of the *Peacock* under the lee of the Island just before dark and were soon surrounded by many canoes. This Schooner is so low in the water that a single step from a Boat or Canoe will place a man on her decks. She has no bulwarks to afford the least protection to her crew, and consequently the persons of all on board are exposed from head to foot to any weapons that might be directed against them. The crew consists of 8 men only, and were we alone, we could not do much to keep off the natives, if they were disposed to attack us unless with a good breeze, when there could be no danger. As the *Peacock* was so near us at this time, [we permitted one canoe to come alongside].

They were the same race as the Elliss Islanders, and like them were affected with a cutaneous disorder that made many of them very dirty looking objects indeed. The skin seemed to lie in rough, horny scales over the entire body & limbs & even on the faces of some, so that the tattooing was hardly distinguishable. Those who were thus afflicted were very unpleasant to look upon, though they did not seem to feel any soreness or inconvenience from it. Our visiters were very desirous & clamorous that we should go ashore, and by their gestures, which were not of the most decent nature, they intimated what they considered as inducements for us to land.

At sundown we left De Peyster's Island but little wiser than we came, and steered to the West for the Kingsmill group. This was now the 18th of March; the wind hung dead ahead, and we had much fruitless beating, as the current carried us to leeward. Job's temper would certainly have given way if he had been in a dull craft, striving against a trade wind, and ours were not in the most amiable train, by any means.

[After we surveyed Sherson's Island on the 24th of March], the same head winds & the same unprofitable & wearisome beating attended a passage of 10 days before we made Drummond Island, in Latitude 1°00 South, and the largest of the Kingsmill group. Many canoes had come off to us during the forenoon and we had beheld their approach with much interest & curiosity, for we were aware that they were a new people, distinct from the De Peyster or Elliss Islanders, and we were all alive with impatience to see what the folks were like.

They were very good looking & reminded me of the Navigators in some instances. They were of a lighter colour than we expected to find them, from their being so directly under the Sun, and beards & mustaches were worn apparently by all who could raise them. Of these, they were very proud. My beard at this time has attained a darker hue than it had when I left Home, & I have suffered it to grow under my chin to a peak of some length. Almost all the natives that came alongside, young & old, noticed it most smilingly, stroking their own faces & pointing to mine in a way to signify their admiration of my taste.

Their canoes were of a totally different build & model from any that we have seen in the Pacific, & a wonderful skill & perseverance must have been employed in their construction. Some of them were made throughout with pieces of board not much larger than the palm of ones hand. These were sewn or lashed together & strengthened into shape by small timbers &

fore & aft pieces, but not a nail or hatchet is used in the whole work. How they manage to produce such excellent & sea worthy vessels with what we would consider *as no materials at all* might well surprise us, and the fearlessness & skill with which they managed them under sail was a proof to us that they passed much of their time afloat. Their paddles were rather insignificant, but the sails were well made & in good order.

We were close by the *Peacock,* and Fifty canoes were darting about us in all directions. We were going so rapidly that the canoes, although they sailed well, could not keep way with us, and as they glanced by us in passing them, with their naked & wild looking crews screaming to us and making all sorts of gestures, the scene was highly animated and afforded us much amusement. As we left the Island, the canoes dropt off from us, and towards evening Captain Hudson spoke us & said he would beat to windward during the night so as to reach the *next* Island, which was then in sight, by daylight.

[After being carried off shore by a fierce current], we made Land again, and at 8 we were close to it. These low Islands are so similar in appearance that they can scarcely be told apart, and as our reckoning was not very exact on account of the current, we were not certain which Island it was until among the canoes that were around us we [realized that] we were at *Drummond Island again* after 36 hours spent in trying to pass it & reach another.

We came upon shoal water at some distance from the land, and I suppose this circumstance aided in determining Captain Hudson to make a survey of the Island. Two of his boats were to proceed in Shore, and the Schooner to run down the reef and look out for the boats. It was Monday when we left the Ship to commence, and it was Thursday morning when we got back to her and dropped our anchor once more. The first thing we learned was that a party had landed from the *Peacock* on the day previous, and one of the Number killed. On the morrow the Boats were to land & burn the town! More War! It seems to me that our path through the Pacific is to be marked in blood.

When [Captain Hudson and his party had] landed, the natives met them in great numbers on the beach, and first & fore-most were a crowd of women, who seemed to have been se-lected for the occasion. These immediately attached themselves to individuals of the party & turned their steps away from the beach. The creatures seemed to have been tutored to the part they were to play, and they clung around the necks of our people so as to completely encumber them & render both limbs & weapons useless, unless by the exertion of violence, while the men swarmed about and picked their pockets & snatched whatever they could grab with the greatest effrontery, as if they were perfectly conscious of the advantage they possessed.

This pilfering was carried to an extent that became of serious consequence, and several were obliged to shake themselves clear of their feminine companions & present their weapons to keep the men off. The men, too, would come up in the most friendly manner & lock arms with our people and attempt to pass one of their own around both elbows and so draw the arms together behind the back, while with their unoccupied hand they would be stealing whatever they could lay hold of.

Matters became very unpleasant, and several who had strayed away entirely alone found themselves so surrounded by natives whose intentions were very evident, that they were con-vinced they owed their escape only to the timely appearance of others who had kept together, & who were obliged to be very resolute and to manhandle some of the most obstreperous na-tives in order to force their way along.

By this time most if not all of our party were very much of the belief that the people among whom they had been so promiscuously huddled, and who had treated them with so lit-tle ceremony, would kill them for what they had about them, and that they had best be getting off to the Boats. This they suc-ceeded in doing, when it was found that one man was missing, and just then shrieks were heard, as if from some person in mortal fear & agony. Two parties were sent to search for him, & his name was called often & loudly without any reply. As they were returning to the boats, they were stoned by the na-tives, who were making all sorts of taunting gestures & bran-dishing their spears in defiance. So the boats returned to the Ship, and it was mere fortune that their loss had been so slight.

There is no doubt in my mind that this calamity would have been avoided, had the party been kept together with [a] degree of order. It is very likely that Captain Hudson's indulgent nature partly influenced him to permit his Officers & men to seek amusement after their own fashion & free from any hindrance that his presence might create—linked with his belief that there would be no disposition on the part of the natives to molest persons so well armed. As the sequel proved, this was a most unfortunate thought and cost John Anderson his life. It is believed that the natives, having inveigled him to a little distance and attracted his attention by the wiles of the women, fell upon him & beat him to death. He had a Musket & a Pistol with him & must have been taken by surprise, & ere he could know his danger or stand on his defence, he fell, a victim to his own heedlessness & to the want of a better example on the part of his superiors.

Drummond's Island is 30 miles in length, but nowhere more than 400 yards wide. More properly it should be considered as a chain of Islets, for it is divided by a number of narrow & shallow channels. It is so thickly populated as almost to defy conjecture, yet from the immense number of houses, which fairly line the whole shore & exceed any thing of the kind that I ever saw, & from the swarms of canoes that we met with, I should estimate that 8000 beings existed on those slender shores. There were several villages on the same strip where the murder was committed, and we expected to meet with considerable opposition on the part of the natives, as they seemed to have reduced fighting to some sort of system among themselves and to have plenty of it.

Like the Hellish Feegees, their thirst for blood & plunder is inherent & too deeply rooted in their dispositions to allow a hope for its change. To extend mercy to such people ere you have read them a severe lesson and taught them to fear you by killing a score or two of them would be absolutely silly. They would despise your forbearance, attribute it to your cowardice, acquire a higher notion of their own bravery, and flushed with the successful perpetration of one murder without loss to themselves, they would have an extra stimulus to further deeds of blood whenever chance would throw any unfortunate vessel in their way. Therefore, much as the occasion for it is to be re-gretted in our instance, it became absolutely necessary to pun-ish them with fire and the sword, and so inspire them with a wholesome dread of the vengeance with which such conduct could be repaid.

At daylight of Friday the 9th of April, we got the Schooner ready for action and took up a position abreast the Town about a mile distant, which was as near as the shoals would allow us to approach. Meanwhile, the Boats of the *Peacock,* conveying a large party, pulled in for the Beach. When we anchored, the canoes came about us to the number of 20 or 30, and we thought we should have our hands full to keep them off.

As this was no time for humbug, when we found that ges-tures with the hand & shouting were of no avail but that they still approached, we took aim at them in such a significant manner and spoke with such earnest meaning in our tones, that they deemed it advisable to desist, for I had taken especial care to show them on the day before, by hanging one of their best pieces of armour[2] to the squaresail yard, that my double barrel would send two balls through it in a second. Just then it seemed to strike them that the Boats must be going on an errand of mischief, and after some consultation among themselves, which, while it was in progress, we had some idea might have reference to an attack on us from the offensive gestures of defi-ance that one gentleman without any clothes indulged in by slapping his long spear in the water, &c., &c., they all at once up with their sails and cleared out for their part of the Island with so much alacrity that we had no doubt they were well aware of the murder and somewhat alarmed as to what might be the consequences. They all stood for villages 6, 8 & 10 miles from the one that was to be attacked.

So we were all alone, and no more canoes approached us, though while the fight was raging there were many alongside the *Peacock,* and the people seemed to think that the burning & killing was great fun. It is likely they were not friends with those who were now to be made the Sufferers.

We watched the Boats with our glasses with much anxiety, & now that we had nothing to care about our own safety, it was most vexatious to be prevented from mingling in the affray that was going on before us. Those whom I loved have been murdered by such Hell Hounds of Islanders as these, & I myself have been put to some trifling uneasiness & inconvenience to keep from being knocked on the head & made a meal of, a most unpleasant mode of making an exit from this world and a most unsatisfactory way of being disposed of after death. So that I regard the bloody fiends as I do the sharks, and would feel the same kind of inward joy in killing them in battle, as I exult in when one of those monsters of the sea is torn from his hold on life.

Curious feelings come over one while listening to sounds that we know are carrying death with them and while we are so distant that we cannot tell whether friend or foe suffers the most. I looked through my glasses until my eyes ached. We saw the Boats draw up in a line abreast the beach, and all the natives in a crowd at the water's edge. A little delay, and a volley ran along the line of Boats. When the smoke blew away, not a native could be seen, but from the scattering fire that was kept up from the Boats we conjectured they were potting away at them among the bushes. Then we saw a rocket making its track through the air, & another, and then a bright blaze leaped up from the nearest House.

Then our people landed, & we saw them separate into divisions & disappear among the Huts, leaving a number on the beach to protect the Boats. Now the flames broke out every where, and from the combustible material of the Houses there was a tremendous glow. The flames mounted as high as the trees, the heated air reached us, & the clouds of smoke obscured the sun. The crackling of the bamboos sounded like the report of guns, and now & then we heard volleys and irregular shots. It was evident that our side had gained the day, but we were in a fever of excitement & impatient longing to know how things were going on with more certainty, & if any had been hurt.

It seemed long to us ere there was a finish made to the business, and it was a relief to us to see that one Boat was pulling direct for us. "No one hurt of our side, and 20 natives killed," satisfied our curiosity until we could learn the particulars, and we got the Schooner underweigh and stood for the *Peacock*.

The natives had been in great numbers on the beach when the Boats approached, and a parley was attempted in the hope to hear something of the fate of the [murdered] Man & perhaps to procure his body. If they gave it up without ransom, the Boats were to return without molesting them. If they demanded so much as a plug of tobacco, the party were to land & burn the spirit house. If they resisted this, the Town was to be destroyed.

The conduct of the Natives frustrated the attempt to hold a parly. They were armed & ready & anxious for a fight. They went through with all their taunting gestures of defiance and even waded out towards the Boats, brandishing their spears, either ignorant of the force of fire arms or despising the handfull of men arrayed against them. Nothing was left to do but to convince them of their error and of the imprudent part they had played, and when a dozen & more of them dropped at the first discharge, the rest fled without stopping to look behind them.

While the party were on shore, Mr. Peale[3] shot two fellows with his rifle who deemed themselves in perfect safety at a distance from him of 200 yards. Some natives who were near would not believe when one dropped that he had been touched, but thought he was playing possum. They approached him, and as they saw that a ball had gone in at the eye and out of the back of the head, they waited no longer but scampered off just in time to save themselves from a similar fate, with all their doubts satisfied &, I suspect, with their fear very much quickened.

The dying and the dead were left where they had fallen, and those whose insatiable cupidity had caused them to put on such a show of welcome to mask their designs of plunder & murder were taught by this lesson how the taking of a single white man's life would be visited on their heads.

When the Boats returned, they were hoisted up, & we made sail from Drummond Island ere the smoke of the burning villages had ceased to ascend.

[In the course of the next few weeks the *Peacock* and the

schooner completed the survey of the Kingsmill group and then continued northwestward toward the Marshall Islands.] It was now the last of April. We had been 5 months from Oahu. Our provisions & water were becoming scant. It was time we were on the North West coast, yet we were a long distance from it, and it was necessary to procure fresh supplies as soon as possible. At Pitts Island Old Emmons came on board & he brought the news that we were to go to Oahu from the Pescadores.

The day after, the 30th of April, was dead calm, and in the Forenoon the Purser[4] of the *Peacock* came on board to get an account of our provisions, &c., & brought an agreeable order which put us on ½ a Gallon of water a day & ¼ lb. of meat, and at this ratio we were to retain 60 days' supply, the Surplus to be sent to the *Peacock*. We were busy all day; 11 Barrels Beef & Pork we gave to the Ship & received from her Whiskey, water & wood of which we were deficient.

[After surveying Bikini and Eniwetok Islands in the Marshalls, the two vessels set sail to the eastward toward the Hawaiian Islands.] Ten days allowance of the sixty was already gone when we made our start, so that we had but 50 days left. We hope to reach Oahu in 6 weeks from the 10th of May, and I suspect that when we anchor there, we will not have water enough on board to drown a fly, or Beef enough for one meal.

The very sound of Oahu brought Home nearer to me, for latterly it has seemed to me as if Home and I were not in the same world! But with the mention of Oahu came the pleasing thought of Letters from our friends, of news that will interest us, and of mingling again with white people, who wear clothes and have no disposition *to kill & eat every body they see.* D——n these cannibal Islands—I am fairly sick of them.

                                                    Monday May 24th

Twenty four days have we been on this allowance of miserable beef, *good* bread, and alas! until to day, of *drinkable* water! But our long indulged suspicions have been verified: the water casks are *full* of *dead mice,* and the taste is—bah! I *cannot* say *what* it is!—horrible—name it not!

The Vulture of Hunger is gnawing at our livers, and we have

nought to solace it. The briny meat that keeps the life within us at the expense of health creates a thirst that we can afford but a drop of water to quench. No—*not* to *quench!* to barely relieve! Can a situation more tantalizing be imagined? Every salty morsel that we eat, parches the tongue. The hot sun streams upon us, calms oppress us, the winds hinder us, and we can hope for *no relief* until a long and weary month shall have passed away.

In this Latitude of 31° North (Would it were in the Atlantic!) we counted with certainty upon meeting with a fresh Westerly wind. We have been grievously disappointed & for the last 8 days have had light winds & calms. We are only 1500 miles from our Port, but we may be a month in reaching it, and we have only 36 days' provisions & water left. We have *Wood* enough now for *two* days more and shall have either to burn up spars that we can ill spare, or eat *raw* the horrible meat that we can scarcely bolt when cooked.

There is no place near for us to make a Harbour, and whatever may happen, we must bear it. I hope we can. We serve out the water by gills, and we each of us keep our allowance in bottles, which we hoard with the most jealous care. For breakfast I boil half a mug of water for my tea in a Lamp that I have, & to accomplish this, I have to use Oil that we strained from a Porpoise caught the other day. Our Lamp Oil & candles will barely serve us a month and can not be *wasted* for a culinary use. I cannot bear to go with merely cold water in the morning, and this hot tea is a wonderful help. I have managed to apply a mite to cleansing my teeth, though it squeezes my bottles dry.

Tuesday 25th May

The mice—the mice—the mice—and the Cockroaches that are like so many Turkey buzzards! As to the latter, they are hideous and overrun every thing. It takes me half an hour to bale their fragments out of my tea every morning, and they scour about the Cabin like so many Horses. As to the mice, so soon as night sets in they commence their revels, and they keep it up till day light.

Now, it is to be made known that *Sleep* in this Schooner is very rarely to be had. Since I joined her six months ago, it is a sad truth that I have never known one single night of sweet or refreshing rest. It is needless to say why this is so. Want of exercise does not help one to sleep. The mice & roaches & the heat have driven me from my berth, & I *"turn in"* on deck or on the lockers to toss & tumble through a most unquiet slumber until morning.

The mice make me nervous; they gallop in crowds over the deck, they fight, they scratch, they screech, they bite the wood work & keep a noisy uproar that sets us half crazy, because we can't stop *it* or *kill them.* We heave shoes at them & kick the bulkheads & get up & take the candle all over, but to no avail. The instant we lay down, the *theatricals* commence again. Last night one rascal came on my pillow three times & nearly startled me into a fit. I have thanked my stars more than once that I am not a man of nervous habits.

Fanny at times makes a rush among the performers and scatters them at the expense of several lives, but they are so numerous that we find their *dead* in the paint pots, in the *Slush,*[5] among our clothes, and at last, in the *water.* One of the men was made sick last night from drinking the water, & to day we were obliged to put what little we had saved up into a breaker & clean our bottles for the new cask that we are now using from. We will make *Tea,* from the *other,* as that will destroy the *taste!* All Knox's Coats & pants have been eaten by these vermin. Mine I left on board the *Peacock* in a tight drawer.

October 23rd

Could not eat any dinner to day, because the beef was so hard & dry. Roused from a most melancholy mood by the cry of "Porpoises! porpoises!" Go on deck. All hands up & Old Medley[6] rigging his harpoon in a fever of excitement. The fish dart across the bows like so many meteors in the water. Several times the Harpoon is thrown without success. Several minutes we pass in the torture of suspense, when a lucky heave sends the iron into one. "Haul in!—hand over the *bowline!*" & we are all engaged in securing the prize. He jumps and struggles fearfully & lashes the water into foam. "*We may lose him!*

No!—the bowline *is over his tail*. Haul in, boys!" and he is landed on deck!

Joy shines in every face at the prospect of a feast, and although the fire has been long put out, it is now got underway at once. The head of the Porpoise is cut off before it has ceased to flop about, and four or five knives are busy in stripping its blubber off and in cutting the meat. In a very short time the carcass is dissected, and the brains & some steaks are hissing in the frying pan. Old Knox & I superintend the butchering, as we had the Capture, with great satisfaction, and at 7 P.M. we sat down to a hot supper that an hour before we had not thought of.

Now, do not imagine that a Porpoise furnishes such morsels as would delight an epicure. Oh, no!—it is fishy & oily, and the meat, though tender, is black as one's hat and coarse as the bark of a tree. But to one in a state of hunger next door to starvation, & who has already eaten Dogs & Kangaroos & Shark and raw pork & *bad* beef & many other *nameless* things, a Porpoise steak does not come so amiss. By the aid of some Oahu wine that is not drinkable, some fish sauce and some pepper vinegar, our fry went very well, & we turned in to sleep with some feeling of internal comfort. But I only slumbered from 10 to 2—no more than four hours.

Sunday June 6th.

This cruize of now more than 6 months has had less to redeem it than any other I ever made, and it has pulled me down in flesh most woefully, if it has not sapped my health. Besides bad grub and the scarcity of it, besides the foul water & the want of it, the confinement has been nearly equal to a residence in a Penitentiary. This state of *non*locomotion has not been by any means a period of rest; the Schooner has dived and pitched, & rolled enough, and has been always on the go. What her masters have missed in walking, she has made up in Sailing, and we have never but once been able to throw aside care & anxiety by seeing her safe in a Harbour. Even then it blew a gale, with rain, thunder & lightning.

The Schooner has been so hardly used that she is all to pieces, and her rigging comes down in every blow. She leaks in her deck, and we have never been allowed time for repairs that were necessary, though we often asked for it & were as often promised it only to be put off. We have been shuffled off to get along as we best might, and, oh! strange to tell, have been treated as if we were begging for personal relief and denied the assistance we required from a public officer for a public vessel, in which were periled the lives of 11 men engaged, not on their own affairs, but on the public service.

The wind continued to be so flawy and unsteady that we were tantalized into the most feverish humour because we could not count with any certainty upon our run. Never were clouds scrutinized more anxiously. We watched the signs in the Sky both day & night, and as often as they failed, the Clerk of the weather was any thing but blessed. It certainly was very provoking. A breeze would come and carry us merrily along for an hour or so, when, just as we had persuaded ourselves with the fond belief that *this* wind *would last,* it would die away. Then when we had fretted a time, back would come the breeze, and the Schooner again show signs of life.

Still we made tolerable progress, and it was with much satisfaction that we observed every day, as we marked our position on the chart, the diminishing of the distance between us & Oahu. At last, on Sunday the 13th of June at 10 in the forenoon, we discovered high land ahead, as good a sight for our eyes as ever the first glimpse of the New World was to the vision of Columbus.

It was a mercy to us that *this* day the wind did *not* fail, but increased so that we carried the lee gunwale under and never took a rag off the Schooner. She was under water most all the while and tore & pitched through the foaming seas in a way that was glorious to behold. Shortening sail was the last thing we thought of, and we cracked on her so that no one could stand upright. It was a cheering excitement to *feel* her *go,* and we were sure we would be off the Port by dusk, all ready to enter it in the morning.

At 4 in the morning Knox & I turned out, & we soon had

the Schooner pointed for the shore. In half an hour we could distinguish "Diamond hill," and at 5 we had the houses plain in view. I went below & dressed to be all ready to go ashore, and by 6 we were entering the passage in the reef. We did not wait for a Pilot, & following the buoys, we got along very well for some distance, so that we were well inside when we took the ground & hung. After a little trouble we got afloat and anchored near the Consul's wharf by 7 o'clock.

After delivering to the Consul sundry letters of requisitions, I went next door to breakfast and had the satisfaction of sitting down to a well spread table that stood still & did not jump about. Before I had made much destruction among the edibles the Consul came in & handed me a letter & a bundle of papers. I had to stop—open the letter—look at its date—a year ago— all well! & I finished my meal.

[CHAPTER 19: TO THE COLUMBIA RIVER]

The second day the *Peacock* came in, and we were very busy in getting ready to sail. The men, however, were allowed liberty on shore for 24 hours to repay them for 6 months of hard work on shipboard, and we ourselves endeavoured by riding, eating & bathing to restore that animation of body & spirits which had been sadly wanting for so long. I was distressed beyond measure to find my weight had fallen from 14[7] to 135 lbs. Yes, 12 lbs. of solid flesh had frittered away by drachmas—enough to have gorged a dozen Shylocks.[1] With the thermometer at 156° Farenheit and food that would have ruined the digestive organs of even the Automaton Chess player;[2] with about the amount of violent exercise that a baby gets in its cradle; with a mind never free from anxiety and a disposition crusty as Mrs. ——, it is not to be wondered at that my shadow should grow less. *But 2 lbs. a month!* There was something terrible in the thought of turning into a second Calvin Edson[3] at this rate; and as I never was in a condition to spare even an ounce, I thought on my fate with tears in my eyes.

Simon Blunt was making a tour round the Islands & on hearing of our arrival, he came post has[t]e to Honolulu. He is one of the very dearest naval friends I have, and I was too happy to meet him so unexpectedly. His health was now restored, and Captain Hudson offered him a passage in his Cabin to the River, but Simon could not think of again putting himself under the command of Captain Wilkes.

Of a very enthusiastic disposition, Blunt volunteered for the Expedition with a heart brimful of devotion for its cause and with his mind zealously bent upon the duties of the cruize. He was prepared to go to all lengths, and there was *nothing* he would have dreaded so much as that which had *now* happened, a separation from the Squadron & his friends before the final termination of the concern. But this particular service, which at the outset we all regarded as a sort of Elysium, has turned into such a Hell & the Commander, whom we deemed as a model of all that was honorable & just, has proved to be such an abominable villain that even Simon Blunt, having once been forced to quit us by his illness, could not dream of returning again. With one of the kindest hearts, with a simplicity of character that rarely survives boyhood in any one, with a soul of honour and truth, Simon Blunt is liked by all who know him, & it is my happiness that he calls me friend or brother!

On the 2nd of June we sailed from Oahu and shaped the course for the Columbia River, the *Peacock* carrying short sail so as to keep us Company, Captain Hudson intending to try the entrance in the Schooner before he ventured the Ship. After being plagued with an Easterly wind for a long time & much farther North than we had expected, we at length got a fresh Westerly breeze, which carried us rapidly towards the Coast.

We looked forward to meeting the Squadron with much interest as we had been so long parted from our friends and as we should learn both what they had been doing meanwhile, & what was *now* to be the destination of us all. At last, on Sunday morning the 18th of July at 4 o'clock, the fog clearing away, showed us the Land at the mouth of the Columbia River only a few miles distant. The *Peacock* was not then in sight, although noises on board her had been heard two hours before.

There was scarcely any wind, & we drifted idly about until near 8 o'clock, when we caught a breeze from the Southward & Westward that put us to leeward of the entrance. The Ship was now in View and not far off but to windward & was making the best of her way to gain a position from whence she could run in.

It was with no slight interest that we made our approach to this portion of our native land. There was *something* in the thought of no longer having an ocean between us & our own *homes* & of being for a brief time upon the sod of America, though the Atlantic was so far away. But "the River" has been on our minds all the cruize. We have always looked to the time we should arrive at it as forming a great era in the history of the Expedition, and the season for visiting it having been once delayed & postponed, an additional twelvemonth had been tacked on to the voyage to enable us to reach the Coast *this* spring. The survey of the River, we always considered, would be the grand finale of our operations, and it over, there would be little else to do but to *get Home* as fast as we could!

Astoria[4] and the voyagers' tales of adventures in this region, some of which were fatal & melancholy enough in their termi-nations, were fresh in our memory, and it would be useless to deny that *we* had a presentiment that disaster & distress or death would happen to some of the vessels, or to some of us, ere our work would be done. I never could get rid of this feeling, and, like the others, could only hope for the best. Surveying, a pur-suit at all times attended with danger, is here from various causes an extremely perilous duty, and from the Experience that we had already known in other places, it was quite certain that our anxiety was not without reason for its existence.

We were off the River, at last, and after a separation of 8 months from our friends in the *Vincennes* & *Porpoise*—a pe-riod which had been fraught with peril to us all—we looked to meeting them with mingled feelings of pleasure and sadness, for as *they* had been three months *here,* we could hardly hope that *all* were safe.

As we expected Captain Hudson on board, we made all ready to receive him this Sunday morning, certain that he would come. In overhauling our clothes to dress up as the oc-casion required, Knox found his coats sadly injured by the mice, and I taunted him by reminding him what a snug drawer, free from all vermin, held all my best apparel on board the *Pea-cock*. Aware that the Schooner was no place to bring clothes to, I had left all my shore going ward robe in the Ship when I quit her in Oahu, and the things had never been in requisition since. Little did I think that before night, my tone of triumph would be so changed.

To our disappointment, the *Peacock* hugged the wind, & they were evidently about to attempt the entrance without waiting until we could work up to her. The weather continued thick at times, and owing to the wind & current, there was a heavy swell running, and the breakers inshore of us were quite high. All was so unfavourable that we did not expect to get in before the morrow.

At 2 o'clock we made out the *Peacock* to be ashore. Her sails were flying adrift & being furled, and on nearing her, we read a signal, which said, *"Aground, I am!"* We saw the sea of wild foam she was among, & *we gave her up for lost, from that moment!*

We continued to stand for her, until she again made a signal that *"We* were running into danger," when we wore off shore & hove to. We saw them hoisting out one Boat to receive an anchor, & a smaller boat was sounding about the Ship. The large boat was smashed instantly & the pieces came floating by us with the tide. The other boat was almost lost. Once she swamped; they had the good fortune to drift out of the breakers, & bale her clear. Finally she got safe back to the Ship, but it was by a very narrow risk. The breakers were tremendous, and they rolled on to the Ship with a force that must soon break her up. The poor thing, too, was lurching badly in her unnatural bed.

Another signal to us, "Act at your discretion." We made sail & tried to find the entrance, for night was fast approaching, & we were doubly anxious to get to a safe berth where we might be at hand to render assistance in the time of need. Now the minute Guns boomed over the waters, but there was no answer from the Shore. All there was dreary & silent, nor could we discern a single indication that there were people on the land.

Our efforts to find the entrance were in vain. A white line of foam appeared to extend from shore to shore & was a barrier over which we had a warning before our eyes not to attempt to pass. Another signal to us of "Danger," & we hauled off shore. It was nearly dark, & by another signal we were directed to stand to sea. With very sad & heavy hearts we stood to seaward & hove to for the night in great doubt as to the condition we should find the Ship in in the morning. They were now sending up rockets & night signals.

At 4 it was broad daylight, & we kept away for the entrance. Soon after we saw the Ship with her upper masts sent down. At 5.30 we were about a mile from her, when she made the old signal to us, of "Danger," so that we wore round & hove to. The breakers were still lashing against her sides and at times going clear over her, her bulwarks were washed away, and she was rolling so deeply that at every lurch it seemed to us as if she would right herself no more. At 6 she hoisted her ensign "*Union down,*" the mark of extreme distress, & to a sailor's eye of all symbols the most sad, the most forlorn. The sight of it fairly made me sick.

We could not approach near enough to be of service or to have any communication with our unfortunate brothers, and we could not learn their chances or their hopes. We feared there had already been some loss of life. The conjectures that chased each other through our minds were various but idle & only added to our distress, for no sooner would a gleam of hope enliven us, tha[n] it would be driven away by some symptom for the worse. Oh! how long & weary were the hours to us, ay, the moments to *us;* but to *them,* a moment was an Eternity.

Still we looked on, with all our eyes, and we knew that in a little while, *all would be over with the Ship!* Presently there was a loud cry from our men, & as the poor old *Peacock* gave her most sickening lurch *her Mizen Mast went by the board.* The rolling of the Ship as the huge seas beat against her was really dreadful to look at, but how much more so to those on her deck. Next, after the American ensign & its support had disappeared, the two remaining masts fell also, and the bare hull was left a wreck amid the breakers that were sweeping over it with a fury that must soon break it up & destroy it as a place of refuge altogether. To see those masts go, was as sorry a sight as ever I looked on, and I had so much of a sailor's feeling for my old Ship, that I regarded her dissolution with feelings that a landsman may not understand.

Again did we experience the distress that was almost maddenning of being so near our friends & debar[r]ed from aiding them. We would gladly have incurred risks if we could have taken the Schooner to a spot where she would have been of service, but as yet we could not distinguish an entrance, and still, even in *such* a crisis watchful upon us, the old signal of "Danger you are approaching" would be hoisted on the *stump* of the mizen mast.

We hung about her, now here, now there, as near as we could keep without getting aground ourselves, and when it was necessary for us to stretch off shore, it was with most unwilling hearts. It was hard to leave them—it was yet harder, to look on. At noon I went to the mast head, and having been drifted to the Southward by the tide, I could see what appeared to be the passage into the River. We determined to try it, and after some narrow risks that brought my heart to my throat more than once, we finally found ourselves *inside* the reef that had proved so fatal to the *Peacock*. We were desirous of anchoring & made a signal requesting permission to do so, but to our surprize it was not granted, and we had, very reluctantly, to run out to sea again. Signal was made to us that a "Pilot would be sent on the morrow," & from this we judged that there was some chance for escape, and that they had had communication with the shore.

At dark we stood off the land & hove too. We believed that all hands were still in the Ship and that they had not boats to take off the half of them on shore. *The Ship must go to pieces or sink* during the night, and we were haunted by horrible fancies of drowning men & by the harrowing question of *who, who shall we see on the morrow?*

I had the middle watch, and *rarely* have four hours seemed to me so long. The weather was not settled & was even threatening, and all the watch I thought of the poor fellows on the wreck. So wearily did the time pass away that when four o'clock came at last, it seemed to me that I had experienced emotions enough to have crowded a week.

At 8 o'clock when I went on deck again, we were *close* in with the reef, *but no ship was to be seen,* though some of the men declared they saw her quite plain much farther up the River, ports & all, with boats pulling around her stern. A glance through the glass made their mistake evident. The refraction had contorted some bushes into the resemblance of a Ship's hull, and in running my search along, I caught a sight of the Bowsprit & the head of the mizen mast just above the water, but *the hull* had sunk for ever. At the same instant we saw a large boat, *full of men,* pulling around a high point of land in the River, & we concluded they must be the *Sole Survivors.* The *Peacock* was gone, and, alas, as we thought, *she must have made herself the grave of an hundred men.*

The wind was so unsteady that it would have been destruction for us to have attempted an entrance at this time, & now, more than ever, we had a dread impatience to know *the worst* that was distressing in the extreme. We determined at all hazards to run in as soon as we had wind enough to fill the Sails, and we felt pretty confident we could hit the passage again.

I looked once more through the glass—"Good God! there is *a man* on the end of the Bowsprit, with the breakers roaring under his feet." Our first impulse was to launch a boat to go to his relief, but a moment's reflection told us that neither of ours would live in the Sea. *What* could we do? One solitary individual hanging by his eyelids, just waiting to be washed away. I never felt so much terror on another man's account in all my life. I looked once more and right happy was I to find I had been deceived. It was the *Cap* of the Bowsprit only; no human form was visible about the wreck.

Yet a while we were tortured waiting for a wind. At last it came, & the Schooner moved. We steered for the entrance, & again I struggled to the mast head to look out for the treacherous breakers which were not clearly distinguishable from the deck. I had not been long in my uneasy berth before I saw a dark object on the water far ahead and directly in the passage. It *might be a boat,* yet we had been deceived more than once by enormous trees that floated past us with the currents of the River. We neared it—I thought I could see the oars flash—I slid down on deck—a glass! There was no longer any doubt, a boat with an American Ensign flying was pulling for us, and in a few moments would be alongside.

Nearer she came, we could distinguish Old Emmons and an

Indian, the only sitters. I was too impatient *to wait,* & jumping on the taffrail, screamed at the top of my voice *to know if all were saved?* There was one moment of silence & suspense ere the answer came back—the very sea seemed stilled. *"All hands safe on shore & well!"* "Hurrah! hurrah!" there was no controlling it. The feeling *would burst out,* and there was another hearty cheer!

Old Emmons was welcomed like one from the dead, but he had no rest until he gave us the whole yarn, while we ran the Schooner in under the guidance of the queerest looking pilot I ever put my eyes on. Nearly all hands had been landed on the second morning by the boats, & taking advantage of the tide & a smooth time. But 30 men, the Captain, 1st Lieutenant, & some other Officers remained on board, & the boats were unable to return for them, though they made the attempt, & after imminent risks were obliged to return to the shore, from whence with fearful anxiety they watched the Ship. Only this remnant were on board when the masts were cut away. The Ship's bottom had stove in during the night, the water was up to the berth deck, and they had had a terrible time.

When we had stumbled upon the entrance to the River on the previous afternoon, these few only were in the Ship, & it was then that the Boats had put back, so that we did not see them, nor did we even think they had been hoisted out, and though matters had been bad enough all had been better than we had dared to hope. About sundown the boats succeeded in reaching the wreck & took all hands away, but it was much as they could do. One boat was turned over & over among the breakers, and the crew were only saved in time by another boat that chanced to be near. Several others were nearly lost, and one boat in particular was reared so upright by a monstrous sea that the man in the bows was thrown out of her, heels over head, & fell in the water astern.

It was a mercy that all were saved. Time pressed them so that no attention could be paid to any thing but the preservation of *life,* and before the first party left the Ship, the order was passed "for every one to leave in the clothes he stood in," not even a change was allowed, and the Boats were crowded as it was.

Of all with which the *Peacock* had been crammed, of all the countless things which constituted the outfit of a vessel of war, of all the personal effects of the Officers, of all the store of curious things collected in the past 8 months, how little was there left! The Captain saved his journal, and the surveys, the Master[5] his Chronometers, the Artist a few of his sketches, and all else was left a prey to the sea. There were some, indeed, who contrived to secure the few relics from which they could not bear to part, as he who cut the portrait of *his wife* from the frame & rolling up the pictured canvass, carried it away in his bosom.

The shore was but 2 miles from the wreck & was high & rocky, overgrown with grass & thick with huge pine trees. Rounding the point that shut the Ocean from the view, there was a cove so quiet, so sheltered & of such picturesque beauty that as the boats pulled close by the rocky shores with the green branches waving over their heads, the vines & flowers reaching even to the water's edge, the birds darting to & fro & the sweet & savoury odour of the land filling the air, the contrast to the wild & thrilling scenes of the wreck was so great & so sudden, that men unused to give way to such emotions found the moist drops to be glittering in their eyes.

And when the Schooner entered this lovely cove and lay as if she were asleep upon its calm waters, *we,* too, fresh from the turbulence of the Sea & the nervous excitement of the past few days, felt the sweet influence of safe & perfect repose. And there before us were the tents, the sylvan huts, the fires & the groups of the shipwrecked men. Another moment, & we had our brothers by the hands.

The majority of the Officers and crew were sent up the River to Astoria, where the [Hudson's Bay] Company have a small Establishment.[6] Here they were to go into quarters until the arrival of Captain Wilkes. The remainder were soon to follow.

There were three or four canoes full of Indians in the Cove, and once again we got a sight of a new people. They were a very curious looking race—within the common height, slender bodied, flat-heads, matted dirty long hair, small eyes, thick noses, big mouths, filthy skins, and copper complexions. Each man had his Gun & hunting knife, &c. Some were robed in blankets, some wore only a shirt, others had shooting jackets on & leggings, & some had nothing at all. Their pouches, moccasins, &c., were embroidered with beads & porcupine quills after the Indian fashion, and the handles of their knives & the stocks of the Guns were curiously ornamented in various ways.

Their Canoes, hollowed out of a single tree, were models of lightness & beauty, but there was that in them that attracted our attention above every thing else: salmon, yet alive, fresh from the River & so huge that one was more than a mess for all hands of us. From four to nearly five feet in length and of a breadth that told well for the fat within, it was a delicious pleasure to contemplate them, and an Epicure would have gone stark mad with joy. A few charges of powder was the price for a fish that was worthy to be paid for in gold, and we had several on our deck in short order.

The dinner that day was superb: venison, salmon & Champaigne, Coffee (with milk) and cigars. Mr. Kone, Emmons, Perry & Baldwin were our guests, and we feasted away as if there had been never a Shipwreck at all. Mr. Kone was a Missionary who, with a Mr. Frost, had settled on the opposite shore of the River about 7 miles from the Cove. They had seen the Ship among the breakers and had hurried over to be of all the assistance they could. Mr. Kone had induced the Indians, by promising them a blanket apiece, to attempt reaching the Ship in their Canoe, but after several trials the breakers were too heavy, & they had to put back to the shore.

The next day every body went away up the River, & we were left alone in the Cove, the very first interval of quiet that the poor Schooner had known for more than 9 months. We made use of it to paint her and to refit the rigging as well as our very limited resources would permit.

Guillou came down to stay a week with us, and his company enlivened our solitude greatly, for by this time Knox and myself were no more society for each other than two sticks. With Guillou I now took [long] walks, penetrating through the wildest part of the Forest over to the Sea beach, & just following our noses for guides. The shore at the sea side was broken into Several hills with deep ravines between them letting out on to the beach. The faces of these hills were complete walls of black rock rising perpendicularly for 500 feet without a single blade of grass to relieve their ruggedness, but their summits were overrun with green & flowers and crowned with the gigantic Pines of the North.

There was just enough of sandy beach at the foot of these wild barriers for good & safe walking at ordinary tides. In some places the bluffs made out into the water so that we could not pass around them, and in others the surf rolled its foam close to our feet. There were many deep caves in the lower parts of the rock into which we entered for several hundred feet, & the whole length of the beach was strewn with huge dead trees brought thither by floods from the River & gales of wind. Mammoths of the forest and of an age tha[t] one could hardly grasp at, they were here mouldering away by the hundreds. The bald Eagles were wheeling over our heads & soaring aloft until they became mere specks against the sky. Myriads of sea fowl were on the wing, now darting into the water after their prey, shrieking & screaming like so many ghosts, now sailing away to secure their feast, safe from the pursuit of the keen eyed Monarchs of the air. Seals, with their uncouth heads just above the surface, were gambolling without the surf, and for miles the white line of breakers extended to where the poor old *Peacock* had found her grave. The whole scene was wild & strange to our eyes, after so long a stay among the soft Isles of the South.

About this time we received orders from Captain Hudson to get underweigh daily and make ourselves acquainted with the passage into the River. We had two Indian pilots on board, and when the weather permitted, we ran out to sea & returned again to the Cove. Ramsey & George, the Pilots, were brothers, and a precious couple they were. Ramsey was very short & very thick, with a head as big as the "Black dwarf's."[7] One eye was entirely closed up, and the other twinkled but faintly amid the folds of wrinkles that surrounded it. His hair was quite grey & fell in long, coarse locks to his shoulders, and, altogether, he resembled the figure of "Jack of Clubs" on a playing card. George was not so much of a picture. He was taller, his head was of the ordinary size, his hair long & black, but he had as villainous countenance as I ever beheld, one of those faces, from which you turn away at the first glance, satisfied that the possessor is, or ought to be, a candidate for the gallows.

Both these interesting individuals spoke broken English, and both were immoderately addicted to drinking rum & telling lies. Their cunning talk when they wanted to "come over us" for an extra glass of grog, was highly amusing, and we often gratified them because we could not resist such barefaced & impudent attempts. These two gentlemen were dressed in jacket & trowsers and, like the rest of their tribe, had several personal habits that rendered them very disagreeable intruders on board our little craft.

We soon tired of our inactive & solitary life and longed for the arrival of the *Vincennes*. The *Vincennes* and *Porpoise* had arrived off the River in May, but the breakers were so heavy that they did not attempt to enter. They kept on to the North for the Straits of Juan de Fuca & Puget Sound and commenced surveying operations there. Captain Wilkes came over to Fort Vancouver[8] by land and thence down the river to the mouth in the hope of seeing us appear. When he returned to his Ship, he left orders for us to commence the survey of the River immediately on our arrival. As May, June & July wore away and brought no word of the *Peacock* or Schooner, they came to the sad conclusion that we had been wrecked on some of the Islands and had made up their minds to have a good search for us before they got Home.

Despatches had been sent across the land to the *Vincennes* informing them of the loss of the Ship, but no[ne] received in answer until the 2nd of August, when young Waldron[9] came with orders from Captain Wilkes, and intelligence that the *Vincennes* & *Porpoise* were on their way to the River.

On the 6th, a quantity of provisions was brought down from Astoria for us to carry outside and await the *Vincennes*. Captain Hudson came on board also, & we got underweigh. We descried two vessels afar off & coming in with a fresh breeze. In less than two hours we were once more in company with our friends whom we had not seen for more than 8 months.

I went on board the *Vincennes* and had the pleasure to find them all well. Great was the hubbub, and all kinds of rumours were flying about. They expected to enter the River, but a little bird had told us that the *Vincennes* would continue on to San Francisco under the Command of Captain Ringgold, while Captain Wilkes remained with the *Porpoise* to survey the River. As we had expected, there had been more difficulties between Captain Wilkes & his Officers. Lieutenant Johnson was now under arrest, and Alden was 1st Lieutenant of the *Porpoise* in his place.

After all manner of backing & filling, boats passing & repassing during the afternoon, towards sundown Captain Wilkes moved aboard the *Porpoise*, and calling us within hail, ordered Knox to join him & leave me to carry the Schooner in. We were fortunate enough to reach the Cape before dark, where I had to heave to & pick up the Launch, so that on anchoring for the night, the Brig was a mile ahead of me. Ramsey was on board her, & George was with me, as neither Knox nor myself knew any thing about the upper channel. At daylight we were underweigh again. In a short time we saw that the *Porpoise* was hard & fast near a sand bank, at which George was much elated. As we passed near to the Brig, I sent the Launch to her assistance, & I chuckled as much as George did to find myself sailing ahead of the grand Commodore.

The morning was warm & clear, the River smooth, and it was a novelty to us to be navigating along shore after so long buffeting with the Ocean. Several Indian lodges & the house of the two Missionaries, having washed clothes hung on lines in front of it, were the only signs of life upon the banks until on rounding a bluff point, we opened the settlement of Astoria spread over the sunny side of the hill, with the big ensign of the *Peacock* waving over the largest shantee.

And so *I* had the honor of anchoring the first public vessel of the United States in the waters of this famous place & felt my importance accordingly. The *Porpoise* soon followed, and after a visit on board her, I landed for the first time on the Southern shore of the River and felt a little like, as if I was in my own countree—not much, however.

[CHAPTER 20: THE PURSUIT OF CORPORAL DEWEES]

Three rough frame & log houses—one a dwelling, the other two for stores—comprise all the edifices, belonging to the Company at Astoria, but there were so many huts & shantees belonging to the Shipwrecked people scattered over the hill side and so many groups in motion that the place had quite a lively, & stirring air.

Mr. Birnie,[1] the Agent of the Company, is a tall, portly, hale looking Scotchman, has an Indian Wife & a house full of children, and was exceedingly kind & hospitable to us all. The *Peacock*'s Officers were messing in common at his house, but almost every individual had his own little hut to sleep in, the work of his own hands, and formed of mats or planks or of both. Some of these were very pretty structures and were even enclosed in miniature yards with the ornaments of winding paths and little groves of transplanted pines. The men had one long shed and a number of smaller tenements, a barber's shop, a hotel, a nine pin alley, and a bakery. They had long streamers & flags flying from tall poles in different quarters, and rude mottoes were painted wherever there was room to stick them. It was quite an interesting colony and as yet only wanted a name.

We were not allowed much rest. More provisions were tumbled on board us & more men & *all* the Midshipmen save one & two or three other officers and Captain Ringgold, also, & the Schooner was crammed. Before dark we were at anchor in the Cove again, and that night we had a small celebration, after which Alden & I slept two in a bed and the rest wherever they could find room. In the morning we stood out, met the *Vincennes*, transfered the men, &c., to her, & away she steered to the South. A thick fog coming up, we could not see the land & were obliged to get an offing. For 3 days the fog continued, and we had an anxious time of it. We wanted to keep our position as nearly as possible, & yet we were very much afraid of the breakers. As it was, we just escaped. We got into 3 fathoms water and were only lucky enough to get clear again.

On the 3rd evening we succeeded in running in with a fresh breeze from the Southward & Eastward, but the weather was still thick at intervals with rain. On the way into the Cove we found a squadron of boats there and Captain Wilkes, who as usual, commenced with his ridiculous signals as soon as he saw us. He was alongside in a very few minutes with Captain Hudson, and although it was then dusk & the fog obscuring the land, he ordered Knox to up anchor, for he must be at Fort George[2] that night. We stared, as well we might, at the idea of such an attempt, but we had nothing to say, and accordingly we were under sail again, flying along at a tremendous rate. I really felt a cold shiver run all through me on finding myself once more alongside of Captain Wilkes. *He* had the impudence to ad[d]ress *me,* not on duty, but as I stood soaking in the rain, "if I had no Pea Jacket?"—just as if he *could* wheedle me into the belief that *he cared for my comfort.*

He seemed to think the Schooner was to find her own way up the narrow Channel, for we could see no land and were going too fast to sound. I expected every moment to strike. Knox would not say a word. The two Pilots proclaimed that they could do nothing, but old Bustamente[3] preserved his stupid & vacant stare, saying, "Look out, we must not lose the Cape until we get hold of the trees," when the fog had shut *all* the land from our view. At last, he appeared to wake up to a faint sense of our situation, and after questioning Knox & finding that we had nothing to guide us, he thought we had better return. Better *return* indeed!—no man in his senses, would have *started.* Great was our relief, to get rid of him when he reached the cove. He went ashore & pitched his tent for the night. Knox & I landed to see the folks, who were lying around their fires. I found Jim Gibson, & we had a long yarn of school boy days and about all the good people at Home.

The next morning was fair & clear, and making an early start, we were at Fort George by 10 o'clock. Dr. McLough[l]in[4] had just arrived from Fort Vancouver, & as he is an important personage in these parts, I was glad of this opportunity to see him.

Before noon we were hurried on board the Schooner to receive Dr. McLough[l]in & carry him down to the Missionaries, and off we went, accordingly. We worked down in a little while, aided by the tide, and having dressed myself for the occasion, I accompanied the Doctor on his visit, which was merely one of politeness, a civil *call* & no more.

As we were landing, we saw several persons walking down the beach at a little distance, who had the appearance of belonging to the crew of the *Peacock*. I supposed they were her men who had received permission to take a stroll and thought no more about the matter. The houses stand only 100 yards from the water, but before we reached them, Mr. Frost met us equipped for a journey, and having a man & a led pack horse with him. He excused himself to the Doctor for not returning to the house with him and hastened on.

I found Mrs. Frost & Mrs. Kone to be very pretty young women, and it really did my eyes good to see them. It was long since I had seen such cheeks & eyes. I set my tongue in motion, but I was soon drowned by the clatter of Mrs. Frost, who was pouring a torrent of words against Dr. McLoughlin about every thing, until they came to the matter of who the men were we had seen in advance of Mr. Frost. The two women & Mr. Kone hesitated & prevaricated in their answers, but the Doctor pushed his questions & much to my surprise, they at last admitted that one of them was a deserter from the *Peacock*'s crew, and that he was going the journey with the Rev. Mr. Frost. I had not even known that there had been a single desertion and was quite astounded.

It further turned out that this man, who was a Corporal of Marines, had been about their premises for several days & had been fed & lodged; that Mr. Frost had intended to send word to Captain Hudson that the man was at his house and that he, Mr. Frost, had been to the Camp but *did not* inform against the deserter, although he had intended so to do; that the Corporal had told them his time had expired several months ago, that he had a right to leave the Service with his Arms, & that he had done so with the design of remaining in the Country.

The Doctor scolded them very sharply for giving shelter to deserters (this was the second instance), as it was encouraging sailors to break their engagements and would bring troublesome persons among the settlers. He did not allude, however, to the peculiar blackness of the present transaction, which was certainly a most rascally affair & terribly unbecoming to one of the profession of the Rev. Mr. Frost. They were very much disconcerted and endeavoured to make apologies. Mrs. Frost's tongue went as fast as ever, but she expended her breath to no purpose, and I came to the conclusion that she was a very sharp tempered woman with no more honesty than her husband. Mrs. Kone was of much milder manners & infinitely more lady like than Mrs. Frost and was a very good, simple hearted creature, easily led by others.

The Doctor shortly made a move, and we returned on board, got underweigh & stood back to Astoria. As soon as the Doctor landed at Astoria, he informed Captain Wilkes of what had occurred, and before I could get ashore & make a report myself, I was ordered to pursue the said Corporal Dewees, until I found him. As there was no time to be lost, in a few minutes I was on my way in one of the *Porpoise*'s Boats with a crew from the Schooner and the Seargant of Marines[5] as my aide. I could not procure any cooked meat on board, and I was afraid we should want it sadly before we returned. My only equipments were my sword, pea jacket and a flask of brandy.

It was nearly dark when we got to the Mission, and landing, I met Mr. Kone on the beach. I told him my errand and asked where I should overtake Mr. Frost? "About 15 miles down the prairie"—that he was glad to find I was going for such a purpose, and hoped I would succeed; it would save much trouble to have the man back & that *he* had refused to have anything to do with him.

I requested him to procure me a guide and to give him directions, which he did. It was necessary to proceed a little farther with the boat as the tide was up and the beach impassible. About sundown we beached the Boat & hauled her up high & dry. I gave the crew all necessary cautions, as there were two Indian lodges at this place, and directed them to await my return.

The guide set out on a fast walk, and the Seargant & myself followed in his wake. Our way lay immediately along the Sea over a hard sand beach from 30 to 100 yards wide. This beach was bounded by the prairie bluff, the ground rising like a wall, and in heavy gales is covered by the Sea, which then throws its spray clear up into the Prairie. This wall or barrier, which looks exactly as if it were a dyke thrown up by men's hands, runs just here for 15 miles in a line almost as unerringly strait as the Compass can indicate, the shore being without a single indentation in the whole distance. It terminates where a high ridge comes down to the Sea & forms a prominent Cape.

On climbing this bluff, you find yourself overlooking a vast extent of Prairie land bounded by mountains in the distance. The Prairie is *"rolling."* Its surface is nowhere level or spread into broad plains, but is broken into a succession of long, undulating swells, and looks for all the world like a sea of green, arrested in its motion and made solid & still. It is overgrown with a tall grass & many flowers, and in many of the vales are clumps of bushes along the margin of the small streams, which here & there swell into gentle lakes. Such a prospect on the one hand & the roaring of the Sea at my feet made up a scene such as I had never before beheld.

Darkness soon overtook us, & we held on our way at a very rapid gate. I could not talk to the guide & had only to follow him in silence. I expected to be completely knocked up ere I could accomplish 15 miles. In the past 9 months I certainly had not walked 10 miles, and I was scarcely in a condition to undergo a hurried journey on foot. I could not guess how my expedition was going to terminate, but I determined to persevere as long as there was a hope of undertaking the Rev. Mr. Frost. I felt considerable spite against this gentleman already, and it increased at every step I took.

The Seargant was a fat, lazy man, even more unfitted than myself for a pedestrian excursion, & he very soon lagged behind, so as to delay us considerably. [My] waterproof boots (this was the last service they were on), now grown old from long & hard usage, began to gall my ancle, and during the rest of the tramp gave me so much pain that more than once, I was on the point of throwing them away & risking my bare feet.

By half past 10 I was so thirsty that I could not hold out unless I could get some water. My limbs were aching, & I felt so terribly fatigued that I had a great mind to lay me down to sleep & give up further progress. However, I could not knock under yet, and making the guide understand that I wanted to drink, he struck off from the beach, clambered up the sandy rampart, and took across the prairie.

We passed several of the swells until we came to a valley where the bushes denoted the existence of a stream. The Indian thrust himself among the thorns in several places, but the water proved *"peshack!"* Disappointed thus, we continued on until the sagacity of our conductor assured him he should not fail, and squeezing himself through a thicket, he called us to follow him.

At the risk of face, hands & clothes, we scrambled in and found him in a marsh, standing on the tufts of grass, which kept him from sinking in the mud. I stumbled & buried my knee, but I plucked myself out & got firm foothold. With the cup part of my brandy flask, the Indian dipped up the water, &, never waiting to inspect its limpidity, I drank about 50 measures as fast as he could fill them. Sweeter draughts I never knew. I took care to add a dash of spirits to the last one and felt wonderfully renovated thereby. I gave the Seargant a dose likewise in the hope that it would put fresh vigour in his frame. We were at the bottom of a snug little dell, protected from the wind, and the attractions of the spot as a place for sleep were so seductive and my weariness was so great, that it was with much difficulty I could muster resolution to proceed.

We now kept along the summit of one of the swells, as I supposed to command a view of the fires of the camp. I thought we might be close to Mr. Frost, and it was most vexatious to me, that I could not communicate a single word to my guide. The Seargant lagged astern so frequently, that I lost patience with him and threatened to leave him alone to the mercies of the wolves if he did not keep up. I half suspected he was desirous of delaying me in order to afford the Corporal a chance to escape.

At half past eleven I felt done up myself. I could walk no longer, & I signed to the guide that I must lay down & sleep. He pointed ahead & said, "fire, smoke." I looked, the Seargant looked, but we saw nothing. The Seargant wanted to drop down where we were, but I concluded the Indian must see what we could not and determined to go on yet a while. The Seargant's groan was very sincere, but there was no help for him.

It was just midnight when the Indian stopped at a clump of bushes & beckoned to me saying, "fire." He put the branches aside, and I saw several sleeping forms around a few live coals and got a glimpse of a sailor's hat. I made sure I had my man, pushed into the circle, & the sleepers starting up showed me the grim & tawny faces of a pack of Indians. There was not a white visage among them.

Disappointed, disgusted & full of bitterness against the Rev. Mr. Frost, I flung myself down on a mat, my limbs so stiff & sore that they gave me great pain. The guide collected a few twigs but not more than barely kept the coals. I would have given my head could we have raised a blazing fire, for the night air was chill & it now began to rain. Fleas attend Indians wherever they go, & there was no scarcity of the vermin here—they bit through my *boots*.

I placed the Seargant as a sort of screen between me & the men on one side, and my neighbours on the other were a young woman & her child. She had a blanket to cover her, but the others were naked and had only the shelter of small mats. The sky was a general pea jacket for us all. I fell into a most unquiet doze, but after 1 o'clock I could not close my eyes. I was shivering from the cold and the drizzling rain was decidedly unpleasant. Poor Seargant Heavisides was in deep affliction and groaned continually in such a dismal style, that wretched & spiteful as I felt myself, I could not help laughing at him under my breath. If I could have kept on my feet, I should certainly preferred doing so to laying down, but irksome as this was, it was the easiest position I could assume, and in spite of the rain & the cold I held out until ½ past 3. If it had not been for the Brandy, I should certainly have taken the Ague, or something worse.

The Indian had been up several times, looking at the sky for the signs of morning, and now he and another prepared themselves to start. It occurred to me that they must be sure we were so near to Mr. Frost as to be able to reach his camp before he moved, and we set off without a word at a terrible pace. The hope of succeeding alone enabled me to keep up with them. We took to the beach again, and until 5 o'clock never slacked our gait. The Seargant was out of sight astern. I felt completely fagged out and came to a dead stand, intending to turn back, but just then the Indians found the trail turning from the beach, and following it, we ascended to the prairie.

With fresh hopes of success, I pushed on, up and down the swells, for nearly a mile, when we came to a valley wider than usual with fine groves of trees scattered over it, and a long, beautiful lake in its midst. Here the Indians pointed ahead and exclaimed, "Smoke." I saw it, got quite excited, and hurrying on, I was close to the tent before I was observed. My sword was naked in my hand, as the sheath had come to pieces. I pulled aside the curtain of the tent and saw the *said Corporal Dewees, sitting on one bed* & the *Rev. Mr. Frost alongside him* on another, both of them having just started from their Sleep.

Without scarcely knowing it, I pointed my sword at the man's breast and told him, he was my prisoner! Much astonished was the Reverend gentleman to see me at all. Much discontented was he at my abruptness, for I did not even take a second glance at him or address to him a word. I ordered the Corporal, who was dumb with surprise at his sudden capture, to hand me his musket, for I was uncertain whether he would submit peaceably. He gave it up immediately, & I took care to hold on to it myself, as it was loaded with ball. It would never have done for me to let him escape, and I had made up my mind to use no half measures, if any difficulty took place. However, without a word he commenced to pack up his things, and I turned to compliment the Rev. Man Kidnapper at my leisure.

"Good morning Mr. Frost!" "Oh! good morning, good morning, Sir." This was enough for civility, & I was dying to let out some of my bile. So I said, very slowly, "If I had known yesterday, Sir, when I met you near your house, that *you had a deserter from the Ship in your company,* you would not have got so far without interruption, and I should have been spared a very disagreeable night walk." The Rev. Mr. Frost winced but had no reply. I stood silent at the door of the tent in the rain. I was afraid to trust my tongue further, for I longed to abuse him for the rascally part he had acted.

He addressed the Corporal with a, "Well Dewees, how do *you* feel about it? *Must* you go?" The answer, was, "Yes!" The Rev. gent. was *sorry* for it, and turning to me, said that the Corporal's *time* was *out,* these four months. I replied that the Corporal was a deserter from the Service, from which he had never been discharged. He repeated, "But *the man says,* his time *is up.*" I told him it was a matter I could not discuss, & he dropped the subject. It seemed to me as if he thought he could argue me into letting the man alone.

By this time the Corporal had his bundle made up and told me he was ready to start. I made a move accordingly, but, on Mr. Frost asking me to stay for some breakfast, I could not refuse. I was hungry, wet & tired; the Seargeant had not made his appearance. We had a long march to accomplish, & unless we took this chance for refreshment, we should not find another, & I doubted if we could hold out. Extreme necessity obliged me to sit down with the Rev. Mr. Frost, or I would have seen him —— first.

He now felt himself privileged to talk, I suppose. He did not attempt to conceal that Corporal Dewees was bound with him to the Willamet[6] and seemed very indifferent about it, too. He said he had not persuaded or bargained with him to go. The flimsy falsity of this assertion was disgusting. The man had been fed at his house, had been furnished with clothes & blankets, and now formed one of the party of which Mr. Frost was the head, whose way led through a wilderness where men had never travelled before, & where resources were necessary that the man himself could never command.

It was evident that Mr. Frost had encouraged & partly inveigled Corporal Dewees to accompany him, and that he had made provision for him, there can be no doubt, for he said to me that he could spare the food for my breakfast, as now he should have the fewer mouths to feed; that he had expected a pursuit before he crossed the plain and had said so, but that having got so far, he had thought the Corporal safe. This was admitting his interest in the matter, but he did not appear in the least disturbed or mortified, though, as I thought, there was so much reason for him to be ashamed. He, a clergyman & a Missionary, to be assisting a man to desert from the Service of his own Nation was under the circumstances a most villainous business, & I hope it will bring him to the disgrace which he richly deserves.

A man & boy composed the rest of the party. They were going on a tedious journey to the settlement at Willamet, making their own path as they proceeded, so that they could pass it with a drove of cattle on their return.

The breakfast, was but slight—some hot water barely tasting of tea, dried venison & ship's biscuit—but it did me infinite good. I was too much amused at the impudence of the boy to be angry, when he proposed to *me to desert,* and go with them, saying, "What a fine lot we should have," for which he was *applauded* by his master. By the way, Mr. Frost had harboured this same youth, who was a runaway from an English brig.

The meal was finished & the Seargant had not appeared—I set out to return, but we had not gone far before we met the poor man coming slowly along & tired to death. So I returned with him, that he might eat & rest. The rain continued to fall & the weather looked very threatening. Mr. Frost concluded to remain in his camp until it cleared up, & I allowed Seargant Heavisides a good resting spell.

It was past seven when we got fairly started. I gave the Indian the musket to carry, and the Seargeant & Corporal trudged along side by side. How weary was the way. I never was so much exhausted, and my body & limbs were sore, stiff & exceedingly painful. I could hardly drag one foot after the other. My brandy was all gone; the sun was obscured, and a cold brisk wind chilled me through. It was luckily on our backs, however, for we could not have stood it in our faces. Persevere! & so I did, for there was no remedy, but it nearly killed me. I never suffered so intensely in all my life. Even the Indian guide complained to me that his legs were sick, & I have no doubt they were.

At half past 11 I felt unable to move & told the guide we must go on to the prairie and sleep. So we ascended to it at once, & selecting a soft tuft of grass in a hollow, down I lay. We were very thirsty, but the Indian said the water here was "*pe-*

shack." He dug up some roots & gave them to me to chew; they were somewhat bitter but they moistened my throat. The next minute I was asleep. In one hour I woke up; all hands were dozing. The wet grass had chilled me through, and though I could have slept on for a week, I thought best to start again to warm us, and so off we went.

We passed 3 large spars on the beach & some planks that had drifted from the *Peacock*. The Corporal told me the Indians had picked up several boxes of candles and had lit up the lodge with them by the hundred.

Between 1 & 2 o'clock we reached the boat. I would not have walked another mile to save my life. It would have been useless to try—I should certainly have died in the attempt.

Now, the orders in the Squadron direct that the boats shall at all times have 3 days provisions & water in them, so that on being suddenly dispatched or unexpectedly detained, the crew would not suffer. But this order, like many others, was *never* put in practise on board either the *Vincennes* or *Peacock*. It seems it was *never neglected* on board the *Porpoise*. My men, in overhauling the chest in the boat, found there enough beef & pork for us all and plenty of bread. We fell to without further delay, and I picked my bone as dry as a chip after drinking about a gallon of water. We launched the boat & made sail with a fine breeze up the River. I stretched myself out in the stern and fancied myself on a bed of down.

The Corporal had to leave his borrowed clothes at the Mission & to procure his own & his bayonet, which he had left there. I landed him in charge of the Seargeant & went into Mr. Kone's house to wait for them. They were very much shocked to hear of my fatiguing journey, and they hastened to set a table for me, which looked so inviting that I made very short work of it.

Another hour brought us alongside the Schooner. The prisoner was put in irons on board the *Porpoise,* and all hands of us went to sleep. I shall never forget my starlight journey after Corporal Dewees. I learned afterwards that this same Corporal had worked for several years with Grid & Brenneman as a shoemaker, that he knew all the *Lancaster* people & had been born in the County.

[CHAPTER 21: LIFE ON THE COLUMBIA]

This was about the middle of August and the survey of the River not yet commenced. Several signals had been erected, however, & the work was now to begin. The two Brigs[1] were to go up the River to Vancouver, and *we* were to remain alone to undertake from "the bar to above Astoria." This was a most unsatisfactory arrangement for us, as we had already seen sufficient of this portion of the River and were very desirous of visiting the interior. There was no help for us, however, and we had to content ourselves with the prospect of two months of hard work, solitude and danger.

On the 19th we ran the first line of soundings near the Cape, and got a taste of what was to follow. The flood tide brought in such a heavy swell as to endanger parting our cables, & we had to heave up in a hurry & run in shore. I was away in a boat & had to pull for the cove. We soon found that the tide would delay us greatly, for we could seldom work except about slack water. Often we had to remain at anchor all night in a bad berth, where the Schooner would roll & work so that to sleep was impossible. After a day of toil & exposure this was rather tough. Then there would be a thick fog for several days, and we had to be idle, which was too annoying, for the good season was fast passing away.

[The loss of the schooner's two boats in a storm necessitated a brief return to Astoria for a replacement.] Dr. Palmer & Purser Speiden had been left at Astoria, the former in charge of the sick & the latter superintending the baking of 18,000 lbs. of bread for the Squadron from flour purchased of Dr. McLoughlin. Bob Johnson & Dr. Guillou, both being arrested, were also living there to await the return of the Brig. These two had had greatly improved the appearance of the place, and the settlement was called Bobville after the first named, who was Mayor of the City. New walks had been cut & graveled, a swing had been put up, new elegant & commodious mansions erected, the bakery was in full swing & various other arrangements had been made which it is unnecessary to mention.

Guillou was Schoolmaster to a tribe of young Birnies, and all hands assembled in the room which was the sitting, eating & sleeping apartment of the whole family every evening to tell stories & play with the children. The little creatures were totally unaccustomed to the society of educated (I mean conversable) persons, and they hung around us & clambered to our laps to hear over and over again the tales that are common to the Nursery at home, the Mother listening with as much interest as the children. The eldest of these was a fair haired girl of 13 & quite tall, but she did not deem herself too old to be fondled and had to be kissed as often & nursed[2] as long as any of the rest. In two only were there any signs of Indian blood. These had dark skins & hair; the others were fair as ourselves. Mrs. Birnie was a half breed and was a most excellent kind, Motherly Woman, as simple hearted as her youngest child. She preferred talking French, but she could express herself very well in English. The young ones were encouraged most in the latter, but they could jabber French & Indian also.

It was too funny to see a parcel of great big men, seated in a ring with this tribe of children, & playing "hunt the slipper," "going to London," &c., &c., the young ones happy beyond measure, & the Mother's eyes streaming with delight, while to the Indian women in the chimney corner, the thing was a mystery beyond their comprehension. It was a pleasant change to us from the rough & uncouth habits of our life to mingle thus with the young, but it only made me long the more to be at home.

There was an old boat laying on the beach that had been my especial eye sore on board the *Peacock,* for she was very crank & looked more like a coffin than any thing else. Several times I had nearly gone to that very respectable gentleman Davy Jones in her. She had been much improved recently from having capsized (at last) among the breakers during the wreck, & after drifting through a very heavy sea for 6 or 8 miles down the coast, had finally drove high & dry on the beach, where the surf was wild enough to break up a Ship.

The *Pearl*'s time had not come yet, and she was brought to Astoria by the Indians. She had not been repaired & was much stove. We launched her, and with sheet lead, tar, white lead, putty & nails we patched her up as well as we could. I was anything but pleased, to see her again & was fearful she would serve us an ugly trick.

We went at our work again, and for some weeks had fair weather. The *Pearl* leaked so badly that she had to be bailed every 15 minutes, but the boat never capsized or swamped entirely, though she came near it several times.

For more than three weeks we toiled on, solitary and alone. Those were weary weeks, & we were sick & tired of the Mouth of the Columbia, as well we might be. Besides, the duty was very dangerous. Once we came within an ace of having to abandon the Schooner & take to the boats, and in fact almost every moment was attended with infinite risk. It was like being under sentence of death, and it was so unpleasant and uncomfortable, that I should have felt a happy relief could I have known with any certainty "that I was born to be hung"—the thought of drowning would not have been so disagreeably intrusive.

Foggy days became more frequent as September advanced, so as to delay us very much. The wild birds were making their appearance, & some of the Indians having returned to the River, we now lived somewhat better on ducks, geese, elk & deer. On the 23rd September, we took advantage of a rainy day to run up to Astoria & land two sick men. We found the *Oregon* there; the *Porpoise* was to be down in a few days. Bob Johnson came alongside of us in a small canoe just as we were anchoring and told me there were four letters for me on shore dated in February, only seven months old.

I could scarcely credit him, though I thought he would not attempt such a cruel jest, but he showed me a letter of his own, and I was crazy to get ashore. It was such an unexpected happiness that it set me wild. The Company's caravan had crossed the Mountains & left our letters at Quebec, & we had given up all hope of receiving any. We were soon landed and I ran into Mrs. Birnie's room to be in quiet to read about Home, all to myself.

Bobsville still flourished and was now much enlivened by the arrival of the Brig. We had a pleasant evening, for we had good news from Home. It gave us new life, & I felt like another man.

We left the next morning & went to work again & kept hard at it, until the 1st October, when seeing the *Porpoise* appear, we joined her at Fort George. Captain Wilkes was creating a great hubbub as usual—doing every thing at once, & retarding the whole. All articles belonging to the Squadron were being embarked, & he was going to get the two Brigs out of the River as soon as possible. The portion of the River which he had allotted to us was yet unfinished, and *we* were to be *left behind* to complete it.

All was now hurry & bustle, & the good people ashore were to lose the inmates whose presence had entertained them so much. The children were all crying, and Mr. & Mrs. Birnie were very sad. A kindliness of feeling had sprung up between us, and our intercourse had been so happy & familiar that it really was quite painful to all of us to say farewell.

There was a devilish act to transpire before we left Astoria. Captain Wilkes, after having tyranized over & insulted Dr. Guillou so long & so often, at last, to cap the climax, to out Herod Herod, *refused to receive him into the Squadron* and was on the very point of sailing & leaving him at Astoria to find his way home as best he could. The sequel to this I will omit here, except that at the latest minute, the Doctor joined the *Oregon*.

Knox was taken on board the *Porpoise* as Pilot, George was on board the *Oregon*, & I was left with half a crew to carry the Schooner down to the cove. I started the last, but as the wind was ahead, the Schooner had the advantage, and passing the others most gallantly, I was the first to reach the Cove. Next morning, the 3rd, an order came out appointing Knox as Pilot to the *Porpoise* & myself as Pilot to the *Oregon* to carry them to sea. Sinclair[3] took charge of the schooner, & Knox & I consulted together & made ourselves as important as pilots generally were. The 3rd & 4th passed, & the wind did not serve. It was our task to round the Cape & look out how appearances were outside.

We persuaded Guillou to transfer himself to the Schooner, where he would be more comfortable than in the *Oregon*. On the 5th in the afternoon a fair breeze sprang up. Immediately after, we were underweigh, and under the skilful guidance of our hard earned experience, Knox & I put the vessels in blue water & safety, the Schooner following in our wake.

We hove to in deep water, & much to every ones surprise, Captain Wilkes transfered himself to the Schooner. Guillou was sent to the *Porpoise* temporarily, Knox & myself returned, and the next morning we stood into the River again, the Brigs keeping in the offing. Two boats had been left behind surveying, & the Carpenters & Sailmakers were still in the Cove at work on the rigging & sails of the *Peacock*'s launch. As we could not take her away, she was to be left with Mr. Birnie for the good of vessels coming to the River.

We hove to in the cove, and Captain Wilkes left us, taking Knox with him to examine a small river in the bay, Blair, myself, and three men only remaining on board to carry the Schooner up to Astoria, in the neighbourhood of which the boats were at work. Much to my delight, we met with no misfortune.

I had nothing to do all next day and lolled about to make the most of my holyday. During the day Captain Wilkes & Knox returned. They had not succeeded in finding the portage, notwithstanding Old Bustimente's boast, while they were searching for it, that he had never *seen* anything, he could not *find!* The blind, presumptuous, vain, ignorant fool—is it possible he does not know how ridiculous he makes himself in the eyes of every one he talks to for 5 minutes?

He seemed at this time to manifest great consideration towards *me*, as if desirous to obliterate the remembrance of the past. We had had no intercourse together since he hurried me out of the *Vincennes*, and now, as the cruize [w]as near its end, he imagined that a few smooth words, false & hollow though they be, will be sufficient to wipe away all sense of the thousand outrages we have groaned under during his tyrannical reign. He has, I am ashamed to say, succeeded with some, who have flung themselves into his arms without thinking that on the least cause he will trample on them again, the same as he has before.

He sent Knox and Blair away to sound in the Launch & our old worn out & leaky whale boat and left me in all the dignity and glory of command. The next morning the boats were employed again, and Captain Wilkes went to work himself, leaving me, with three men only, to take the Schooner down the River. Now, the duty on which he sent Knox belonged to me, and it was evident to us all that he was *trusting* the Schooner to *me* to flatter me up to the top of his bent. I thank my stars that I am not of so *gullable* a nature, as to be so easily duped.

This was the 8th October, & we saw Astoria for the last time. The Schooner came within a hand's breadth of getting on the beach just after I got underweigh. She drifted so close that I could have spit upon the sand from the deck, and I thought there was no chance to scrape clear. But the craft herself has a natural antipathy to making a monument of her bones, and aided by an eddy tide, she managed to just get by the point. This was the only place in the whole river, where the Shore could be approached so closely, there being 6 & 7 fathoms at the water's edge.

Although we had no boat, I was ordered to land on my way down and observe [angles] at several stations. To accomplish this, I borrowed Mr. Birnie's canoe and managed to do all that was requisite. The wind being ahead, after a most tedious beating I was obliged to anchor abreast the Missionary houses when the tide turned to the flood and lay there for the night. Soon after dark, the weather became very bad. A fresh wind from the West came directly in the River and raised a heavy swell, and squalls of wind & rain followed each other without intermission. The Schooner rolled so heavily that had I been free from anxiety, I could not have slept; as it was, I remained on deck nearly all night on the lookout and added another wrinkle to the number already crowded about my eyes.

On the 9th the weather moderated, & I beat the Schooner over to the [opposite] shore, where the Boats joined us, and we had a famous supper of wild fowl and also a good night's sleep. The next day the last lines' soundings were run, and after a hard tug at the sweeps & towing with the boats, we got the Schooner safely over the bar and out to sea. Only one of the Brigs was in sight, but from light winds & the currents we could not near her, and on the following afternoon Captain Wilkes took his Boat & pulled to her. He was too important to stay in the Schooner, & we were not at all sorry at his departure. On the 12th, at noon, the *Porpoise* joined us, when all our passengers left us, and we received orders to remain, and finish the bar, and then survey the Coast down to the line of our possessions. Further orders were not to be opened until this duty was performed, and we were on no account to re-enter the River.

The two Brigs made all sail with a fresh breeze for San Francisco, and we were left alone to do the work that the Brigs should have performed, instead of laying off & on in perfect idleness. This was just like "Bustimente." He kept himself and the Brigs clear of the bar when the weather was good & now left us there in the poor Schooner, just as the blows were coming on. We knew we should have a wretched & dangerous time, and our sails & rigging were so rotten, that we could put no trust in them whatsoever. Knox asked to be allowed to go in the River & refit. The answer was, "Refit at Sea"—we *did* "refit at Sea," with a vengeance.

We were in no pleasant mood, therefore, and as we thought of the fun & *fresh beef* to which the others were hastening at San Francisco, a place we were most eager to visit, we were miserable, indeed. After five days of unfavorable weather, we managed to sound a few short lines, when we were obliged to anchor in a very dangerous berth near to the North breakers, the wind having died away. There was a monstrous swell on, but we thought we'd try the boats & launched them, with some risk of staving them.

Blair & myself started. It was like going over the Alps. I never pulled in such rollers in my life, and I had some anxiety as to whether we should get back in safety. We *did* reach the Schooner without accident, but the swells had increased and on the bar the rollers now broke with huge tops of foam. The Schooner happened most luckily to be just beyond the bar in 8 fathoms water, and even there, it was now just touch & go.

I wanted Knox to get underweigh at once & go to sea, for it really was a frightful berth to ride a night in, with breakers on three sides of us and a strong tide on to them at times. Knox determined to hold on & be ready for a start if matters should become worse. We hoped the morrow would be a better day and that we could finish the bar & be done with it.

We had now been detained 6 days, and unless a chance soon offered, we would have to leave it incomplete, for the weather would grow worse & worse as the season advanced, & we had no time to delay. Vexed with our detention, mad that we were picked on for this work, the most important of the whole survey, without the means or opportunity of doing it faithfully, we were besides in great distress & uncertainty about our future destination, whether the Schooner was to be sold, & where we were to join the Squadron.

No rest this night either. 19th: the same tremendous swell setting in, nearly rolling the Schooner overboard & turning into *breakers* so close inside of us as really to alarm us all. A mist obscured the Land, so that we could not survey, & all day we were idle and *anxious*. Towards dark the rollers became worse, and the schooner lay in an unfavourable position, for she was broadside in to them, & they came in like young mountains, each threatening to sweep our deck. I urged Knox to get underweigh, but he refused. Now, however, *"the old men"* of the crew came to him, and at last, he concluded that we would be much better off at Sea, and that if we got out clear, we would do well.

Watching the best chance, we hove up the anchor and made sail. There were some moments of intense anxiety during which we did not know whether we should succeed or fail. Once all of us held our breath as we saw a most tremendous sea rising immediately ahead of us, and advancing toward us like a high wall of water ready to tumble over the first obstruction in its way. The helm was put down, and every one took hold of some rope to save himself by.

I jumped up the Main rigging & held on, like a salt. I felt that if that *"wall"* *should* break over us, it would sweep us all away & swamp the Schooner in an instant. The hurry & crowd of thoughts that come over a man in such moments, and which have oppressed me so often, now troubled me again, and I waited the result in a suspense that words cannot paint. The Schooner had some way on, & to our surprise & joy, she rose & crawled over the roller in safety & just in time, for it broke just under her stern, & the whole line of sea there was white & shining with its foam. A smaller one followed which took us off our legs for a moment, but the men worked like heroes. We got the Foresail set and without more danger got safely to sea.

Dry clothes, some salt beef, & a glass of whiskey set us to rights, but while we congratulated ourselves on being clear of this scrape, we could not help wondering what was to happen next. Knox determined that if the bar did not smooth down in one or two days, he would leave & proceed to obey the sealed orders with all despatch. 20th: light winds during the day. Towards night anchored off the bar. But little swell. 21st: fair weather & water perfectly smooth. Took a berth just outside the bar & started with the boats for all day to do all we could. Got alongside at sundown, heartily tired but satisfied that the bar was done at last, and that we had lived to see it.

So after a delay of 10 days we succeeded in doing 8 hours' work, which could & should have been done by the Brigs when they were idle & when there was no risk. The next day was foggy, so that we could just discover the Cape, and we made sail to the Southward, right glad to take our final departure from the Columbia River after a stay there of more than 3 months.

[October] 25th: the wind was now out [of the] South East & increased to a gale, with thick weather. Kept to the Southward & Westward under the Foresail & anticipated no harm. At 7 bells in the evening, I turned in & was enjoying a little vision of Home before going to sleep, when I & the rest, who were sitting up, heard something *snap* & the men singing out that the "Forestay had gone." My vision was rudely disturbed. The disastrous consequences likely to ensue from the accident presented themselves very disagreeably as we hurried on deck, but there was no time for delay. What was to be done, must be done quickly. The rope that was now parted and flying in two *supported both the masts,* & every moment until we could complete the remedy there was the most iminent risk of being dismasted.

I stood forward by the Foremast to be among the men who were at work, and while directing, bawling & helping, the sad pickle we were in presented itself at every stray moment that offered. The Schooner possesses no resources within herself, & from her rig, if one important thing goes, she is disabled. Doing our best, as we were, the men were obliged to work under water at the risk of being washed away, & we were very doubtful how our temporary securities would answer. If they lasted out this gale, they might part the next, & all hands of us felt that we were in a very uneasy predicament. Most fortunately the Jib had been taken in (the tack having carried away) 15 minutes before or the Foremast would have gone when the stay parted, & then we should have been a helpless wreck.

We did not think it *too* uncharitable to wish, that "the man" who told us *"to refit at sea"* had been lashed to the said stay when it blew away, & Captain Hudson ought to have kept him company, for Knox asked him for a new stay in Oahu & was refused. This was the commencement of a series of troubles that came near sending us after the poor *Sea Gull*, & caused me more anxiety for some days than I ever knew in my life before, or hope to know again.

26th & 27th: The gale continuing with heavy squalls, rain and a large sea. Spliced the Fore stay & secured it afresh. Went on ½ a Gallon of water, and by our reckoning we had a good offing from the Land.

28th: Blowing harder than ever, with an awful sea—my morning watch. The Schooner behaving bravely & straining very little. It was impossible not to admire the way in which she rode it out. At 7 very much surprised to make land ahead & all along under the lee. Wore ship instantly & did not feel much uneasiness, as the wind was dead off shore. During the forenoon the wind hauled to West, which altered our position entirely & brought the land under our lee. The change was attended with rain, thunder, lightning & hail, and as if these were not sufficient to contend with, there came a whirlwind in the clouds which threatened to sweep over us but luckily changed its gyrative course & went astern. It was certainly the most angry looking sight I ever saw among the clouds, & we were very much alarmed at its rapid approach.

We now found that we were in a sort of bay & that we were drifting ashore *a little*. The Seas were higher than any we had been among since we left Cape Horn, & the squalls blew as if the Heavens were coming asunder. We could carry but one sail, & that was our only hope, the Foresail, on the mast supported by the wounded stay. We were afraid this sail would split, and we watched the land, the sky, sea, & schooner during this *longest* day with an anxiety that was sharpened to torture. We dreaded the coming night.

We did not appear to gain an inch. The sea was tumbling us right into the bay, & getting desperate, we ventured to set the Jib, manoeuvering all the time as the wind veered a point or two to keep her on the tack which permitted us to head most off the shore. In 10 minutes the Jib was badly split, and we had to unbend it for repairs. It was lucky we did repair it, for during that night the Jib & Mainsail *saved us.* Darkness came on in this way, with the land as near as ever.

I lay down to sleep a little, for I was very much fagged out, and after taking in a restless doze until 9 o'clock, I awoke from a change in the Schooner's motion, and poor Guillou, who was sitting on the lockers the image of sad despair, told me that *the Foresail had split clear across,* and that we were under "bare poles." I roused out at once & went on deck. The wind had suddenly ceased, the sail gave two flaps & split & now, without a rag set, the Schooner was rolling & drifting at the mercy of the waves, which were still of an enormous height and coming on board on all sides. Old Knox was quietly at work bending the Jib, and one hand was stitching the Foresail together as he best could with the light the moon afforded, when she was free from clouds. The noise of the wind was hushed, and the tremendous heaving of the sea seemed unnatural in the calm.

Knox & I talked a little about our condition, and the men were labouring in that desperate & earnest silence so usual to them in times like this. Every now and then, as some monster of a sea would raise up & threaten to fall on board us, we warned the men to look out for themselves, and took care to secure *our*selves by the firmest hold we could obtain. Once our attention was otherwise directed, and the man at the helm, happening to observe a large wave was rising far above us, cried out in such thrilling tones, "Save yourselves!" that we turned to look at him as much as at the sea. He had cowered down nearly on his knees, and was grasping the tiller like grim death, his face white with terror, and distress, agony, despair on every feature. All this time the sea was heaving us into the bay, and when we thought on *what* was going to be the *end* of *this* scrape, we had to admit the possibility of total shipwreck by daylight, at which time, we allowed, we should be drifted close to the beach.

At 11 o'clock, we finished bending the Jib, and in mercy to us just then the wind came up strong from the North of West, and we gave her the double reefed Mainsail & Jib with the bonnet[4] off, rather doubtful how she would stand such sail, but it was *all* that we could do. Heavy squalls came over every half hour to which we had to lower the Mainsail, hoisting it as soon as they passed. The Schooner exceeded our expectations, and behaved wonderfully. She walked ahead at a rapid rate, & by a watchful and tender management of the helm she escaped the heaviest seas. At midnight Knox turned in, completely worn out. It was my watch, I was excited to a pitch that drove all idea of sleep away & I kept the deck until after six in the morning, having had about one hour's sleep in twenty-six.

I thought I could carry the Mainsail through some of the squalls and ran the risk accordingly, for I was bent on running the Schooner out of sight of the land by daylight. It was not that I feared she would capsize or ship too much water, but there was the wounded stay & the rotten rigging fore & aft. The danger was that the ropes would carry away again, & we should become once more helpless. I felt that it was a critical matter, though, and more than once, as the Schooner yielded to the blasts, I found myself, by that involuntary nervous action which affects men at such times, compressing my teeth until my jaws ached. Once, the men asked me, to lower the Mainsail, but I could not bear to do it and held on to every thing. I shall never forget this night. By six we had made nearly 30 miles & were satisfied there would be no land in sight at daybreak. So I made me a cup of chockolate by *my lamp* & turned in, weary yet happy, too happy, *that we had been saved again!*

When day broke, there was nothing but sea & sky around us, and towards 8 the wind moderated & finally died away, leaving a very heavy & uncomfortable swell. The Mainsail tore out of the clue before we could lower it, and as we had as much mending as we could attend to, we hauled down the Jib and set every body at work, helping ourselves to rip, cut out, pull the stitches, &c., &c., the Schooner rolling tremendously and the deck afloat with water. We expected another gale, and by night we had progressed with the sails so that we could set them by taking in a reef. With our *only* sails going at this rate and the rigging rotten, we actually contemplated the prospect of our being obliged *to winter somewhere* to the Northward, wherever we might be fortunate enough to bring up, and we felt very curious about this indeed.

The next morning, the 30th, the wind came out from South East and blew as violently as ever, so that we had to lay to under the Foresail. We did wonder *when* our troubles would cease. At 5 in the evening the gale suddenly ceased, and a calm succeeded, attended of course with a monstrous swell. We lowered every thing at once, "stripping the Schooner naked to *save* her clothes." All that night, the next day & night, and until 11 A.M. of the 1st November, we lay with the masts bare, rolling so as to nearly drive us frantic and water pouring over the vessel in floods. We were obliged to keep her *before* the swell with her head to the North & Westward, the very opposite to our course, and we were wretched and *almost* disheartened.

Until the afternoon of the 3rd, the winds played us fickle, breezing up for a few hours & then dying away calm with the same heavy swell, forcing us to lower the sails and drift at the mercy of the weather. It was now 13 days since we had finished the bar & thought ourselves fairly clear of *iminent* risks. As yet we had made so little progress on our way to the Southward that we could not consider ourselves as having obtained a start.

After this specimen of the weather & in our distressed condition, we had no intention to venture near the land again. The Sealed orders were opened, and they directed us, to proceed to Oahu & *sell the Schooner.* The Squadron would join us there. This was good news. We were all most anxious to be rid of the *Flying Fish,* because she leaked badly, was ill found, much strained & not calculated to keep up with the other vessels on the passage home, & because we were heartily wearied of her narrow limits & longed for a larger craft & a more numerous mess.

[CHAPTER 22: ACROSS THE PACIFIC]

On the 3rd [of October] we got a fresh wind from North West & to the infinite delight of all hands, the Schooner was at last pointed fair for Oahu & running 9 knots the hour. The change was blessed indeed, & we were not without hopes that this breeze would carry us clear into the trades. It *did* continue steady & strong, & though we pressed the Schooner with sail, even to some risk, & though the swell was still heavy & caused her to roll so that we could have no comfortable rest, we did not care, we were speeding from storms, fogs & rains, into a milder clime, & we firmly trusted that our perils in the Schooner were ended for ever. Now that we were clearing away from the North West Coast, safe & sound, we consoled ourselves with the belief that we should have a *direct, safe & speedy* passage home along a frequented route, & free from the anxieties of navigation among unknown seas. We were cruelly deceived.

The North West wind that came so opportunely held on gloriously, & carried us rapidly into the Trades. We were not distressed by the breeze ever failing, and on the 16th, only 13 days after we had taken the fair start, at 11 P.M. in my first watch, we made high and ahead the Island of Morotori, just to the [ea]stward of Oahu. Hove to, to wait for daylight.

We could not sleep for thinking about the morrow, and towards morning made sail with a fresh wind along the Southern shore of Morotori. The Schooner went roaring along with as much sail as she could stagger under, to our infinite delight. At 2 o'clock we were close to Oahu & steering for the Anchorage. All doubts about the [whereabouts of the] *Vincennes*, were ended, as we descried a large ship with a Broad pennant & American Ensign flying, at anchor in the Roads.

At 3 we came to between the *Vincennes* & *Porpoise* & were surprized to find that they had only arrived a few hours before. I went with Knox on board the *Vincennes* & got some dinner of chicken, potatoes, &c., and a glass of good wine, luxuries that had been rare with us of late. Captain Wilkes was on shore, and Knox pulled into the Harbour, taking Guillou with him, both of them receiving particular directions to bring back all the eatables the Hotel might afford in a state for instant mastication, and a dozen of fat ale. About 8 the Boat returned with a well-filled basket, from which Blair & I crammed ourselves until we could gorge no more. There were no letters for us, but several bags had been forwarded to Manilla, nor was the news from the United States very recent.

In the morning we went into the inner harbour, and hauling immediately alongside the wharf, we commenced discharging the Schooner, preparatory to heaving her out. [She] was to be turned bottom up, & the crew transfered to the *Oregon,* which vessel came in the day after our own arrival. But to our horror, grief, surprise, ominous whispers were already afloat *that the Schooner was not to be sold.* We were in the most cruel, tantalizing suspense.

The Schooner's rigging was overhauled & condemned, & we found some of the Shrouds to be hanging by a *single* strand, of which *all* the yarns *were rotten.* Her repairs went on from day to day, but we were still in doubt about her being sold. We did not know whether to lay in mess stores until two days before we finally sailed.

Knox was taken sick the second day we were at the Wharf, and all the work fell on my shoulders. From daylight until sunset I was on the sandy wharf, almost broiled to death in the sun, and worried into a fever from directing the operations & looking out for the men, but I generally found time to ride in the evening, & after a bath enjoyed a good night's sleep.

Guillou was to leave the Squadron here, and he had a companion in Lieutenant Bob Johnson, who was also going home under arrest, & charges preferred by our amiable Commander in Chief. These two fixed themselves in a town house at first, but soon increased their Establishment by occupying a cottage belonging to the French Consul, at a pleasant ride from the Town. We had two very delightful dinners there, which I managed to attend, as one was on Sunday & the other was by night.

Time wore on, and as there seemed to be no idea of disposing of the Schooner, I laid in a supply of stores, & we prepared ourselves for another cruize in her, with the sweet & calm resignation that has become our distinguished characteristic under all circumstances of disappointment or distress. Blair was transfered to the *Vincennes*, & Sanford joined in his place.

On the 28th November, the *Vincennes, Porpoise* & *Oregon* stood out of the harbour and anchored in the roads. We were not yet ready for sea, deck & rigging all adrift, and the pitch defiling the sides. In this state we sailed at 4 in the afternoon and came to near the *Vincennes*. After dark we all weighed together, run under the lee of the Island & hove to.

The next morning boats were passing & repassing, and all kinds of signals flying until 2 in the afternoon when the *Porpoise* & *Oregon* made sail to the Northward & Westward on a wind, & we kept away to the South West in the wake of the *Vincennes*, with a fresh breeze & a heavy sea after us. The Schooner rolled very heavily, and her rigging being new, stretched so, that at 3, as she made a tremendous lurch, we heard a crash, the main boom went up strait & the mast bent like a bow. We were sure it had sprung and luffed to, lowered the Mainsail, made signal for "assistance" to the *Vincennes,* and commenced to set the rigging up.

We almost hoped the mast *was* sprung, for Oahu was still in sight, and we could easily reach it under the Foresail. We soon had a plan fixed that we would have a nice time in Honolulu, refit thoroughly, and then go home by way of Tahiti and the Straits of Magellan. But we were not to be so favoured, for though the seams in the deck were opened & the partners split, the Mast proved to be sound, & we continued on with the *Vincennes* under short sail after undergoing an insulting interrogation from Captain Wilkes.

The next morning he hove to & told us we would part company, as he could not delay. So he sent us arms, stores, orders & Dr. Whittle. We were happy enough to get clear of *him*, and old Whittle, one of the very noblest fellows in the world, made us up a most sociable mess of four miserable, discontented wretches as ever were seen. Our orders were, much to our astonishment, to proceed to the Southward "to Strong & Ascension Islands lying in 0° 58' North Latitude and thence to Manilla, examining every thing on the route and arriving in that port by the 10th of January without fail." This route carried us out of the trade winds into the Variables and was extending the passage much beyond the common run of vessels pursuing the direct track in the strength of the trades.

We had not dreamed there were to be any more delays, but had fondly hoped, trusted, believed that all our work was ended, and that *now* we would go Home as fast & as straight as we could. We gave up this hope, however, and made our minds up that the same old, accursed system of humbug & delay would continue until our arrival in New York. As it was, we consoled ourselves by the prospect of a pleasant visit to Ascension, which Island we had a yearning desire to see, and which is a very Paradise in itself.

The trades were quite fresh and raised a large sea. The day after we parted from the *Vincennes* we carried away the Squaresail yard, and thereafter could only run under the Mainsail when before the wind. That sail, with its heavy boom of 40 feet in length, projecting at right angles from the mast, made the Schooner very uneasy & wet and rendered *"carrying on"* a matter of some delicacy. Its eternal thrashing & jumping, together with the rolling of the vessel & the floods of water that came over the decks & into the cabin, made it utterly impossible to get a decent night's sleep, or to sit, stand, eat, or exist in any comfort. Besides, we were passing through an unfrequented sea and only had *luck* & a *look out* to trust to, to keep from running down some Island in the dark.

As we got down towards the parrallel of 10° North, the wind fell light, as we expected, and thenceforward our progress was slow. We had seen but one Island, small & uninhabited. I celebrated my 26th birth day with roast pig & champaigne, but it was a monstrous sore point to think I was only a Midshipman still.

On the 16th December, we hauled to the Westward along the Southern Mulgraves, having them in sight. They are low, coral Islands, and were the resort of the mutineers of the Whaleship *Globe*.[1] The natives came off in their canoes, but we outsailed them & had no disposition to delay or to let them come alongside. On the 17th we passed Boham's Island and made Hunter's Island. This latter was not on our chart, and as it was nearly dark when we discovered it, we had to heave to for the night. 18th passed it & also Baring's Island, where the horrid massacre on board the *Awashonks*[2] occurred; saw no people, but many fires along the shore after dark.

It now wanted but 23 days to the time appointed for our arrival in Manilla, and Knox was afraid he should not reach there in season unless he *gave up Ascension* and hauled to the North at once. I did all I could to persuade him to the contrary, but it was of no avail, and we had to submit to the miserable disappointment once more, just when we were at the very door, if I may say so, of the Island.

On the 29th, we made Mackenzie's Islands, a chain of the low, coral formation, and enclosing a sea of a lagoon. We tried to find a passage about the centre of the Island to save doubling the Southern point and succeeded in getting into the lagoon, but could see no opening on the opposite side. It was near sunset, the canoes were too numerous around us to permit us to anchor, and we had to beat out again where we entered & gain an offing for the night.

In the morning, we made sail again to the Southward & Westward, and passing around the Southern end of the Island with a light wind, a canoe came alongside containing only two men & a boy, from whom we purchased a mess of fine fish & some cocoa nuts for some Tobacco, of which they were very fond, and a segar, which the boy smoked with much gusto as if he were accustomed to it.

Leaving the Isles, the winds carried us along famously & we had now no doubt we should reach Manilla *before* the time. On the 3rd of January *1842*, we were well up with Cape Espir-

itu Santo and had had a current of 30 odd miles in our favour
setting to the Westward. On the 4th, we had no observations
for Latitude or Longitude, and at the rate we were running, we
would be up with the Cape at Midnight if we allowed for the
same current that we had felt during the two last days. By *dis-
regarding* the current, the rate of sailing would not bring us in
sight of the Cape until daylight, and Knox got a very strange
idea in his head that this current ought to *slacken* as we neared
the land, while Sanford & I were sure it ought to be increasing.

We had a warm argument about this, as the consequence of
trusting to Knox's plan would most likely end in our *getting
ashore* before we knew it. He determined *to run for the Cape*
with the expectation of making it at daylight, and it was as unfortunate an expectation as he could possibly have relied on.
The Northern shore of the straits was more than 100 miles distant to the North West, thus forming a wide & deep gulf at the
entrance. Into this gulf Sanford & I wished the Schooner to be
run by altering the course two points, and then at all events, we
would be *safe*, without losing ground, either, for in the morning we would be ready to enter the narrows. The wind was
blowing a smart gale, with frequent heavy squalls & thick
cloudy weather, thus rendering Knox's course imprudent beyond excuse, & fairly deserving to be termed insane.

Knox, Whittle, & myself turned in at 8, & Sanford had the
first watch. The wind was on the quarter, and the Schooner was
going 7 & 8 knots. At 10.30, the Jib was taken in on account
of the squalls & the heavy sea. At 11 a low, dark, thick squall
passed over & settled in the horizon on the lee bow, leaving
there a wall of blackness, so that sea could not be distinguished
from sky. At 11.30 this gloom *lifted a little,* and those on the
lookout *saw land & breakers, close aboard,* & just where all
had been so indistinct the moment before. I was awake &
heard the cry, but could not understand it until it was repeated
by Sanford down the hatch. The helm was instantly put down,
the Schooner brought by the wind, & the fore sheet hauled aft.
But before this was accomplished, Knox & I were on deck, just
as we turned out with not a rag on, save a shirt.

The sight was frightful, and at the first glance, it seemed impossible we should be saved. The night was very dark, yet we could see the land & the horrible breakers, oh! so close. 150 yards is the *farthest* off that I can venture to name. The wind fairly howled in its violence, and the swell was enormously high, increased twofold by the shoalness of the water, for *now* we were *in the rollers & could see the bottom*. It was do or die, and most likely would be do *and* die with us, in spite of all.

All hands were hurried on deck, and we commenced clearing away the Mainsail & Jib, for under the foresail only the Schooner had scarcely any way, if she even held her own against the seas, although if the force of the wind were considered, the one sail was quite sufficient canvass to show. But it was our *only* chance—we might *possibly* claw off under a press of sail, & we might whip the masts out of her, yet to let her lay under the foresail 5 minutes, and there would be an end of us.

They soon got the mainsail clear abaft, where Knox & Sanford remained, but I had difficulty enough with the Jib to drive me wild. Turn after turn of the *downhaul* had been passed around the sail to secure it from being washed from the bowsprit. We worked away at it as hard as men could work, but we only fouled it, and I ordered it cut. There was no knife—the men had come up in such haste. Some one brought a knife, and the rope was cut.

"All clear now! hoist away!" Hoist, pull, strain, it was, but the sail did not go up. "What holds?" A cursed stop, away out on the stay. This cut, and hoist away again. It was like hauling a "rope yarn over a nail," the Jib went up so heavily & by inches. *What* can be the matter now? Barnard,[3] my right hand man, who had been using the knife, thought the others were not exerting their strength, & he sung out, "This is no time to trust the God Almighty's interference—you must pull, haul for your lives!" and pull & haul, it was. By a long hard tug, the Jib was hoisted nearly up, and we found that the *halliard block* had split & come out of the strap, thus destroying the purchase altogether.

I do not know how many minutes, we were engaged with the Jib, but many or few, they were dreadful & I thought I should go mad. It was evident that we had neared the breakers, &

their white foam was terribly distinct & in strong contrast to the surrounding blackness of land, Sea & sky. The men, as they came up from below, were very much startled to find the danger so iminent, and, "Oh! God, we are right among them," broke from several, as they hurried to work. I cannot describe my own feelings, they were too horrible to tell.

The peak of the Mainsail had been raised at first, to keep the Schooner to the wind, and as the Jib was finally hoisted, the whole Mainsail was shown to the gale. The effect of this pressure of canvass on the little Schooner was tremendous, and she drove through & under the seas at a rate that any other time would have been fearful. The masts switched like willows, and the water came over the bows just as it falls over a *mill dam* ashore, in torrents. Several of the crew were, like myself, holding on to the Foremast and receiving the shock of all the water on our devoted heads, and the Schooner trembled, jumped, pitched, as if she was shaking herself to pieces.

Had she not have been the most glorious model of a sea boat that ever *was* built, she could not have borne this sail an instant, but she was true as gold and was making a rapid progress & heading a little clear of the breakers. But yet it seemed impossible for us to escape, and feeling *certain* that the Schooner would *strike* & go to pieces, I went below in the cabin for a life preserver to take even so poor a chance to be saved.

Whittle had not turned out; he had no idea matters were so bad. I told him to be quick about it or he would be drowned in his berth, which set him in motion at once. I was not long in finding what I wanted, but every instant I expected to feel the Schooner settle on the rocks, and my thoughts were *choking* me. I had no confidence that my voice would serve me, but I found that I could talk quietly enough, and without betraying any want of composure. Whittle wanted me to put on drawers or trowsers, but I told him there was *not time* & if the worst came, I would be better without them.

I hurried again on deck. We could *not* fetch by the breakers, and the Schooner *must be stayed or lost*. She had behaved wonderfully, but it was almost *too* much to expect that she would *tack* in such a sea. For a square rigged vessel, or for one of her own class but wanting her qualities, destruction would have been inevitable. I had a sickly sort of a belief that she would stay, but every one of us felt how critical was the chance. We tried, she refused, we began to shake, there was no room to miss *often*. Again the helm was put a lee, and the sail tended with all the care that we could bestow. To our infinite joy and relief, she *did* come about, beautifully, *and we knew we were saved*. By the compass, the mariner's blessing, we saw that we headed the very opposite course to the one on which we had approached the land.

I was forward again, undergoing a shower bath that would not have disgraced Niagara, and looking with a sad eye on the Jib, as it was fast splitting to rags from the force of the water that dashed into it, but in a perfect glow to think that I, that all of us, might yet *get home*. We took in the Mainsail as soon as we could, and when we had got at a safe distance from the Shore, we began to get the Jib, or rather its remains, in, for it was split from the foot to the head, but as the *downhaul* was cut, we were a great while about it, and nearly lost a man from the bowsprit.

We now went below, and after taking a good look at each other to make sure we were all alive, and mingling our thanks for our preservation, we took a strong drink of brandy & dried & dressed ourselves. I had the middle watch to keep and remained on deck until 4 o'clock, the wind blowing a hard gale with frequent, tremendous squalls, and a very heavy sea. This mattered not—there was no land under our lee, and wind & sea we could stand forever. The weather continued the same all the next day, and after a trial to go to the Westward, we found the current setting so strong on shore that under the foresail alone we could not make any progress, and we had to wear & gain an offing until the gale would break, & the Jib be repaired.

It was not until the 7th that we were ready to run for the straits, and *avoiding* the Cape, we got safely in the narrows on the morning of the 8th and were in smooth water & fine weather, to our infinite delight. Towards night it fell dead calm, and we drifted slowly with the tide between two high Islands that were about 10 miles apart.

A more lovely sight never fell from the Heavens. The atmosphere was transparently clear, not a star was absent from its place, and the waters were brilliantly illumined from the reflection of those lamps of the skies. Huge fires were burning along the highest summits of the land, and the glow that arose from them shed a vivid light adown the hills. Quietly the Schooner floated along, and to us poor seaworn mortals, it seemed as if we had entered into a New World, and a new existence.

Light winds rendered our progress slow, and it was not until the morning of the 13th January that we got off the Entrance to the Bay of Manilla. We were very much afraid that we should find the *Vincennes* just ready *to sail* and be walked off to sea again before we could get a piece of clothes washed. We passed an English brig off the Capes, sailing two feet to her one, and *beat in* with the wind blowing right in our teeth.

The Bay, which is not more than 12 miles wide at its mouth, with a large Island laying midway, expands into an immense circular sheet of water 40 miles in diameter, the City standing on the Eastern shore. At 11 o'clock, we made a large ship in the wind's eye of us. At 1 we had gained on her, so that we made her out to be the *Vincennes,* the English brig being still outside & just visible above the horizon. At sundown we were well to the Northward in the bay and communicated by signal with the *Vincennes.* At midnight the wind failed, and we anchored without knowing exactly how far we were from the town. Captain Wilkes hailed us, and Knox went on board.

At daylight we went on deck to look for the town & were glad to find the Shipping plain in sight, about 8 miles distant. Both Vessels were soon underweigh, and at 8 we were anchored once more. Three or four American merchant vessels had their ensigns up, and a large Bombay Ship, painted to resemble a line of battle ship, lay nearest to us. The Shore was low & about 2 miles distant. We hauled alongside the *Vincennes,* at once, to have our main mast lifted, and Whittle & I prepared to go ashore.

Captain Wilkes had sent three boats in, one for the Consul & the other two for the marketing, quite forgetting that he was now in a port where Quarantine laws & health & custom house

Officers were in vogue. The boats were ordered back to the Ship before they reached the river, and we had to wait for some hours before the Custom house barge came alongside, and the Authorities authorized us to land. Then we waited until the letter bag was brought on board, and I had the happiness to receive one letter a few days later in date than those that came overland to the Columbia River.

The afternoon was somewhat advanced as, after a tedious pull in the sun, we entered the river, the mouth of which is about ½ a mile from the town. The current was running out strong, and as our boat was crammed full, we were quite glad when we landed at last & took up our march for a Hotel. It was now nearly two years since we had been in any built up Towns, and it was quite a novelty to us to walk between tall houses and among crowds of people, & to see artisans busy at work.

When we reached the Hotel, the first step was to order dinner, & while this was preparing, we walked to the shops of the China merchants, but bought nothing save shoes, of which my feet were sadly in need. Then, as we had still more than an hour to spare, we took Carriages & set off for a drive. The vehicles were gig bodies on four wheels, drawn by two horses, a postillion with boots up to his neck and a spur on his left leg riding the near horse. I felt as much delight at being whirled along, as I used to when a child.

[After we toured the city and the nearby countryside,] the last turn we took was along the beach & just outside the ramparts, where it seems the fashionable of Manilla take their evening drives. Two carriage tracks run parrellel & close to each other for about half a mile, and two streams of vehicles heading different ways pass & repass each other by following these, so that you can review at your leisure the same beauties half a dozen times over, before the cavalcade breaks up & winds its way into the town. The Ladies bore staring very heroically, and even smiled a return to our earnest glances. None wore bonnets or caps, and the raven hair, which was common to all of them, was very simply and tastefully dressed, with no other ornament than white flowers just plucked from the garden.

It was with the most singular and excited feelings that we beheld this array of beauties. I cannot help thinking on the time, when I shall once again mingle with the fairer sex without feeling some misgivings as to my ability to behave with propriety, nor without believing that I shall fancy every woman I see to be an angel of beauty & goodness & myself to be in an Elysium which it would be death to leave.

We have led such a rugged life during these four years that the somewhat coarse & familiar habits we have acquired by this eternal, unvaried intercourse with each other have become rather deeply seated to be readily abandoned, and they are certainly such as will not be tolerated beyond the limits of a Ship. I hope for the best & shall throw myself on the mercy and protection of the feminines under whose gentle influence I may trust to acquire or regain sufficient polish to enable me to appear in society without making a display of rudeness that might better suit an Ourang Outang than a young man very much in want of a wife.

As I could only go ashore on alternate days, I remained on board the morrow all alone, reading the newspapers & my letter over & over again and indulging in thoughts of Home. My solitude was enlivened for a while by the arrival of Madame Barbara, one of a class of female merchants peculiar to Manilla, who bring off to vessels the various curious things that the country affords. Madame Barbara was a native of the Island & *had been* good looking, was still very lively & active, and was well recommended for her honesty, which we never found cause to doubt. She had shells, Birds of Paradise, embroidered slippers, segar cases, China boxes, Grass Cloth, Hats, shoes, handkerchiefs, calicoes, ribbons, and as she said, "Every thing, *got!*"

Her way of talking was very amusing, & she became great friends with all of us and visited us every day. Once she brought her guitar and treated us to music. The Style in which she sang "Oh! give me but my Arab Steed,"[4] I shall certainly never forget.

On the 21st of January at daylight we got underweigh with a light breeze and stood out of the Bay. A Ship was standing in for the anchorage, and as we neared her she hoisted American Colours. The *Vincennes* spoke her in passing and continued on her course. When we had got some distance beyond her, Signal was made for us to speak her, and we tacked to follow her. We were soon alongside, & she proved the *Ianthe*, Captain Steele, 4 months from Boston. We sent our Boat to her & procured some newspapers, which we commenced to overhaul, as we turned after the *Vincennes*.

I think it was the second paper I opened that contained the Navy promotions of the 8th of September 1841. My astonished glance fell at once on *my own name* among the Lieutenants! I remember, but I cannot describe, what I felt! I was confounded. Joy and surprise made me dumb! I had not had even the shadow of a hope for such good fortune but had schooled myself to the prospect of waiting for 3 long years before I should receive any advancement, and the miserable prospect was almost death. Yet here I had been made a Lieutenant more than a month ago! It was too unexpected, too much, to bear it with any composure, & when I found my voice, I screamed the glorious news aloud, but the utterance nearly choked me. I never felt so proud or happy in all my life—no, not even when I first heard I was a Midshipman.

I took care to draw black lines around the paragraph & folded the paper up so that it remained on the outside, in full view, & then it was sent to Captain Wilkes. I could not quiet myself for days.

The usual passage from Manilla to Sincapore, during the favourable Monsoons, is from 7 to 10 days. We could not believe in a rumour that was afloat which stated we were to go out of the direct route, & even to survey Islands & passages on the way. As the most straitforward Navigation & the utmost expedition could *only* carry us Home *before* the time pledged most solemnly to be the termination of this eternal cruize, and as any delay would be *certain* to detain us *beyond* that time, we had ventured once more to place some Confidence in Captain Charles Wilkes, & had trusted that our course from Manilla would prove that he intended to fulfil his bond. We were, as usual, deceived.

When we cleared the Bay of Manilla, we steered to the Southward at once & pursued a track which is rarely, if ever, enlivened by a passing sail. He left us when we had been several days out to survey Appo Shoal & named two places of rendezvous, where we were to rejoin him. Light winds detained us several days before we finished the work, and not meeting the *Vincennes* at the first appointed spot, we proceeded to the second at the entrance to Balabac Straits. No Ship to be seen, but as we had no further orders except that the *Vincennes* would meet us there, Knox determined to lay "off and on" for a reasonable time before he kept on for Sincapore.

We remained there from the 30th of January until noon of the 8th of February without seeing any thing like a Ship. We were in a fever of impatience & disgust & were somewhat concerned for our safety besides. Shoals were as thick around us as blackberries, and we could scarcely avoid them. Indeed, once we run hard & fast aground & had much trouble to get clear again. We anchored at Midnight, and in the morning found *the rocks* above water all around us, and only the Schooner's length from us. Again, at sundown, with a fresh wind, we got entangled amid the shoals, so that we could not tell how to get clear. We scraped the bottom & then would find ourselves in deep water, and immediately afterwards came right on the reef again. We had to anchor, & trust to good weather during the night. Luckily the wind, though fresh, did not increase.

This was rather nervous work, & we heartily wished Shoals, Wilkes & all at the very Devil. Besides, the people around were the most notorious, bloody pirates in the world, & we saw their fires every night. We dreaded an attack from them, & we knew we could not hope to resist or escape unless we had a stiff breeze, which was rarely the case. With the many chances for Shipwreck that beset us, our resources were equally bad, for we had but one small unseaworthy boat, and there were 16 full grown men on our decks.

On the 13th, we spoke the English Brig *Black Joke* from Macao bound to Sincapore, and on the evening of the 15th we were inside of Sincapore straits, having experienced some anxiety lest we should have been swept by them by the current.

The wind left us at sundown, when we were about 20 miles from the town, and until midnight we drifted along the Shore of the Island, having a strong current in our favour. We could not discern any signs of the port, but heard a most thundering noise of gongs beating, which sounded like the roar of surf, and the beach was lined with lights. The Chinese were keeping up their New Year. At 12, we anchored, having passed several Chinese junks as if they were tied fast to the bottom.

In the morning, we found we were about a mile from the Shipping, and soon discovered the *Porpoise & Oregon,* but no *Vincennes!* We could not imagine what had become of her. We tripped the anchor and were soon in a berth near the *Porpoise.* Alden boarded us before we came to, & thought he would surprize me with the news of our promotions, but we bluffed him off. The Brigs had been here 26 *days!*

Whittle, Knox & myself went to breakfast on board the *Porpoise,* and to overhaul the letter bags for our treasures from Home. I found many letters, but they were all old. They filled up vacancies, however, and told me much that I had wanted to learn.

Three days after our arrival, the *Vincennes* came in, & great was the uproar in consequence. They had been away down to Sooloo, surveying and humbugging to the discontent & disgust of all hands, & had arrived at Balabac Straits the day after we left there. To our utter surprise, to our ineffable disgust, Captain Wilkes ordered a "court of enquiry" on Knox, for not looking for him at a *third* rendezvous, which *he said* he had appointed *but which he had not named.* Incapable as he is, of the slightest feeling of gratitude, reckless as he is, of all regard to truth, this act of his was as black a deed as any that have disgraced him during the cruize. Knox has served Captain Wilkes most faithfully for five years, and no one knew his value more than the man himself who was prefering accusations, which he must have been aware were false. The Court sat for several days & found not the shadow of a cause for either enquiry or censure.

Knox was of course suspended from his Command during these proceedings, and as he was unwell, he lived on shore, so that the charge of the Schooner devolved on me. An English gentleman had been on board to look at her and was so pleased that he declared he must have her, if she was to be sold. We encouraged him all we could, & he went to the *Vincennes* to see Captain Wilkes forthwith. A day or two afterwards, a survey was held on her, & it was recommended not to trust her to go round the Cape in the hurricane season, which was at hand. It was determined to sell her at Auction without reserve, & the day was fixed.

I was delighted at the prospect of leaving her for many reasons, though among them was *not* the fear to trust her round the Cape. Sanford & Whittle were detatched, & I was left to clean her out, carry her inshore & deliver her up. The day of sale came, & for the last time the *Flying Fish* was got underway with the American ensign at her peak. The breeze was fresh up & she beat in, in gallant style, to a berth among the Junks. About 4 P.M. the new owner came alongside & soon after, receiving orders from Captain Wilkes, I hauled down the ensign myself and delivered her up.

The crew were unwilling to leave her, for they were very much attached to her & were the best set of men that ever belonged to her. We all left her together, & I could not help feeling some sorrow at leaving her in the hands of strangers. I had the same sort of regard for her tha[t] a man must entertain for a gallant horse that has carried him safely through the fight, & I almost repented that the poor little craft had been so rudely bartered away.

This was January 24th. My orders were to the *Porpoise* and were just what I wished. I should have got the Hydrophobia on board the *Vincennes* with Captain Wilkes, and as to the *Oregon,* she was even to be dreaded more. Alden, my right hand friend, was the Lieutenant of the *Porpoise,* and I was quite happy to finish the cruize where there was the prospect of the most peace.

[CHAPTER 23: HOMEWARD BOUND]

On the 26th [of February], at day light, the Squadron weighed & stood out of the Straits. Head winds obliged us in the afternoon to run thro' the Straits of Rhio instead of Sincapore Straits, and we followed the *Vincennes* through the narrow belts of water between Islands of the most lively scenery, until night coming on obliged us to anchor; the navigation was too intricate to be attempted in the dark. The next day we continued on through the Straits of Banca & then through those of Sunda, anchoring frequently each day & night. On the 7th March we cleared the Straits of Sunda & entered into the Indian Ocean, quite glad to be once more in a clear Sea.

By being favoured with fresh & fair winds *all the way,* it was just possible that we should arrive in the United States by the 31st May, the time solemnly pledged for the expiration of the cruize. We could hardly hope for extraordinary breezes, but we were prepared to make the most of every breath that stirred. We did, now, at this time, venture to hope that *all* the vessels would at last be ordered to pursue the most direct route home & that we would rendezvous at the Cape of Good Hope.

We were not prepared for such a diabolical arrangement as was now made public! The *Vincennes* was to touch at the Cape & then sail for New York via St Helena, as strait a course as could be shaped, while *we* were to go away over to Rio de Janeiro *for nothing,* and to stop at St Helena, which was 3 or 500 miles out of the track, merely because he would like to hear how we were coming on!

His miserable motive was too transparently veiled to be hidden, & was apparent to every one. To make sure that *he* should get Home *first* with his own Ship, he could adopt no other scheme than this vile one, for which he would deserve hanging, only that he deserved impaling, long, long ago. Such an abominable arrangement we had never supposed even *he* could execute, and the black hearted treachery of the act fairly appalled us. A further & most ingenious method of torture was also adopted in requiring the temperature of the Sea to be tried every day at the depth of 100 fathoms, and lest this should not suffice, he told Captain Ringgold to keep company with the *Oregon*, as far as the Cape. She sailed dull on a wind & delayed us considerably.

The breeze was tolerably fresh, and we made a fair progress across the Indian Ocean until the 19th, when we were annoyed by four days of calm weather attended by a very heavy swell, and during which we lost much ground by keeping company with the *Oregon*. We were amply repaid for this during the following six days, for the wind came up fresh & fair, and we ran 1300 miles in that time. This was glorious, and watch keeping was no hardship but most happy excitement.

Off the Cape we had a current of 80 miles in one day, but light winds kept us longer in doubling it than we had expected. On the 12th April we passed the Meridian & hauled up for St. Helena with a fair breeze that lasted four or five days & gave us hopes of a quick passage, but it failed then, and it was not until the [24th of April] at one hour after midnight, that, by the light of a full moon, we caught the first glimpse of this famous Island, being about 15 miles distant from its Southern point.

I heard the cry of "Land O," & turned out to have a look; there it was, a blue mass, heaped up against the sky. All hands in the ward room were awake, and shortly we were startled, and in great distress, to hear them stripping the Brig, first of one sail & then of another, until they reduced her to her naked Topsails. We could see no reason for this. The roadstead was perfectly accessible at night, and, as there was now a light almost equal to that of day, we were distracted at the delay, which we feared would cause us to arrive late in the forenoon, and thus we should be cheated out of time which we could ill afford to throw away. I could sleep no more but tossed restlessly in my berth in no very amiable feelings to the Captain, waiting until 4 o'clock, when my watch commenced.

Now, we had parted with the *Oregon* to the Eastward of the Cape & left her astern. A few days afterward, in my morning watch, as day broke, we found her alongside of us again, though we were going 9 knots the hour. We lost her soon after and never met until *this* time, when as we lay with scarcely any headway, up came the *Oregon* close alongside of us with studding sails set on both sides and passed us, as if we had been at anchor. I took the deck at 8 bells, stamping & chafing with vexation, and this was not lessened by the Captain's saying to me that the *Oregon* was doing very strangely. *I thought* they were doing the sensible thing, and we! it was too hard to see that Brig pass us, and I could not talk for anger.

It was nearly 5 o'clock before he allowed us to commence to make sail, & then the canvass was spread much too gradually to suit my impatience. If we had been approaching "Hell gate"[1] we could not have been more slow or cautious. However, as the thing resulted, we might have been spared all our uneasiness, but we are & have been in such a state of mind on account of *real* evils that, on the least appearance of delay, we go into fits. The breeze held & I packed on all the sail that would draw, so that by seven o'clock we had opened the Shipping at anchor & were only a few miles from the Roads. The shores were steep, rocky & barren, with the exception of a green & cultivated plain on the very summit of the Island, in the midst of which shone the white walls of "Longwood!"[2]

At 8 we were quietly at anchor, close to the beach, with the guns of the batteries right over our heads. A stouter heart than Napoleon's might have sickened at the first view of this Rocky pile as a prison for life. From our anchorage, there was scarce a blade of grass to be seen. The valley that makes back of the town was shut out from us, and all we saw were the black rocks & red earthy cliffs rising perpendicularly from the water to a height of 2000 feet, frowning with ramparts and artillery; a very limited strip of beach, lined with a parapet of stone which was bristling with huge guns; & a few houses, some of which were excavations in the face of the rock, in its rear. It was as cheerless a scene as can be found in the wide world.

The health officer, the Consul's Son, & the Commander of her Majesty's Brig *Brisk* visited us a few moments after we came to, & the harbour master (who rejoiced in the famous name of Gulliver) coming soon after, we learned that all our wants could be supplied before night, though the day was Sunday. Accordingly it was determined that we should sail in the evening, and the *Oregon* came to anchor to keep us company, although they had intended to get on without any delay.

As there was no time to be wasted, all of us who could be spared left the Brig by 9 o'clock to make a hurried visit to "the Lions,"[3] and return on board to relieve those who kept the Ship in season to give them a chance. A few strokes of the oars carried us to the Landing steps, where there was some swell on, & we had to swing ourselves ashore by laying hold of a rope which hung from a crane, a most undignified manner of presenting ourselves, "epauletted & sworded," in the dominions of Her Majesty, Victoria the 1st.

A score of her red coated soldiers were assembled there as lookers on, and it cost us no little trouble to answer their punctillious & never failing salute. We turned short to the right & passing above the heavy guns that form the water side defences, we came to the draw-bridge and gates, which front the principal street & the only square of the town.

Turning into this miniature square, the houses around which were remarkably neat & well built, we soon came to the residence of Mr. Carroll,[4] whose consulship was indicated by a golden eagle, blazing with stars, &c., over the doorway. A tall, well looking, gray haired gentleman met us in the passage with the expression, "I'm proud to see you, Sir," and a shake of the hand to each of us, and ushered us into a sitting room, where, as we were too many for conversation, we employed ourselves in looking over the lithographic prints of the exhumation, &c., &c., of Napoleon's remains, two very fine sets of which were laying on the tables. In the mean time carriages & horses were preparing to take us to "the Tomb" & "Longwood," the Consul making all the arrangements himself.

While Alden & myself were busily intent upon the prints, we were startled by the entrance of two young ladies from behind us, whom the Consul named as his daughter & Miss Legge!

Their appearance was the first intimation we had of there being such attractive personages in his family, & their sudden introduction had somewhat of a theatrical effect. Both were tall & very tastefully dressed in pure white. Miss Carrol is handsome, with fine eyes & teeth & beautifully black hair, which she wore in a cluster of curls down her neck. Miss Legge, without being pretty, had a clear complexion, & the two were quite a sweet pair of roses to have bloomed in such a desert as this.

I made my best bow and, putting my best foot forward, came to anchor close aboard the fair convoy in two seconds after they hove in sight. They were full of talk, & we rattled away in a short time on very familiar terms. After a time, Alden joined company & told the ladies he had heard Mr. Carroll say they would accompany us on our drive. They protested they had heard nothing of it, but the old gentleman settled the matter & said he had arranged it all with Mrs. Carroll before we came ashore. So they ran for their bonnets, as the Carriage was coming, & we tried the temperature of the Consul's decanter.

"The Carriage" turned out to be a very small "double dearborn,"[5] with a seat in front for the driver, & mounted on the lowest possible wheels, the only description of vehicle in use upon the Island. Miss Carrol, in a very sweet little straw bonnet, was safely stowed by my side, & Miss Legge & Alden occupied the seat in front.

I was in an extraordinary thrill of pleasurable excitement, for, during nearly four of the *longest* years, a *"tete a tete"* with a lady has been as far from my lot, as the hopes of a Savage are from Heaven. I told the girls so. They laughed & said Matters were nearly as bad with them. Brother John had knocked at their door before breakfast & told them an American man of war was coming in. *They thought the news too good to be true.* And sooth to say, society in their lonely Isle can scarce be more enlivening than the weary intercourse of Shipboard.

Neither of these girls *had ever seen the outside of the Island.* Their world was but a few miles square, & from infancy to womanhood they had known no other. With rocks & sea & sky they were familiar, but with the grand sights that are common among us—railroads, steamers, mighty cities, wide spreading, cultivated plains & rushing rivers—they knew of them only by hearsay and had in regard to them the curiosity of children.

When we had gained the whole ascent & reached the summit, the second carriage overtook us, & Alden resigned his seat to Sinclair, as a courtesy due from a married to a single man. In a little while, we came in sight of the "Valley of the tomb," and descending from the ridge, the Carriages halted some short distance above the bottom of the gorge. A shower of rain that came sweeping over the hills hurried us into a neat cottage, where a lady in deep mourning welcomed us with the easy manners of one accustomed to the frequent visits of strangers.

She lived in the Cottage while Napoleon was in existence, and almost every day *He* came to the valley to rest in its shade and to drink of the spring, which after his death[6] watered the grass around his grave. He would drink no other water than this, and often sent his *Valet* with a Silver flagon, that he might rely on having it pure and fresh. "He did not like to be observed," the good lady said, "yet many a time he had come into the house, and thrown himself upon the very sofa you are sitting on; yes, and that young lady there (Miss Legge), often did he nurse her on his knee, before she was old enough to walk" (thereby hangs a tale, I suspect).

The great Exile had chosen this valley for his burial place and had indicated the very spot beneath his favorite willows and close to his favorite spring, where he wished his grave to be. He had so much anxiety about this that, just before he died, our lady's husband was sent for & taken to Napoleon's bedside to assure him that the ground he so coveted for this melancholy purpose would be willingly parted with and his request faithfully fulfilled. Strange, that he who had conquered a world should have to bargain for six feet of earth to lay his bones in.

When the rain ceased, we walked to the grave [and entered the tomb]. When we ascended, we pulled a twig from the willows which overshadowed the grave as memento of our pilgrimage to a spot, which has now lost its greatest claim to celebrity.[7] While this valley held the ashes of him who shook the world, the sight of that humble slab must have been singularly affecting. A rough stone, without a letter to record who slept below, was all that met the eye.

The ride to Longwood was over the summit of the ridge, which was flat pasture ground, and commanded a prospect of the Ocean. We went first to the old house, where Napoleon died. The rooms were all going to decay, the plaster falling off & the floors littered with straw & dirt. In one large apartment was a thrashing machine, and, *"just where that black horse stands,"* said the man who showed us round, *"just there Napoleon died!"*

The new house, which was built for the Captive Emperor, stands but a few steps from this, and is a very fine edifice, occupying, I should think, the most favourable situation on the Island. A profusion of rose trees in full bearing surrounded the house, and the Ladies were kind enough to gather a boquet for each of us. It seemed strange, yet there could be no doubt of it, for there I, William Reynolds, was, with a very sweet & very pretty girl at my side pulling flowers, under the windows of Longwood. The whole of that ride was like a dream.

It was just three o'clock, when we got down to Mr. Carroll's, again. Alden had hurried on before us and had gone on board to relieve the others, and in a few minutes they came on shore & started up the Hill. The ladies had gone up stairs to make their toilettes, as the wet grass had sadly disarranged their dress, and we now only waited for their reappearance to make our adieus and return to the Brig. They soon came down, bringing with them the *boquets* eloquently fixed with ribbons, & were kind enough to express their regrets that our parting was to be so abrupt. It was with the most sincere truth that I told them this had been to me the very happiest day of the cruize. A very cordial shake of the hand, a very kind adieu, and I saw no more of Miss Ellinor Anne Carroll or Miss Legge.

The Officers on shore dined at the Consul's and came on board about 9 o'clock. In an hour, we were underweigh and out at Sea.

We expected a passage of 15 days [to Rio], & at first, the winds favoured us so that we had hopes of making the run in 12 days. It is amusing to watch the solicitude we all feel and express every hour during the day about the winds, the speed of the Brig, the termination of the passage, the stay at Rio, and *arrival at Home!* The instant the observations are worked out at noon, the position is marked on the chart, and the distance still intervening measured with anxious eyes, as well as scale & compasses.

Since leaving the *Flying Fish,* I have improved in appearance and in disposition. My mess mates tell me I look 10 years younger than when I first joined the Brig, & I am conscious that a horde of wrinkles beneath the eye & several alarming gashes in the cheeks & about the corners of the mouth have disappeared under the influence of better living, better accommodations, sound sleep, four watches & a mind free from the fear of a dozen deaths. But there are still very visible wrinkles and marks on my front, which far from adorn it, and I turn from a mirror in utter sorrow & even disgust. Were it not that they should be considered as *honorable scars,* obtained from hard service & exposure to winds & seas, in all latitudes & in all weathers, I should really be ashamed of them. I look upon the hardships, dangers & servitude that we have undergone in this Expedition as parrallel in their extent to the worst years of the Revolutionary War, & if its operations had been protracted for 48 months longer, every one of us would have been *expended* from a *wearing out* of the system, if from no other causes.

The weather has favoured us very much. Very little rain & generally a smooth Sea have allowed us dry decks most of the time—quite a contrast to the long & heavy rollers of the "Pacific." During my watches, my first care is to see that every sail that will draw is set & set properly, & then, not to take a rag in unless there is danger of blowing it away. Every mile brings us nearer Home, and *"Carry on her"* is the principal which governs us all.

As the squalls rise, I shorten sail until I think I have prepared the Brig to run through them, and then await the result screwed up to the necessary pitch of determination *to hold on* to the rest, but ready to reduce more, if requisite. The cloud is overhead—we have got its weight. The vessel heels to the increase of wind and trembles from the speed with which she parts the waters. The excitement is rapturous, & when the squall has passed, it is with the most exulting satisfaction that I dwell upon the accuracy of my judgement & upon *the fact* that I have driven the Brig an *extra mile* or *two* on her course.

Light winds near the Land lengthened our passage so that it was the night of the 11th of May when we made Cape Frio light.[8] The next night we anchored outside the mouth of the harbour on the ebb tide. In the morning we found an American Brig close to us, & boarding her, she was just from New York, with papers to the 26th of March & even with one letter for our Purser, so that we had lots of news before breakfast. The slow-sailing *Oregon,* from which we had separated several weeks before, was also at anchor near us, & in the afternoon with the sea breeze, the *Porpoise* & *Oregon* entered the harbour together.

As we passed under the stern of the Old *Deleware,* I shoved off to board her & report our arrival to Commodore Morris.[9] At the same time, the rigging was manned, & *three cheers,* the only salute in our power to offer,[10] were given to the Broad *Pennant* & returned. The *Deleware*'s Officers looked at me as if I were a natural curiosity. They had not seen *an Explorer* in full bloom, and in questioning me, almost forgot that *I* might have some inquiries to make. They brought a few letters up, among which I was rejoiced to find one for "*Lieutenant* William Reynolds." A large bag was on shore. The Commodore remembered me & was very kind, gave me a huge mass of newspapers & two Navy registers for 1842, which were treasures to us indeed.

When I left the *Deleware,* I hurried on shore for the letter bag and had the satisfaction of getting three or four more, one as late as February 14th, just 12 months after those received at Columbia River & Manilla. These were a most grateful addition to my stock of family news.

Our stay in Rio was very unnecessarily protracted until the 22nd. All our wants were supplied *in one day,* and when the *specimens* (to procure which, was the ostensible object of our orders) came on board, they were contained in five small boxes, light enough to be all lifted by one hand! The *Oregon* came *for nothing,* b[r]ought *nothing* and went away as wise & as empty as she came in. *Why* did the fool *send* the *two* Brigs & only *use one?*

I amused myself, like the others, in purchasing little things to take Home, but we were obliged to curtail our list of intended purchases on account of a difficulty in procuring money & from a very serious apprehension that our Extra pay will be checked against us & we reduced to the condition of unfortunate bankrupts. If this should be the case, my plans will all be knocked on the head. I will off Jacket & go to work until Uncle Sam & I are once again Square Yards. Marriage or a tour in Europe will be entirely out of the question. I find this a very pleasant state of uncertainty to remain in, but a few days will decide matters, & meanwhile I am not disturbed in my appetite or sleep.

On Sunday the 22d May, the wind came up fresh from the South West, a very favourable quarter for carrying us clear of Cape Frio and enabling us to make Northing at once, which is rarely the case when the trade winds blow home to the Harbour. At 1 P.M. the glad sound of "All hands up Anchor, for Home!!!" bellowed with the greatest unction by the Boatswain & his mates, set every body astir, and the chain was soon coming in faster than it had been accustomed to for years. The Topsails were hoisted before the Anchor was loosed from the bottom, and we were hoisting up a Boat, the last boat, with the live stock from Rat Island, when the Brig as if she were impatient of even this delay broke the hold of the anchor herself & commenced to pay-round on her heel. She was hawsered, and the anchor was hove up, *not to be let go again,* as the men said, *until for the last time, off the Navy Yard at New York!* We passed close under the *Delaware*'s stern, cheered them & were cheered in return, their band playing "Sweet Home" as loud as they could blow, and a great excitement there was all round.

I had the mid watch that night, and when I took the deck, the Brig was going 9½, with skysails & studding sails on both sides, Cape Frio being plain in sight on the bow. The sky was clear, & the full moon gave a light equal to that of day. In half an hour,

I had to take in the skysails & the lighter Studdingsails, & by 1 o'clock a squall was rising rapidly to which I had to shorten more sail.

We were flying by the Cape, & I considered the Brig prepared for all the harm the squall could do, when the Captain came upon deck. "Mr. Reynolds, I am astonished at the situation the vessel is in, furl this, & take in that, &c., &c., &c." Of course I did as he ordered & said nothing. The result proved that his flurry had been unnecessary, and I had to make sail again before he went below. At 3 the light on the Cape was out of sight, & we kept away to the Northward & Eastward at once, a piece of good fortune that does not happen to one vessel in ten.

For two days we made good progress to the North, when we had light winds for four days but still made something on our course. On the 25th got an Easterly breeze that just enabled us to lay clear of the land, & was attended with frequent squalls. The Captain became less nervous, and we carried sail hard, running the *Oregon* completely out of sight. As we advanced to the Northward, the Land made out farther to the Eastward, but fortunately the wind kept hauling so that we could lay up higher, as there was the necessity for so doing & on the 2nd of June, we were off Cape St. Roque & had a clear sea under our lee.

The 4th we made a very short run, the 5th a tolerably fair one & crossed the line. Until the 9th we only made 2 or 3 miles the hour, and frequently not so much. The weather squally & rainy—you would have thought a second deluge was at hand. My head ached from the never ending beating of the heavy drops upon it, and at the end of a four hours' watch, I really felt as if I had been *wet through* from breast to back! A ducking with salt water is nothing, but to be drenched by rain is the very devil!

On the 9th we got a glorious breeze, and until the 19th, made from 160 to 200 miles a day with as beautiful sailing as I ever saw—skysails set, and the Ocean as smooth as a summer lake. We confidently expected to arrive in New York on the 25th, but we were grievously disappointed, for on the 20th the wind died away, and until the 23d it was nearly dead calm, though we fanned a little to the Northward. Our average of 170 miles a day was sadly destroyed.

On the 24th, we were again favoured by a smashing wind, which carried us to the Northward of Bermuda, & again our hopes were raised. "How fast is she going?" were hourly questions by night & by day, and the intensity of our anxiety was such as can scarcely be appreciated by those, who have never known a four years' absence from the Home they love. The 25th the wind was baffling, & we were worried, but several vessels were in sight, & we beat them all. Sunday the 26th, the day of the present writing, we have made 130 miles, are now, at noon, going 9 knots, and are 338 miles from New York. We are to live off *fresh Pig* & *Champaigne,* and now no one ventures to name a *later* period than Wednesday morning for our arrival in New York, though the majority give her Tuesday evening to accomplish the remaining distance by.

Monday 27th June

We have had another very rude slap in the face, from a North West wind, and our high hopes of yesterday are ruined! Until 9 o'clock last night, the wind held at South West and drove us along at 9 knots the hour, but after that, amid rain, thunder & lightning, the breeze died away & finally shifted to the North West, or dead ahead. As we are in the Gulf stream, the current is carrying us to the Eastward, and our prospects are very unfavourable. *Saturday* is now the *last* day named for our arrival. It would have been high treason to have even *thought* so yesterday!

It makes me shudder still to recal some of our escapes [in the course of the past four years]. I often think of them in my night watches, & it actually was a *strange* feeling to me when I began to admit, with some degree of confidence, the almost forlorn hope *that we should reach Home, after all!* The dread of the *contrary* has weighed upon us like an incubus, in spite of every effort to drive such an unpleasant fear away.

Tuesday, [June] 28th, 1842

This has been a terrible day. We have been becalmed most of the time. Again, have had hopes encouraged by the aspect & motions of the clouds & by intervals of breeze that would last for an hour or two, & then, when we began to count upon a steady wind, die away to an idle calm, but worse than this, we are in the influence of the Gulf Stream, *and it has carried us 90 miles North East by East, directly away from the land!* Patience is very necessary with us *now!* We think, or rather fear, we may have to pass the *Fourth of July* at Sea.

Wednesday, June 29th noon

Expect to be more to the Eastward, than we were yesterday. Light winds continuing & most of the time from the North West, or dead ahead. Several vessels in sight, but all bound *from Home to the East,* none like us, striving almost helplessly to make westing against the Current.

We have gone off to the Eastward, the same as yesterday, by the set of that mighty current, which must run at the rate of nearly four miles an hour, and the wind hangs most provokingly in the very quarter to which we wish to steer. *What* would we *not* give for an *Easterly* blow? I have thrown away all my old shirts & shoes and whistled myself out of breath, & all other nautical resources have been attempted to raise a wind, but in vain. We are helpless Victims of a hard fate, but we still try to keep cheerful faces, and with some success, unless we think of *Mr. Lieutenant Charles Wilkes!* The Vincenneses are all snug at Home, & *we,* in serving a most despicable purpose, are <u>*Here*</u>*!!!*

I feel very curious, when I endeavour to picture the changes that have occurred at *my own home!* Four years have had their effect there, and I have to witness this yet. James, Jane & Kate,[11] at 20, 18 & 17, *must* be very much altered from what they were at 16, 14 & 13, & I cannot fancy their looks, try as much as I may. All the others I expect to find but little changed, and I am only too happy to know that of all the faces belonging to *that hearth,* not one has yet been taken away. As to myself, I am thin as a shadow, and ugly as thin. My general title of "*Old* Reynolds" is no misnomer; I look old & feel accordingly.

Thursday, June 30th

Very light winds still. Yesterday we had been set *180 miles* to the East by the current. We think we are now to the Northward of it, but we are not certain, & there is not the slightest symptom of a coming breeze. My mid watch last night, clear weather, dead calm & a heavy sea. At noon found we had made 30 miles to the Westward, which has helped us a little, and we have now a light breeze that sweeps us along four & five miles the hour. Hopes are rising a little for Saturday evening!

In one thing, I have reason to be thankful—I have never been unwell, not for an hour for the last five years, and have not missed a single watch, by day or night, on account of my health. Among the Sea Officers, not another one has been as fortunate in this respect as myself, though none of them have ever been dangerously ill. I am overjoyed to find that I have recovered entirely from the effects of that Batavia sickness, which so nearly made an end of me, and I think there can be but little wrong in the constitution that has borne all the hardships, climates & privations of this cruize.

Friday July 1st

Fortune favours us. We have been going 6 & 7½ knots the hour, with a South West wind & a smooth sea. My morning watch. Hopes high for making *the light* at daybreak in the morning, & being safe at anchor before to-morrow night. At noon 113 miles from Sandy Hook. My watch from 6 to 8— have just come below—"Sounded in 26½ fathoms, coarse grey sand"—rubbed my fingers on America, the first man. Going 7 knots & a half. *Almost* positive of seeing the light during the night as it is only 65 miles distant, though the weather is thick & smoky & quite cool.

Made the light house in the morning watch. Got a pilot on board. Passed Sandy Hook after breakfast with a light breeze, which seemed about to die away altogether to our great disgust. Hoisted a signal for a Steamboat, but the fog hung over the land too thickly for the telegraph to work. Heard that the *Vincennes* had arrived early in June, and our companion, the *Oregon, three days before us!* She had taken the proper course of crossing the Gulf Stream off the Delaware—not like our Captain's nonsense about making a strait course for New York!

Good luck to the breeze, it freshened and drove us fairly up the harbour. My watch on deck—off the quarantine ground shortened sail and called all hands. I went below to shave and dress. About 11 anchored off the Navy Yard, not without fouling the brig *Somers.*[12]

We had hoped we would be set free from all duties and from the Brig entirely as soon as we arrived—that the Commodore would from mere kindness of heart, release us and give the vessel in charge of the Navy Yard people, particularly as all our men went on shore as soon as they had moored the vessel, except four men whose times had not expired. We were sadly disappointed and had yet to undergo the misery of *keeping watch in New York!*

On the 4th July morning, Sam Reynolds[13] and Sam Witmer came on board, altogether unexpected, of course. Did not recognize Sam until he opened his mouth and had to ask, "Which of you is it?"

Went with them ashore at New York in my horrible, long-tailed, greasy, antiquated uniform coat. Streets alive with processions, soldiers, and people. Boys firing pistols, guns, & fireworks in our faces & under our feet. Terrible hubbub—but saw no drunken men.

Dine and sleep at the American Hotel. Get my new clothes and leave of absence on the 6th July.

The return home! cannot be written here.

Notes

CHAPTER I: TO THE SOUTH ATLANTIC

1. **Vincennes:** The flagship of the squadron, a 700-ton ship-rigged sloop of war. The other vessels of the expedition at its outset were the 559-ton ship-rigged sloop of war *Peacock,* the 468-ton store-ship *Relief,* the 224-ton brig *Porpoise,* and two refitted New York pilot schooners, the 110-ton *Sea Gull* and the 96-ton *Flying Fish.*

2. *the Captain:* Lieutenant Charles Wilkes (1798–1877) of New York, commander of the expedition.

3. *the Secretary of the Navy:* The newly appointed New Yorker James Kirke Paulding (1778–1860), novelist and politician. Paulding's order of 11 August 1838 required "the surrender of all journals" to the Navy Department at the end of the voyage.

4. *her commander:* Passed Midshipman James W. E. Reid of Georgia, later lost with his schooner.

5. *the lucky bag:* The receptacle of various items left unattended about the vessel and periodically auctioned off to the crew.

6. *the Scientifics:* The members of the corps of civilian scientists and artists attached to the expedition.

7. *George Porter:* Porter survived this horrendous experience only to die of a fever at sea on 3 March 1842, shortly before the expedition's return.

8. *"all of which I saw, part of which I was":* A slight misquotation of Virgil's *Aeneid* 2.8 (Dryden translation).

9. *Mr. Drayton:* Joseph Drayton, a Philadelphia engraver and portrait painter.

10. *Mr. Pickering:* Charles Pickering, a thirty-three-year-old Harvard-educated naturalist, served the expedition as both botanist and zoologist.

11. *Buonvista & Mayo . . . St. Jago:* In the Cape Verdes.

12. *the First Lieutenant:* Thomas T. Craven (1808–1887) of Washing-

ton, D.C., with whom Reynolds had served previously in the schooner *Boxer* and the *Peacock.*

13. *working "dead horse out":* Earning enough money to pay off an advance from the government.

14. *the Purser:* Richard R. Waldron (d. 1846) of New Hampshire, the official responsible for the accounts of the *Vincennes* and for issuing provisions and clothing. He was as well a personal friend of Wilkes's.

15. *the Furnace Fire:* A reference to Cornwall Iron Furnace, twenty miles northwest of Lancaster, where Reynolds's family resided at the time of the expedition.

16. *false fires:* The term can apply either to the ignition of wooden tubes containing combustible materials that burn brilliantly for several minutes or to blank discharges of the guns.

17. *Captains Parry, Ross, Franklin, Beechy:* Sir William Edward Parry (1790–1855), Sir John Ross (1777–1856), Sir John Franklin (1786–1847), and Frederick William Beechey (1796–1856), British naval officers and Arctic explorers.

18. *"vi et armis":* By force of arms.

19. *"Pyrosomia":* Pyrosomes, tiny phosphorescent marine animals that form themselves into a free-swimming colony in the shape of a hollow cylinder closed at one end.

20. *Admiral Krusenstern:* Adam Johann von Krusenstern (1770–1846), celebrated Russian navigator, who contributed his advice to the Navy Department during the planning stages of the expedition.

21. *Mr. Johnson:* Lieutenant Robert E. Johnson (d. 1855) of North Carolina.

22. *Potomac & Delaware:* a forty-four-gun brig and a seventy-four-gun ship of the line, respectively.

23. *Norfolk School . . . Examination:* After studying at the school at the Gosport Navy Shipyard in Norfolk, Virginia, Reynolds successfully took the examination that qualified him as a "passed midshipman" and made him eligible to be promoted to a lieutenancy when a vacancy should occur.

24. *Pennsylvania:* The largest vessel in the U.S. Navy, rated at 120 guns.

25. *Washington:* Reynolds worked at the Depot of Charts and Instruments, forerunner of the Navy Hydrographic Office. Here he first met Wilkes, who was superintendent of the depot at the time.

26. *slip my cable:* Die.

CHAPTER 2: RIO AND THE ARGENTINE COAST

1. *Whittle:* Dr. John S. Whittle (d. 1850), assistant surgeon of the *Vincennes.*
2. *Sam Patch:* Rhode Island daredevil jumper, the first to leap Niagara Falls and live. A month later he died attempting a leap of the Genesee Falls, 6 November 1829.
3. *a Prize:* According to Reynolds's letter of December 1838 to his sister Lydia, the slaver had been captured by a British sloop of war in the ongoing effort to enforce the ban on the slave trade enacted by Great Britain in 1807; see *Voyage to the Southern Ocean: The Letters of Lieutenant William Reynolds from the U.S. Exploring Expedition, 1838–1842*, ed. Anne Hoffman Cleaver and E. Jeffrey Stann (Annapolis, Md.: Naval Institute Press, 1988), p. 41.
4. *the [American whaler]* Leader: a bark commanded by Charles Ball.
5. *Captain Ringgold:* Lieutenant Cadwallader Ringgold (1802–1869) of Maryland, commander of the *Porpoise.*
6. *Tide Staffs:* Measuring rods for gauging the rise and fall of the tide.
7. *the Cornet:* A signal flag.
8. *Shags:* Cormorants.

CHAPTER 3: ORANGE HARBOR AND THE FAR
SOUTHERN ISLANDS

1. *Lieutenant Alden:* James Alden (1810–1877) of Maine.
2. *Captain King:* Philip Parker King (1793–1856), British naval officer, who surveyed the southern coast of South America with Robert Fitzroy 1826–1830.
3. *Camera lucida:* A device for projecting an image onto a blank sheet of paper, where it may be traced.
4. *stop water:* A drag towed astern to retard the motion of a vessel through the water.
5. *Jim Gibson:* James H. Gibson, Reynolds's boyhood friend and classmate in the Young Gentlemen's Academy at Lititz, a village eight miles north of Lancaster; Gibson was rated a coxswain in the crew of the *Vincennes.*
6. *our Gun:* A small cannon, mounted on a carriage.
7. *"Of a winged & Sea Girt Citadel":* Byron, *Childe Harold's Pilgrimage,* II.249.

CHAPTER 4: BOAT DUTY OFF CAPE HORN

1. *the flesh pots of Egypt:* See Exodus 16:3.
2. *Scotch Cap:* A sturdy, woolen, brimless hat, decorated with two tails or streamers.
3. whose *name:* Surely that of his Lancaster neighbor Rebecca Krug, whom he married a few weeks after his return to the United States.
4. *a slow match:* A hempen cord soaked in a solution of saltpeter and used to ignite the guns.
5. *"Peter Wilkins":* The hero of the fictional *Life and Adventures of Peter Wilkins* (1751) by Robert Paltock; the shipwrecked Wilkins reaches a land where the inhabitants can fly.
6. *Gannymede:* Ganymede, cupbearer to the gods in Greek myth.
7. *an altitude:* A measurement of the angular distance between the horizon and a heavenly body (in this instance the sun), used in the determination of position and time.
8. *any definite meaning:* According to Charles Wilkes, *Narrative of the United States Exploring Expedition,* 5 vols. (Philadelphia: Lea & Blanchard, 1845; facsimile ed., Upper Saddle River, N.J.: Gregg Press, 1970), vol. 1, p. 125, the phrase was delivered in a sing-song manner by the natives when asking for presents.
9. *the days of Cook:* Captain James Cook explored Tierra del Fuego in 1768 and again in 1774.
10. cap: Percussion cap, a device recently developed to replace flint as a means of igniting the charge in small arms.
11. *"Fly up the creeks":* Local name for the American bittern and green heron.

CHAPTER 5: THE RETURN TO ORANGE HARBOR

1. *Betsy Baker:* One of the names commonly applied by seamen to a gun.
2. *Bacon:* Passed Midshipman Frederick A. Bacon of Connecticut, later lost with the *Sea Gull.*
3. *the* Beagle's *stay:* The British exploring ship *Beagle,* commanded by Captain Robert Fitzroy, first visited Lennox Island in 1830 and again in 1833, when Charles Darwin was on board as official naturalist.
4. *John Sac:* The Maori chieftain Tuatti, who, after an absence of eight or nine years from New Zealand, joined the expedition in the United States as a seaman; see Wilkes, *Narrative,* vol. 2, p. 378, and Reynolds, *Voyage to the Southern Ocean,* p. 12.

5. *Slipped:* Instead of taking the time to retrieve her anchor, the brig let loose the anchor cable, typically attaching a buoy to it so that the anchor might be recovered at some later time.

6. *Walker:* Lieutenant William M. Walker (d. 1866) of Maryland, commander of the *Flying Fish* during this first exploration of Antarctic waters and afterward first lieutenant of the *Peacock*.

CHAPTER 6: TO VALPARAISO

1. *William Johnson fell overboard:* Evidently the seaman Johnson was saved, for the "List of Officers and Men" in Wilkes, *Narrative,* vol. 1, p. xlv, reports that he was sent home in the *Relief.*

2. *Captain Hudson:* Lieutenant William Levereth Hudson (1794–1862) of New York, commander of the *Peacock* and second in command of the expedition. Four years older than Wilkes, Hudson was senior to him on the navy's lieutenants list.

3. President *(once our own):* The forty-four-gun *President* under Commodore Stephen Decatur was captured off New York Harbor by a British squadron on 15 January 1815.

4. *night heads:* Knightheads, heavy timbers that rise just inside the stem and support the inner end of the bowsprit.

CHAPTER 7: THE PACIFIC ISLANDS

1. *anchored forever:* The *Sea Gull* never did rejoin the squadron, apparently lost in the gale of late April 1839.

2. *The* Falmouth . . . *by us all:* The helpful Captain Isaac McKeever had curried Wilkes's favor in order to install his nephew, Edwin DeHaven (1816–1865), in the officer corps of the expedition. Wilkes appointed DeHaven acting master of the *Vincennes,* ignoring the claims of some of his own officers, Reynolds among them, to the post.

3. *The* Relief . . . *in the Squadron:* Anxious to rid himself of the slow-sailing store ship and its commander, Lieutenant A. K. Long (1804–1866) of Maryland, Wilkes ordered the *Relief* home after consigning to her several other officers with whom he was displeased. Among the other changes in the personnel of the squadron at this time, Thomas Craven, the very competent first lieutenant of the *Vincennes,* was ordered to remain in Callao and take command of the *Sea Gull,* when and if she should appear. He was replaced by Wilkes's favorite, Lieutenant Overton Carr (d. 1886).

4. *There has been . . . the swallowing:* On 20 August Wilkes had issued an order forbidding fraternization between the lieutenants and the midshipmen of the *Vincennes*. Bravely, if not wisely, Reynolds wrote a reply in which he defended their right to associate off duty.

CHAPTER 8: THE SOCIETY ISLANDS AND SAMOA

1. *this place, so famous in the eyes of all Navigators:* Cook observed the transit of Venus from this point in 1769.
2. *the* **Arreay:** The Areoi, a secret religious society, reputed by the missionaries to practice infanticide and human sacrifice and to conduct grossly licentious ceremonies.
3. *the affairs of the consul Mr. Blackler:* Blackler had complained to Wilkes of discrimination against American maritime interests by Tahitian officials.
4. *paid rather dear for their whistle:* An allusion to Benjamin Franklin's "The Whistle" (1779), a bagatelle cautioning against the sacrifice of true values for false ones.
5. *a* **White Man:** William Gray, or Grey, who had lived on Tutuila eleven years and was to serve the expedition as interpreter and pilot in Samoa.
6. *Lieutenant Underwood:* Joseph A. Underwood (1809–1840) of New York transferred to the *Vincennes* from the *Relief* at Callao.
7. *Papalangi:* White person.

CHAPTER 9: TUTUILA, UPOLU, AND AUSTRALIA

1. *A white man:* Edward Cavenaugh of New Bedford, Massachusetts.
2. *Midshipman Henry:* Wilkes Henry of New York, the young son of Charles Wilkes's sister Eliza.
3. **David Smith:** Listed in Wilkes, *Narrative,* vol. 1, p. liii, as an armorer.
4. *missed stays:* Failed to cross the eye of the wind while tacking, a mishap particularly common in square-rigged vessels like the *Vincennes*.
5. **Our first Luff:** Lieutenant Carr.
6. *weather it:* Pass to windward of it without tacking.
7. *stayed:* Tacked.
8. *the man with the trumpet:* The officer of the deck (possessor of the speaking trumpet, the symbol of his authority), in this case Lieutenant Carr.

9. *gangway:* In this context, one of two walkways running fore and aft on either side of the vessel and linking the forecastle and the quarterdeck.

10. *the booms:* The rack holding the spare spars.

11. *Lieutenant Case:* Augustus L. Case (1813–1893) of New York; like Underwood, he was transferred from the *Relief* to the *Vincennes* at Callao.

12. *Mr. Knox:* Passed Midshipman Samuel R. Knox (d. 1883) of Boston.

13. *May:* Passed Midshipman William May (1814–1861) of Washington, D.C., Reynolds's cabinmate and longtime friend.

14. *my old Ship:* Reynolds had served on the *Peacock* in the Arabian Sea and the East Indies in 1833–1834.

CHAPTER 10: ANTARCTICA

1. *eclipse Cook, & distance the pretender Weddell:* Cook's most southern latitude, attained in 1774, was 71° 10' south; the British navigator James Weddell claimed to have reached 74° 15' south in 1822.

2. *Mr. Eld:* Passed Midshipman Henry Eld (1814–1850) of Connecticut.

3. *our discovery will be verified:* Reynolds and Eld were eventually credited with being the first in the expedition to sight the Antarctic continent.

4. *"Kill Biscuit":* One of several irreverent titles that Reynolds applies to Wilkes.

5. *Clark:* Midshipman George W. Clarke.

6. *the Frenchman:* Captain Jules Sébastien César Dumont d'Urville (1790–1842), leader of a rival French exploring expedition.

7. *pintles . . . gudgeons:* The male and female parts, respectively, of the hinges by which the rudder swings.

8. *Fore Foot . . . palm lashing:* The forefoot is the timber that connects the stem of a vessel to the keel; the bill port is where the tip of the fluke of the anchor rests when it is stowed; the palm lashing is the means by which the broad part of the fluke is secured to the vessel's side.

9. *Spanker boom:* The spar that extends the bottom edge of the fore-and-aft sail set from the mizzenmast of a square-rigged vessel.

10. *Taffrel:* The upper works of the stern.

CHAPTER 11: SYDNEY AGAIN AND THE PASSAGE TO FIJI

1. *Simon:* Passed Midshipman Simon F. Blunt (d. 1854) of Virginia, transferred from the *Porpoise* to the *Vincennes* at Orange Harbor.
2. *Pinckney:* Lieutenant Robert F. Pinkney (1812–1878) of Virginia, who prepared formal charges against Wilkes when the squadron reached Honolulu. Wilkes retaliated by arresting Pinkney and having him court-martialed when the expedition returned to the United States.
3. *Dr. Fox:* John L. Fox (d. 1864) of Massachusetts, one of the two assistant surgeons on board the *Vincennes.*
4. *Thompson:* Midshipman Egbert Thompson (1822–1881) of New York, who had transferred from the *Flying Fish* to the *Vincennes* at Rio.
5. *Old Emmons:* Lieutenant George Foster Emmons (1811–1844) of Vermont.
6. *boarding nettings:* Nets extending fore and aft on each side of a vessel to prevent an enemy from jumping aboard.
7. *Pilot:* Tom Granby, who lived on the island of Ovelau in the Fijis; see Wilkes, *Narrative,* vol. 3, pp. 40–41.
8. *New Hollanders:* Australian aborigines.
9. *Guillou:* Dr. Charles F. B. Guillou (d. 1897) of Pennsylvania, assistant surgeon of the *Peacock* at this time.
10. *"The King of the Cannibal Islands":* The title comes from an immensely popular comic song written by the British performer A. W. Humphreys around 1830 and set to a tune composed by John Charles White.
11. *a patent rifle:* The breech-loading Model 1819 Hall rifle.
12. *his native name:* Tanoa.
13. *Elliott:* Midshipman Samuel B. Elliott.
14. *the Parson:* The Reverend Jared L. Elliott of Washington, D.C., chaplain of the squadron, who was later disgraced and sent home from San Francisco in October 1841.
15. *J. W. W. Dyes:* John W. W. Dyes (d. 1855), assistant taxidermist in the scientific corps of the *Vincennes.*
16. *Cunningham:* Jacob Cunningham of Nantucket.
17. *Bich la Mar:* Bêche-de-mer, or sea cucumber, like sandalwood, was a valuable commodity in the China trade.
18. *angling:* Measuring angles with the sextant.
19. *Columbus & the Eclipse:* Reynolds recalls the incident recounted in Washington Irving's *Life and Voyages of Christopher Columbus* (1828), book 16, chapter 3, in which Columbus overawes Jamaican natives by pretending to control a lunar eclipse.

CHAPTER 12: FIJI

1. *taunt:* Tall masted.
2. *The D[octo]r:* James C. Palmer (1811–1883) of Maryland, surgeon of the *Peacock.*
3. *"Sa vour nan Deelish":* "Savourneen Deelish," a traditional Irish melody; the words that Paddy and Reynolds recalled were written by George Colman the Younger for his opera *The Surrender of Calais* (1791).
4. *patent logs:* Mechanical devices towed astern to measure the distance sailed; a rotor spun by the motion of the vessel through the water actuates a dial that records mileage much as an automobile odometer does.
5. *the said Jonah is the Rev. Mr. E[lliot]t:* Elliott had been temporarily assigned to the *Peacock;* parsons brought bad luck according to sailors' lore.
6. **Captain Belcher:** Sir Edward Belcher (1799–1877), commander of the survey ship *Sulphur.*
7. *rudder braces:* Gudgeons; see chapter 10, note 7.

CHAPTER 13: PORTENTS

1. *The mate of the* **Leonidas:** The second mate, Joseph Baxter.
2. *firing the guns of that ship to measure a base:* The expedition regularly measured the base line used in triangulation by noting the difference in time between the flash and the report of a gun fired at one end of the base line as they were seen and heard at the other end; by multiplying that time difference by the speed of sound, the surveyors could determine the length of the base line.
3. *Budd:* Lieutenant Thomas A. Budd (d. 1862) of New York.
4. *fighting Captain of the Forecastle:* Officer in charge of the forecastle, or forward part of the deck.
5. *a person:* The seaman William Dunbar.
6. *the Compressor:* A device, sometimes called the stopper, through which the chain cable passes as the anchor is raised; when the lid of the compressor is closed, a bar may be inserted through it in order to jam the cable and check its movement.
7. *Jack nasty face:* The common seaman.
8. *John Theodore Beaton:* Or Beton, rated an ordinary seaman.
9. *Captain Eagleston:* J. H. Egleston, master of the *Leonidas.*
10. *McBride:* Hugh McBride, who had joined the expedition at Upolu

as an ordinary seaman; McBride was eventually found at Muthu-ata, where he had been hidden by the natives.

11. **"hlígoó":** Or *liku,* an apronlike band made of bark, worn at the waist.

12. **Monkey face passage:** A narrow channel dominated by a huge rock formation resembling a monkey's face in profile.

13. **James Thomas Gauntt:** Or Gant, a house servant of the Reynolds family.

14. **Thomas Mizer:** Or Mizir, who had joined the expedition in Tahiti as a first-class boy.

15. **John Minnie:** Or Meiney, master-at-arms of the *Peacock.*

16. **Perry:** Lieutenant Oliver Hazard Perry (1815–1878) of Rhode Island, son of the hero of the Battle of Lake Erie.

17. **Blair:** Midshipman James L. Blair, transferred from the *Relief* to the *Peacock* at Rio.

18. **Sir Joshua [Reynolds]:** (1723–1792), British portrait painter.

19. **Mr. J[eremiah] N. R[eynolds]:** (1799–1858), Ohio newspaper editor, who lobbied vigorously for more than a decade for the creation of an American exploring expedition.

CHAPTER 14: CRIME AND PUNISHMENT

1. *umquhile:* Erstwhile.

2. **"Faca bete" fashion:** In accord with Fiji custom.

3. **Baldwin:** Passed Midshipman Augustus S. Baldwin (d. 1876) of New Jersey, transferred from the *Porpoise* to the *Peacock* at Callao.

4. *a few rockets:* In combat the squadron fired incendiary Congreve rockets, not the signal rockets to which Reynolds refers earlier.

5. **Davis:** Passed Midshipman Alonzo B. Davis (d. 1854) of Louisiana, transferred from the *Relief* to the *Peacock* at Callao.

6. **one tot of grog a day:** The standard allowance of spirits in the U.S. Navy was one-quarter pint each day, served out twice a day in small tin measures called "tots."

7. **Dana:** James Dwight Dana (1813–1895), the expedition's geologist.

8. **go on the list:** Report oneself sick.

9. **the siege it sustained in the East Indies:** Reynolds nearly died from a fever contracted in Batavia (now Jakarta) in 1834.

10. **Sandford:** Midshipman Joseph P. Sanford (1816–1901) of Virginia, assigned to the *Porpoise* at this time.

CHAPTER 15: AFTERMATH

1. *Carter:* An English member of the small community of European men resident at Ovalau, five of whom were employed by the expedition as interpreters and pilots.
2. *Bowie Knife Pistol:* The cutlass pistol patented by George Elgin in 1837 and manufactured by Morrill, Mossman and Blair of Amherst, Massachusetts.

CHAPTER 16: HONOLULU

1. *Esau sold his birth right:* See Genesis 25:33–34.
2. *the Locusts were in Egypt:* See Exodus 10:4–19.
3. *"roll off":* Drum roll.
4. *"Pierce's":* The residence of Henry Augustus Peirce (1808–1885), a prominent Honolulu merchant.
5. *"soon changed into dangling heaps of clothes":* Quoted from Charles Dickens's *Oliver Twist* (1837–1838), chapter 52.
6. *Couthouy:* Joseph P. Couthouy (1808–1864) of Boston, conchologist of the expedition.
7. *pendular experiments:* The cumbersome pendulum was used to measure the effects of gravity at various points in the course of the voyage in an effort to determine the precise shape and mass of the earth.

CHAPTER 17: RETURN TO SAMOA

1. *like the unfortunate Starling, "We can't get out! We can't get out!":* An allusion to Laurence Sterne's novel *A Sentimental Journey through France and Italy* (1768), "The Passport. The Hotel at Paris."
2. **Salt horse:** Beef preserved by salting.
3. *the* Pandora . . . *Mutineers of the* Bounty: The British Admiralty dispatched the frigate *Pandora* to the Pacific Ocean in November 1790 to search for the *Bounty* mutineers. Passing within a few days' sail of Pitcairn Island, where the fugitives had settled, the *Pandora* succeeded only in retrieving and imprisoning the fourteen members of the *Bounty* crew whom the mutineers had left at Tahiti. On 28 August 1791 she struck a reef off the northern coast of Australia and sank.

4. *Judge, Chase:* "Judge" was the nickname for Emmons; "Chase" is evidently a misspelling of Case.

5. *a certain Lieutenant:* Pinkney.

6. *an American Whaler, the* John Howland: a ship from New Bedford, commanded by William H. Whitfield.

7. *I had to sweep the Schooner:* The schooner was so small that it could be propelled in a calm by long oars called sweeps.

8. *Harrison:* Passed Midshipman George W. Harrison, assigned to the *Peacock.*

9. *Mr. Heath's congregation:* At this time Thomas Heath was the senior missionary in Samoa, sent there by the London Missionary Society.

CHAPTER 18: RETURN TO OAHU

1. *Mr. John Effingham:* A character in James Fenimore Cooper's novel *Home as Found* (1838).

2. *armour:* According to Wilkes, *Narrative,* vol. 5, p. 47, the body armor of the islanders was "made of plaited cocoanut-fibres, woven into as solid and compact a mass as if it had been made of board half an inch thick, and was as stiff as a coat of mail."

3. *Mr. Peale:* Titian Ramsey Peale (1788–1885) of Philadelphia, one of the two naturalists attached to the expedition and son of the painter Charles Willson Peale.

4. *the Purser:* William Speiden (d. 1861).

5. *Slush:* The fat remaining after boiling meat; it was saved and used for cooking, making candles, and greasing the spars.

6. *Old Medley:* Joseph Medley, seaman, who joined the expedition at New Zealand.

CHAPTER 19: TO THE COLUMBIA RIVER

1. *a dozen Shylocks:* In *The Merchant of Venice,* 1.3, the money-lender Shylock demands a pound of the borrower's flesh as a forfeit for nonpayment of a debt.

2. *the Automaton Chess player:* A supposed robot in the guise of a turbaned Turk, invented by Wolfgang von Kempalen and first demonstrated before the Austrian court in 1770. In the first half of the nineteenth century Johann Maelzel displayed the device in Europe and America, where it attracted a number of skeptical ana-

lyst, Edgar Allan Poe among them, who correctly ascribed its
workings to the manipulations of a concealed human operator.

3. *Calvin Edson:* Widely exhibited American "living skeleton"; in
1830 Edson, who was five feet, four inches tall, was said to weigh
sixty pounds.

4. *Astoria:* An account by Washington Irving of the operations of
John Jacob Astor's American Fur Company; the book, published
in 1836, is regarded as the first corporate history.

5. *the Master:* In the navy, the officer responsible for the navigation
and stowage of a vessel.

6. *Astoria . . . [Hudson's Bay] Company . . . Establishment:* The
trading post was taken over by the British Northwest Company
during the War of 1812. By the time of Reynolds's visit to the Columbia, the Northwest Company had amalgamated with its great
rival, the Hudson's Bay Company.

7. *the "Black dwarf's":* Reynolds refers to the deformed Sir Edward
Mauley in Walter Scott's novel *The Black Dwarf* (1816).

8. *Fort Vancouver:* Headquarters of the Hudson's Bay Company in
the Northwest, situated a hundred miles up the Columbia near
present-day Vancouver, Washington.

9. *young Waldron:* Thomas W. Waldron, captain's clerk of the *Peacock;* he was the son of R. R. Waldron, purser of the *Vincennes.*

CHAPTER 20: THE PURSUIT OF CORPORAL DEWEES

1. *Mr. Birnie:* James Birnie (ca. 1799–1864).

2. *Fort George:* The British name for Astoria.

3. *old Bustamente:* This epithet for Wilkes apparently derives from
the name of Anastasio Bustamante (1789–1853), Mexican general
and successor to Santa Anna as president in 1837.

4. *Dr. McLough[l]in:* John McLoughlin (1784–1857), the able superintendent of the activities of the Hudson's Bay Company in the
Northwest.

5. *the Seargant of Marines:* Aaron Walmsley.

6. *the Willamet:* The fertile Willamette Valley in present-day Oregon, settled in the 1830s by French Canadians brought in by
McLoughlin and American farmers under missionary supervision.

CHAPTER 21: LIFE ON THE COLUMBIA

1. *The two Brigs:* The second brig was an American merchantman, renamed the *Oregon,* that the expedition had purchased at Astoria as a replacement for the *Peacock.*
2. *nursed:* Tenderly held.
3. *Sinclair:* Lieutenant George T. Sinclair, transferred from the *Relief* to the *Porpoise* at Callao.
4. *the bonnet:* An extra piece of canvas laced to the foot of a sail to increase its power in light winds.

CHAPTER 22: ACROSS THE PACIFIC

1. *the mutineers of the Whaleship* Globe: On 26 January 1824, mutineers led by Samuel Comstock massacred the officers of the Nantucket whaler *Globe,* eventually landing on Mili Island in the Mulgraves, where Comstock, who hoped to establish a private kingdom, was murdered by his companions. Of the seamen who remained on the island, all but two were later killed by the natives.
2. *the horrid massacre on board the* Awashonks: On 5 October 1835 the master and the first and second mates of the whaler *Awashonks* of Falmouth, Massachusetts, were slaughtered by visiting natives using the ship's own cutting spades.
3. *Barnard:* Probably Robert C. Bernard, rated quartermaster, who joined the expedition at Valparaiso.
4. *"Oh! give me but my Arab Steed":* A drawing-room song by Thomas Haynes Bayly (1797–1839).

CHAPTER 23: HOMEWARD BOUND

1. *"Hell gate":* An infamous rock-strewn narrows in the East River of New York Harbor.
2. *"Longwood!":* Napoleon's residence during his exile on Saint Helena.
3. *"the Lions":* The major points of interest.
4. *Mr. Carroll:* William Carrol, a British subject.
5. *"double dearborn":* A light four-wheeled wagon of a type common in the United States.
6. *his death:* On 5 May 1821.
7. *lost its greatest claim to celebrity:* Napoleon's remains were returned to France in 1840.

8. *Cape Frio light:* About seventy-five miles east of the entrance to the harbor of Rio de Janeiro.

9. *Commodore Morris:* Charles Morris (1784–1856), commander of the Brazil Squadron.

10. *the only salute in our power to offer:* The vessels of the expedition were forbidden to fire their guns unnecessarily in order not to disturb the delicate chronometers on board.

11. *James, Jane & Kate:* Three of Reynolds's seven living siblings.

12. *the brig* Somers: Less than five months later, on 26 November 1842, the brig was to be the scene of the climax of the so-called *Somers* mutiny, when three of her crew accused of a mutinous conspiracy were summarily hanged at sea.

13. *Sam Reynolds:* Samuel Moore Reynolds (1814–1888), William's older brother, for whom he had a special affection; he regularly celebrated Sam's birthday throughout the years of the expedition.

A Glossary of Place-Names

The following list supplies the current equivalents of Reynolds's place-names in those instances in which his terms are incorrect or have fallen into disuse.

Ascension Island	Pohnpei
Banca	Bangka
Baring's Island	Namorik Atoll
Bete Leb	Viti Levu
Boham's Island	Jaluit Island
Boqueroon	Boquerón
Buonvista	Boa Vista
Cantab	Kandavu, Kadavu
Capa de Verde	Cape Verde Islands
Carlshoff	Aratica
De Peyster's Island	Nukufetau
Drummond Island	Tabiteuea
Duke of York Island	Atafu
Eimeo	Moorea
Elliss Island	Funafuti
Fegee	Fiji
Huaheine	Huahine
Hunter's Island	Kili Island
Kingsmill group	Gilbert Islands
Lebooca	Levuka
Mackenzie's Islands	Ulithi Islands
Maquaries Island	Macquarie Island
Marli	Mali
Mayo	Maio
Mololo	Malolo
Monono	Manono
Morotori	Maui

Motorita .... Motu-iti
Mouna Roa .... Mauna Loa
Mudwater .... Mathuata, Macuata
Mulgraves .... Mili Atoll
Navigator group .... Samoa
New Holland .... Australia
Nuca Murray Bay .... Rukuruku Bay
Noloa .... Ngaloa, Galoa
Organ Mountains .... Serra dos Orgãos
Otaheite .... Tahiti
Ovelow .... Ovalau
Papahite .... Papeete
Parri .... Nuuana Pali
Pitts Island .... Makin
Rahwa .... Rewa
Raya .... Praia
Rhio .... Riau
Rooka Rook .... Rukuruku
Rotomah, Rotumah .... Rotuma
Salufato .... Safata
Sandal Wood Bay .... Mbua, Bua Bay
Sandwich Islands .... Hawaiian Islands
Saunders .... Tupuaemanu
Savie .... Savaii
Sherson's Island .... Nanumanga Island
Sincapore .... Singapore
Somi Somi .... Somo-Somo
Sooloo .... Sulu
St. Jago .... Säo Tiago
Strong Island .... Kusaie Island
Tavia .... Tavea
Tonga Taboo .... Tongatapu
Veuna Leb .... Vanua Levu
Whahoo .... Oahu
Wylea Rock .... Wailea Rock

Printed in the United States
by Baker & Taylor Publisher Services